D0883370

Seven American Utopias

Seven American Utopias

The Architecture of Communitarian
Socialism, 1790-1975

Dolores Hayden

The MIT Press

Cambridge,
Massachusetts,
and London, England

This book was set in IBM Composer Press Roman by
Techdata Associates, and printed and bound by The
Murray Printing Company in the United States of America.

Second printing, 1977

Library of Congress Cataloging in Publication Data

Hayden, Dolores.
    Seven American utopias.

Bibliography: p.
Includes index.
    1. Utopias—United States. I. Title.
HX653.H39   335'.973   75-23148
ISBN 0-262-08082-6

Leap and shout, ye living building
Christ is in his glory come
Cast your eyes on Mother's children
See what glory fills the room!

—Shaker hymn

III Learning from Utopia

Acknowledgments

Funds for research were provided by a Beatrix Farrand Fellowship from the Department of Landscape Architecture at the University of California, Berkeley, in 1972-1973, and by a grant from the American Institute of Architects in 1970. The Department of Architecture at MIT helped to support the expenses of manuscript preparation.

I am especially grateful to John Coolidge of Harvard University for incisive, detailed criticism throughout every stage of research and writing. His advice was invaluable. I would also like to thank Roslyn Lindheim, who made it possible for me to develop some of the themes of the book in a seminar at Berkeley in 1973; and Peter Marris, who helped me to pose theoretical dilemmas as well as to resolve some personal ones.

Many other people have read and argued over sections of the manuscript with me, including Christopher Alexander, Donald Appleyard, Jeremy Brecher, Clare Cooper, Sheila de Bretteville, Albert Fein, Chaviva Hosek, J. B. Jackson, Kevin Lynch, Carl Sauer, Leland Vaughn, Gwen Wright, and the late Shadrach Woods. Discussions with other communitarian historians, including Arthur Bestor, Robert Fogarty, Rosabeth Moss Kanter, and Benjamin Zablocki, helped me to clarify many of the arguments. So did discussions with students at Berkeley and students at MIT.

Each case study depended upon historians and local residents who generously gave me the benefit of their expertise: for Hancock, Sister Mildred Barker, Theodore Johnson, Robert Meader, John Harlow Ott, and Amy Bess Miller; for Nauvoo, Paul Anderson, Leonard Arrington, Richard Bushman, Carl Haglund, Robert Flanders, T. Edgar Lyon, and Lillian Snyder; for Phalanx, Donald Drew Egbert, Alyce Lathrop, Ann Miles, Nicholas Riasanovsky, Eric Schirber, Michael Sorkin, and Ann Vernell; for Oneida, Mary L. Beagle, Imogen Noyes Stone, Geoffrey Noyes, and Jerome Wayland-Smith; for Amana, Betty Blechschmidt, Frank J. Lankes, Rudolph Pitz, Madeleine Roehmig, Charles Selzer, and Dan Turner; for Greeley, Florence V. Clark; for Llano del Rio, Robert Hine, Paul Kagan, Albert Kapotsy, and Kali le Page. All errors, of course, are my responsibility alone.

Members of many Boston area communes provided information for my first research in 1969. Members of my commune—Jim Ault, Barbara Bliss, Ebe Emmons, Tony Giachetti, and Huck White—offered moral support as well as experience and observations.

I am very grateful to staff members in all of the libraries and archives cited in the notes who located material for me. I would especially like to thank Bill Logan, an architect and Harvard classmate who took many of the contemporary photographs, and Eleonor Hellman-Sogin of the Rotch Library at MIT, who provided invaluable help in locating many of the historic photographs. I owe a great deal to William R. Tibbs, who contributed skill and architectural judgment in drawing maps and building plans, and to Margo Jones, who helped with that work. Alice Paley, Alice Tyler, Maritza Leal Banchs, Lynne Rutkin, Elizabeth Morrison, Renate Majumdar, and Katharine Mills typed the final manuscript; Wyn Tucker and Anne Shepley helped coordinate the typing. The editorial staff and the design staff at the MIT Press provided advice, criticism, and creative expertise throughout the publishing process.

Finally, I would like to thank my women's group and the members of WALAP (Women in Architecture, Landscape Architecture, and Planning), who supplied personal encouragement when I was getting started, as well as my colleagues at MIT who provided hospitality and support during the last month of writing.

I Seeking Utopia

1 Idealism and the American Environment

I saw a new heaven and a new earth. . . . And I John saw the holy city, new Jerusalem, coming down from God out of heaven. . . .

—Revelation 21:1-2, John the Evangelist describing the millennium

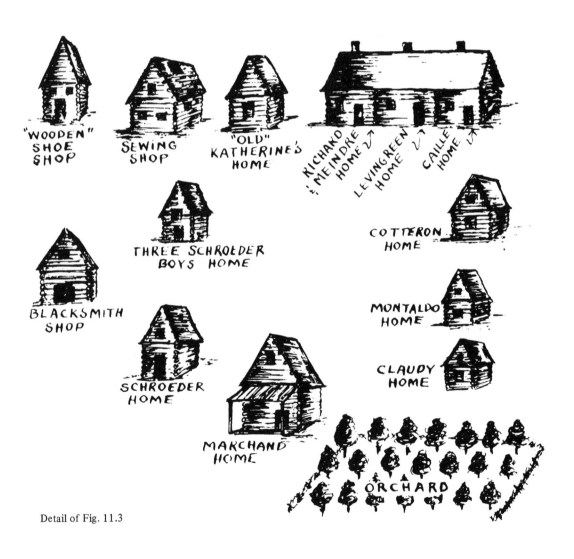

Detail of Fig. 11.3

Drive through Jerusalem Corners, New York, or Promise City, Iowa; pass the freeway exits for Elysian Valley and Arcadia in California; stop at the "Garden of Eatun" restaurant in Cozad, Nebraska. American place names revive settlers' visions of the New World as earthly paradise, dreams about the apocalyptic properties of the American landscape first expressed when Columbus claimed to be the discoverer of a "new heaven" and a "new earth."[1] The rhetoric of paradise embellishes an adventurer's map of Eden, Virginia; it decorates the stern sermons Puritan leaders preached to their covenant communities; it obscures the industrial order established in early corporate towns; it suffuses the balance sheets of land speculators with romance. It lingers, ironically, in the title of a recent study of the contemporary American landscape, *God's Own Junkyard*.[2]

Paradisiac preoccupations in the United States have usually rested on the assumption that salvation and material prosperity are earned through an individual approach to the land of promise and its physical resources. This book is about dissident idealists who looked upon the New World as a potential paradise, but insisted on realizing this potential through collective organization and ownership. To demonstrate how the New World should be settled, several hundred groups established communistic societies which planned and built model towns. The Shakers, one of the largest and most successful of these groups, called their society a "living building"; and this metaphor encapsulates the subject of this book, the relationship between the members of these experimental communities, their forms of social organization, and the complex, collective environments they created.

At the same time that experimental communities sought viable forms of social and environmental organization, they sought suitable terms to describe themselves: "socialist," "communist," "communionist," "communitist," "communistic," "communitarian," "commune."[3] Marx and Engels, who studied American communistic societies with an eye to supporting "scientific" socialism, ultimately gave these communities their most familiar, if least appropriate, name: "utopian socialist." In their haste to embrace a collective life style, the members of American communes did anticipate or share the political naïvete of utopian socialist writers who proposed to unite all classes in the immediate construction of ideal communities, but even the most optimistic commune members had to come to terms with real people and real places. Engels pointed out the paradox which utopian theorists such as Robert Owen and Charles Fourier ignored: "The more completely ... [their plans] were worked out in detail, the more they could not avoid drifting off into pure phantasies."[4] Communards encountered a different paradox: the more their communities were worked out in detail, the more they became particular solutions for particular groups and the less they seemed applicable to the larger society.

Even though the communards' strategy can be criticized, some of their model communities were prodigious feats of consistent social and physical design. Their common sense contrasts with the dreamy extravagance of much utopian writing; their imagination and inventiveness distinguish them from the regimentation of much state socialism. Since the communards' collective dwellings and workshops were constructed in an American context, they are steeped in our national lore of earthly paradise, frontier self-reliance, democracy, and moral superiority.

Thus they challenge American family life styles and American capitalist industries more directly than communes in China, *kibbutzim* in Israel; or *ujamaa* villages in Tanzania: they turn our own cultural and historical assumptions upside down. Even more provocative than their collective organization is their feminist organization: those few communes which attempted to change the role of women were designed to include facilities for communal child care, communal cooking, and communal housework. Here one finds arrangements for egalitarian living which possess a liberatory potential unmentioned in most utopian writing and unrealized in most socialist states.

During the past ten years in the United States, communal strategies have been revived by thousands of groups. Some are rural communities attempting to become economically self-sufficient, others are urban groups of individuals working in traditional jobs but living communally to find support for their ideas. Along with the new communes has come new theoretical support for the argument, first advanced by Owen and Fourier, that revolution must replace existing industrial conurbations with decentralized, self-sufficient communities combining industry and agriculture. Although the site plans and housing designs published here may be of use to existing communes and other organizations dedicated to this ideal, I did not seek them out primarily for that purpose. So many architects prescribe novel housing to preclude political conflict that I feel I must disclaim any connection with these utopian "soft cops" and their Corbusian blackmail, "Architecture or revolution?"[5]

My main purpose in this research was to explore the relationship between social organization and the building process in particular community groups. I began this research as an architecture student and working designer. I had been involved in designing self-help housing for migrant workers, cooperative housing sponsored by trade unions, and communal housing for divinity students working with dropout teenagers. I wondered what involvement in environmental design could mean to groups which were committed to larger processes of community organization, and to groups which saw themselves as countercultures. And I wondered what would result from the process of creating an environment to reduce and collectivize traditional "women's work."

Historic communal groups had mobilized their economic and personal resources to attempt to answer such questions. By focusing on groups of communards involved in the building process, I hoped to document an idealistic aspect of American history and a realistic aspect of architectural history. Most of the literature on historic communes deals uneasily with the relationship of people to their physical surroundings. Sociologists and historians lacking visual inclinations have often taken communitarian landscapes and buildings for granted, treating them as background settings for their particular concerns, although building was the major collective activity for many groups. In contrast, when architectural historians have abandoned utopian design (a favorite subject) in favor of experimental utopian communities, they have chosen to look at monumental buildings such as the Mormons' temples or the Harmonists' Great Hall. They have usually analyzed these buildings as aesthetic objects isolated from the residential, commercial, and industrial buildings and the landscapes which establish their social context. If the "invisible environment" of history and sociology is not fully enlightening, the monument-dominated environment of architectural criticism is far more misleading.

Making such allegations and defying traditional disciplinary boundaries provokes anxiety, my own as well as my readers'. I think that what I have gained by taking a broad look at ideology and built form compensates for some difficulty with purists who do not accept this material as "architecture." I have used the terms "physical planning," "landscape architecture," and "environmental design" quite interchangeably and loosely, and I am not prepared to recognize any traditional aesthetic distinctions between the terms "architecture" and "building." I am concerned with the changing, continuous relationship between life style and life space. I am asking, with the communitarian theorist Murray Bookchin, "How does the liberated self emerge that is capable of turning time into life, space into community, and human relationships into the marvellous?"[6]

To organize some extended explanations about the ways that communal groups define their life styles and their life spaces, I pose three communal dilemmas. Every group must achieve a balance between authority and participation, community and privacy, uniqueness and replicability. These are crucial areas of political choice which lead to problems of physical design whenever any settlement is built. Since the spatial organization of dwellings and workplaces makes questions of order, sharing, and viability very explicit, self-conscious communal groups often used the design process to explore the transition between socialist theory and practice. It is this transition, expressed in terms of the design process, which I have tried to report and analyze.

Because historic communistic societies defined themselves as models of social and physical design, many of them kept detailed records of their design processes. Model communities were usually bounded, socially and geographically, and their favored list of accomplishments was an inventory of the buildings and the landscape of the domain. While this is all very tidy in terms of substantiating a group's activities, it is necessary to balance the general optimism of members against the more caustic comments of outside observers in order to get at conflicts and problems. Sometimes historic communitarian buildings and sites themselves provided the best clues of what was going on in a community at a given time; discrepancies between what I read and what I saw were the most frequent sources of new interpretations of the history of various communes. The graphic evidence here is arranged to reveal development of each community over time; drawings have been made at similar scales to allow comparisons between communities.

I chose seven groups (Shakers, Mormons, Fourierists, Perfectionists, Inspirationists, Union Colonists, and Llano Colonists), and seven sites (Hancock, Massachusetts; Nauvoo, Illinois; Phalanx, New Jersey; Oneida, New York; Amana, Iowa; Greeley, Colorado; and Llano del Rio, California). Four were religious communities, three were nonsectarian; together they provide a fair representation of the ideological and geographical spread of the communitarian movement, between 1790 and 1938. Their approaches to economic sharing varied widely. Five owned all land communally; two mixed private and communal ownership of land. Three shared all income equally; two equalized wages but offered some return for capital invested; one started on the basis of total sharing but ultimately permitted private property; one started with private property mixed with cooperative ventures. In terms of financial stability and longevity all seven groups would rank somewhere between average and outstanding experiments. Two communal industries, Oneida silverware and Amana woolens, are still the basis of active corporations. All of the groups did a substantial amount of building, and ultimately I selected them because their history was well documented by both inside and outside observers, their buildings were sufficiently well preserved, and their members' approach to the environment was animated with idealism and inventiveness.

Frequently I have been asked, "Weren't all these people crackpots?" or "Weren't all these experiments hopeless failures?" By the third or fourth generation, members of even the most stable experimental societies usually grow restless and choose to rejoin the outside world. But failure, I think, is attributable only to the most unimaginative experiments, and I am willing to define as a success any group whose practices remain provocative even after the group itself has disbanded. Nathaniel Hawthorne, who lived at Brook Farm, provided an eloquent statement of a communard's purpose: "My best hope was, that, between theory and practice, a true and available mode of life might be struck out; and that, even should we ultimately fail, the months or years spent in the trial would not have been wasted, either as regarded passing enjoyment, or the experience which makes men [and women] wise."[7] John Humphrey Noyes, founder of the Oneida Community, offered a more assertive justification: "We made a raid into an unknown country, charted it, and returned without the loss of a single man, woman, or child."[8]

The communitarians' ventures in collective, experimental design are fraught with problems to balance their triumphs. Their idealistic ventures in synthesizing all aspects of community design gain in relevance, as contemporary community groups, as well as planners and architects, become more conscious of the power of environmental design to support or contradict other forms of community organization. The records of early communal "raids into an unknown country" provide us with substantial experience of the rewards and problems of building for a more egalitarian society. Any group involved in environmental design, as part of a broader campaign for societal change, has much to learn from them.

1 Charles Sanford, *The Quest for Paradise*, Urbana, Ill., 1961, p. 40.

2 Peter Blake, *God's Own Junkyard: The Planned Deterioration of America's Landscape*, New York, 1964.

3 The historical antecedents of these terms are discussed by Arthur E. Bestor in "The Evolution of the Socialist Vocabulary," *Journal of the History of Ideas*, 9 (June 1948), 259-302, and in *Backwoods Utopias: The Sectarian Origins and the Owenite Phase of Communitarian Socialism in America: 1663-1829*, 2d enl. ed., Philadelphia, 1970, pp. vii-viii. I will rely on the terms "communistic society," "communitarian" and "commune," since their meaning has changed least in the past century.

4 See Lewis S. Feuer, "The Influence of the American Communist Colonies on Engels and Marx," *Western Political Quarterly*, 19 (Sept. 1966), 456-474; Friedrich Engels, *Socialism: Utopian and Scientific* (1880), tr. Edward Aveling, New York, 1969, p. 36.

5 The term "soft cops" is Robert Goodman's, from *After The Planners*, New York, 1971. "Architecture or revolution" is the rhetorical finish of Le Corbusier's influential work, *Vers une Architecture*, Paris, 1928, p. 241.

6 Murray Bookchin, *Post-Scarcity Anarchism*, Berkeley, 1971, p. 44.

7 Nathaniel Hawthorne, *The Blithedale Romance*, Boston, 1859, p. 76.

8 John Humphrey Noyes, quoted in Constance Robertson, ed., *Oneida Community: An Autobiography, 1851-1876*, Syracuse, 1970, p. 26.

2 The Ideal Community: Garden, Machine, or Model Home?

Now if we can, with a knowledge of true architectural principles, build one house rightly, conveniently and elegantly, we can, by taking it for a model and building others like it, make a perfect and beautiful city: in the same manner, if we can, with a knowledge of true social principles, organize one township rightly, we can, by organizing others like it, and by spreading and rendering them universal, establish a true Social and Political order.

—Albert Brisbane, *A Concise Exposition of the Doctrine of Association, or Plan for a Reorganization of Society*, 1843

2.1 "We are all a little wild here with numberless projects of social reform"; locations of United States communitarian settlements by type and decade of founding, to 1860, are shown here and on following pages. Present state lines are drawn to aid identification; see Appendix B for exact locations, keyed to numbers on map.

1663 - 1780

■ Non-sectarian; foreign leaders
● Non-sectarian; American leaders
▲ Sectarian; foreign leaders
◆ Sectarian; American leaders

"We are all a little wild here with numberless projects of social reform," Ralph Waldo Emerson commented to Thomas Carlyle in 1840. "Not a reading man but has a draft of a new community in his waistcoat pocket."[1] Emerson was referring to the second of several phases of communitarian excitement which swept the United States during the nineteenth century and involved at least one hundred thousand idealistic citizens in hundreds of communistic experiments. Although these idealists have often been dismissed as dreamers, their intense involvement with environmental design demonstrates the practical energy behind their movement. These reformers advocated diverse programs ranging from absolutism to anarchy, spiritualism to atheism, speculative land development to collective industry, but they agreed on their strategy. All believed that social change could best be stimulated through the organization and construction of a single ideal community, a model which could be duplicated throughout the country.

As the creators of model communities, some communards described themselves as "Social Architects" redesigning society. They proposed a complete restructuring of city and country in response to the environmental problems created by the Industrial Revolution. Their goals incorporated both social and physical design. They tried to equal the visionary scope of philosophers who attempted to define human nature and describe programs for its finest expression, and they wanted to match the promotional successes of inventors and entrepreneurs who had influenced American land development and American industry. By adopting the encompassing symbols of the model community as garden and as machine, the communitarians hoped to synthesize many aspects of pastoral and tech-nological idealism which characterized American attitudes toward land and life. In the equally powerful symbol of the ideal community as model home, they hoped to fuse idealism about family and society displayed in facade, hearth, and plan.

Although there were precedents for the communitarian strategy—monasteries established in Europe as models for a new Christian society, and Puritan covenant communities founded in New England in the colonial period—widespread secular and religious acceptance of communitarian tactics occurred for the first time in the United States during the first half of the nineteenth century. Settlers were pushing the line of the frontier westward very rapidly, and it seemed to many reformers that a mobile, expanding society existed which could easily be influenced by new concepts of community design. Victor Considérant, a French socialist and a disciple of Charles Fourier, expressed the communitarian view of America's development quite plainly: "If the nucleus of the new society be implanted upon these soils, to-day a wilderness, and which to-morrow will be flooded with population, thousands of analogous organizations will rapidly arise without obstacle and as if by enchantment around the first specimens. . . ."[2]

Communitarian thinking was most popular in the United States between 1820 and 1850 (Fig. 2.1), decades of agitation for abolition, labor rights, equitable land distribution policies, women's rights, educational reform, and penal reform. Citizens and reformers of various persuasions chose communitarian experiments to express their ideas about social change because alternative strategies of individual dissent, revolution, or gradualist reform seemed ineffectual. Communitarian reform was novel. It was non-

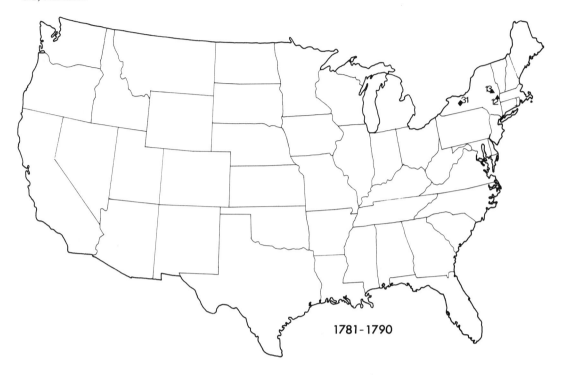

1781-1790

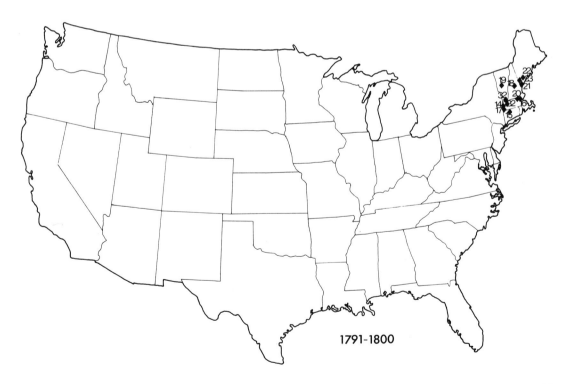

1791-1800

1801-1810

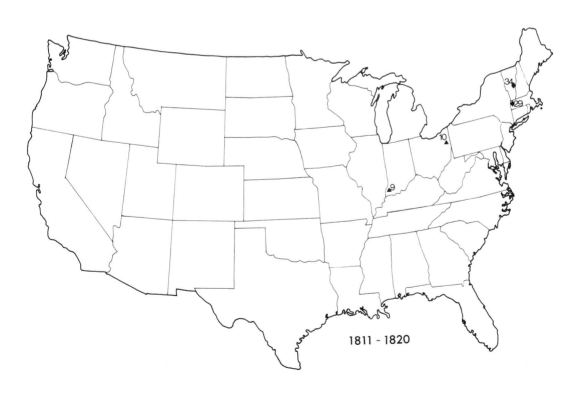

1811 - 1820

2.1, continued

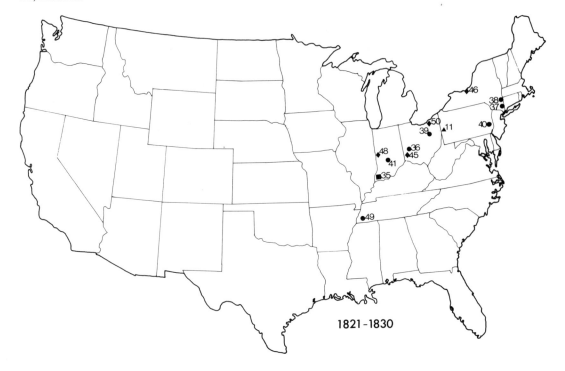

1821-1830

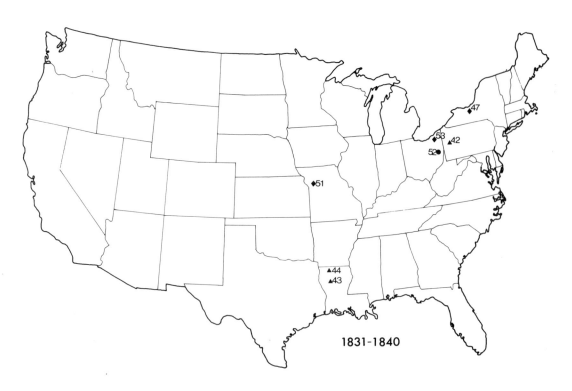

1831-1840

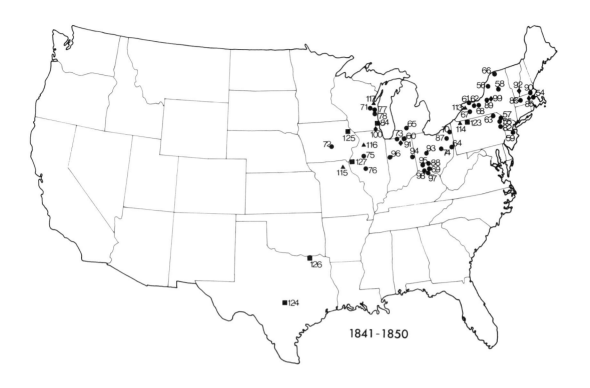

1841-1850

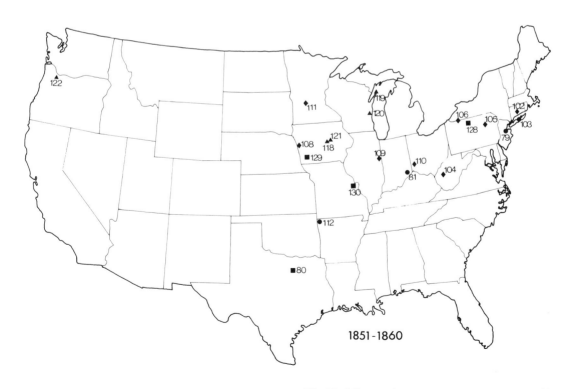

1851-1860

violent, yet total in scope. Thus it offered hope to those Americans, skeptical of violent conflict after the wars of 1775 and 1812, who were committed to developing new institutions through reasoned choice. It was supported by those conservatives who believed that new communities founded in the West would serve as a safety valve to preclude class conflict generated by urban workers in the East. At the same time it appealed to activists who felt that the social and environmental problems created by industrialization were beyond individual effort or gradual reform. The strategy gained adherents in times of economic distress—after depressions of 1837, 1854, 1857, 1873, and 1893—when desperation motivated farmers and workers to call for complete social reorganization. Middle-class citizens were more curious than desperate. Two Presidents and various members of the Supreme Court, the Cabinet, and Congress attended addresses by Robert Owen in 1825; business leaders and intellectuals followed Fourierist propaganda on the front page of the New York *Tribune* in the 1840s.

Not only Americans felt encouraged to launch communal ventures. Although most American communards were native born, a substantial minority were emigrants from England, France, Germany, Scandinavia, and eastern Europe, whose leaders considered the United States the best location for their experiments. Frequent encouragement came from European tourists like James Silk Buckingham and Harriet Martineau. Although the seaboard cities offered educated Europeans limited entertainment, experimental communities provided them with lively anecdotes and the occasional profound insight. Journalists' firsthand reports of successful ventures then encouraged other European groups to follow these examples.

The appeal of communistic societies was not restricted to American reformers or touring Europeans. The ideal community became a symbol of broad persuasive power. It could be presented as "garden," in terms of horticultural and agricultural productivity and its placement in an idealized landscape. It could be presented as "machine," in terms of its efficient design, industrial productivity, and its relationship to an American tradition of political inventiveness; or it could be presented as "model home," in terms of its design and life style. Sectarian communities tended to emphasize pastoral themes; nonsectarian ones, technological themes; but most successful experiments united pastoral and technological symbolism in support of the larger goal of an ideal home. If they joined design practice to theory, their ideals sometimes became surprisingly real.

The American continent was often conceived of as heaven on earth, a new or rediscovered paradise. C. W. Dana, for example, in an essay of 1856 entitled "The Garden of the World, or The Great West," described the area between the Allegheny Mountains and the Pacific Ocean as "The *Land of Promise*, and the *Canaan* of our time. . . . with a soil more fertile than human agriculture has yet tilled; with a climate balmy and healthful, such as no other land in other zones can claim."[3] In the first half of the nineteenth century this was a land scarcely known, mapped along a few trails cut by trappers and explorers, a spatial vacuum on which hopeful idealists imposed an imaginary geography of fecundity, equality, and self-sufficiency.

Such idealism could be rather literal and inhibiting to communal groups. Some German pietist sects were anxious to locate their experiments on the site of the original Garden of Eden. The spiritualists who founded a community at Mountain Cove, West Virginia, in 1851 also claimed that their site was Eden's original location.[4] In an equally literal vein, readers of a Los Angeles communitarian paper were encouraged to join the "People's Army" which would cultivate a farm of 1,000 acres "called the People's Garden, also called the Garden of Eden," where they would enjoy "work in the garb of play."[5] Recruits joining the Union Colony of Greeley, Colorado, were offered an analogy between their irrigation ditches and the river which watered Eden. And this same colony was described as a garden in miniature, where the residence lots were flower beds and the streets, garden paths.

Abandoning literal Edenic references in favor of more diffuse pastoral fervor, many communards posed the virtues of the country against the vices of the American or European city. Images of the communitarian settlement as a pastoral retreat were introduced by the Shakers in contrast to the "great and wicked cities" of the world, and by the Fourierists in contrast to the "unnatural life of our crowded cities."[6] Yet settlements were also described in the religious tradition of the Sermon on the Mount: "Ye are the light of the world. A city that is set upon a hill cannot be hid."[7] The Shakers dealt with the conflict between city and country very neatly, by giving each of their settlements two names, one corresponding to the rural village where it was located, and the other, a "spiritual name" suggestive of the Heavenly Jerusalem, such as "City of Peace," or "City of Love." A similar uncertainty existed, but was not resolved, among the members of the anarchist Kaweah colony, who built "Arcady" and "Progress" side by side.

With the exception of a few religious groups which eschewed industry as worldly or corrupting, most communards wished to establish self-sufficient settlements, based on both industry and agriculture, offering the advantages of both city and country. For many early sectarians, the ideal was a tidy village with a range of craft industries, but later experiments attempted more elaborate settlements with communal dwellings and factories surrounded by collective gardens and fields. Even the most isolated communes created centers of community life which were far more urbane in character than the isolated homesteads which surrounded them. Charles Nordhoff, a traveling journalist, cited cheerful, busy people, small shops, and musical performances as communal assets, and claimed that in the 1870s Amana, Iowa; Zoar, Ohio; Icaria, Iowa; and Aurora, Oregon were all "more like a small section cut out of a city"[8] than like villages (Figs. 2.2, 2.3).

At least part of the conflict between pastoralism and urbanism was resolved by where the communards chose to locate. Expansionist communes based their optimism on the idea of a spatial vacuum beginning at the frontier and extending west, but they did not often establish themselves there. Most groups selected sites in the settled areas short of the frontier, sometimes moving their communities farther west with each succeeding generation. They had to be close enough to civilization to proselytize new recruits and to demonstrate the superiority of their way of life to that of the cities which they denounced. But they could not risk being overrun with visitors. A few communes, such as Oneida and the North American Phalanx, set up urban branches as agencies marketing their products, but urban-based communes, like Stephen Pearl Andrews's "Unitary Home" in New York, were very rare. Most groups settled into the "middle landscape" of agrarian republicanism, that area of cultivated farms, midway between the cities and the wilderness, which has been described by Leo Marx in *The Machine in the Garden* as representing the ideal life style of the colonial period.[9] But instead of a middle landscape of independent farmers, each pursuing his or her own livelihood, the communitarians wanted a collectively owned and organized middle landscape with industry to complement agriculture, a middle landscape organized on a scale to resist the pressures of change and urbanization.

Whatever form a communitarian group decided that its settlement was to take, the members committed themselves to developing land, which they saw as unique and perfectible, something for which they were accountable. In this respect communitarian practice was closer to the careful, balanced land use practiced by the seventeenth century Puritan groups than of the more careless, individualistic approach typical of many nineteenth century homesteaders. In the first half of the nineteenth century, the difference between communitarian attitudes toward the land and the attitudes of other Americans seems striking. In that period most American farmers made money through the rising prices of land, not through successful cultivation. Thus, while many farmers waited for a chance to sell out at a favorable price and move west, they impoverished their land by cropping it constantly to its most lucrative staple.[10]

In contrast to mobile, independent farmers, the communards became very skillful cultivators, concentrating their energies in chosen places. Nordhoff observed:

I know of some instances in which the existence of a commune has added very considerably to the price of real estate near its boundaries. . . . Almost without exception the communists are careful and thorough farmers. . . . Their tillage is clean and deep; in their orchards one always finds the best varieties of fruits. . . . A commune is a fixture; its people build and arrange for all time; and if they have an ideal of comfort they work up to it.[11]

Communitarians could not always afford to purchase good land, but they almost always transformed the land they were able to obtain. In successful communes, scientific methods of agriculture and horticulture were studied diligently. The most up-to-date practices were put into effect by the Shakers, the Mormons, the Perfectionists, the members of the North American Phalanx, and the Greeley Union Colony (among others). Experiments to develop new techniques were also conducted. Sometimes

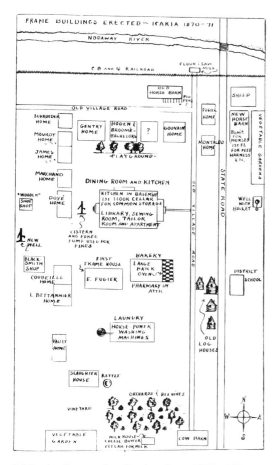

2.2 Icarian Community, Corning, Iowa, 1870-1871.

2.3 A communal village centered on a symbolic garden with evergreen trees representing eternal life and the twelve gates of heaven: Zoar, Ohio, founded 1817.

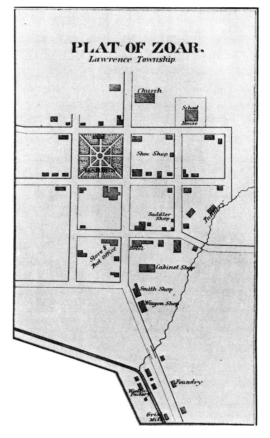

communards made mistakes—the Harmonists thought Lombardy poplars would improve the fever-ridden Indiana climate and the Silkville Fourierists followed the silk culture fad of the 1870s in Kansas—but misconceptions were clarified when communal groups joined in public debates on agricultural and horticultural topics.[12] The Shakers published guides to farming and gardening; other groups submitted articles to well-known agricultural journals.[13]

The art of landscape design also interested communards. Oneida Perfectionists were constantly involved with ornamenting as well as improving their land. Theosophists in Point Loma, California, collected exotic plants from all over the world to develop their domain as a replica of Eden, although their technique was more suggestive of Noah filling up the Ark.[14] Mormons, who were also preoccupied with Edenic imagery, planted thousands of fruit trees. Harmonists built greenhouses and developed elaborate garden plans (Figs. 2.4, 2.5) symbolic of the community's relationship with the outside world; a Zoar garden reflected the members' religious beliefs with a radiating geometrical pattern (Fig. 2.3). Residents of Zion City, Illinois, combined radiating streets with picturesque landscape elements reminiscent of Frederick Law Olmsted's plan for the suburb of Riverside, Illinois.[15] Cemeteries were another preoccupation of communitarian landscape designers, and communal projects included Hopedale's attempt to imitate the picturesque planting of Mount Auburn Cemetery,[16] Amana's even rows of identical graves surrounded by evergreens, and Salem's reflection of the Moravian choir system in cemetery landscaping.

In all these practical ways, communistic societies planted and pruned their way to earthly paradise. Thus the founders of communes who first revised traditional utopian thinking in light of their collective vision of the American landscape, then enriched and developed the American landscape with their collective efforts. The ideal of a paradisiacal garden provided a symbolic explanation for each settlement's location and sustained the members' commitment until their domains had been developed. Then the communards could draw strength and inspiration from their own landscapes, the real gardens which they had developed.

The Ideal Community   18

2.4 Harmonist garden maze with meditation hut, New
Harmony, Indiana, founded 1814.

2.5 Harmonist garden, meditation hut, Economy,
Pennsylvania, founded 1824.

The Community as Garden

When communitarians described a model settlement as an "invention," it was as a social invention, analogous to a mechanical invention which could be designed and then mass produced. In 1820 the British social theorist, Robert Owen, presented a plan for a model community (Fig. 2.6) in this light: "If the invention of various machines has multiplied the power of labour . . . THIS is an invention which will at once multiply the physical and mental powers of the whole society to an incalculable extent, without injuring anyone by its introduction and its most rapid diffusion."[17] In the same vein Albert Brisbane prophesied that Fourier's theory of communal "Association" (Fig. 2.7) would do for household organization "what the mariner's compass did for navigation, the telescope for astronomy, and steam for machinery."[18]

In terms of politics, the communitarian analogy between social and mechanical inventions had been drawn before. The Constitution had been described by its framers as "the most beautiful system which has yet been devised by the wisdom of man."[19] Several heroes of the revolutionary period were inventors in a broad sense: Thomas Paine (who designed bridges), Benjamin Franklin, and Thomas Jefferson. Thus, the communitarian socialist Robert Owen was more credible in American society as an inventor than as a corporate manager; and Charles Fourier carried more weight as a "Social Architect" than as a psychologist. In terms of the physical environment, the invention analogy, popularized by the Utilitarian Jeremy Bentham with his "Panopticon" in 1791 (Fig. 2.8), enjoyed credibility untarnished by the confusion of physics and psychology.

The assertion that the invention of a settlement pattern could solve social problems also reflected Americans' wider confidence in environmental inventions. Jefferson's 1785 Land Ordinance established a physical grid as a social equalizer. Between 1820 and 1850 prison reformers vaunted the social and moral benefits of more architectural "inventions," the punitive designs of the Auburn and Pennsylvania penitentiaries. American mental asylum directors invented curative environments during the same period, often based on qualities sought by communal experiments: isolated sites, buildings designed to express stability, and advanced mechanical equipment.[20] Communitarians had the advantage of belonging to voluntary societies which could resist inappropriate designs; prisoners and the mentally ill were, in some cases, helpless victims of mad inventors (Fig. 2.9).

If the model community plan represented an inventor's theory, the settlement itself represented a working prototype, a "patent office model"[21] which proved that the theory would work in practice. A pioneering spirit, coping and practical, sustained experimental communities in the short run. In the long run, as an extension of the "invention" simile, the successful prototype was expected to inspire national demand. Here theory changed from practicality to vagueness with groups like the Oneida Perfectionists, who ultimately relied upon "the silent action of truth and the Providence of God."[22] Only communities which actively organized duplication of the model, such as the Shakers, the Moravians, and the Mormons, succeeded in reproducing the original settlement to any great extent.

Like the concept of the community as garden, the ideal of the model community as invention found its best expression in practical, direct efforts. The communitarians who be-

2.6 Community designed by Robert Owen, model by
Stedman Whitwell, 1825. The model is raised off the
prairie on a platform; family houses under peaked
roofs surround the square; dining halls and communal
facilities extend toward a central greenhouse; corner
buildings are schools and "conversation rooms."

2.7 Phalanstery designed by Charles Fourier, view by
Jules Arnoult, ca. 1848. Industrial buildings and dove-
cote tower in foreground, across open square from
communal dwelling with enclosed courtyards.

The Community as Machine   21

2.8 Section and plan of a "Panopticon," designed as
an "industry house" (workhouse) or jail, where a single jailer using mirrors can supervise 2,000 inmates. By
Jeremy Bentham, 1791.

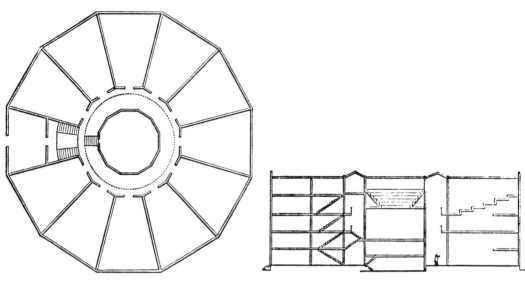

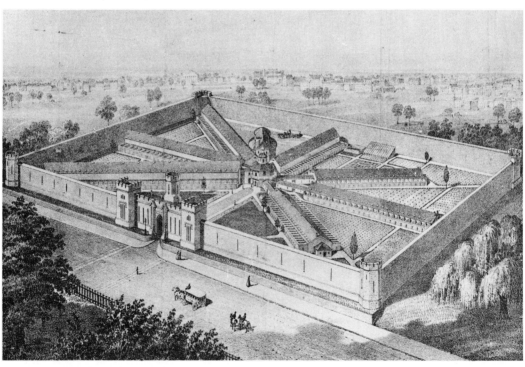

2.9 Communitarians could resist inappropriate designs
(Fig. 2.6), but prisoners and the mentally ill were, in
some cases, helpless victims of mad inventors: Eastern
State Penitentiary, Philadelphia, designed by John
Haviland, 1829. Each prisoner is isolated in a private
cell with private exercise yard.

The Ideal Community   22

2.10 Improved Shaker washing machine, 1878.

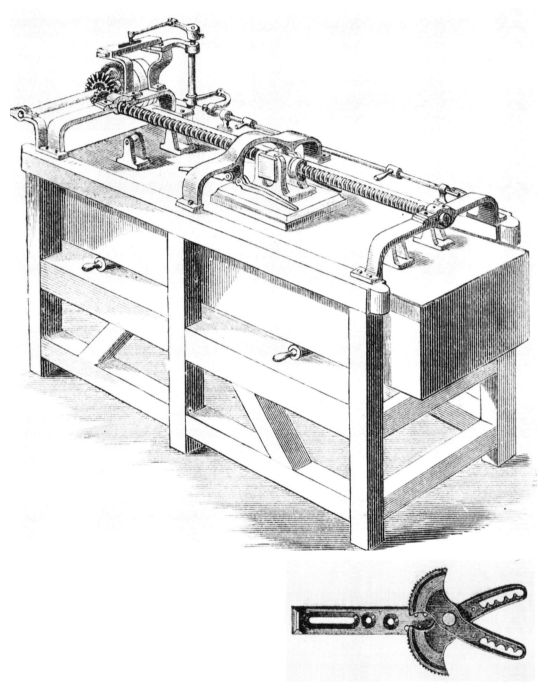

2.11 Shaker window sash lock, 1878.

lieved in inventions developed supportive communal industries which enhanced creativity immensely. They produced dozens of real mechanical devices designed by men and women who considered their patentable inspirations as justification for their social optimism. Among the Shakers (Figs. 2.10, 2.11), inventions were considered gifts from God; among the Oneida Perfectionists, inventions provided the basis of the community economy and filled their mansion with labor-saving devices. Josiah Warren, a member of the New Harmony community and the founder of Modern Times, an experiment in anarchism on Long Island, designed a web press and a variety of stereotyping devices. Other communitarian inventors include Tabitha Babbitt, a Shaker who designed a circular saw and cut nails; Jonathan Browning, a Mormon who designed a repeating rifle, and Sewell Newhouse, a Perfectionist who invented animal traps. Nordhoff observed that "the communist's life is full of devices for personal ease and comfort . . ." and also that "ingenuity and dexterity are developed to a surprising degree in a commune. . . ."[23] Viewed in light of the multiple environmental perfections achieved by the communitarians, the concept of the community itself as an invention seems less naïve or simplistic. Whatever the theorists' intentions, the analogy became the symbolic framework for developing, in concrete ways, the most innovative possible groups.

Garden and machine represent nature and technology; home symbolizes family, in hearth, facade, and plan. When communities issued tracts or posters to recruit new members, they often illustrated them with sketches of their dwellings as tangible proof of their achievements. Along with these illustrations, slogans appeared on the mastheads of communal papers. Oneida's *American Socialist* was "devoted to the enlargement and perfection of home." Topolobampo's *The New City* declared itself for home, "home money, home employment, home protection, home franchise, home virtue, home worship, home ideals, home people, and home day."[24] Communal affection and security could be evoked by a hearth; prosperity and permanence projected on a facade; equality and efficiency suggested by a plan. The model home directed attention to sexual politics, and, like garden and machine, found its truest expression when idealism influenced life style.

In choosing an ideal dwelling as a symbol of social and economic success, communards emulated other Americans, but they resisted the national acceptance of isolated family dwellings located on individual farms. Those communes which favored model family homes wanted them clustered in model villages, reminiscent of Puritan covenant communities. Those communes which advocated small collective dwellings were a bit more unorthodox; those which aimed to house hundreds of communards in a single collective dwelling aroused the greatest incredulity and outrage among their neighbors.

All groups criticized isolated, individual houses as lonely, wasteful, and oppressive; many groups compensated for this attack by attempting to exceed the standards of private dwelling design. Oneida Perfectionists complained of "the gloom and dullness of excessive family isolation," or the "little man-and-wife circle," where one suffered "the discomfort and waste attendant on the domestic economy of our separate households."[25] A Shaker Eldress was unwilling to "bend over the cradle and sing lullabye" as her work; a Llano designer criticized the traditional home as a "Procrustean bed" which maimed women, an "inconceivably stupid" arrangement which confiscated women's labors.[26] When communards described the model community as an ideal home they predicted a place where conviviality, collective economy, and some leisure for women would prevail. The ideal hearth was expected, in the words of the Oneidans, to "knit us together mentally and spiritually," as a "love organization."[27] The ideal facade would inspire respect and aesthetic pleasure. The ideal plan for collective services would enable all to live better together than in isolation, with the reorganization of domestic work lightening the toil of the women of the community.

Images of garden and machine were often summoned to support testimonials for communards' model homes. At Oneida and the North American Phalanx, members were constantly at work improving the gardens adjoining the collective dwellings. In Nauvoo, Greeley, and Amana, colonists competed in planting trees and flowers on private plots surrounding the houses. This form of beautification was straightforward; at Economy and Harmony gardens created a complex symbolic context for a model home. Hedges and shrubs formed mazes, suggesting the paths of life. At the center of the mazes were meditation huts, symbolic houses, reminding members that the community provided a model home in a confusing world.

Mechanical inventions combined with beautiful or symbolic gardens to reinforce the view of the community as an ideal home. Heating, lighting, and sanitation devices contributed to perfect health. The Shakers made domestic labor lighter with removable window sash for easy washing, round ovens for more even cooking, conical stoves for heating irons more efficiently. The Harmony Society constructed floors which could be removed so that it was never necessary to carry furniture up or down stairs in a dwelling.[28] The Oneidans created "lazy susan" tables so that food could be turned instead of passed. In the case of their "pocket kitchen," described in Chapter 7, domestic perfection came not from a new invention, but from recognizing the singular virtues of an old, symbolic hearth.

Domestic inventions were perhaps the communitarians' best advertisement. In most nineteenth century communes "women's work" remained sex stereotyped, but men and women benefited when cooking, cleaning, and child care were collectivized (Figs. 2.12, 2.13, 2.14, 2.15). Labor-saving devices and regular schedules allowed communal domestic workers to enjoy far more leisure than individual homemakers, and this aspect of communal life was reported in detail in popular illustrated magazines.

An indication of how much communal model homes were admired is offered by Catharine Beecher's and Harriet Beecher Stowe's domestic economy manual, *The American Woman's Home*, published in 1869.[29] Although the authors are not sympathetic to communal experiments, they adopt the concept of the ideal community as a model to be mass produced when they describe the single-family home (Fig. 2.16) as a Christian "commonwealth," a model which can be duplicated to achieve the "Heaven-devised plan of the family state."[30]

2.12 The model home directed attention to sexual
politics: communal child care facilities, Familistère,
Guise, France, founded 1859.

2.13 Communal laundry, with Shaker-designed conical
stove to warm flatirons, New Lebanon, New York,
1873.

2.14 Women in the communal bakery, Oneida, 1870.

2.15 "If you have pleasure and love for anything all effort and labor are light." Men and women working in a Moravian bakery, surrounded by Christmas loaves.

This description is accompanied by excellent plans for a cottage equipped with flexible furniture, a streamlined kitchen, and a range of heating, ventilating, and sanitary inventions similar to those enjoyed by communal groups. Elsewhere Catharine Beecher suggests that these "model family commonwealths" can be grouped in model neighborhoods around cooperative bakeries and laundries.[31]

Another attempt to emulate communes' model housekeeping arrangements was launched by the Cambridge Cooperative Housekeeping Society in 1870-1871. Members organized a cooperative bakery, general store, and laundry service available to subscribing housekeepers in Cambridge, Massachusetts, and they argued for the inclusion of such facilities in the new apartment buildings then being constructed for the middle class.[32] The effect of these proposals was mixed: they influenced new groups of communards to reexamine the "unitary home" (Fig. 2.17) and idealize the single family house and cooperative housekeeping, more than they influenced private families to adopt any cooperative practices (Fig. 2.18).[33] The architecture and domestic inventions of the Shakers, Fourierists, Oneidans, and Inspirationists remained a challenge to American domestic design which has not yet been met.

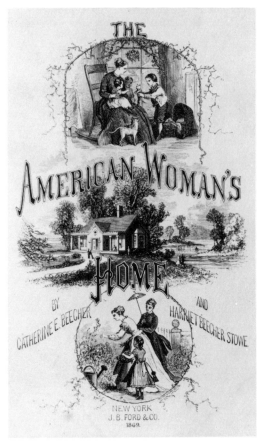

2.16 The single-family home, presented in a communitarian vein, as a Christian "commonwealth," a model which can be duplicated to achieve the "Heaven-devised plan of the family state": *The American Woman's Home*, 1869.

2.17 The Resident Hotel or "unitary dwelling" designed by Albert Kimsey Owen with Deery and Keerl, Architects, Philadelphia, proposed for the Pacific Colony (Topolobampo), Sinaloa, Mexico, ca. 1885-1895.

2.18 An alternative to the unitary dwelling, "model family commonwealths" grouped in "model neighborhoods," with centralized kitchens and laundries, proposed for the Pacific Colony.

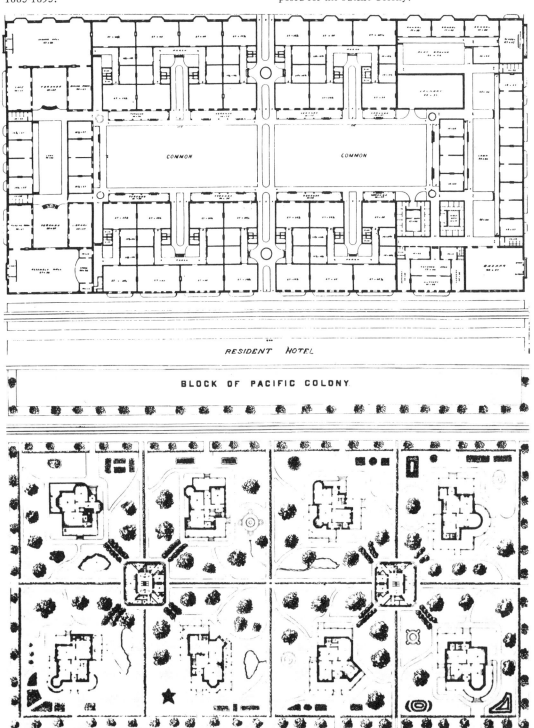

1 Ralph L. Rush, ed., *The Letters of Ralph Waldo Emerson*, vol. 2, New York, 1939, p. 353.

2 Victor Considérant, *The Great West: A New Social and Industrial Life in Its Fertile Regions*, New York, 1854, p. 58, quoted in Arthur Bestor, "Patent-Office Models of the Good Society," supplemental essay to *Backwoods Utopias, The Sectarian Origins and the Owenite Phase of Communitarian Socialism in America: 1663-1829*, 2d enl. ed., Philadelphia, 1970, p. 249.

3 [C. W. Dana], *The Garden of the World, or The Great West; Its History, Its Wealth, Its Natural Advantages, and Its Future, also comprising A Complete Guide to Emigrants*, by an Old Settler, Boston, 1856, p. 2.

4 John Humphrey Noyes, *History of American Socialisms* (1870), New York, 1966, p. 569.

5 *The Industrial Democrat*, 1.1 (Aug. 21, 1914), 1.

6 "Millennial Laws" (1845), reprinted in Edward Deming Andrews, *The People Called Shakers*, 2d ed., New York, 1963, p. 258, and Julia Bucklin Giles, "Address before the Monmouth County Historical Association on The North American Phalanx," MS, n.d. (1922?), Monmouth County Historical Association Library, Freehold, N.J.

7 Matthew 5:14. This same Biblical phrase is quoted in the Covenant of the Massachusetts Bay Colony, which defined the first Puritan covenant community.

8 Charles Nordhoff, *The Communistic Societies of the United States* (1875), New York, 1966, p. 405.

9 See Leo Marx, *The Machine in the Garden: Technology and the Pastoral Ideal in America*, Oxford, England, 1964. For the locations of communitarian settlements, see also Ronald Abler, "The Geography of Nowhere: The Location of Utopian Communities, 1660-1860," unpublished paper, Department of Geography, Pennsylvania State University.

10 Paul Gates, *The Farmer's Age: Agriculture, 1815-1860*, vol. 3, The Economic History of the United States, New York, 1960, pp. 398-399.

11 Nordhoff, *Communistic Societies*, pp. 391-392.

12 William E. Wilson, *The Angel and the Serpent: The Story of New Harmony*, Bloomington, 1964, p. 41; also see Garrett R. Carpenter, "Silkville: A Kansas Attempt in the History of Fourierist Utopias, 1869-1892," *The Emporia State Research Studies*, vol. 3, no. 2 (Dec. 1954).

13 James Holmes, *Useful Hints in Farming*, West Gloucester, Maine, 1850; *The Gardener's Manual*, New Lebanon, 1843. See also Russell H. Anderson, "Agriculture among the Shakers, Chiefly At Mount Leba-

non," *Agricultural History*, 24 (July 1950), 133-120, and "New Lebanon, Its Physic Gardens and Their Products," *American Journal of Pharmacy*, 24 (Jan. 1852), 88-91.

14 Emmett A. Greenwalt, *The Point Loma Community in California, 1897-1942: A Theosophical Experiment*, University of California Publications in History, vol. 48, Berkeley, 1955.

15 Philip L. Cook, *Zion City, Illinois: John Alexander Dowie's Theocracy*, Zion City, Ill., 1970, p. 7.

16 Daniel Bluestone, "A City Which Cannot Be Hid," unpublished paper, Department of Architecture, M.I.T., Jan. 1974.

17 Robert Owen, "Report to the County of Lanark," May 1, 1820, in *A New View of Society and Report to the County of Lanark*, ed. V. A. C. Gatrell, Harmondsworth, England, 1969, pp. 253-254.

18 Albert Brisbane, "Association," New York *Tribune*, August 3, 1842, quoted in Eric Schirber, "The North American Phalanx, 1843-1855," unpublished paper, Department of History, Princeton University, p. 8.

19 Gordon S. Wood, *The Creation of the American Republic, 1776-1787*, Chapel Hill, 1969, p. 594.

20 See David J. Rothman, *The Discovery of the Asylum: Social Order and Disorder in the New Republic*, Boston, 1971. Ellen T. McDougall has traced some of the architectural implications of asylum design in "The Retreat of the Retreat," unpublished paper, Department of Architecture, M.I.T., Jan. 1974.

21 Arthur Bestor, "Patent-Office Models of the Good Society," *Backwoods Utopias*, p. 230.

22 *The Oneida Community: A Familiar Exposition of its Ideas and Practical Life, in a Conversation with a Visitor*. Wallingford, Conn., 1865, p. 19.

23 Nordhoff, *Communistic Societies*, p. 401, p. 415. See also John S. Williams, *Consecrated Ingenuity: The Shakers and Their Inventions*, Old Chatham, N.Y., 1957.

24 *The American Socialist*, 1-4 (1876-1879); *The New City*, 1.1 (Dec. 8, 1892), 1.

25 Goldwin Smith, *Essays on Questions of the Day, Political and Social*, New York, 1893, chapter on "The Oneida Community and American Socialism"; John Humphrey Noyes, *History of American Socialisms* (1870), New York, 1966, p. 23.

26 Mary Antoinette Doolittle, *Autobiography of Mary Antoinette Doolittle,* Mount Lebanon, 1880: see also Chapter 10, n. 31.

27 John Humphrey Noyes, address on "Dedication of the New Community Mansion," Oneida *Circular*, Feb. 27, 1862, p. 9.

28 Wilson, *The Angel and the Serpent*, p. 41.

29 Catharine E. Beecher and Harriet Beecher Stowe, *The American Woman's Home, or Principles of Domestic Science; Being a Guide to the Formation and Maintenance of Economical, Healthful, Beautiful, and Christian Homes*, New York, 1869.

30 Catharine E. Beecher, "How to Redeem Women's Profession from Dishonour," *Harper's New Monthly Magazine*, 31 (Nov. 1865), 716.

31 Catharine E. Beecher, "A Christian Neighborhood," *Harper's New Monthly Magazine*, 34 (Apr. 1867), 575.

32 Cambridge Co-operative Housekeeping Society, *Prospectus*, Cambridge, Mass., 1869. See also Chapter 9, n. 30.

33 See the proposed combination of single family homes and resident hotels in Ray Reynolds, *Cat's Paw Utopia*, El Cajon, Calif., 1972, a discussion of the Topolobampo community. Another work which suggests a combination of unitary dwellings and single-family cottages is Beta (E. B. Bassett), *The Model Town*, Cambridge, Mass., 1869. See also Bradford Peck, *The World A Department Store* (New York, 1890) and Henry Olerich, *A Cityless and Countryless World: An Outline of Practical Co-operative Individualism* (Holstein, Iowa, 1893), both republished in New York in 1971 in a series on utopian fiction edited by Arthur Orcutt Lewis. Both recommend cooperative apartment houses with many of the features of Fourierist unitary dwellings.

3 The Communal Building Process

Every force evolves a form.

—Shaker proverb

What is unusual about the Bruderhof is that its chief sacred object is not a mountain, or a stone, or a book, but the community itself.

—Benjamin Zablocki, describing the Bruderhof, in *The Joyful Community*, 1972

Detail of 10.23

As theoretical reformers, some communards called themselves "social architects"; as committed settlers, most of them intended to create what might be called an "architecture of social change," environmental demonstrations of their programs for society. When communitarians began to build a settlement, the contradictions inherent in their strategy—that the model community must be controlled but innovative, collective but voluntary, unique but replicable—became design dilemmas. With much of their credibility depending on their skills as community builders, communitarians became intensely concerned with planning, landscape design, and architecture. If their model communities were to be successful as both social and physical inventions, they needed design skills as well as organizing skills to resolve the dilemmas they encountered as builders.

In their critiques of existing society, communitarians often cited architecture as an eloquent language which made very clear statements about social structure. Describing marble bank facades and shoddy tenements in New York, the Fourierist promoter Albert Brisbane exclaimed: "The spirit of a society is stamped upon its architecture. Do not the inanimate constructions which surround us proclaim the want of a new social order? Do not they speak to us . . . of the falseness of society and the urgent necessity of a great Social Reform?"[1]

Asserting that their existing environments proclaimed the ideology of capitalism and shaped behavior to suit that economic system, many communitarians concluded that radically different environments were necessary to meet their personal and collective needs. But criticisms of existing environments fell short of new approaches to design. Symbolic concerns were often sources of attitudes toward design: the concept of the community as a garden expressed the communitarian commitment to the wise use of land and natural resources; the concept of the community as a machine expressed the communitarian belief in creating ingenious inventions; and the concept of the community as an ideal home expressed the communitarian interest in extending the family spirit and collectivizing homemaking. But these various symbolic concerns did not always add up to a coherent approach to planning and building. Communards' struggles to achieve a synthesis of their ideological and architectural concerns are the subject of this chapter and the successive case studies; the processes are of as much interest as some of the eventual products.

Sectarian groups looked first to the Holy Bible, especially to passages about the Heavenly Jerusalem, for guidance in shaping their communities. The description of the Heavenly Jerusalem, "and the city lieth foursquare, and the length is as large as the breadth"[2] inspired many square town plans, including the Mormon "Plat of the City of Zion." Descriptions of the Temple of Solomon inspired the Shakers to develop metaphorical equivalents of its sequence of courtyards and gates, and led the Pietists of Ephrata to use wooden joints rather than nails in imitation of the Temple's construction without the sound of hammers.[3] The Ephrata group also created doorways that one must stoop to enter, since they believed that "low and narrow is the way," and their literal interpretation of scripture led them to extreme asceticism.

Nonsectarian socialists found that utopian writings and architectural designs furnished the most provocative visions of what their communities could look like. For a bizarre model of efficiency they could look to the utilitarian philosopher Jeremy Bentham, and his plan for a "Panopticon," a workhouse for two thousand people supervised by a single jailer manipulating a system of mirrors (Fig. 2.8).[4] Robert Owen offered descriptions of "parallelograms" which Stedman Whitwell, his architect, presented in model form to President John Quincy Adams and exhibited in the White House in 1825. One of Bentham's and Owen's more imaginative ideas was extending bunks from the walls at night and pulling them up to the ceiling to free the space by day.[5] Charles Fourier described the architecture of a model phalanstery at length, and was perhaps the best source of architectural advice. He was concerned about creating spaces which fostered stable human relationships and made so many specific archi-

tectural recommendations, that a modern systems designer calls him a "detail man par excellence."[6] Etienne Cabet provided some general architectural descriptions of his utopian city of Icar, but he resorted to promising a prize for the best design of a single-family house with prefabricated parts, rather than suggest how dwellings might be built.[7] The work of Bentham, Owen, Fourier, and Cabet suggests the problem of rigid, geometric plans conceived by visionary writers and architects—they are designed for imaginary space, not for the life space of communities (Figs. 3.1, 3.2). In the style of Thomas More, whose Utopia is an island of identical houses and identical gardens flourishing in balmy weather, these designers provided ideal plans for ideal places, and they were often too unrealistic to offer much guidance to communitarian settlers (Figs. 3.3, 3.4, 3.5).

Although some communitarians were determined to create plans based upon the Bible or the suggestions of utopian writers, other communitarians looked around to decide what contemporary monumental or vernacular architecture was worth imitating. Joseph Paxton's Crystal Palace in London, built in 1851 (Fig. 3.6), was much admired, perhaps because of its associations with greenhouses and gardens symbolic of Eden, or its prefabrication, symbolic of easy replication, but it was almost as remote from communards' resources as the utopian prototypes. Fourierists who hoped to create large communal dwellings or "combined households" admired the palace of Versailles, and, on a more local level, looked to grand hotels as prototypes of collective dwellings.[8] One anonymous Fourierist illustrated Alcander Longley's book, *Community Homes*, with pictures of the "White City," the Columbian Exposition of

1893 in Chicago, showing how exhibition pavilions could be used as communal dwellings and workshops.[9] Some other groups also admired this eclectic, neoclassical architectural assemblage as a demonstration of the virtues of determined urban design, but the Fourierist's point was more polemical: he or she seems to have intended to take over the exhibition, not imitate it.

For prototypes of less than landmark quality, communitarians turned to pattern books. The first Mormon Temple in Kirtland, Ohio, was based on a plate from Asher Benjamin.[10] Andrew Jackson Downing's books on rural landscape gardening and architecture were popular with the members of the Oneida Community, and they built Italianate facades adapted from Downing's illustrations.[11] The octagonal house plans (Fig. 3.7) published by the eccentric phrenologist, Orson Squire Fowler, were admired perhaps because of their uniqueness, perhaps because polygonal forms suggested equality.[12] The Hopedale Community in Massachusetts and Modern Times, in Brentwood, New York, actually built octagons;[13] Brook Farmers expressed interest in Fowler's ideas, but did not build in this manner. Catharine Beecher's books on the ideal home were also well regarded, for she dealt with ideal interiors and advanced mechanical equipment, as well as overall building design.[14] By the turn of the century Ebenezer Howard's plans for *Garden Cities of To-Morrow* were in favor.[15]

Vernacular traditions of building influenced the communitarians even more than published plans. Many of them launched their settlements with log cabins or sod houses out of necessity. When their finances improved, they adopted local building traditions based upon familiar materials and techniques. Shaker designs owe much to the New England Puritan village, and other American groups also revered this model. Foreign groups of communitarians, like other immigrants, often wished to retain the building traditions of their homelands. The Moravians, Harmonists, Inspirationists, and Separatists created German villages; the Jansenists recreated some Swedish building types; colonists at Icaria and Réunion imitated French prototypes.

After the communitarian movement was fairly well established in the 1840s, groups could look to each other for architectural inspiration. The Shakers' village designs were too intimately connected with their ideology for easy imitation, but their furniture seems to have been purchased by other groups, including the Harmonists.[16] The Harmonists' towns were imitated by the Mormons, who in time had their own imitators, the Union Colony of Greeley, and by the Llano Community. Various Fourierist groups traded plans for communal dwellings, and their plans strongly influenced the Oneida Perfectionists, who then gave advice on building to everyone who read their journal, *The American Socialist*. The phalanstery design introduced in the New York *Tribune* in the 1840s lived on even beyond Oneida—a similar building was planned for Fountaingrove, California, in the late nineteenth century, and another was erected in Newllano, Louisiana, in 1934.

Given the influence of contemporary building, both American and foreign, monumental and vernacular, what chance did the communistic societies have of creating something different or distinctive? Communal design became distinguished because of the collective purpose inherent in the design process. Communitarians sought consistency which was most uncommon in other rural American towns, where isolated farms and a few crossroads shops formed rather

3.1 Rigid, geometric plans, designed for imaginary space, not for the life space of communities: Sforzinda, by Filarete, 1457-1464.

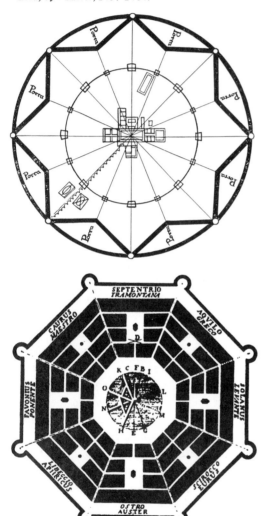

3.2 "Ideal City," by Galiani, after Vitruvius, seventeenth century.

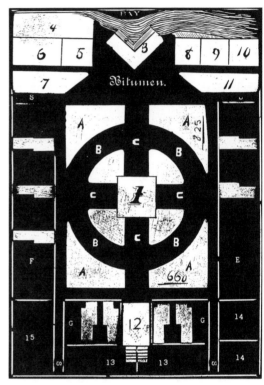

3.3 Some communards favored geometric designs: a circular park serves as town center in the plan proposed for Winter's Island, California, 1895. A, lawn; B, drive; C, walks; 1, hotel; 2, wharves; 3, warehouse; 4, lumberyard; 5, blacksmith shop; 6, machine shop; 7, cannery; 8, power house; 9, waterworks; 10, laundry; 11, sheds; 12, schoolhouse; 13, playgrounds; 14, stores; 15, hothouse and seed beds; S, street; E, four-room cottages; G, six-room cottages. Building lots one-quarter acre; hotel, $12 \frac{1}{2}$ acres; whole plot, 34 acres. "The whole open space between the square and the warehouses to be macadamized or bitumenized."

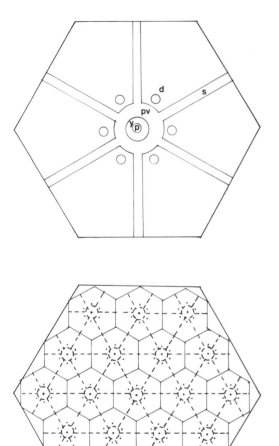

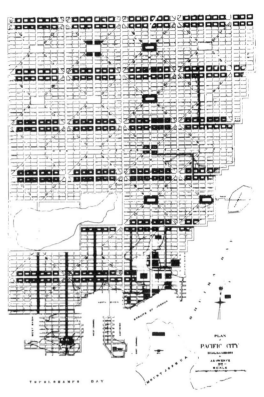

3.5 Grid with diagonal circulation, proposed for the
Pacific Colony (Topolobampo), Sinaloa, Mexico,
1880. Resident hotels and rowhouses are darkened in
a grid of single family homes.

3.4 Hexagonal block and grid by J. Madison Allen,
1873, published by Josiah Warren, founder of Modern
Times, New York, and Utopia, Ohio. Plan shows one
section of a city: p, public building; y, yard; pv, pavil-
lion or circular street; d, private dwellings; s, streets.
Plan of the whole city shows these blocks repeated.
Each private lot is 3-5 acres.

3.6 Greenhouses and gardens symbolized Eden; prefabrication suggested industrial mass production: thus
the Crystal Palace, 1851, by Joseph Paxton, was a
favorite prototype for communards.

3.7 Octagons combined the geometric symbolism of
ideal cities with the phrenological virtues of "construc-
tiveness," and "inhabitativeness" which appealed to
communards: the octagonal dwelling of Orson Squire
Fowler, Fishkill, N.Y., 1854.

The Communal Building Process   38

incoherent settlements. Their search for consistency was expressed in their programs to plan and build entire towns, using their collective resources to construct a range of communal facilities from public meeting places to private dwellings. Consistency was also expressed in their efforts to create a balance of industry and agriculture, which differentiated their patterns of land use from those of company towns like Lowell or Pullman, coherent architectural statements of the restrictive structure of industrial capitalism. Despite ideological variations within the communitarian movement, environmental design presented similar problems to all groups with similar strategies. All groups faced choices: authoritarian versus participatory processes; communal versus private territory; unique versus replicable designs. These dilemmas derived from the communitarian definition that an experimental community must be controlled but innovative, collective but voluntary, unique but replicable. Only if communities resolved these contradictions in the process of design and building could they achieve their ideological and architectural goals.

When a communitarian group began its experiment, the design and construction of buildings first made the ideal society seem real. Like new settlers anywhere, communitarians asked themselves what physical planning their new life style required. How much money should they spend on land? On buildings? The answers depended upon full examination of their needs. Was housing to be designed for nuclear families or for a communal family? What communal gathering spaces did they need? Should they concentrate effort on agricultural facilities or on manufacturing facilities? And how was agreement on these issues to be reached?

Although all communes involved their members in making such decisions, attitudes toward participation and leadership in design varied in sectarian and nonsectarian groups. Cohesiveness in religious communities was often enforced by the implicit threat of damnation for those members who defied the divine authority embodied in the leaders or prophets. In such groups charismatic leaders often wielded absolute authority over all spheres of community life including the planning and design of the settlement. Sometimes their decisions were justified as God's own designs. Shaker leaders claimed the Millennial Laws concerning building were revealed to them by God; Amana elders received building directions from God through their prophets; George Rapp asserted that an angel had shown him the plan of the Harmonists' Economy church.[17] Joseph Smith, the Mormon prophet, announced that God gave him first a plan for the Kirtland Temple, then the "Plat of the City of Zion," and then the plan for the Nauvoo Temple. His followers were so concerned with interpreting the divine will accurately that they were afraid they had been expelled from Nauvoo because they had not built the city correctly according to the Divine Plat.[18] In general, those sectarian groups under the most authoritarian rule produced the most coherent architectural statements of their beliefs. Product was much more important to them than process. But, correspondingly, these groups had the greatest trouble balancing doctrinaire approaches to building with enough openness to members' criticisms to encourage growth and change.

Nonsectarian communes found it much more difficult to develop effective community leadership, and this problem is reflected in their architectural design. In the secular community almost all issues were open to discussion and compromise, and many groups disavowed individual or committee leadership in favor of government by consensus. When cohesiveness was lacking, it was difficult to develop consistent plans or a coherent architectural style. Designs tended to result from pragmatic compromise, typified by the Llano del Rio General Assembly's decision to accept one woman's design for the facade of a new school and another man's plan for its interior. To the casual observer buildings designed by consensus may often present a much weaker architectural expression of the communal ideal than the more authoritarian communities achieved. To heighten the contrast, secular groups usually avoided building churches and symbolic monuments of any sort. But paradoxically, the process of design was sometimes more important to these secular groups than it was to the sectarians, since it assisted collective exploration of various communal alternatives.

The importance of design compromises as expressions of the group's consensus should not be underestimated. The overall cohesiveness of many communities depended upon the contin-

ual, voluntary involvement of the people in decisions which epitomized their idealism. The Llano del Rio community lost cohesiveness when discussions turned away from the buildings which were actually needed and under construction. When Llano's leaders introduced the chimera of the "ideal socialist city" of the future, the working out of current problems in assemblies was ended. Members of the Greeley Union Colony found that the cohesiveness of their community lessened when the group stopped arguing over their communal irrigation system, which served as a focus of discussion about equality, and turned their attention to the construction of private homes and different bits of symbolic architecture—a Methodist church, a Baptist church, a Masonic lodge.

At least a few groups insisted upon design by consensus throughout their existence, and tentatively changeable plans served this need better than rigid, monumental ones. The residents of the North American Phalanx rejected a large symbolic edifice which their patrons urged upon them in favor of a smaller dwelling, with wings added every year. Their patrons' dogmatic refusal to understand this choice resembles the authoritarianism of many sectarian leaders, and reveals their unwillingness to see design as both process and product. At least one religious community institutionalized design by consensus. At Oneida, evening meetings were often devoted to dwelling and landscape design, and the community's building program, stretching over thirty years, was a constant expression of its social stability. When at last they consulted an outside architect, breakup was impending. As the example of Oneida demonstrates, although planning and design by two hundred members was extremely slow, it was a source of continued communal satisfaction.

Contemporary advocate planners offer the warning that participation is no substitute for control,[19] but in small, voluntary communities like Oneida or the North American Phalanx, participation reflected real support for the building decisions which were made.

Moving from design to construction, the differences between authoritarian and participatory styles were often resolved in building practice. Almost all communities built their own buildings. In addition to performing routine construction jobs, community members often set high standards of craft and inventiveness. Members constantly involved in improving a community's land or adapting its buildings were less possessive of their personal space than they would otherwise have been, and members who were urged to express their creativity through inventions had less reason to fear loss of individual identity in other spheres of collective life. Participation in building was especially effective when it was linked to Perfectionist religious beliefs, uniting the desire to do something effective in the present with the desire to serve as an example for the world in the future, explicitly relating the best construction to the keenest communitarian idealism.

Perfectionism did not imply the creation of perfect landscapes or buildings at any one moment, for its complement was patience. The route to perfection was usually adaptation, coaxing and developing ideas to fruition, building upon advances made by other members of the community. When there was scope for improvement—an older member's brainstorm, a new recruit's sudden observation—a much higher level of quality in overall design was achieved. At the same time a sense of community was fostered by the multitude of small individual contributions which made communal life perceptibly more perfect. The preceding chapter suggested some of the ways that perfectionism helped make ideals real: linking the pastoral ideal with improvements to land; the technological ideal with refinement of tools and environments; and the domestic ideal with elaboration of the comforts of home. Perfectionism in building incorporated all of these symbolic activities. It could help to resolve the dilemma of authoritative versus participatory design by uniting many diverse individuals in a constant cycle of design, construction, and adaptation, a process of making the communitarian ideal into a functioning collective settlement.

All communal groups needed a strong sense of their collective identity if they were going to develop a cohesive community, yet most recruits who were willing to isolate themselves from society were strong-willed, independent individuals. Oneidans piously exhorted each other to develop the "we-spirit" instead of the "I-spirit."[20] Nathaniel Hawthorne, who lived at Brook Farm, was a bit more cynical about the dilemma of creating the voluntary, yet cohesive experiment: "Persons of marked individuality— crooked sticks as some of us might be called— are not exactly the easiest to bind up into a fagot."[21]

A design process emphasizing adaptation and participation helped build cohesiveness, but in spite of collective building activity, questions of communal and private space remained. The communitarian group required an isolated, defined place for its experiment, collectively developed as an expression of the group's ideology, which could not be worked out without keen intuitive understanding of environmental psychology. An explicit discussion of territoriality could avert friction over questions of private property and privacy; an innate understanding of the social properties of spaces could promote community. The concepts of "sociofugal" and "sociopetal" spaces, which discourage or encourage the formation of relationships by making it difficult or easy for groups to gather, were well articulated by the Shakers, the Oneidans, and the Fourierists, long before these ideas became the basis of discussions about twentieth-century psychiatric ward design.[22] Understanding the properties of spaces and individuals' reactions to space, self-conscious groups could negotiate a balance between communal and private territory, an essential part of subordinating old concepts of

private property to new concepts of communism. At least three main areas of design can be identified: boundaries, approaches, and vantage points which helped to define the communal territory; communal buildings and housing which sheltered communal activities; and circulation paths which linked a variety of indoor and outdoor spaces.

Boundaries, Approaches, and Vantage Points

Distinct boundaries, controlled approaches, and elevated vantage points emphasized a community's territory as a symbolic whole, separate from society. Literary and architectural utopias often stress isolation achieved by fantastic devices: the canals surrounding Plato's Atlantis; the channel separating More's Utopia from the mainland; the platform lifting Owen's New Harmony off the prairie (Fig. 2.6). Communitarians had to seek real rather than imaginary methods of delineating their borders.[23] Communities at Beaver Island, Michigan, and Point Loma, California, achieved the maximum ecological insulation of an island or a peninsula, while other groups like Kaweah and Llano del Rio depended upon watersheds. Although geographical isolation could offer a community a chance to develop undisturbed, as the Mormons did in the Great Basin, it also brought problems of transportation and communication, such as those encountered by the Llano del Rio community in the Mohave Desert, or the North American Phalanx, whose markets could be reached only over ten miles of bad roads covered in heavy sand.

Whether or not geographical borders delineated a community's territory, approaches to the community were usually marked and controlled. Distinctive fences, prominent features of Shaker landscapes, were also erected by the

Harmonists, the Inspirationists, the Separatists, the Mormons, and the Union Colonists.[24] The Theosophists designed massive ceremonial gates leading to Lomaland (Fig. 3.8). Even more effort was employed to give visitors a sense of transition from ordinary landscapes to consciously composed ones. Crossing the border of the Shaker community at New Lebanon, New York, Horace Greeley reported that the Shakers' roads were better paved than the town highways which led into them, and commented that a monarch could envy their lawns.[25] A visitor to the North American Phalanx commented on the charm of the entrance road winding amid grapevines and wild blackberry bushes before reaching the community dwellings in a romantic, sequestered location overlooking gardens and a small lake. The same reporter also claimed that the soil changed color when one crossed the Phalanx border.[26]

Within the well-defined borders of the experimental community, vantage points allowed members to survey the whole of their model domain.[27] The Shakers established mountain sanctuaries; the Oneidans built towers; the Mormons constructed a promenade atop their Nauvoo Temple; the Amana Inspirationists used a windmill as a vantage point (Figs. 3.9, 3.10). From here they observed their landscapes, where the recycling of water and waste within closed systems restated their boundaries. They could also observe a range of services defining their self-sufficient economies. A typical commune would include a blacksmith shop, a machine shop, a sawmill, a gristmill, a printing plant, a communal store, a school, a church, and perhaps a hotel. Delight in self-sufficient community facilities was keenest among the Shakers, who assigned one or more special facilities to each communal family of thirty to one

hundred people, then sited and painted these buildings according to their uses, establishing a color code of services.

Communal Buildings and Housing

Boundaries, approaches, and vantage points defined the communal territory as a self-sufficient whole, emphasizing collective land use, but within the domain a variety of communal and private activities took place, each requiring its particular territory.

Every community required ceremonial space for its collective activities. A church sheltered a community's worship; a dining hall, its feasts; an assembly hall, its decision making; a dance hall, its social life. If these buildings were carefully designed and constructed, they enhanced the rituals. If they were attractive places, members frequently assembled in the collective territory and made the community a lively and pleasant place to live. If they were neglected, members were likely to retreat to their dwellings and group spirit would flag.

Providing community facilities filled a fairly obvious communal requirement, but creating housing raised innumerable questions about the advantages and disadvantages of private and communal space. As the discussion of the commune as an ideal home indicated, communards included proponents of the communal dwelling, who argued that dissolution of the nuclear family was a prerequisite of community, as well as proponents of the private dwelling, who claimed that retaining the nuclear family within the communitarian settlement was necessary for stability and long-term growth. The inherent dangers of both kinds of housing were predictable. The groups inhabiting communal dwellings tended to break up over issues of sex or of personal privacy. A Bruderhof convert,

3.8 Gates to Lomaland, Theosophical community at Point Loma, California, framing the glass and steel domes of the "Homestead," ca. 1900.

3.9 A windmill used as a vantage point: Inspirationist community, Amana, Iowa.

3.10 Within the well-defined borders of the experimental community, vantage points allowed members to survey their model domains: Oneidans in the north tower of their community's mansion, ca. 1868.

for example, is reported to have apostatized after a nightmare about having to live in a dwelling which was surrounded with constricting steel bands made by his fellow communards.[28] The groups who built private dwellings often broke up quarreling over private versus public ownership. Some communities were skillful enough to design accommodations which combined some of the best features of both communal and private dwellings, but developing such designs usually required years of experience with communal living.

Striking a balance between communal and private territory was the basis of many Fourierist designs to promote the "passional attraction" described in Chapter 6. The North American Phalanx tried to include a variety of housing options—dormitory rooms, family apartments, or land for private dwellings—but they found that the inhabitants of private dwellings withdrew themselves from the communal territory more than was desirable. Less choice, and more control, were the goals of the Amana Community, which built small communal houses without kitchens, and of the Llano del Rio Colony, which planned to build single-family houses without kitchens. Members dined communally, balancing the privacy of bedroom and parlor against the required sociability of the dining room.

Most of the communities which believed that the abolition of private space would strengthen group cohesiveness, in time refined their designs to develop more of a balance between communal and private space. Early Shaker dwellings, with three converts sharing one bed, gave way to the family system where converts increased their use of communal space in three stages of membership. The first Oneida Mansion House, with its communal "Tent Room," ex-

cused because members were forced to learn forbearance, was replaced with a second Mansion where most adults had private rooms. Similarly, members of the Woman's Commonwealth in Belton, Texas, who ran a hotel and often sacrificed their personal rooms to guests in busy seasons, eventually retired to a mansion near Washington, D.C., with private rooms for all.[29]

Those communities which emphasized private family dwellings also were forced to develop more balanced designs over time, complementing privacy with community. Mormons in Nauvoo, Illinois, were commanded to build single-family homes of brick on an ambitious pattern which strained private resources, yet tied every builder to the town where so much labor had been invested. In a similar manner the founder of Greeley, Colorado, constructed a large, expensive home in the first year of the experiment and encouraged others to make similar investments. When the Mormons had moved from Nauvoo to Salt Lake, they gave more careful thought to the balance of communal facilities to serve private homes; the Greeley colonists did not, and it proved their undoing. At Llano del Rio the first move away from private homes was the creation of a separate dwelling for teenagers; in the second Llano Colony communal dwellings were provided for single adults and for children of all ages.

Circulation Paths

Whatever combination of communal and private territory a community developed, circulation paths connecting communal and private spaces offered opportunities for encouraging community without regimentation. Organized group activity could best be promoted in structured spaces for community ritual, but more casual social involvement flourished in more ambiguous spaces. Communal stairs, porches, stoops, and corridors offered just enough space for socializing yet were not identified with any particular person or activity.[30]

At the North American Phalanx, dwelling entrances were connected by covered porches, one version of the corridors recommended by Charles Fourier where people would meet between work assignments. A similar purpose lay behind the design of the boardwalks at the Trumbull Phalanx which linked apartments built around an open courtyard. At Oneida underground tunnels connecting the Mansion to nearby buildings served a similar purpose, as did an entrance hall with a barometer and a bulletin board, where members could linger until others stopped to chat with them. Eventually Oneida created small sitting rooms adjacent to corridors to formalize the tradition of casual sociability. At Amana a network of "foot streets" on the interior of each block united the buildings lining the periphery into a neighborhood. The paths plainly expressed the residents' collective use of a communal kitchen house or other facilities, but they extended this collective use of space with the possibility of more informal contacts. Even today they are favorite play areas for Amana children.

In all these circulation spaces members could socialize, if they chose, without the compulsory collective activity typical of a church or dining hall, and without the possible violations of privacy or propriety threatened by entertaining in a bedroom. In contrast to the Phalanxes and Oneida, where the benefits of socializing were appreciated, the Shaker communities prohibited members from loitering in circulation spaces, such as the halls or the doorsteps of buildings. They did use these spaces for rituals, such as the "Cleansing Gift,"[31] and they allowed processions along the exterior circulation paths of their domain during religious ceremonies, so one can infer that they understood the power of such places, but found them inimicable to the strict maintenance of celibate discipline.

If a communistic society had a clear plan for a settlement (whether it had been dictated by a single leader or achieved by consensus), if it conscientiously encouraged members to adapt and perfect the collective plan, and if the plan allowed for an adequate balance between communal and private territory, then the settlement was quite likely to survive. But such an experiment would remain isolated and removed from the problems of society it had set out to correct, unless it could be duplicated. Although the communitarians' ultimate goal was to cover the earth with communities modeled on the original experiment, less than half of all experiments reached the point of constructing the second community, and very few got beyond the creation of a handful of new settlements. If the first hurdle for communitarians was to distinguish the unique qualities of their particular experiment from a mass of vague utopian ideas, the second was to distinguish the limitations of their unique experiment (which had, perhaps, become a utopia) from the broad applicability of its design.

A unique environment could invite celebration: it could reinforce its creators' sense of themselves as a chosen people preaching a new social gospel and it could convey this identity to outsiders, consolidating and enlarging the effects of special dress, language, and customs. A replicable environment, on the other hand, was essential to development of the original settlement, as well as to the establishment of new settlements based on the original model. A Shaker village, for example, could grow by adding one or more "families"; a new Shaker settlement would begin with a single "family" and gradually develop by replicating these environmental and social units. Some groups, seeking uniqueness, became simply eccentric. Others

made too many gestures in favor of replicability, and wound up with nothing visually distinctive or worth duplicating. The Union Colonists of Greeley hoped to inspire a hundred imitations and produced an absolutely mediocre grid town which was, in fact, nearly indistinguishable from hundreds of others in Colorado.

Achieving a balance between unique and replicable plans was necessary in terms of site selection, building program, and building style. For some groups uniqueness began with symbolic descriptions of the site as a special place. For the Mormons, it was important that Nauvoo, Illinois, was midway between the Rockies and the Allegheny Mountains; for the Perfectionists, Oneida was described as the center of a circle outlining the state of New York. The Koreshans picked Estero, Florida, as the point which "the vitellus of the alchemico-organic cosmos specifically determines."[32] A Bruderhof poet described his community's location as "the city where the South and the North shall meet."[33] Of course, if the site was unique, the settlement was not, in principle, replicable. If it was in some way at the center of the universe (whether the universe was defined as America, New York, or the cosmos), then additional settlements would be satellites and slightly inferior. The resolution of this dilemma of site selection could be found only in the realistic assessment of the site as a particular, rather than a unique, place. If its topography, soil, water resources, climate, and possibilities for transportation and communication were pragmatically assessed, the communitarian settlers could deal with resources and problems which were uniquely theirs. And they were much more likely to deal with them wisely, if they were able to see beyond symbolic justifications.

After asserting the uniqueness of their locations, some communitarians went on to attract attention to their experiments through distinctive architectural massing, ornament, materials, and scale, employed both with and without skill in design. The Theosophists of Point Loma developed bold and dramatic round buildings (Fig. 3.8) surmounted by colored glass domes illuminated at night and topped with golden flaming hearts.[34] The community of Topolobampo favored Moorish arches.[35] The Mormons in Nauvoo ornamented their temple with suns, moons, and stars, rather than classical Ionic or Corinthian capitals. Traditional architectural motifs were used in the palaces designed for Fountaingrove, California (Figs. 3.11, 3.12), and for the dwellings of Zion City, Illinois (Fig. 3.13), but in such profusion and confusion that the results might appear unique. Certainly Holy City could claim to be unique— in *kitsch* per square inch (Figs. 3.14, 3.15). Sheer size was sometimes called upon to demonstrate uniqueness, as when the Llano del Rio colony boasted of the West's "largest and most modern rabbitry," and the "largest political card in the United States," a mountaintop advertisement for Socialist candidates.[36] Mobility was the unique feature of a house on wheels, designed by the Harmonists for their shepherds.[37]

Naïve eagerness to be unique could easily lead to pomposity and narcissism in design. Grandiose and unique buildings could attract recruits, publicity, and contributions to the original settlement—but these same structures could suddenly become a group's greatest handicap rather than its greatest asset. An overambitious design, like the $750,000 Mormon Temple for Nauvoo, could bankrupt a community trying to complete it, or exhaust members' enthusiasm, if not their finances. Even if extremely ambitious building projects were carried out successfully, like the Oneida Mansion House, members might lose their desire to build again. After thirty years of work on their Mansion, Oneidans knew the collective cost of a building "perfected" by two hundred community members and resigned themselves to guiding tourists through the model which they could never duplicate. When the Oneidans said, in justification, "What if there is not another bright spot in the wide world, and what if this is a very small one? Turn your eye toward it when you are tired of looking into chaos, and you will catch a glimpse of a better world,"[38] they sounded a bit defensive.

In terms of architectural style and building program, finding a balance between unique and replicable plans required a consistent approach to many diverse social and architectural issues. Most of the communities which were able to duplicate their first settlement developed consistent styles of building. And most of them developed coherent networks of buildings rather than single edifices, networks which corresponded to the various social groups within the community. Thus, the unit of reproduction was the cluster or neighborhood of six to thirty people rather than the settlement itself, and the clusters within the settlement were unified by a consistent style of vernacular building.

How did communitarians develop a consistent vernacular style? One anthropologist defines vernacular styles of building as typified by a small number of building types, adapted to various needs, arranged with emphasis on the connections between volumes rather than the volumes themselves, integrated with the site, and constructed in local materials by members of a defined culture who build in a tradition agreed upon by all.[39] This is a definition often applied to building by primitive cultures remote from industrial civilization, but it has some relevance to building by communes in isolated settlements. The definition emphasizes adaptation and connections. The comparison gains significance from the communards' interest in adaptation as a form of "perfecting" structures, and in social connections created by circulation spaces.

Perhaps the communitarians who formed intentional communities could be described as seeking an *intentional vernacular* architecture. Groups of strangers who united to pursue their religious or political beliefs by forming a new community needed to create a distinctive community form, borrowing from literal Biblical imagery, visionary utopian inventions, and whatever established building traditions they knew or fancied, American or European. Despite the odd mixture of design sources, the self-conscious communitarian struggle to unite social and architectural ideals made rapid fusion possible. Once a satisfactory prototype had been created, community discipline could encourage its duplication.

Economic pressures and the need for equality encouraged communitarians to standardize their building types. The need for orderly growth led them to standardize procedures for making additions and adaptations to existing buildings. In the settlements of the Shakers, the Inspirationists, and the Harmonists, such procedures clearly operated, aided in some cases by standardized preparation of lumber, hardware, doors, and windows. Prefabrication suggested mass production of the social "invention" of the community, so it was enthusiastically pursued by communitarians before its general acceptance in American construction. Taken together, standardized plans, procedures, and ma-

terials allowed for flexible principles of site planning, such as those institutionalized in the Shakers' Millennial Laws. A wide latitude could be granted for members' judgment regarding site planning in new terrain, since fairly fixed rules governing building form, size, color, placement, and ornament ensured that each new settlement would be similar to the model in its visual effect.

Communitarian consistency in building and site planning could still be very fragile, especially if members were overly concerned with uniqueness or inventiveness. No vernacular style can survive unless it is clearly accepted by members of a culture as essential to their way of life. In primitive communities this sense of essentials might be built up over hundreds of years. In communitarian settlements, vernacular style survived because the indoctrination was often intensive. The physical process of building was identified with the process of spiritual and social development of the community. The members of Shaker communities considered themselves part of a "living building," and their history reveals ideological and architectural consistency which most other communities achieved only in part.

Examining the environments created by groups which developed a coherent vernacular style of building, it is striking to see how much uniqueness they were able to achieve within the limits of highly replicable style. The collectively agreed-upon framework reinforced the limits of the community by emphasizing its architectural consistency. Unusual symbolic or perfectionist details are infinitely more impressive when set within such a disciplined framework. The Shakers' meetinghouse interiors in red, blue, and gold gain from contrast with severe, confined exteriors. The Harmonists' decorated doorways

3.11 Grandiose Fourierist plans to house spiritualist
ritual: design for the south facade of a Social Palace or
Symposium, Fountaingrove, California, 1894-1895.

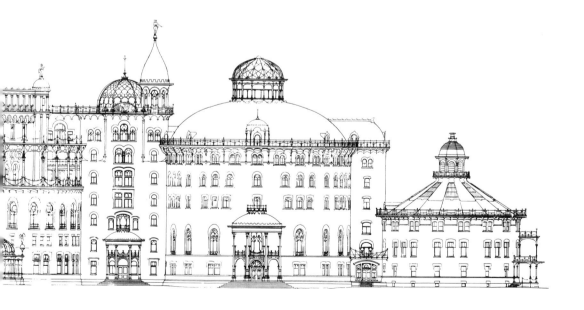

3.12 Portico, vestibule, Rotunda of the Dance, with
water arches and pivotal pavilion, Hall of Ascent, Hall
of the Feast ("above are a hundred bowers of Love's
Repose"), and kitchen, section of Social Palace, designed for Fountaingrove, California, 1894-1895.

PORTICO   VESTIBULE   Water Arches   Pivotal Pavilion   Water Arches.
                                              ROTUNDA OF THE DANCE

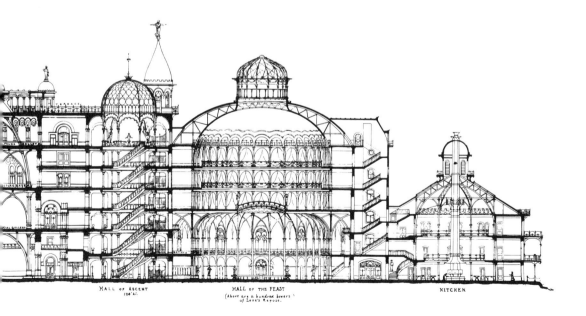

HALL OF ASCENT
120 ft.

HALL OF THE FEAST
(Above are a hundred bowers
of Love's Repose.

KITCHEN

Unique versus Replicable Plans   53

3.14 Holy City, California, communal gas station, ca. 1918.

3.15 "Headquarters for the World's Perfect Government," Holy City, California, ca. 1918.

3.16 Head of an angel, lintel from a doorway in Harmony, Pennsylvania, ca. 1811.

3.17 Cemetery gate, Harmony, Pennsylvania.

3.13 Eclectic use of traditional motifs: Zion Hotel, Zion City, Illinois, 1902.

(Fig. 3.16) stand out against a background of similar brick houses; their cemetery gate, swinging on a silent hinge, is a more striking sculptural object for being set against a purposely vacant, grassy communal enclosure (Fig. 3.17). Reviewing the dilemma of unique versus replicable plans, one can compare a community housed in a single, large, eccentric building with one housed in a complex of related, coherent, connected buildings. In terms of persuasion, this is the difference between expletive and argument. When the usual caricature of an experimental community is contrasted with the reality of successful, long-lived communitarian groups, the dilemma is illuminated. The opposing states of uniqueness and replicability are not so incompatible after all.

The dilemma of developing a unique but replicable community can be analyzed in terms of physical design. But since I have argued that the resolution of the dilemma lies in a vernacular style of building, I would like to venture a further argument about underlying styles of spatial perception. All communities attempt to create social commitment during the indoctrination of new commune members. Some groups, I believe, also attempt to foster what can be called spatial commitment as part of this process.

A recent sociological study by Rosabeth Kanter analyzes communes in terms of their use of commitment mechanisms which include two components, detachment from outside society and attachment to the commune. Kanter postulates three types of commitment: instrumental (or cognitive) commitment, which supports group continuance; affective (or cathectic) commitment, which supports group cohesion, and evaluative (or moral) commitment, which supports social control. The twin components of instrumental commitment are sacrifice and investment—the cost of leaving the community is balanced against the profit of staying. The components of affective cohesion are renunciation and communion—the rejection of outside relationships is balanced by the emotional satisfaction provided by the community. The components of evaluative commitment are mortification and transcendence—the loss of one's private identity is balanced against the gain of a collective identity and purpose.

When these three types of commitment coalesce in an intentional community, according to Kanter,

. . . processes of giving up and getting make the group a clearly focused object for commitment. . . . This process contains the first principles of a "gestalt psychology": to develop maximum commitment in its members, a group must form a unity or a whole, coherent and sharply differentiated . . . a figure clearly distinguished from the ground, whether the ground is the outside society or excluded options for behavior.[40]

This behavioral process seems to find its direct, environmental equivalent in the construction of the model community, a defined physical form which takes shape as a "figure" in the ground of the wider society and the broader landscape. Thus I speculate that the types of commitment which Kanter describes in sociological terms have approximate spatial equivalents.

People make instrumental, affective, or evaluative commitments in objective, personal, or imaginary space. If objective space is defined as space which can be quantified, or measured in feet and inches, this is the space of land-use planning and construction, the space where practical gains or losses of community membership are experienced. If personal space is considered to be physiologically or culturally defined space, the territories and "hidden dimensions" which determine whether people perceive themselves as isolated or invaded, then this is the space where the emotional satisfaction of community is enhanced or eroded. If imaginary space is defined as unmeasurable space, the sense of being or the sense of vastness of heaven, then this is the space of theoretical designs and visions, where moral dedication to a transcendent cause is cultivated.

The preceding discussion of the dilemmas which communitarians faced as builders drew upon examples from the areas of objective space and personal space. Imaginary space is

more mysterious, but there is a body of material which suggests communal concern in this area. Several groups perfected unorthodox systems of spatial reference, assigning special significance to left and right, horizontal and vertical, forward and backward, or near and far locations. When these unusual properties were incorporated into the group's way of relating to the rest of the world, the results affected both personal space and imaginary space.

Because the intuitive meaning and expressive character of space varies from one culture to another, the counterculture which transforms its members' sense of space has found a very distinctive way of shaping their approach to life and to environmental structuring. The new systems of spatial ordering would be not only unique, but also replicable, as the socialization process would orient all new members to the communal codes. The Hutterian Brethren altered their personal space by reversing traditional concepts of "inside" and "outside," placing their barns and outhouses nearest the roads, and their houses and lawns in seclusion, symbolically turning their backs on the world.[41] The "cellular cosmogony" of the Koreshan community (Fig. 3.18) was a system of imaginary space which specified that the earth is hollow and that humans walk inside the sphere, where they are stabilized by centripetal force under a horizon which curves upward.[42] In both cases the message seems to be that salvation is accessible only to those who reject a false or worldly spatial orientation by turning themselves upside down or inside out.

The Shakers developed not one but two unorthodox codes of personal space. They dressed the right side first, stepped first with the right foot when ascending the stairs, folded hands with the right fingers uppermost, knelt and rose with the right knee first, and harnessed the right-hand beast first in a team. This was part of a set of strict rules concerning posture and directions of movement, orienting members to the structuring of "earthly" space in orthogonals. "Heavenly" space was unconfined, the space of whirling dances and ecstatic visions, symbolized in circles and bright colors. The alternation of these two uses of space to express Shaker eschatology is described at length in Chapter 4. While both earthly and heavenly space could be defined as systems of personal space, heavenly space was also a system of imaginary space.

In contrast to the Shakers, some modern communes where systems of personal space seem very casual employ the spatial discipline of yoga or *tai chi* to set the tone for various communal activities. A change of style in the use of personal space may always help in attaining a vision of imaginary space, whether one moves from discipline to release, with the Shakers, or from release to discipline, with the hippies.

Communitarians, because of their strategy for social change, involved themselves in complex collective processes of design with many more social implications than the building projects usually undertaken by professional architects. Coping with paradoxical demands for authoritative and participatory processes, private and communal territory, unique and replicable plans, communitarian builders dealt with a full range of social and environmental structures in new settlements. This chapter has only begun to suggest what understanding the totality might imply. Looking at the design process in terms of three dilemmas has allowed me to emphasize the ways that life problems become building problems. Dilemmas imply conflict and reflect the open-ended nature of the building process in a communal settlement. Design, use, and redesign are vital to the life of the community, as constant, human approaches to achieving cosmic, communitarian goals.

Discussing dilemmas by citing physical design solutions related to paradoxical program requirements does not imply a series of pat answers: one group's solution may be another group's problem. This becomes clear in the following seven case studies, where I am able to treat the design processes conducted by various groups more fully. It has been necessary, however, to focus on selected aspects of design which were stressed by particular communities in order to try to convey the spirit of involvement, to emphasize the process as much as the results. I have given almost as much space to troubles as to triumphs; more, in the case of Nauvoo, Greeley, and Llano del Rio. For the communitarians, changes in their own life styles were slow and difficult, and an architecture reflecting those changes could evolve only as an integrated part of the total process of community building.

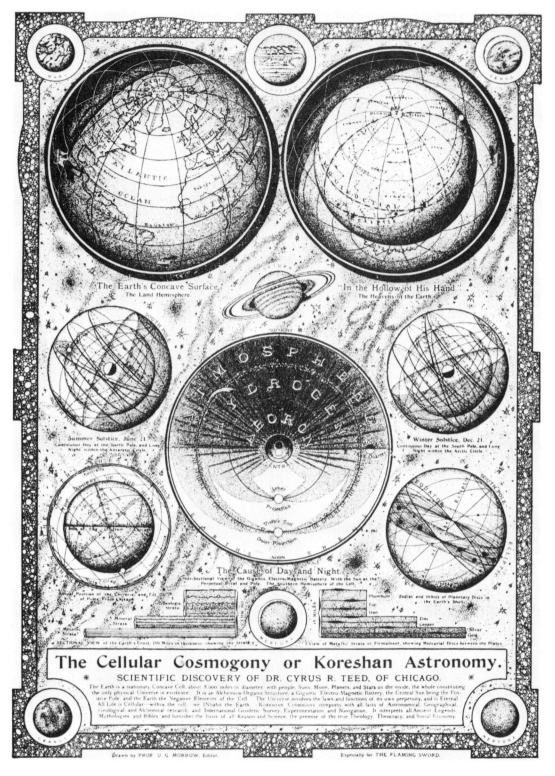

3.18 "Cellular Cosmogony," diagrams of the earth as a
hollow globe, illuminated by a central sun, Cyrus
Teed, Koreshan community, Estero, Florida, 1901.

1 Albert Brisbane, *A Concise Exposition of the Doctrine of Association, or Plan for the Re-organization of Society*, New York, 1843, p. 23.

2 Revelation 21:16.

3 Donald Drew Egbert and Stow Persons, *Socialism and American Life*, vol. 1, Princeton, 1952, p. 626.

4 Jeremy Bentham, *Panopticon, or, The Inspection House*, London, 1791.

5 Bestor, in *Backwoods Utopias*, p. 129, cites *Description for an Architectural Model from a Design by Stedman Whitwell, Esq. for a Community upon a Principle of United Interests, as Advocated by Robert Owen, Esq.*, published in London in 1830 (which I have been unable to locate) as the fullest description of Owen's model. See also Everett Webber, *Escape to Utopia: The Communal Movement in America*, New York, 1958, p. 45.

6 Robert Boguslaw, *The New Utopians: A Study of System Design and Social Change*, Englewood Cliffs, N.J., 1965, p. 11.

7 Robert Daughters, "Icaria-Speranza: The Last Try at Icarian Communism," unpublished paper, Department of Architecture, University of California, Berkeley, June 6, 1973, p. 12, includes a general description of Cabet's ideal community. See also Egbert and Persons, *Socialism and American Life*, p. 632.

8 In *The Bostonians* (1886), Harmondsworth, 1973, p. 91, Henry James portrays the former communard, Selah Tarrant, as always hanging about in hotel lobbies, hoping to be in the center of things.

9 Alcander Longley, *Community Homes, A Narrative of the Relief Community* (alternate title, *What Is Communism?*), 2d ed., rev. and enl., St. Louis, 1890. The Western Reserve Historical Society, Cleveland, owns a copy with illustrations of the "White City" (1893) pasted onto the pages.

10 See Chapter 5, n. 49.

11 See Chapter 7, n. 55.

12 Orson Squire Fowler, "Associative Houses" in *A Home for All, or, The Gravel Wall and Octagon Mode of Building*, New York, 1854, pp. 90-92. See also Walter Creese, "Fowler and the Domestic Octagon," *Art Bulletin*, 28 (June 1946), 89-102.

13 Daniel Bluestone, "A City Which Cannot Be Hid," unpublished paper, Department of Architecture, M.I.T., Jan. 1974, includes photographs of three octagons built at Hopedale; one is a large communal dwelling, and two are smaller family homes. Ellen McDougall visited the Modern Times octagon and described it to me. *The Harbinger*, Nov. 11, 1848, published an octagonal plan for a communal dwelling, cited in Egbert and Persons, vol. 1, p. 632.

14 See Chapter 2, n. 29.

15 Ebenezer Howard, *Garden Cities of To-Morrow* (1902), London, 1970.

16 William E. Wilson, *The Angel and the Serpent: The Story of New Harmony*, Bloomington, 1964, p. 53. The author's anecdotal account includes many notes about buildings and their uses which I have been unable to verify elsewhere.

17 William E. Wilson, "Social Experiments on the Wabash: New Harmony, Indiana," in Thomas C. Wheeler, ed., *A Vanishing America: The Life and Times of the Small Town*, New York, 1964, p. 83.

18 See Figure 5.3.

19 Sherry Arnstein, "A Ladder of Citizen Participation," *Journal of the American Institute of Planners*, July 1969, pp. 216-224.

20 Rosabeth Moss Kanter, *Commitment and Community: Communes and Utopias in Sociological Perspective*, Cambridge, Mass., 1972, p. 41.

21 Nathaniel Hawthorne, *The Blithedale Romance*, Boston, 1859, p. 75.

22 Humphrey Osmond, M.D., "Function as the Basis of Psychiatric Ward Design," *Mental Hospitals*, architectural supplement, 8 (1957), pp. 23-29. See also Edward T. Hall, *The Silent Language*, Garden City, N.Y., 1959, on territoriality.

23 In the realm of imaginary delineation: the Mormon plan to take over Missouri and the Brotherhood of the Cooperative Commonwealth plan to take over Washington.

24 On Mormon fences, see Mark. P. Leone, "Archeology as the Science of Technology: Mormon Town Plans and Fences," in Charles Redman, ed., *Research and Theory in Current Archeology*, New York, 1973.

25 Horace Greeley, "A Sabbath with the Shakers," *The Knickerbocker*, 11 (June 1838), 533.

26 (Nathan C. Meeker?), New York *Tribune*, October 23, 1844.

27 Points of surveillance could also assure that every member's whereabouts were usually known. Charles Nordhoff reported that at Oneida anyone leaving the Mansion stuck a peg in a pegboard to "tell all his little world where he may be found" (in *The Communistic Societies of the United States* (1875), New York, 1966, p. 410). In the same vein, Elders were expected to know the whereabouts of every Shaker all day long, and watchtowers on the roofs of some dwellings were constructed. Rappists' labors were supervised by their leader from a cave overlooking the fields of Harmony.

In contrast to this sort of surveillance, some communities sanctioned an occasional vacation at the community's own resorts, distant from the original site but contained by communal boundaries nevertheless. Oneida, for example, maintained a sloop on the Hudson, a hunting lodge at Joppa, and a cottage called Cozicot on Long Island Sound, while Llano del Rio established a lodge at Jackson Lake. Shakers and Mormons did not have resorts but they could be sent to other branches for a change of scene. Such vacations were probably rewards for good behavior, not remedies for wanderlust.

28 Benjamin Zablocki, *The Joyful Community*, Baltimore, 1972, p. 180.

29 Gwendolyn Wright, "The Woman's Commonwealth: Feminism's Success Story in Texas," unpublished paper, Department of Architecture, University of California, Berkeley, 1973.

30 On spaces where casual social involvement is likely to be perceived as appropriate or inappropriate, see Erving Goffman, *Behavior in Public Places: Notes on the Social Organization of Gatherings*, New York, 1963, pp. 50-59.

31 The ritual of the "Cleansing Gift" is described in David R. Lamson, *Two Years' Experience Among the Shakers*, West Boylston, Mass., 1848.

32 Cyrus Teed, quoted in Kanter, *Commitment and Community*, p. 36.

33 Philip Britts, "Song for the Present Day," frontispiece, in Zablocki, *The Joyful Community*.

34 Universal Brotherhood and Theosophical Society, *Lomaland*, Point Loma, Calif., 1908, is a good collection of photographs.

35 Ray Reynolds, *Cat's Paw Utopia*, El Cajon, Calif., 1972.

36 Llano Publications, *Llano Viewbook*, Llano, Calif., 1917; *Western Comrade*, 5.3 (June-July 1916).

37 Wilson, *The Angel and the Serpent*, p. 41.

38 John Humphrey Noyes, *History of American Socialisms*, quoted in Kanter, *Commitment and Community*, p. 139.

39 Amos Rapoport, *House Form and Culture*, Englewood Cliffs, N. J., 1969, pp. 4-8.

40 Kanter, *Commitment and Community*, p. 71.

41 Victor Peters, *All Things Common*, Minneapolis, 1965, p. 78. Many communes attempted to redefine units of time, and the relationship between communal theories of space and time would be a good subject for further research along the lines of Robert Flanders's article on Mormon concepts of space and time, cited in the bibliography for Chapter 5.

42 Cyrus Teed, *The Cellular Cosmogony, or, The Earth a Concave Sphere* (1905), Philadelphia, 1974.

II Building Utopia

4 Heavenly and Earthly Space

Leap and shout, ye living building
Christ is in his glory come
Cast your eyes on Mother's children
See what glory fills the room!

–Shaker hymn

4.1 Communards whose community building skills
became legendary: a group of Shakers, 1875.

As a young girl, Ann Lee worked fourteen-hour days in a cotton-spinning mill in Manchester, England. In 1762, when she was twenty-five, she married a blacksmith, Abraham Standerin. Her first three children died in infancy; the fourth was stillborn, and she lay in the agony of delivery for hours, screaming that sexual intercourse was the cause of all the world's evil. Finding some solace in a local sect called "Shaking Quakers," she began to experience visions of an earthly paradise located far from the slums of Manchester and populated with angelic, sinless beings. In 1773, she proclaimed her special powers as the female counterpart of Christ who was destined to establish a "millennial church" in America. With the financial backing of one rich convert, forty-four-year-old "Mother" Ann Lee and eight followers embarked for New York in 1774. Two years later, at Niskayuna, near Albany, they established a small settlement based on the principles of chastity, community of goods, confession of sins, and separation from the world.

The group at Niskayuna called themselves the Millennial Church or the United Society of Believers in Christ's Second Appearing, but they were commonly known as "Shakers" because of the frenzied shaking which accompanied their religious services. Numerous millennarian sects flourished in the United States in the eighteenth and nineteenth centuries. All predicted an imminent, catastrophic second coming of Christ which would initiate the millennium, a period of one thousand years when Christ would reign on earth, as prophesied by John the Evangelist. What distinguished the Shakers was their assertion that the millennium had already commenced.[1] They described it as a slow, progressive redemption of the world effected by the members of the Millennial Church.

"We travel with Christ," said James Whittaker, one of Mother Ann's disciples, "in the resurrection and in the work of regeneration."[2] Shaker missionaries traveled, in fact, a few days behind revivalist preachers who announced an imminent second coming. In Massachusetts in 1780, in Kentucky after 1805, in New York and New England in 1827, and again after the Millerite excitements in 1843, the Shakers made thousands of converts, offering them earthly employment in the Millennial Church to assuage the anxiety generated by other preachers.[3] Mother Ann exhorted members, "Do your work as if you had a thousand years to live and as if you were to die tomorrow."[4] Patient perfectionism was thus coupled with revivalist urgency. Converts developed into communitarians whose community building skills became legendary (Fig. 4.1).

Between 1780 and 1826 the Shakers founded twenty-five settlements from Maine to the Ohio frontier.[5] These well-built and prosperous villages greatly enhanced the credibility of the communitarian strategy for social change in the United States. The existence of over two dozen model Shaker communities was cited by communards everywhere as proof that it was possible to construct a satisfactory model community and then to duplicate such an environment on demand. Robert Owen knew of them through W. S. Warder, a Philadelphia Quaker, who felt that news of their success would encourage Owen to attempt a practical test of his own theories.[6] Karl Marx and Friedrich Engels followed their activities closely.[7] John Humphrey Noyes, leader of the Oneida Community and author of a *History of American Socialisms*, praised the Shakers' demonstration that "... successful Communism is subjectively possible," and he claimed that communitarians were more indebted to the Shakers than to "any or all other social architects of modern times."[8] Henry George cited their settlements as successful precedents for agrarian socialist communities.[9]

Although the Shaker approach to community building proved one of the most persuasive and durable of any offered to the American public between 1780 and 1900, their success was not sustained after 1860. Millennial doctrines won them converts and insured a supply of eager workers building communities and toiling in the fields, but celibate living restricted their numbers. This was a helpful discipline in early years of poverty, but one that made self-perpetuation impossible in years of few conversions. A fanatical willingness to purchase land in order to redeem the earth, coupled with unwillingness to engage in heavy industry, eroded their prosperity after the Civil War. The years 1860 to 1900 were a period of decline; 1900 to 1970, a period of contraction. The United Society still exists, but today its more than 17,000 recorded members are represented by a few venerable sisters living at Sabbathday Lake, Maine, and Canterbury, New Hampshire.[10]

The gradual decline of the United Society can be explained partially by the national transition from a rural, agricultural economy to an urban, industrial one, a change which denied them recruits. Their success is much harder to explain. Other groups approached the Shakers' achievement in creating model communities, but few were able to emulate the Shakers' ability to produce satisfactory replicas of the first ideal settlement. In evaluating the Shakers' achievements, one must inquire how they were able to replicate a successful initial experiment. This is the critical test for any communal group which claims to have a strategy for social, rather than personal, reform.

Traditional explanations rest on the authoritarian religious discipline of the sect or on their missionary zeal. Equally authoritarian communities such as the Amana Inspirationists or the Oneida Perfectionists proselytized less; equally zealous missionaries, such as the Millerites or the Mormons, were less adamant about communitarian isolation or discipline. Such explanations lead only to another question. How were the Shakers able to sustain discipline while recruiting a large number of new members and while encouraging the simultaneous development of many new settlements? The answer seems to lie in the way that the physical process of designing and building new settlements—the communitarian goal—was fully integrated with the Shaker religion. Members found in environmental design the only activity broad enough in scope to accommodate their aspiration to turn the earth into heaven.

Other communitarians held the physical environment in high regard. Robert Owen, for example, wished to utilize architecture to reinforce social design, but for the most part he was too concerned with physical display, with spatial inventions conceived as rather facile analogies of social inventions. He sensed the power of environmental design as a force for social change without understanding how to harness it. In contrast to communitarians who emphasized the merits of particular designs, the Shakers chose to concentrate on the design and building process. They probed the perceptual questions which link social behavior and environmental design. Their writings concerning building deal with "order and use," organization and activities. This chapter will explore the complex interweaving of social and physical goals in the life of the Society. A picture emerges of Shaker communal life, paradoxically totalitarian and anarchic, ascetic and sensual. In defiance of these contradictions is a driving sense of communitarian purpose, which unites people, land, and buildings in a mission of millennial redemption.

The Shakers' plan for the gradual redemption of the world aimed at nothing less than transforming the earth into heaven. This allowed them to maintain two simultaneous visions of an ideal community. In what they called the earthly sphere, they envisioned rural settlements of millennial believers based on Mother Ann's precepts; in the heavenly sphere they projected a New Jerusalem as described by the evangelists. Daily work and religious rituals were designed to foster belief that both spheres were accessible to members. The believers experienced earthly millennial life and simulated the experience of heavenly life. Only an intricate theory of community structure, encompassing the temporal and spatial contradictions of an earthly society which was becoming heaven, could resolve the excruciating tension.

The authors of this theory, Joseph Meacham and Lucy Wright, succeeded Ann Lee and James Whittaker as the leading ministers of the United Society of Believers in 1787. They organized believers into ascetic communal households called "families" which consisted of thirty to one hundred persons in a similar condition of spiritual "travel."[11] Meacham and Wright distinguished three types of families: the novitiate, the junior order, and the senior order. These orders contained new believers, cooperators, or communists, since economic union progressed with spiritual development. Most settlements had at least one family of each type.

Definition of the heavenly sphere also developed under Meacham, Wright, and their successors. The details of life in Heavenly Jerusalem were made vivid and concrete during worship. In 1824, David Benedict visited New Lebanon where he observed a meeting with worshipers executing "a figure of marching the heavenly road and walking the streets of the New Jerusalem."[12] All communities were frequently referred to as "Zion" in Shaker writings, as well as by their local designations. Between 1838 and 1854, a period of special spiritual fervor, all communities assumed additional heavenly names—City of Peace, City of Love, City of Union, Holy Mount, Holy Land, Pleasant Grove. Dual names and frequent acting out of life in paradise probably underlie the report of "a magnificent spiritual city, densely inhabited, filled with palaces and fine residences," which was alleged to be "at but a little distance from the terrestrial buildings of the Church Family" in one of the Shaker settlements visited by Charles Nordhoff around 1875.[13]

The parallel developments of ascetic community order and fanciful mystical worship converge in the imagery Meacham employs to describe the concept of the Shaker family, the unit of both social and physical organization for the society. He compares the three categories of Shaker families to the three courts of the Temple of Jerusalem described in the Old Testament.[14] The twelve Shaker virtues are the twelve gates of the Temple.[15] A later author, Richard Pelham, elaborates this theme, describing the sect as constructing a temple with God as "the great Architect" and the Believers as "master builders." "Generators," that is, "worldlings" with children, are relegated to the role of brickmakers.[16] The central metaphor is the same as Meacham's—people are equated with the physical elements of the Temple.

Because the Temple was a common symbol used to represent the Heavenly Jerusalem, Shaker social and physical organization was, by transference, heavenly organization. An early Shaker hymn makes this message more explicit when members are addressed as a "living building":

Leap and shout, ye living building
Christ is in his glory come
Cast your eyes on Mother's children
See what glory fills the room![17]

The family system, which allowed for graduated levels of spiritual and economic participation in the society, made assimilation of new members an orderly process. Expanding the practical rationale for the family system into the concept of the "living building," Joseph Meacham demonstrated his communitarian genius. Meacham identified the personal, spiritual growth of each member of the sect with the external, physical growth of the community. A "Hymn of Love" celebrates this union:

Love the inward, new creation,
Love the glory that it brings;
Love to lay a good foundation,
In the line of outward things.[18]

The "living building" developed into a living, building process.

Behind the spiritual metaphor linking earthly and heavenly building lay practical, intuitive understanding of methods for creating sectarian commitment. The role of the Shakers as master builders, described by Richard Pelham, involved making each convert a building block suitable for the "living building." This implied developing each member's capability to experience the dual life of the earthly and heavenly spheres. Dozens of commitment mechanisms were used by communes to involve members in all-encompassing life styles, such as unorthodox sexual practices, isolation from family members or friends, or use of special names and secret languages. The Shakers employed many of these devices, but the "master builders" specialized in skillful manipulation of their converts' perception of personal space and spheres of movement in order to simulate experience of the dual spheres.

Earthly Space

A sampling of Shaker rules concerning orientation and posture reveals consistent orthogonal ordering. At meals printed signs called table monitors warned, "Bread and meat are to be cut square."[19] Diagonal reaching was discouraged by the provision of serving dishes for every two to four persons.[20] For members walking on the domain diagonal shortcuts were forbidden in favor of the right angle paths.[21] Vertical alignment of movement was also prescribed. Erect meditation positions were specified for "a true sense of . . . privilege in the Zion of God," and anyone who slouched or nodded was required to make a public apology.[22] At the end of a day of right angle discipline, Millennial Laws dictated that members should "retire to rest in the fear of God . . . and lie straight."[23]

Distancing regulations created envelopes of space and imaginary barriers to separate brethren from sisters and believers from "worldlings." Different spheres of activity—agricultural, horticultural, and mechanical occupations for the men; domestic work, tailoring, garden, and craft activities for the women—discouraged personal contact, since members could not visit workplaces of the opposite sex without a specific reason. Within the dwelling houses, an "invisible boundary"[24] separated men's rooms on the west from women's rooms on the east. Double sets of stairs and doors (Fig. 4.2) articulated the division between male and female territory.[25] A distance of five feet between brethren and sisters was specified for the assembly in the meeting room.[26] During "union meetings" members crossed the line to gather in small groups in retiring rooms (Fig. 4.3), but "a respectful distance between brethren and sisters was required."[27]

Should members encounter the "world's people," spatial regulations encouraged them to preserve their personal distance. At a special trustees' office outsiders who wished to do business with the Shakers were received; most members were removed from casual contact with such visitors. Shaking hands with an outsider was discouraged. Any two members walking out on an errand in the world were enclosed by a double spatial envelope. Millennial Laws required that ". . . you should keep so close together that there would not be room for even as much as a dog to run between you and your companion."[28]

Enforcement of regulations concerning personal space varied. The rules became stricter between 1800 and 1850, then after 1850 observance seems to have been less punctilious. Differences between communities were great. In some communities, surveillance seems to have enforced discipline—peepholes in the meeting houses enabled the Elders to watch the worship[29] and watchtowers on the roof of the dwelling house at Pleasant Hill are reported.[30] Yet an apostate mentions young Shakers sneaking downstairs after hours for a bit of "sparking."[31] A Shaker song about old "Slug," who pesters sisters working in the kitchen and falls asleep during meditation, has a gently chiding tone which suggests that infractions were fairly common.[32]

Shaker spatial discipline was enforced less by surveillance or admonitions than by Shaker design and crafts. Attention to each individual's personal needs provided constant physical reminders of posture and distancing regulations. Often skeletal measurements were used for the design of chairs and beds.[33] At least one visitor felt the pervasiveness of spatial discipline expressed in the furniture and found it foreign to his own sense of personal space. Charles

4.2 Pairs of stairs and doors for the separate sexes,
Center Family dwelling, Pleasant Hill, Kentucky.

4.3 "Ranged against the wall were six or eight stiff,
high-backed chairs, and they partook so strongly of
the general grimness, that one would much rather have
sat on the floor than incurred the smallest obligation
to any of them": chairs arranged for a union meeting,
communal dwelling, Church Family, Hancock, Massachusetts.

Dickens visited New Lebanon in 1842 and reported: "Ranged against the wall were six or eight stiff, high-backed chairs, and they partook so strongly of the general grimness, that one would much rather have sat on the floor than incurred the smallest obligation to any of them."[34] In addition to Shaker furniture, Shaker tailoring of uniform clothing involved use of individual patterns, and cobblers made individual lasts for members' shoes.[35] This was common practice in rural communities, but when furniture and apparel encased each member perfectly and completely, few additional exhortations were necessary. Members were physically surrounded by the handiwork of other believers. Social control was thus achieved through careful articulation of personal identity, a synthesis quite at odds with modern bureaucratic control and anonymity.

Heavenly Space

The spatial constraints of the earthly sphere provided a springboard to heavenly space. During religious meetings constraints on posture and movement were suspended, although a sexual division between men and women was usually maintained. This release from the earthly spatial discipline seems to have helped members to enjoy a mystical, abandoned experience of a "heavenly sphere" where flowing movement was possible, a world illustrated by drawings filled with rich decoration and fanciful constructions (Figs. 4.4, 4.5).

In Shaker religious rituals, dance and pantomime were common. Imaginary garments were donned; visitors included Indians, devils, George Washington, the deceased Mother Ann. Right angle order was superseded. The same members who walked straight, tiptoed, and never raised their voices were suddenly singing and shouting, whirling in dizzy circles. Their hymns give some sense of this kinetic release, such as "Limber Zeal":

Let the gift come as 'twill, I am ready to move,
To be twisted and turned any way in Mother's
  Love.
Now in Limber Zeal I will twist and reel.[36]

or a song about stepping out in the New Jerusalem:

We love to march the heavenly way
And in it we can dance and play,
And feel our spirits living.[37]

An account of a typical meeting suggests how the transition from earthly to heavenly space was made. David Lamson, an apostate who lived in the community at Hancock from 1843 to 1845, describes a family meeting in the hall of a dwelling house, where brethren and sisters enter through double doors, forming two opposing phalanxes on opposite sides of the room, according to the discipline of the earthly sphere. The imaginary line which divides the dwelling extends through the space between the two groups. Lamson explains: "The space between these two bodies is called the altar. Or, there is an imaginary, or spiritual altar in this space."[38] The altar seems to provide the crucial transition between the earthly space of the dwelling axis on which it rests and heavenly, imaginary space, since the worshipers' acknowledgment of the invisible altar precedes the elaboration of imaginary spatial experiences during the service. Sketches made by observers of Shaker meetings serve as "before" and "after" illustrations of this practice (Figs. 4.6, 4.7).

4.4 "A Present from Mother Lucy to Eliza Ann Taylor," New Lebanon, 1849, ink and watercolor drawing, showing a Shaker dwelling house with double doors, transformed into a heavenly building of precious stones, surmounted by single eye of wisdom and a "crown of bright Glory."

4.5 "An Emblem of the Heavenly Sphere," ink and watercolor drawing, Hancock, 1854, trees and gardens surrounding Shaker saints in heaven, accompanied by Mother Ann, apostles, prophets, the Savior, Virgin Mary, and Christopher Columbus. "Rejoice, go on, you'll yet obtain the sight/An entrance in those regions of delight."

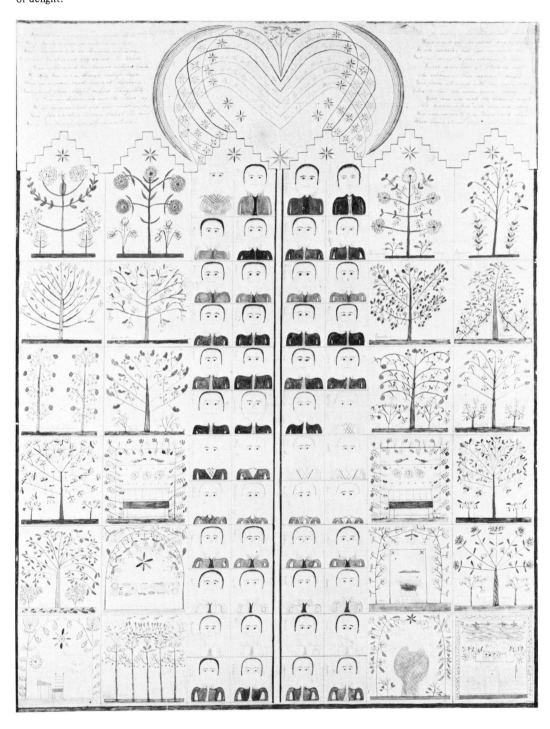

4.6 Shakers in formation at the start of a meeting; outsiders in foreground.

4.7 "The Whirling Gift," Shaker formation breaking up.

The "master builders' " manipulation of members' perceptions of personal space fostered experiences of constraint and release which distinguished the earthly and heavenly spheres and united members as parts of a "living building." Members became, at the same time, both the building and the builders. As their general sensitivity to physical space was heightened by the Shaker socialization process, skills and interest in spatial design were developed, qualities which could be drawn on for the practice of environmental design. In their village planning the Shakers tried to achieve the same kind of balance between rigid order and joyful celebration which characterized their personal lives. Order was established by a set of general Shaker attitudes toward community design expressed in the Millennial Laws which prescribed certain principles for physical organization. Celebration was made possible by allowing each community to develop in harmony with its natural site, under the direction of its members, as the development of Hancock, Massachusetts, demonstrates.

Nothing less than an image of Hell itself, the polluted, crowded, unhealthy industrial sprawl of Manchester, England, with a few rich residents and thousands of poor ones, could have inspired the Millennial Laws which regulated community design. Mother Ann and her English comrades seem to have retained a strong aversion to the urban life prevailing in the English factory towns of the 1750s and in American industrial cities of a later date, for the settlements they envisaged were to be sited far from "the great and wicked cities."[39] A Shaker hymn described it more lyrically:

In a hamlet, remote from the thronged thoroughfares
Where business and pleasure with folly abound

I dwell in retirement and breathe the pure airs. . . .[40]

The basic principles of Shaker community planning opposed economic exploitation and the despoliation of nature, advocating careful use of land and economical planning of buildings in order to provide essentials for all.[41]

The acquisition and cultivation of land dominated the economy. William Hinds describes Shaker "land mania,"[42] their willingness to buy all land that joined them and more in anticipation of their need for new community sites. In 1874, their home farms totaled 50,000 acres; their overall holdings, 100,000 acres.[43] Much of this acreage was "cold and sterile," marked with "rocks and boulders bare."[44] Careful landscaping and cultivation soon changed its appearance. They improved the roads in their domains, planted trees, built fences, flagged neat paths. Horace Greeley claimed that a monarch might envy their lawns.[45] Only ornamental planting of flowers was forbidden, since flowers were reserved for heaven.

Agriculture provided their sustenance; its position as the supreme practical art was unchallenged in their communities. The Shakers cultivated only those crops suitable to the soil and climate in a given community.[46] Crop rotation and contour plowing made the most of the soil; woodland and pasture land they cared for as carefully as their tilled acreage. Benson Lossing describes the slopes at Mount Lebanon as "enriched by the most perfect culture."[47] Harriet Martineau declared, "The earth does not show more flourishing fields, gardens, and orchards, than theirs."[48] The editors of *The Cultivator* could not decide which pleased them more, the Shakers' ingenious agricultural implements and buildings, or the neatness evidenced in their care and use.[49] The editor of the *Sani-*

tary Engineer, Charles Wingate, noted that rain-water was channeled into laundry tubs, kitchen waste was circulated to the orchards, and waste in earth closets used for compost heaps,[50] all aspects of a sacred, closed system to redeem the land through intense, careful use.

The building process in a typical Shaker community was an activity subsidiary to agricultural organization and site planning. Buildings were designed to be overcapacious, eliminating crowding, anticipating the future growth of each family.[51] The details of their construction were so painstaking, according to Wingate, that the permanence of the structures "would bring tears to the eyes of a jerry-builder."[52] Their forms, however, were forbidden to be "odd or fanciful," and their siting was deliberately methodical and antipicturesque.[53]

This emphasis on traditional planning and sound construction became the basis of a distinctive vernacular style of building. The Shakers were acutely sensitive to the effects of the physical environment on the life of their communities. They wished buildings to house their activities and display them accurately to members and the world at large, and they perceived that an orderly but nonmonumental development of traditional rural building types would serve these needs better than any elaborate or fanciful designs they could devise. Just as they decried the arts of music, drama, and painting,[54] the Shakers denounced "architecture." In 1875 Charles Nordhoff, who found Shaker buildings homely, asked Elder Frederick Evans if Shakers building anew "would not aim at some architectural effect, some beauty of design." Elder Evans replied: "No, the beautiful, as you call it, is absurd and abnormal. It has no business with us. The divine man had no right to waste money upon what you would call

beauty, in his house or his daily life, while there are people living in misery."[55] For Evans, all physical resources were a sacred trust, part of a total physical system for redemption. "Architecture" as aesthetic "effect" was close to irrelevant, since the Shakers dealt with a broad range of design goals, varying in scale from heightening basic environmental perception to prefabricating new communities. It is no surprise to learn that there were no self-styled "architects" among the Shakers, only builders, members whose skills included masonry or carpentry, who took a very modest view of their contribution to community design.

The history of the design and building process in one typical Shaker community, Hancock, Massachusetts, between 1780 and 1960, reveals constant change and adaptation taking place within the overall framework created by Millennial Laws concerning buildings. It displays the contrast between the highly developed and replicable pattern followed by all Shaker communities and the freedom of interpretation which allowed members to make Hancock a unique place. What is most impressive is the solemn, evolving unity of buildings and landscape. The total physical environment serves as a dramatic backdrop for daily rituals of work and prayer, as well as for ecstatic ceremonies using visual, earthly epiphanies to suggest the life of the heavenly sphere.

"Thou art idle and slothful," complained Father James Whittaker to Josiah Talcott, a recent Shaker convert. "I charge thee before God to mend thy ways. . . . Get thy farm in readiness. . . . For you have land enough to maintain three families or more, well improved."[56] Whittaker's letter, dated February, 1782, was sent to Talcott at Hancock, located in the Berkshire Hills, three miles east of New Lebanon, New York, the central and leading Shaker settlement. In 1786 the Shaker converts at Hancock built a meetinghouse; in 1790 Joseph Meacham sent Calvin Harlow and Sarah Harrison to Hancock to organize about forty believers into a communal family system supported by farms donated by Talcott, Daniel Goodrich, and John Deming.

At its height, the Hancock community owned about thirty-five hundred acres of land in Richmond, Hancock, and Pittsfield, including woodland, pasture, orchards, and tilled land (Fig. 4.8). The northern part of the domain reached into the Taconic Mountains, including Shaker Mountain, where a holy sanctuary was established in 1843. David Lamson describes this area as "well wooded, with beech, maple, and hickory." The eastern and southern portions of the domain consisted of "those beautiful swells or undulations which are always productive; including a considerable extent of bottom lands, which make very valuable natural mowing."[57] Large barns, a dairy, and a garden house for drying and packing seeds and herbs were located south of the main road through the village, adjacent to the fields. A sawmill and factory on the northern side took advantage of the waterpower of Shaker Brook. Although many herbs were grown in square, half-acre plots adjacent to the garden house, others were gathered wild in the northern woods. Orchards lined the highway between groupings of buildings.

Building began in the location of Church Family, described by Rebecca Clark in 1791 as including a hundred believers, gathered into a few existing farm structures, crowded three to a bed at night. According to her the group was "much engaged to build buildings."[58] By 1803, the characteristic pattern of Shaker development was evident in division of the community into six families (Fig. 4.9). Each family included one or more dwellings, barns, and workshops, plus one or two buildings which provided services for the entire community. Thus, the Church Family had the meetinghouse and the schoolhouse, the East Family had woolen mills and later an iron mine, the Second Family made cloaks, the West Family, chairs.

The family system provided, besides the advantages of slow degrees of socialization and gradual levels of economic participation, a system of village planning which included the advantages of neighborhood density, command of the agricultural landscape, and possibilities for growth afforded by a linear plan. It demonstrated a radical departure from the grid layout of such neighboring villages as Barkerville or Hancock, yet retained coherence as a planned community.

The "order and use" or organization and activities of the Hancock settlement were extremely legible because of the right-angle alignment of landscape boundaries and buildings, the hierarchical positioning of buildings according to functions, the distinctive shapes accorded to special functions, and the color coding prescribed by the Millennial Laws. Barns and service buildings were dark colors, deep reds or tans; workshops and dwelling houses slightly lighter in color, yellows or creams; and the meetinghouse, white.[59] Meticulous fencing, in

4.8 Each communal family included one or more dwellings, barns, and workshops, plus one or two buildings which provided services for the entire community: site plan, Hancock, in 1840, showing approximate community boundary.

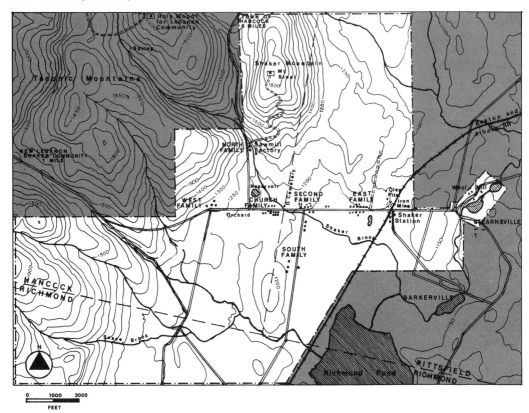

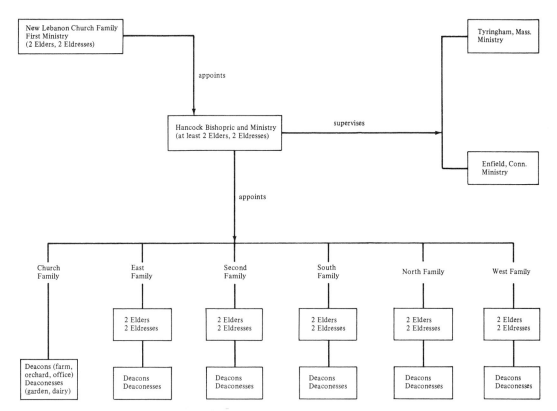

New Lebanon Church Family
First Ministry
(2 Elders, 2 Eldresses)

Tyringham, Mass.
Ministry

appoints

Hancock Bishopric and Ministry
(at least 2 Elders, 2 Eldresses)

supervises

Enfield, Conn.
Ministry

appoints

Church
Family

East
Family

Second
Family

South
Family

North Family

West Family

2 Elders
2 Eldresses

2 Elders
2 Eldresses

2 Elders
2 Eldresses

2 Elders
2 Eldresses

2 Elders
2 Eldresses

Deacons (farm,
orchard, office)
Deaconesses
(garden, dairy)

Deacons
Deaconesses

Deacons
Deaconesses

Deacons
Deaconesses

Deacons
Deaconesses

Deacons
Deaconesses

4.9 Shaker organization, ca. 1840, Hancock, Massachusetts.

4.10 View of Church Family, Hancock, 1839, showing meetinghouse, shops, large communal dwelling, and round barn with conical roof.

4.11 Church Family, Hancock, 1883, showing shops, 1830 brick dwelling, and round barn with twelve-sided clerestory and cupola added.

iron, stone, and wood, defined the boundaries of the Hancock domain and emphasized the pattern of land use. The scale and size of the buildings changed over time, but the basic pattern remained constant (Figs. 4.10, 4.11).

The legible arrangement of the Hancock village facilitated analogies to various spiritual structures, such as the Temple of Jerusalem. It also facilitated knowing one's place within the community, identifying with a particular family or neighborhood as well as with the entire Society. The sense of identification which a member enjoyed was enhanced by the orderly exposure of the functional qualities of buildings and spaces. A precise definition of order in time and space, a sense of aptness—red barn for cows, white house for church—characteristic of some New England villages, and caricatured in toy villages, found a very systematic expression among the Shakers.

A building-by-building description of even part of Hancock, with thirty-four buildings in the Church Family in 1820 (Fig. 4.12) and thirty-two different buildings on the same land in 1878, would be tedious because of the high degree of regularity in design and the frequent rebuilding or adaptation of existing structures. Examination of a few typical buildings in the Church Family shows the limited repertoire of building types assembled to form a typical family configuration and gives some idea of how each type was designed and used.

The Church Family's brick dwelling, built in 1830 under the direction of Elder William Deming, a mason and carpenter, accommodated one hundred members (Figs. 4.13, 4.14). The materials were Shaker-made brick and marble hewn from nearby quarries.[60] A portfolio of basic plans at Hancock includes an axonometric drawing of a slightly larger dwelling (Fig. 4.15) which was probably scaled down by Deming to suit the Hancock program,[61] and which may also have been used for a similar dwelling at Enfield, Connecticut. Siting on a small rise allowed direct front entrance into the formal meeting room (Fig. 4.16) and dining room of the first floor and rear entrance into kitchen areas a level below. The dwelling was equipped with the traditional double circulation system—west stairs for men, east for women—leading to their bedrooms on opposite sides of the second and third floor corridors. Communal sinks in these corridors were augmented by a small brick bathhouse near the dwelling.

The construction details of the brick dwelling emphasize orthogonal ordering and easy maintenance. A wooden strip with pegs spaced twelve inches apart lines all walls about seven feet above the floor, providing a place to hang clothing, implements, or furniture. In the upstairs halls these strips were hung with bonnets or hats, displaying the principle of sexual segregation (Fig. 4.17). By providing consistent orthogonal organization these strips constantly prevented more casual methods of using and storing objects. Large built-in storage cabinets provided more permanent storage in drawers of all sizes. Ever-present concern for economy of motion and materials is demonstrated by double-hung windows, fastened with wooden pegs, which could be unscrewed for quick washing (Fig. 4.18) and by stairs built with small metal clips to hold strips of carpet on the treads, preserving the wood at points of wear (Fig. 4.19).

Near the brick dwelling were several workshops based on standard Shaker framing patterns similar to the pattern for a typical barn (Fig. 4.20) preserved in the Hancock portfolio.[62] Earliest of these is the Machine Shop and Wash House, erected in 1790, a four-story

4.12 The scale and size of the buildings changed over
time, but the basic pattern remained constant: plan of
Church Family, Hancock, 1820.

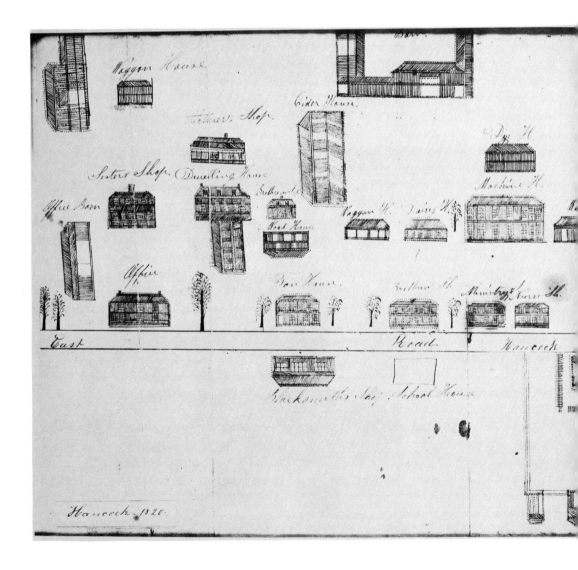

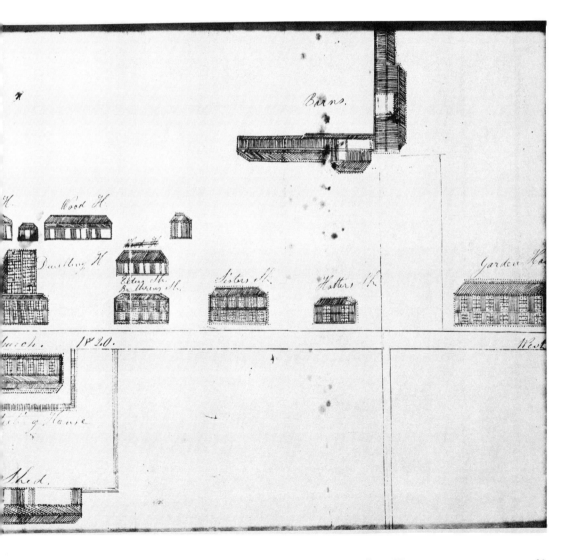

4.13 Communal brick dwelling, Church Family, Hancock, 1830.

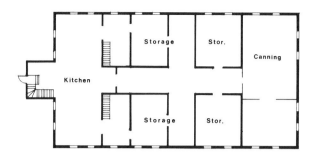

Basement

N

0   8'   16'

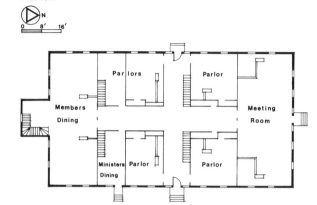

First Floor

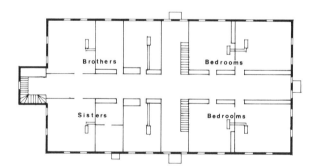

Second & Third Floor

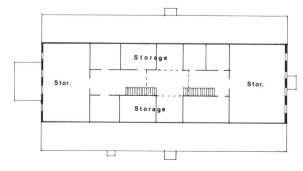

Attic

4.15 Shaker axonometric drawing of a dwelling house, from a portfolio of plans carried by traveling Shaker builders. It may have been used for dwellings at Hancock and Enfield, Connecticut.

4.16 Meeting hall, Hancock dwelling, showing Shaker
stove, orthogonal stovepipe, and storage cabinets.

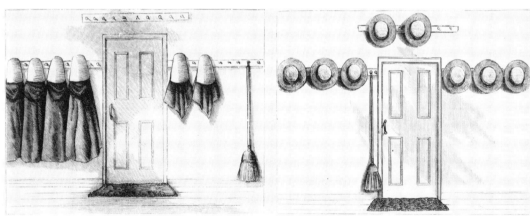

4.17 Entrances to men's and women's rooms, opposite
sides of main hall, Shaker communal dwelling, New
Lebanon, New York, 1873.

4.18 Window, meeting hall, Hancock dwelling. Panes unscrew for easy washing.

4.19 Stair to attic, Hancock dwelling. Small metal clips hold carpet on treads at points of wear.

4.20 Framing pattern for barns and workshops, from a
portfolio carried by Shaker builders.

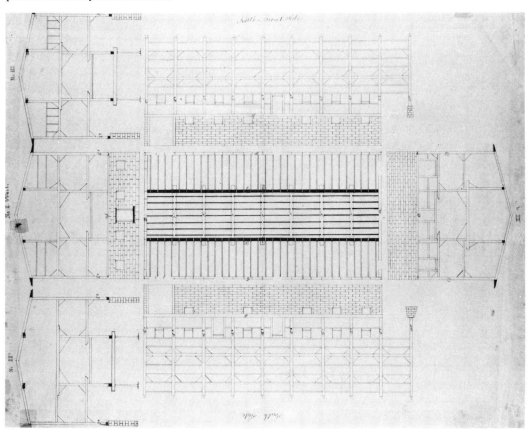

4.21 Schematic sections showing adaptation and additions, Sisters' Shop and Machine Shop and Wash House, Hancock.

Laundry & Waterworks

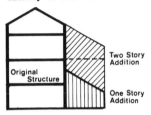

Original Structure

Two Story Addition

One Story Addition

Sisters' Shop

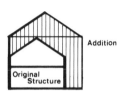

Addition

Original Structure

0   16   32

4.22 Machine Shop and Wash House, north facade, Church Family, Hancock, 1790, and later additions. Original paint, dark tan.

4.23 West facade of 4.22.

frame building painted dark yellow to which single-story and three-story sheds were added (Figs. 4.21, 4.22, 4.23). The interior equipment included sawmill machinery, washing machines, and iron-warming devices. The Sisters' Shop, built around 1810, was a smaller structure designed for storage, then expanded to accommodate the medicinal herb and garden seed industries, a sewing and weaving shop, and a dairy shop (Fig. 4.24). Less successful adaptation occurred in the Trustees' House, one of the original farm buildings occupied by the community's founders. Numerous late nineteenth century additions, including a turret and a Palladian window, reflect the uneasy life in a declining community. With no new buildings under construction, adaptation of an existing structure became an unconscious parody of the spare, functional changes effected in earlier workshops (Fig. 4.25).

The Round Barn of the Church Family (Figs. 4.26, 4.27), built in 1826 by Daniel Goodrich, departed from the Shaker tradition of well-sited, capacious barns in its distinctive shape, which allowed laborers to minimize all motion. Hay was pitched into a central mow (Fig. 4.28) from which fifty-two cattle, housed in radiating stalls, could be fed by a single hand. Gravity eased the work—hay wagons circled on a raised grade and manure collectors circled at a level below the stalls. The Society deemed the barn an inspired design, a gift of God in the same category as the great New Lebanon meeting-house with its curved roof. Both buildings defied the Shaker orthogonal order, but the barn is a remarkable architectural statement of the Shaker passion for perfect, closed systems. Although worldlings copied it extensively, no Shaker community was allowed to duplicate it.

Visitors to Hancock often mistake the Round

Barn for a Shaker church. The actual meeting-house, one of ten designed by Moses Johnson, a traveling Shaker builder, was a rather unassuming building erected in 1786 and distinguished by a gambrel roof and a white painted exterior (Fig. 4.29). The top floors housed the ministry. The meeting room occupied the entire first floor, a clear interior space thirty feet by sixty feet achieved with concealed wooden trusses (Figs. 4.30, 4.31). Millennial Laws prescribed dark blue-green woodwork, red-brown benches, blue-white plaster walls and ceiling, and a yellowish stain for the wood floor. The visual impact of a large, dazzling space inside what appears to be a small white house reveals a desire, if not to force the transition from earthly to heavenly space, at least to provide a setting for worship which would suggest its inevitability.

Hancock can be seen as an assemblage of six families, each family a linear collection of small, colored wooden buildings set down at right angles to the main road. What is missing from this view is a sense of people inhabiting the village and using the outdoor spaces. The shaping of outdoor spaces between families or between buildings did not concern Hancock's builders, since loitering outdoors was not permitted. Stopping to converse at likely places for casual meetings—steps, dooryards, railings, halls—was expressly forbidden, and means of progress through these spaces were carefully defined. They were to be fenced square, and believers were not allowed to "cut up the dooryards into little cross paths and by roads."[63] Visiting between families was also discouraged.

Experience of the visual sequence of the village was reserved for religious rituals. Marching through the orchards or along the highway was a common part of Sunday meetings.[64] Other

4.24 Sisters' Shop, Church Family, Hancock, ca. 1810,
original paint, light tan.

4.25 Trustees' House, Church Family, Hancock, before 1790, with late nineteenth century additions.

4.26 Round Barn, Church Family, Hancock, 1826.

4.27 Plan and section, Round Barn. Hay wagons circled on the top level; hay in the central mow was pitched to radiating stalls; a manure wagon circled below stalls.

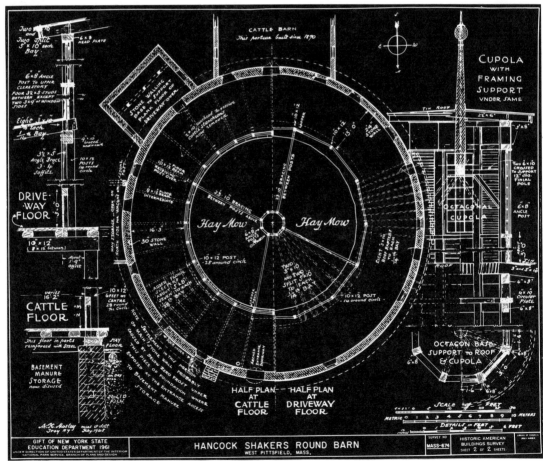

4.28 Haymow, clerestory, and roof framing, Round Barn, Hancock, showing alternate roof beams split to distribute load more evenly.

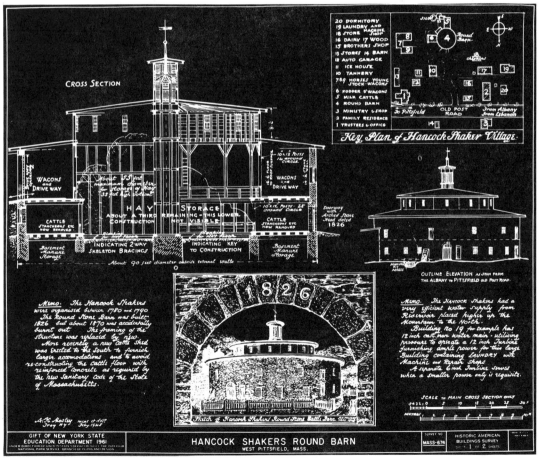

4.29 Meetinghouse, Church Family, Hancock (replica of 1786 Hancock building erected at Shirley, Massachusetts, and moved to site as part of museum village).

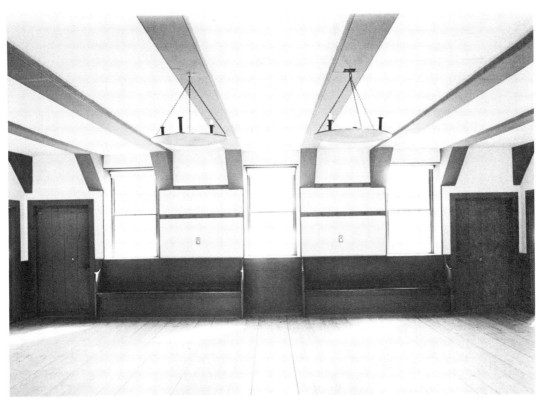

4.30 Meetinghouse, interior.

4.31 If not forcing the transition from earthly to heavenly space, at least suggesting its inevitability: Meetinghouse, interior.

ceremonies made more specific use of the environment. The "Cleansing Gift," instituted in September, 1843, included processions through all the buildings and grounds, sweeping and tidying for an imminent heavenly visit. Lamson describes two bands of roaming singers at Hancock, male and female, entering every building and yard to search for dirt and evil and encourage those cleaning.[65] Elder Hervey Elkins, leader of another Shaker community, recounts a more elaborate version of this ritual:

It was announced that Jehovah—Power and Wisdom—the dual God, would visit the inhabitants of Zion, and bestow a blessing upon each individual as their works should merit. A time was given for us to prepare for his coming. Every building, every apartment, every lane, field, orchard, and pasture, must be cleansed of all rubbish and needless encumbrance; so that even a Shaker village, so notorious for neatness, wore an aspect fifty per cent more tidy than usual. To sweep our buildings, regulate our stores, pick up and draw to a circular wood-saw old bits of boards, stakes, and poles that were fit for naught but fuel, and collect into piles to be burned upon the spot all such as were unfit for that, was the order of the day. Even the sisters debouched by scores to help improve the appearance of the farm and lake shores, on which were quantities of drift-wood. Thus was passed a fortnight of pleasant autumnal weather. As the evenings approached, we set fire to the piles of old wood, which burned, the flames shooting upward, in a serene evening, like the innumerable bonfires which announce the ingress of a regal visitant to monarchical countries. Viewed from the plain below, in the gray, dim twilight of a soft and serene atmosphere, when all nature was wrapped in the unique and beautiful solemnity of an unusually prolonged autumn, these fires, emerging in the blue distance from the vast amphitheatre of hills, were picturesque in the highest degree. How neat! how fascinating! and how much like our conceptions of heaven the whole vale appeared! And then to regard this work of cleansing and beautifying the domains of Mount Zion as that preparatory to the visitation of the Most High, is something which speaks to the heart and says: "Dost thou appear as beautiful, as clean, and as comely in the sight of God as do these elements of an unthinking world? Is thine heart also prepared to be searched with the candles of him from whom no unclean thing is hidden?"

The following words were said to have been brought by an angel from Jehovah, and accompanied by a most beautiful tune of two airs:

"I shall march through Mount Zion,
With my angelic band;
I shall pass through the city
With my fan in my hand;
And around thee, O Jerusalem,
My armies will encamp,
While I search my Holy Temple
With my bright burning lamp."[66]

The "Mountain Meetings," celebrated in May and September, also took advantage of the best New England weather. David Lamson describes the occasions:

The day for meeting upon this mountain, is with the Shakers, a glorious day, a day of rejoicing, and a feast of fat things. All are elated with the idea of going onto the mountain; both old, and young, seem equally elated, all go who are able to walk, and some who are not able to walk, ride, though it is a steep and difficult way for the horses and carriages.[67]

4.32 "Mountain Meeting," woodcut showing Shakers on Mount Sinai at Hancock, 1848, where imaginary banquets took place in imaginary gardens and orchards.

4.33 Environmental order, caricatured in toy villages, found full religious expression in the Shaker domains: Church Family, Hancock, aerial view from the direction of Mount Sinai, 1960.

The sanctuary for feasts of love at Hancock, established on Shaker Mountain (called Mount Sinai) was reached after a slow procession through the domain and along a tortuous path winding up the side of the mountain (Fig. 4.32). From the summit, members could look down on their village (Fig. 4.33), and, even more amazing, they could look across to the sanctuary of the New Lebanon community, situated one peak west. Members of the two communities waved. And the Hancock people, dressed in imaginary golden robes, approached a fenced enclosure containing an imaginary fountain, bathed in imaginary tubs, and partook of an imaginary feast of exotic fruits gathered from imaginary gardens and orchards.[68] They also had imaginary liquor, but surely they got drunk on the environment.

Although Harriet Martineau found Shaker houses "in all respects unexceptionable,"[69] Charles Nordhoff called them "homely," and other visitors described them as grim, factorylike structures. Modern historians agree with Martineau about Shaker style. As twentieth century Bauhaus design became popular, the Shakers were "discovered" as early adherents of the functionalist aesthetic. One critic who expresses this point of view most succinctly compares Shaker buildings to those of Mies van der Rohe, adding Mies's famous aphorism, "God is in the details."[70] Mother Ann's insistence on "hands to work and hearts to God" figures as the theme of several other essays which describe the sect's ascetic piety and explain their physical designs in terms of a work ethic exploded into fanatical functionalism.[71] Such scholarship misses the peculiar passion and vitality of the Shaker design process.

Every Shaker design expressed its makers' internal dual sensitivity to real and imaginary, earthly and heavenly space. Each member, part of the living building, was engaging in a physical labor fully identified with life's ultimate purpose, translating visual concepts into physical reality, helping to transform earthly millennial communities into the New Jerusalem. The socialization process made the design process accessible to all, made it possible. Thus the sequence of two dozen splendid Shaker villages becomes comprehensible, as does the magnificent unity of landscape design, buildings, furniture, and crafts. And the wonder that any human process could generate, on demand, such complete and pervasive, convincing yet unassuming, physical design syntheses is somewhat explicated.

The Shakers' ability to produce a satisfactory communitarian environment, wherever they chose, provides the ultimate proof of their full mastery of the design process. Many groups struggled to design for themselves a responsive environment which would both meet their physical needs and stimulate their daily lives. The Oneida Community solved this problem by identifying some aspects of environmental design as expressive and some as regulative. Their design process and their buildings were delicately poised, complicated, singular to themselves and their site. In comparison the Shaker process and buildings appear to represent pure discipline. But in the closed system of Shaker life, every physical design made possible a responsive, opposite spiritual action. To appreciate the straight chairs, one must know the whirling dances. To understand the rigid alignment of buildings, one must envision members marching through their orchards or rolling woodlands (Fig. 4.34) singing of a procession in their Heavenly City. The most telling comparison is that, despite its complexity, the Shakers' closed system was not unique, but replicable. It could be recreated anywhere that new members gathered to form a "living building."

4.34 Envision members marching through the fields, singing of a millennial procession in the heavenly City of Peace: Church Family, Hancock, view from the fields.

1 Charles Sanford, in *The Quest for Paradise*, Urbana, Ill., 1961, pp. 75-93, describes the development of millennial eschatology in the United States and traces it to the European belief that America was a new continent where the Reformation was to be perfected. Henri Desroche, in *The American Shakers: from Neo-Christianity to Presocialism*, tr. John K. Savacool, Amherst, Mass., 1971, discusses differences between premillenarian and postmillenarian strategies, pp. 76-77. Desroche concludes, ". . . the Shakers were seeking transcendence in immanence itself . . . by creating a world which would no longer be 'of this world,' yet nevertheless would be here, now, and real" (pp. 86-87).

2 James Whittaker, quoted in Edward Deming Andrews, *The Hancock Shakers*, Hancock, Mass., 1961, p. 5.

3 Desroche describes the Shakers as parasites feeding on other sects' revivals, pp. 103-106. Mother Ann's feminist doctrines must have had a special appeal, however, presaging current works such as Mary Daly, *Beyond God The Father: Toward a Philosophy of Women's Liberation*, Boston, 1973.

4 There was no escape—the heavenly reward for Shakers was "glorious employment." Calvin Green and Seth Y. Wells, eds., *A Summary View of the Millennial Church or United Society of Believers, Commonly Called Shakers*, 2d. ed., Albany, N. Y., 1848, p. 130.

5 Edward Deming Andrews, *The People Called Shakers*, rev. ed., New York, 1963, provides a useful statistical table of Shaker settlements with an appendix of short-lived attempts at community founding, pp. 290-291. Andrews also notes that during this period a settlement which appeared to be floundering, like Busro, Indiana, or Darby Plains, Ohio, was sold with despatch and its members reassigned (p. 87). This is the best single work on Shaker history, and I relied upon it for much general information.

6 W. S. Warder, *A Brief Sketch of the Religious Society of People Called Shakers*, London, 1818.

7 Lewis S. Feuer, "The Influence of the American Communist Colonies on Engels and Marx," *Western Political Quarterly*, 19 (Sept. 1966), 456-474.

8 John Humphrey Noyes, *History of American Socialisms* (1870), New York, 1966, pp. 669-670.

9 Desroche, *American Shakers*, pp. 276-277.

10 Membership records are held by Western Reserve Historical Society, Cleveland.

11 Fifty persons was considered the ideal family size. Andrews, *The People Called Shakers*, p. 107, quotes Arthur Baker, *Shakers and Shakerism*, London, 1896, p. 15.

12 David Benedict, *A History of All Religions*, Providence, R.I., 1824, p. 254.

13 Charles Nordhoff, *The Communistic Societies of the United States* (1875), New York, 1966, p. 251.

14 Andrews, *The People Called Shakers*, p. 57. Anthony Vidler's work on Freemasonry has led me to believe that Masonic writings provide a source for this concern with Solomon's temple and with the hierarchical structuring of landscape.

15 Green and Wells, *A Summary View*, p. 297.

16 Richard Pelham, *What Would Become of the World If All Should Become Shakers?* East Canterbury, N.H., 1868, pp. 3-4.

17 "The Living Building," *Millennial Praises, Containing a Collection of Gospel Hymns, in Four Parts*, Hancock, Mass., 1813, p. 158.

18 Edward Deming Andrews, *The Gift To Be Simple: Songs, Dances, and Rituals of the American Shakers*, New York, 1940, p. 51. Hymn first published in 1812.

19 Andrews, *The People Called Shakers*, p. 183.

20 Benson J. Lossing, "The Shakers," *Harper's New Monthly Magazine*, 15 (July 1857), 165.

21 "Millennial Laws" of 1845, part 3, sec. 6.4, reprinted in Andrews, *The People Called Shakers*, p. 283.

22 Nordhoff, p. 174.

23 "Millennial Laws," of 1845, part 3, sec. 7.8, reprinted in Andrews, *The People Called Shakers*, p. 284.

24 Andrews, *The People Called Shakers*, p. 78.

25 An elaborate etiquette prevailed in a building with only one stair—a brother was to ascend first, a sister to descend first, in order to avoid any unseemly show of the sister's ankles. "*Authorized Rules of the Shaker Community*," Mount Lebanon, N. Y., 1894, p. 1.

26 David Lamson, *Two Years' Experience Among The Shakers*, West Boylston, Mass., 1848, p. 52.

27 "Authorized Rules," p. 1.

28 "Millennial Laws" of 1845, part 1, sec. 4.16, reprinted in Andrews, *The People Called Shakers*, p. 258.

29 Lamson, *Two Years' Experience*, p. 84.

30 Andrews, *The People Called Shakers*, p. 178.

31 Lamson, *Two Years' Experience*, p. 192.

32 Nordhoff, *Communistic Societies*, pp. 215-221.

33 Elizabeth McCausland, "The Shaker Legacy," *Magazine of Art*, 37 (Dec. 1944).

34 Charles Dickens, *American Notes*, New York, 1841, p. 79.

35 McCausland mentions this. Also an anonymous poem in *The Shaker* (Mount Lebanon, N.Y.), 1 (May 1871), 36, boasts, "Our shoes are for comfort and made to the feet."

36 Hymn from Enfield, N. H., 1848, quoted in Andrews, *The Gift to be Simple*, p. 64.

37 Early hymn (ca. 1810?), quoted in Andrews, *The Gift to be Simple*, p. 56.

38 Lamson, *Two Years' Experience*, pp. 52-53.

39 "Millennial Laws" of 1845, part 1, sec. 4.9, reprinted in Andrews, *The People Called Shakers*, p. 258. Desroche describes Manchester in Chapter 2 of *American Shakers*.

40 *The Shaker*, 1 (May 1871), 36.

41 Desroche refers to the Luddites smashing machines in Manchester and wonders if they influenced Mother Ann (*American Shakers*, p. 41).

42 William Hinds, *American Communities*, Chicago, 1902, p. 27.

43 Nordhoff, *Communistic Societies*, p. 117.

44 Otis Sawyer, *Who Built Our Shaker Home?* undated imprint, Shaker Museum, Sabbathday Lake, Maine.

45 Horace Greeley, "A Sabbath With the Shakers," *The Knickerbocker*, 9 (June 1838), 533.

46 "Millennial Laws" of 1845, part 3, sec. 8, reprinted in Andrews, *The People Called Shakers*, p. 284.

47 Lossing, "The Shakers," p. 165.

48 Harriet Martineau, *Society in America*, vol. 1, New York, 1837, p. 310.

49 *The Cultivator*, cited in Andrews, *The People Called Shakers*, p. 120. An indication of the importance of scientific agriculture in Shaker communities was their training for children. Agriculture and agricultural chemistry were incorporated in the school curriculum after 1840. For practical experiments the girls were usually given a garden and the boys a small model farm. Andrews reports that the Shakers' role as teachers extended beyond their own community, since they taught good farming practices to local residents. He cites Ralph Waldo Emerson, who claimed the Shakers filled the role of a local aristocracy in this regard. *The People Called Shakers*, p. 89, p. 120.

50 Charles F. Wingate, "Shaker Sanitation," *The Sanitary Engineer*, New York, Sept. 1880.

51 Lamson, *Two Years' Experience*, p. 17.

52 Wingate, "Shaker Sanitation."

53 "Millennial Laws" of 1845, part 3, sec. 9.2, part 3, sec. 1.2, reprinted in Andrews, *The People Called Shakers*, p. 279, p. 285.

54 Desroche, *American Shakers*, p. 292.

55 Nordhoff, *Communistic Societies*, pp. 164-165.

56 James Whittaker, "The Shaker Shaken," letter to Josiah Talcott, 1782, reprinted by Bibliographical Press, New Haven, Conn., 1938.

57 Lamson, *Two Years' Experience*, p. 15.

58 Rebecca Clark, quoted in Andrews, "The Hancock Shakers," p. 22.

59 "Millennial Laws" of 1845, part 3, sec. 9, reprinted in Andrews, *The People Called Shakers*, pp. 285-286.

60 Andrews, *The Hancock Shakers*, p. 30.

61 "Portfolio 9783," collection of Shaker Community, Inc., Hancock, Mass.

62 Ibid.

63 "Millennial Laws" of 1845, part 2, sec. 5.12; part 3, sec. 1.2; part 3, sec. 6.4, reprinted in Andrews, *The People Called Shakers*, p. 267, p. 279, p. 283.

64 Andrews, *The People Called Shakers*, p. 142.

65 Lamson, *Two Years' Experience*, pp. 105-107.

66 Hervey Elkins, quoted in Nordhoff, *Communistic Societies*, p. 239.

67 Lamson, *Two Years' Experience*, p. 56.

68 Ibid., pp. 56-73.

69 Martineau, *Society in America*, p. 310.

70 Hilton Kramer, "God Is in the Details," *New York Times*, July 25, 1971, Arts and Leisure Section, p. 1.

71 D.M.C. Hopping and Gerald R. Watland, "The Architecture of the Shakers," *Antiques*, 72 (Oct. 1957), 335-339; Edward Deming Andrews, "The Shaker Manner of Building," *Art in America*, 48 (Mar. 1960), 38-45; Die Neue Sammlung, *The Shakers: Life and Production of a Community in the Pioneering Days of America*, Munich, 1974.

5 Eden versus Jerusalem

Let the division fences be lined with peach and mulberry trees, . . . and the houses surrounded with roses and prairie flowers, and their porches covered with grape vine, and we shall soon have formed some idea of how Eden looked. . . .

—editorial addressed to Mormons in Nauvoo, *Times and Seasons*, 1842

And the city lieth foursquare, and the length is as large as the breadth. . . .

—Revelation 21:16, describing the Heavenly Jerusalem

Detail of 5.34

The Shakers visualized splendid heavenly cities, while they built ascetic, earthly villages; the Mormons also conceived two simultaneous visions of millennial architecture, but they attempted to construct them side by side. When the first Mormon settlements were built in Ohio, Missouri, and Illinois between 1830 and 1846, two competing images of the ideal Mormon city emerged. Eden, a model of earthly paradise, is a garden city of single-family dwellings; Jerusalem, a model of heaven, is a cult center dominated by twin monuments, the temple and the prophet's residence. Conflict between these two ideals, which were never fully articulated, is expressed in the ambiguities of Mormon town plans and architectural styles, as well as in explosive debates about city scale and the role of central buildings in Nauvoo, Illinois.

Ultimately the Mormons transcended this unconscious dual idealism. From the small group of disciples recruited in 1830 by Joseph Smith, Jr., in upstate New York, the church grew in fifty years to include over 140,000 members gathered in 400 new communities, a record equal to the most optimistic projections of any communitarian theorist. When they migrated to the Great Basin of Utah after sixteen years in the East and Midwest, Mormons encountered an unsettled, barren environment, the geographical "vacuum" all communards dreamed of finding beyond the frontier. Here they were isolated and felt less need to distinguish themselves as unique by erecting unusual and costly buildings. They gave priority to town and regional planning, supported by church-sanctioned methods of vernacular building, irrigation, and horticulture, and they reserved monumental architecture for special symbolic purposes which allowed them to recall the continuity of Mormon experience, without repeating the earlier builders' mistakes. When the preoccupation with monuments of the heavenly Jerusalem which had confused earlier settlements took second place to the development of the landscape of an earthly Eden, they had established an approach to environmental design which would sustain them for over a century.

The "burned-over district" of New York State, fired by a succession of religious revivals in the first half of the nineteenth century, provided the setting for the establishment of the Church of Christ, later termed the Church of Jesus Christ of the Latter-day Saints.[1] Joseph Smith, its prophet and founder, was born in Sharon, Vermont, in 1805, the fourth child of poor parents. His father alternated between unsuccessful farming and storekeeping. In the village of Manchester, near Palmyra, New York, where the family lived after 1816, frequent religious conventions gave Joseph Smith an opportunity to study the rhetorical and theological styles of various Methodist, Baptist, and Presbyterian evangelists. Smith's uncle, Jason Mack, who founded a communistic religious community in New Brunswick, introduced his nephew to communitarian ideas, but Shakers from Sodus Bay and disciples of Jemimah Wilkinson, the "Universal Friend" from Jerusalem, New York, probably preached in Palmyra as well.[2]

In 1820, when Smith was fifteen, he announced that angels had appeared to him to denounce the falsity of existing religions. In 1827, Smith proclaimed his discovery of golden plates inscribed in a cryptic language. Donning special "spiritual spectacles," he translated the plates as the Book of Mormon, which he published in 1830. When Smith's family and friends recognized him as a prophet, he began to preach about the need for salvation in the "latter days" before the second coming of Christ. A basic tenet of the new faith was that the "latter-day saints" were a modern Israel, and that they must gather to await the second coming in Zion, a holy city equivalent to Jerusalem which must be constructed in the Western Hemisphere.

The Mormons might have remained just one more obscure millennial sect, but Joseph Smith's imaginativeness and eloquence were bolstered by the communitarian experience of Sidney Rigdon, Smith's first convert from another religious ministry. A Campbellite Baptist, Rigdon preached in Pittsburgh until 1825 and then in Kirtland, Ohio. From his years in Pittsburgh, Rigdon surely knew of the Harmony Society, a group of ascetic German communists who had built the towns of Harmony and Economy, Pennsylvania, in 1805 and 1824. Since the Harmonists had prospered in both locations, their towns were known as successful millennial settlements constructed in this world. Rigdon also espoused many of the ideas advanced by Robert Owen between 1824 and 1830. Proof of his commitment to building a model community was his Kirtland congregation, which formed a communistic living group known as "the Family."

After converting Rigdon in 1830, Smith decided to move his own following west to unite with Rigdon's existing congregation and community (Fig. 5.1). In Kirtland, Ohio, the Saints began to work out the economic and environmental arrangements of the earthly kingdom they hoped to create, according to the authoritarian process of "inspired" planning.[3] Regulations were often presented by Smith in the form of religious revelations. In February 1831, Smith promulgated the Law of Consecration and Stewardship (later known as the United Order, or the Order of Enoch). He called for the consolidation of all Mormon property in communal storehouses administered by bishops who would redistribute the goods according to members' needs, "for if ye are not equal in earthly things, ye cannot be equal in obtaining heavenly things."[4] Bishops were to bestow an "inheritance" or "stewardship" on members (a house with a store, some farmland, or some tools), so that members could be economically self-supporting. Each "steward" had complete license to engage in economic competition but surplus profits were to be dedicated to the community. These new economic arrangements were designed to bridge the gap between the communism of Rigdon's original "Family" and the individualist orientation of Smith's followers from New York. Communal living was discouraged, perhaps because of conflicts in the Family, but the appeal to individual initiative was made within the framework of income redistribution and accountability.

In developing the Law of Consecration and Stewardship, the Mormons attempted to eliminate inequalities between rich and poor while maintaining a certain amount of competition to spur economic growth. Poor converts liked the system better than rich ones, and disaffected converts had difficulty reclaiming their consecrated property. After three and a half years the law was suspended, ostensibly because the Saints in Kirtland, Ohio, and Independence, Missouri, were not ready for it. Beginning in 1838 Smith reduced his demands to the consecration of surplus property. In 1841 he imposed a tithe of ten percent on income or labor for the support of the Mormon church organization and the Nauvoo Temple. With the elimination of the transfer and retransfer of property, the Law of Consecration became an ideal rather than an actuality. The concept of property "as a life-lease subject to beneficial use and social direction" was retained, but individual ownership came to dominate the Mormon economy.[5]

Although Joseph Smith did challenge capitalism as a system which created inequalities harmful to the full development of the human personality, he never challenged the patriarchal family, which supported it. Traditional sex-stereotyped roles were glorified (much the same way that economic initiative was prized) as stable supports of Christian society, an attitude which made it possible for the Saints to gather new members far more rapidly than less conventional communities. The family home was sanctified in articles and sermons which defined homemaking as women's proper sphere.[6] For men, the isolation of the family was countered by participation in the two orders of the Mormon priesthood, Melchizedek and Aaronic. The hierarchy of the priesthood provided both spiritual and temporal authority for all adult males; the Temple offices and the Seventies Hall, for missionaries, provided communal territory for the men (Fig. 5.2). A woman could but share the reflected glory of her husband's office. In the 1840s when a sort of "consecration and

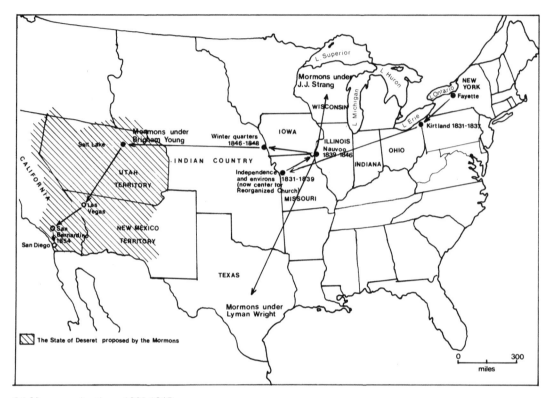

Figure labels (on map):

L. Superior

Mormons under
J. J. Strang

WISCONSIN

L. Huron

L. Michigan

NEW
YORK
Fayette

Mormons under
Brigham Young

Winter quarters
1846-1848

IOWA

Salt Lake

L. Ontario

L. Erie

Kirtland 1831-1837

INDIAN COUNTRY

ILLINOIS

Nauvoo
1839-1846

OHIO

CALIFORNIA

UTAH
TERRITORY

Independence
and environs 1831-1839
(now center for
Reorganized Church)

INDIANA

Las
Vegas

NEW MEXICO

MISSOURI

San
Bernardino
1854

TERRITORY

San Diego

TEXAS

Mormons under
Lyman Wright

The State of Deseret proposed by the Mormons

0   300
miles

5.1 Mormon migrations, 1830-1847.

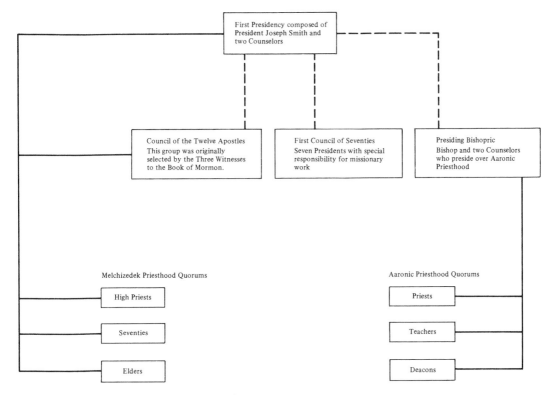

First Presidency composed of President Joseph Smith and two Counselors

Council of the Twelve Apostles
This group was originally selected by the Three Witnesses to the Book of Mormon.

First Council of Seventies
Seven Presidents with special responsibility for missionary work

Presiding Bishopric
Bishop and two Counselors who preside over Aaronic Priesthood

Melchizedek Priesthood Quorums

High Priests

Seventies

Elders

Aaronic Priesthood Quorums

Priests

Teachers

Deacons

5.2 Mormon organization in Nauvoo.

stewardship" of the women of the community was introduced in the form of polygamy, the bonds of brotherhood became even closer. One can view Nauvoo as a commune of men only, sharing rituals, territory, and sexual privilege. Mormon women, caretakers of the men's private homes, are isolated from collective decision making. This is perhaps the least egalitarian and most traditional approach to the dilemmas of authoritative versus participatory processes and communal versus private territory proposed by any communal group.

Efforts to develop a community building program accompanied the Saints' attempts to create a collective economy. On June 25, 1833, Smith sent the "Plat of the City of Zion" (Fig. 5.3), delineating a grid town approximately one mile square, to converts in Independence, Missouri. Blocks were divided into half-acre residential lots, with a central area reserved for at least twenty-five communal temples and storehouses to assist "consecration and stewardship." Each residential lot was to contain one brick or stone house set back twenty-five feet from the street and surrounded by a garden. Mormons were ordered to live in the city and travel to the fields outside it. Identical satellite towns called "stakes" of Zion were to surround the central settlement at an unspecified distance. The communitarian command for duplication of the model read: "When this square is thus laid off and supplied, lay off another in the same way and so fill up the world in these last days, and let every man live in the city for this is the city of Zion."[7]

The Mormons' desire for architectural coherence was somewhat unusual on the American frontier, although Puritan covenant communities in New England had established a precedent for farm villages surrounded by tilled land.[8] The "Plat of the City of Zion" was drawn by Smith; the order to implement it was signed by Smith, Sidney Rigdon, and Frederick Williams. Rigdon's knowledge of town building undertaken by the members of the Harmony Society can only be surmised from circumstantial evidence,[9] but comparison of the plan of Harmony, Pennsylvania (Fig. 5.4) with the "Plat of the City of Zion" reveals similarities of goals, conception, and detailing.[10] Both were considered earthly versions of the Heavenly Jerusalem described in Revelation 21:16. Both were oriented to the cardinal points of the compass and employed a grid pattern of streets. The plans share more unusual features as well: the concentration of dwellings in towns and fields outside and the establishment of a village center with communal buildings. Both plans incorporate gardens, coupling the pastoral symbolism of Eden with the urban symbolism of the Heavenly Jerusalem.[11] Both plans rely on standard materials, setbacks, and zoning (Fig. 5.5) to create a uniform town fabric. Even the one "unique" feature of Smith's plan, the alternation of lot orientations to provide maximum privacy for homeowners, is suggested by the different orientation of the communal buildings from most of the dwellings in Harmony.

The chief difference between the plan of Harmony and the plat of Zion is one of scale, significant in light of the Mormons' later inability to deal with city scale in Nauvoo. Harmony covered fourteen square miles but accommodated approximately 900 people in a dense, central area. All land was communally owned and the boundaries of the settlement were clearly defined. Within them the members of the Harmony Society felt accountable for establishing a self-sufficient cycle of production and consumption. It was a single "kingdom" with a couple of outlying farm villages. Although the Society changed its location three times, members did not wish to expand their membership through the duplication of the model town.

Although Harmony seems to have provided a prototype for the "Plat of the City of Zion," Smith's belief in forceful, active recruitment led him to speculate about expanding Zion beyond the scope of a single settlement. In the same utopian vein as Robert Owen and Charles Fourier, Smith envisioned Zion as a Mormon world order, for he expected the first model settlement to generate an infinite number of identical copies. Thus he prophesied a global network of "stakes of Zion" all based on the plan of the first settlement.[12]

An arithmetical problem further complicated the uncertain scale of Zion. In 1833 Smith stated that the plat of Zion could accommodate fifteen to twenty thousand people. With less than a thousand lots, this assumed a density of at least seventeen people per half-acre lot.[13] In revising this estimate, Smith decided to retain the target population of Zion rather than the ideal territorial size of one square mile. In 1837 he produced a plan for Kirtland, Ohio, which included 4,500 lots, an alteration which established a precedent for growth by expansion rather than by duplication of the model, and emphasized the town fabric at the expense of the town center. When in 1838 the Law of Consecration and Stewardship was rescinded and communal storehouses were no longer required by Mormon bishops, the existence of any center at all for the city of Zion was in doubt. Far West, Missouri, platted in 1838, reflects this change, as does Nauvoo. Despite confusion about city scale, methods of duplication, and the role of the town center, the "Plat of the City of Zion" established the Mormons' intention to build coherent communities. The problems of actually constructing Zion remained to be demonstrated in Nauvoo and resolved in the Great Basin, but their initial achievement as planners was substantial.

Smith's plan to reorganize Kirtland, Ohio, according to a revised, centerless version of the "Plat of the City of Zion" was never implemented because the Saints' sojourn there was ended after the collapse of a wildcat Mormon "anti-bank." Simultaneous attempts to develop

5.3 "When this square is laid off and supplied, lay off another in the same way and so fill up the world in these last days." Plat of the City of Zion, drawn by Joseph Smith, sent to Independence, Missouri, June 25, 1833. Central numbers refer to storehouses and temples.

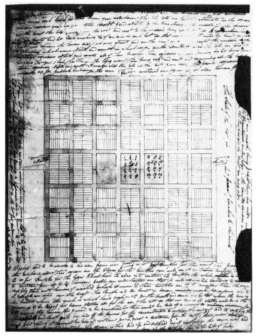

5.4 Another attempt to build a millennial kingdom, Harmony, Pennsylvania, founded 1805, showing town center with communal buildings surrounded by houses. Brick buildings are shaded.

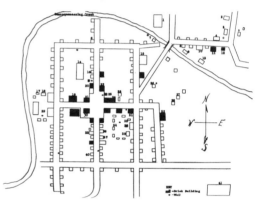

5.5 Harmonist brick houses, ca. 1825, Economy, Pennsylvania.

a Mormon community were occurring in Independence, Missouri, where a group of Mormons struggled to develop a settlement between 1831 and 1833. One source of friction in Independence was the Mormon newspaper, the *Evening and Morning Star*, whose editor concentrated on news of fires, floods, wars, and other disasters which the Mormons believed signaled the Second Coming.[14] Neighbors who feared their religious doomsaying and their political power forced the community to seek another site, Far West, Missouri, seat of Caldwell County. Religious and political persecution continued, exacerbated by Smith's announcement in 1838 that the Mormon Church planned to develop all of Caldwell County as "stakes of Zion," and his prophecy that in time, all of Missouri would be Mormon.

The winter of 1838-1839 saw 5,000 Mormons chased across the Missouri state line by hostile neighbors, to regather in the spring around the sites of Commerce and Commerce City, Illinois, paper towns platted on marshy riverbank land by speculators in 1824 and 1837. The depression following the Panic of 1837 had punctured the Illinois real estate boom, and the land owners offered the Mormon settlers easy terms. Smith renamed the place "Nauvoo," announcing that it meant place of beauty and repose, and set out once again to create the city of Zion. His enthusiasm undiminished by enforced wanderings, he preached: ". . . Blessed are they that continue to the end *faithful*, for whether they have builded a city in Ohio, or Missouri, or Illinois, they shall enter into the joys of their lord, and inherit the Kingdom prepared before the foundation of the world."[15]

Nauvoo possessed a commanding location on the Mississippi River, a peninsula created by a broad westerly bend in the river, bounded on the east by bluffs offering distant views of the Mississippi Valley (Figs. 5.6, 5.7). Below Nauvoo the Des Moines Rapids extended twelve miles downstream, making the site a natural terminus for traffic on the upper Mississippi. A serious disadvantage was the malarial lowland to the south which required immediate drainage. Still, John Kirk, correspondent for the New England communitarian paper, *The Harbinger*, called Nauvoo one of the prettiest places for a city he ever saw,[16] and John Warner Barber, the peripatetic author of *Our Whole Country*, concurred.[17]

During the seven years the Saints spent developing Nauvoo, it grew to be the largest city in Illinois, with a population in 1845 estimated between twelve and twenty thousand.[18] Beginning in January, 1841, all Mormon converts were commanded to move to Nauvoo immediately to build up the kingdom, a policy which brought the community far more members than most communitarian groups were able to recruit, but did not allow for careful screening or for intensive socialization. Converts included many New Englanders eager to identify themselves as a chosen people, perhaps because of their upbringing in Puritan covenant communities. English immigrants to Nauvoo numbered almost five thousand, including many dissatisfied urban workers entranced by Parley Pratt's hyperbole: "Millions on millions of acres lie . . . unoccupied, with a soil as rich as Eden, and a surface as smooth, clear, and ready for the plow as the park scenery of England."[19] A steady stream of newcomers arrived in Nauvoo and Mormon leaders simply tried to orient them to broad community building goals

5.6 "The great Emporium of the West, the center of
all centers . . . a suitable home for the Saints," Nauvoo, Illinois, site plan, ca. 1844, including proposed
dam and canal.

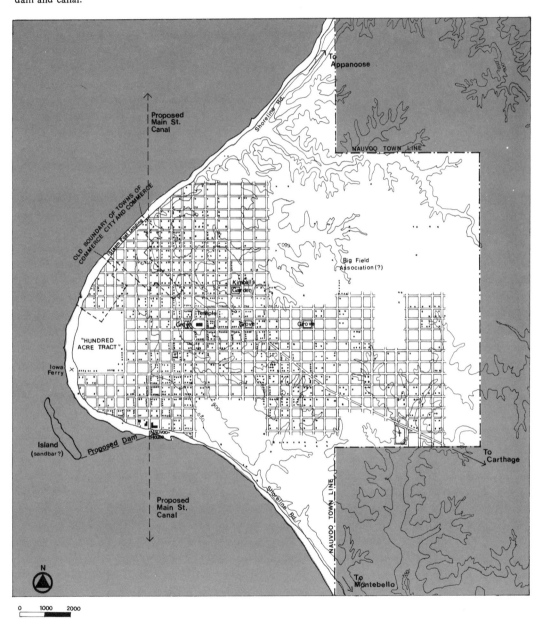

5.7 "Nauvoe [*sic*], Illinois," showing Nauvoo House, on shoreline at right, and Temple on bluffs.

5.8 "Nauvoo is the hub": regional plan, Nauvoo and proposed "stakes."

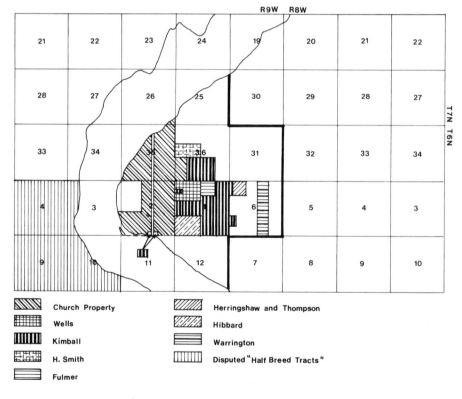

Church Property

Wells

Kimball

H. Smith

Fulmer

Herringshaw and Thompson

Hibbard

Warrington

Disputed "Half Breed Tracts"

5.9 Diagram of land ownership in Nauvoo, showing various church and private holdings.

couched in religious terms. Since all expected an imminent Second Coming of Christ, and the destruction of the rest of the world outside the holy city, the atmosphere was charged with eagerness to do God's will.

Community building in Nauvoo was a confused mixture of religious and secular, public and private enterprise. Given its favorable location and large numbers of settlers, Nauvoo promised to become a successful river city, perhaps as prosperous as Saint Louis. Joseph Smith, in an expansive mood, planned for "stakes" or satellite towns (Fig. 5.8) and envisioned Nauvoo as the center of a great wheel:

Nauvoo is the hub: we will drive the first spoke in Ramus [Macedonia, Ill.], second in La Harpe, third in Shokoquon, fourth in Lima; that is half the wheel. The other half is over the river . . . .[20]

Smith also talked of Nauvoo as the "workshop" of the Midwest. In 1841 he applauded John C. Bennett's proposal to build a canal along Main Street, creating a millrace and a harbor and allowing boats to deliver goods to the front doors of commercial establishments. Smith himself designed a dam extending west across the Mississippi in order to develop a harbor "accessible at all times to the largest class of boats." He hoped the same dam would develop the "best mill privileges in the western country."[21] He saw Nauvoo becoming the

great Emporium of the West, the center of all centers . . . embracing all the intelligence of all nations, with industry, frugality, economy, virtue, and brotherly love unsurpassed in any age of the world . . . a suitable home for the Saints.[22]

Yet in 1842 the city's facilities included only

two sawmills, two gristmills, a foundry, and a tool shop.

One problem was the holy conviction held by both Mormon leaders and Mormon converts that Nauvoo was unlike all other American cities because it was a sacred city existing outside the laws of secular society. Short-term rather than long-term solutions were usually applied to problems of economic and environmental planning, often backed by the fiat of the prophet. He rationalized them with the ingenuousness of a rural farm boy who acknowledges no city slickers' conventions and, indeed, has no idea of what a great city is like. In particular, Smith dealt fast and loose in land speculation, confident that either the Lord would enable the church to pay for land used for the kingdom, or would wipe out all of the Saints' debts with His timely advent. As Trustee-in-Trust of the Mormon Church, Smith bought land on credit and sold it to converts arriving in the city; all of Smith's speculation was compounded by that of other residents. Receipts from land sales financed the construction of the Nauvoo Temple and the Nauvoo House, which was to be both the Prophet's residence and a large hotel.

In terms of his preaching, he promoted private land sales in Eden (the residential city, a gridded garden, infinitely expanded) in order to capitalize public works in Jerusalem (the sacred city of monumental architecture). The consequence of the first activity was hasty expansion of town fabric to cover an area four miles square (Fig. 5.9) without a clearly defined center. The consequence of the second was that when creditors demanded continued payments on the Nauvoo land, all available capital was tied up in construction of the Temple and the Nauvoo House. As a delaying tactic Smith tried to acquire and sell even more land, but the bigger Nauvoo grew, the less rational was its planning and the more indebted was the church. The Temple and the Nauvoo House were vertical monuments of communal significance amid the horizontal spread of private houses. But the sense of place offered by such monuments carried too high a price. Collective pride might be fostered by unique, grandiose buildings, but the economy could not withstand their cost.

As might be expected, the settlers' millennial expectations were called upon again and again to justify the frantic rush of vernacular and monumental building in Nauvoo. Many converts complained, as did James Greenlaugh, the author of an anti-Mormon pamphlet criticizing economic planning in the city.[23] Yet most were faithful, convinced that herculean efforts to develop their own lots and build the two great monuments would improve their standing in the eyes of the Lord. The process of public and private building, with its components of sacrifice and investment, seems-to have generated remarkable commitment to the community. An examination of that process reveals that the successes of the Nauvoo Mormons as builders were almost as great as their failures as financiers.

The rectangular grid system of land surveying established by the Land Ordinance of 1785 has been described as "the blueprint for an agrarian equalitarian society"[24] reflecting the Jeffersonian social ideal of a democracy of small independent landowners. In Nauvoo, the Mormons tried to elevate their portion of the national grid system to a more transcendent level by emphasizing gardens and family homes. The grid was an egalitarian framework. The gardens functioned as Edenic infill, symbolizing the Mormon commitment to redemption of the earth. Distinctive brick dwellings built by the more prosperous converts stood surrounded by gardens, expressive of Mormon determination to unite earthly and heavenly rewards.

The Rhetoric

Edenic imagery transformed concern for private homes and gardens into a collective force for land development, uncontrolled, threatening to non-Mormon neighbors, but crucial to communitarian expansion. Missionaries had used the rhetoric of Eden—Parley Pratt's "park scenery," "ready for the plow"—to sell Nauvoo to converts. Journalists in Nauvoo continued to elaborate such themes, celebrating what they called their "city" by stressing its pastoral qualities such as a "delightful landscape" with lowing cattle,[25] or the "elegant gardens" of the "beautiful plantation" called Nauvoo.[26] In 1842 the editor of the *Wasp* wrote:

The wilderness has been made to blossom as the rose; and where hazle brush grew and muskitoes [*sic*] cousined, gardens decorate and the saints rest. . . . The country for several miles around is already risen into the great mass of a city, built by the only people of the earth, that while they labor incessantly to make this earth like the garden of the lord, labor also . . . to make men fit subjects for his kingdom and coming.[27]

Seven months later the sentiments expressed were similar:

. . . Our city now presents a lively and beautiful appearance. While it is adorned by the hand of nature in its richest dress, all hands seem engaged in adding to the comforts of the inhabitants. Numbers are employed in improving the streets and in removing every nuisance, whilst others are engaged in ploughing, digging, fencing, etc. The female part of the inhabitants are busily engaged in their flower gardens, and all around is health, peace, and happiness; and the songs of Zion are to be heard on every hand, united with those of the feathered tribe in almost every tree.[28]

The journals of Emily Coburn date the Mormon garden mania at least as early as Independence, Missouri, where "our homes . . . presented a prosperous appearance—almost equal to Paradise itself—and our peace and happiness . . . were not a great degree deficient to that of our first parents in the garden of Eden." She also asserts that in Independence "no labor or painstaking was spared in the cultivation of flowers and shrubbery," and seedlings from a commercial nursery in St. Louis were being imported to improve the landscape.[29] In Nauvoo similar effort was prescribed by *Times and Seasons*, February 1, 1842, with the command that "each citizen fill his spare ground with fruit trees, shrubbery, vines, etc., tastefully arranged and properly cultivated; . . . we shall soon have formed some idea of how Eden looked."[30] An element of individualism was introduced by the assurance that "we may each sit under our own vine and fig tree, and enjoy richly the fruits of our own industry."[31] Small consolation to the poor was the note that flower gardens would make even humble dwellings seem "fragrant and fair."[32] All of this horticultural excitement reached a pitch of millennial fervor in 1843, when the *Nauvoo Neighbor* advised: "Set out trees both useful and ornamental—now is the moment—there is no time to lose."[33]

Successful agriculture was a natural extension of concern with Edenic gardens. Advice to farmers from the *Cultivator* of Albany was commonly quoted in the Mormon press, and almost every day a new reprint was offered for the farmer. English converts were commended for their knowledge of hedging and ditching and encouraged to teach these techniques to Americans.[34] Any farmer who could not afford land was invited to join the "Big Field Association,"[35] a Mormon agricultural collective, also begun in Independence, which attempted to achieve increased yields through intensive cultivation of the land, revered as efficient stewardship of Christ's kingdom on earth.

The Architecture

Even more than gardens, homes represented the achievement of earthly paradise. The town was divided into rectangular blocks,[36] and each block divided into four lots to allow every homeowner a corner location. Superior houses, symbols of solid, prosperous Mormon families, were to be habitations which Brigham Young hoped "angels may delight to come and visit."[37]

Although dwellings in Nauvoo usually began as log cabins, members of the church were encouraged to build themselves more substantial houses as soon as possible. Twelve hundred log houses (some as large as twelve rooms), three to five hundred frame houses, and two to three hundred brick houses (some as small as two rooms) were built in the city.[38] Builders brought skills learned in New England, New York, New Jersey, Pennsylvania, Ohio, and England, yet a Nauvoo vernacular developed, since brick houses often were characterized by stepped gables. Imported to the banks of the Mississippi as a decorative form, the stepped gables sometimes incorporated chimneys but often simply aggrandized a dwelling or storefront facade. The James Ivins Printing Complex (Fig. 5.10) and the Brigham Young House (Fig. 5.11) are typical examples of the stepped gable style and its use in houses and commercial establishments.

Pleasing variations were developed by some builders. David Yearsley created a boxy, four-story brick house (Fig. 5.12). The Nathaniel Ashby-Erastus Snow (Fig. 5.13) and Winslow Farr (Fig. 5.14) houses were designed as duplexes, but they incorporate the same scale and materials as the single-family dwellings. Two small institutional buildings, the Masonic Hall (Fig. 5.15) and the Seventies Hall, also utilized the domestic idiom with slightly more elaborate window and facade treatments. The range of architectural effects achieved with brick construction and white wooden trim was substantial, but the siting of each building on an identical picket-fenced lot, cultivated as a garden, reconciled many possible inconsistencies. Since shops often adjoined houses, crossroads service neighborhoods developed, counterpoint to the grouping of four families per block. Urbanity and variety combined with privacy and greenery in Nauvoo at its best. Disorderly rows of shacks built by the poor lined the streets of the worst sections, a challenge to the Eden of privacy and private property which was never taken up, since quarrels over the town center

disrupted the entire settlement.

Eden: The Consequences

A resident, Irene Hascall, summed up her reaction to the unique combination of equal lots, evenly spaced houses, and cultivated gardens in a letter written in 1845:

I cannot describe the beauty of it on paper. . . . It is the prettiest place I ever saw for such a large place; as far as we can see either way are buildings not in blocks like other cities but all a short distance from each other. The ground between them is all cultivated . . . like a perfect garden.[39]

Despite their partial realization of the town fabric described in the "Plat of the City of Zion," the citizens of Nauvoo had serious problems which Irene Hascall did not perceive. "Such a large place" had no strongly defined center and no limits. Lack of a center caused rival factions to develop within the city, competing for prime commercial locations. Lack of boundaries aggravated the lack of a center and worried neighboring non-Mormons, who feared the rapid expansion of Nauvoo. The grid, for all its paradisiacal infill, demanded limits in time and space.[40]

The site of Nauvoo rises 300 feet between the flats, the area of the Mormons' first land purchases, and the bluffs, the area of later expansion. The first plat for the city, in 1839, showed a grid of streets on the flats, with the two widest, Water and Main, intersecting at the future site of the Nauvoo House, near the location of Smith's general store. The Nauvoo House, designed as both the Prophet's residence and a grand hotel, was expected to be the civic and commercial center of Nauvoo and the focal point for a dam and a canal. The bluffs, ac-

5.10 James Ivins Printing Complex.

5.11 Brigham Young House.

Eden: The Gridded Garden City

5.12 David Yearsley House.

5.13 Nathaniel Ashby-Erastus Snow duplex.

5.14 Winslow Farr House.

5.15 Masonic Hall.

Eden: The Gridded Garden City 123

quired in 1840, were intended by Smith to be a raised and secluded religious site, but several citizens were attracted by the commercial possibilities of the area. Land costs were lower, drainage problems fewer, and workers laboring on the Temple needed food, tools, materials, and shelter.

As the commercial and residential development of the bluffs began to rival that of the flats, Smith faced a challenge to his authority. The Temple site was accepted by all as a religious center where the resources of the city should be dedicated. He wanted the Nauvoo House recognized as an equal focus for investment, and objected to the construction of a market on Mulholland Street on the bluffs. In February, 1843, he complained that "the upper part of town has no right to rival those [sic] on the river."[41] He also supported plans for a walled sacred garden in the area of the Temple which would have had the effect of reducing the available land in the area. Nevertheless, new subdivisions were platted, and landowners on the bluffs continued to develop commercial facilities until Mulholland Street was the equal of Main. (Today Mulholland is the center of town.)

The locational conflicts created by uneven topography in the centerless city contributed to the development of an anti-Smith faction within the church. Led by William Law and Robert Foster, church leaders who worked as building contractors developing commercial and residential properties on the bluffs, a dissident group challenged Smith's allocations of funds to the Nauvoo House. He in turn accused them of making it impossible for the church to sell its land on the flats. They muttered of his profiteering. Doctrinal as well as financial issues divided the factions, and quarrels led to the ex-

communication of Law and Foster after they published the Nauvoo *Expositor*, which contained an offer to reform the Mormon Church from the "vicious principles of Joseph Smith."[42] Smith ordered the destruction of the *Expositor*'s press, an act which led to his confinement in the county jail. Encouraged by this schism within Nauvoo, anti-Mormon groups from neighboring towns seized the opportunity to halt the growth of the city. The events are well known. Joseph Smith and his brother, Hyrum Smith, were martyred in Carthage, Illinois, on June 29, 1844, by a hostile, anti-Mormon posse. This violence was followed by an order from the state government, which feared bloody reprisals, commanding the Mormons to evacuate their garden city and leave Illinois.

Unlike residential building in Nauvoo, which sparked competition for land among residents, religious building inspired almost unanimous support. Participation in creating monumental buildings was a source of pride in the city and, more important, was thought to be a guarantee of collective salvation.

The Rhetoric

Resounding revelations concerning the construction of the Temple and the Nauvoo House were uttered by Smith on January 19, 1841. He prophesied that kings from the four corners of the world would come to Nauvoo, and that the city should prepare to receive them:

Let my servant George, and my servant Lyman, and my servant John Snider, and others build a house unto my name, such as one as my servant Joseph shall shew unto them; upon the place which he shall shew unto them also. And it shall be for a house for boarding, a house that strangers may come from afar to lodge therein; therefore let it be a good house, worthy of all acceptation, that the weary traveller may find health and safety while he shall contemplate the word of the Lord; and the corner-stone I have appointed for Zion.
. . . .
And again, verily I say unto you, let all my saints come from afar; and send ye swift messengers, yea, chosen messengers, and say unto them: come ye, with all your gold, and your silver, and your precious stones, and with all your antiquities; and all who have knowledge of antiquities, that will come, may come, and bring the box tree, and the fir tree, and the pine tree, together with all the precious trees of the earth; and with iron, with copper, and with brass, and with zinc, and with all your precious things of the earth, and build a house to my

name, for the Most High to dwell therein. . . .[43]

The whole revelation covers fourteen pages with a curious mixture of styles. Concrete details are given for the Nauvoo House, such as the naming of contributors and stockholders. But for the Temple, a paraphrase of a Biblical description of the Heavenly Jerusalem is coupled with vague promises of special revelations and rituals when the Temple is completed, and warnings of heavenly wrath if it is not. The tone of the revelation is both demanding and cajoling. The promise of regal pilgrimages to the new Jerusalem is countered by the request for provision of a comfortable hotel. The exalted descriptions of a new Temple of Solomon are accompanied by the promise of offices in the Temple for named members of the priesthood. As the Mormons' spirits soared, Smith furnished them with lists of things to do and hopes of personal privilege.

The design and construction of Nauvoo's monuments provided the chance for daily commitment to millennial ideals. The editor of the Nauvoo *Wasp* stated the collective goal on October 29, 1842: "Speedy approximation to opulence and architectural grandure [*sic*]."[44] Frontier settlers, some of them semiliterate, exhausted themselves to create a distinctive Mormon style of building, sustained by their confidence that as a chosen people they were entitled to an architecture as good as any in America. They were sure that in time regal and divine visitants would confirm the worth of their architectural preparations.

The Nauvoo House, begun in 1841, shared equal importance in Joseph Smith's revelation with the Nauvoo Temple. Yet its main effect on the city was to aggravate the split between the two rival centers previously described. Labor

5.16 Design for the Nauvoo House, south elevation,
probably by Lucian Woodworth.

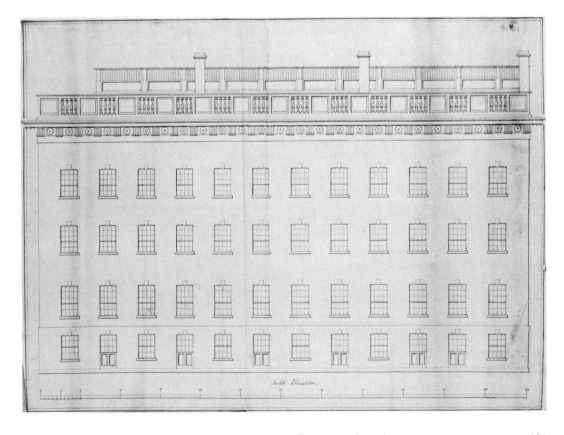

5.17 Unfinished Nauvoo House, painting by David H. Smith.

5.18 First Mormon Temple, Kirtland, Ohio, 1833-1836.

5.19 Kirtland Temple, pulpits of Melchizedek priesthood and yoke-shaped communion table.

5.20 Kirtland Temple, nave and aisles.

5.21 Drawing, "Elevation of the Temple, Now In Erection at Nauvoo," 1842.

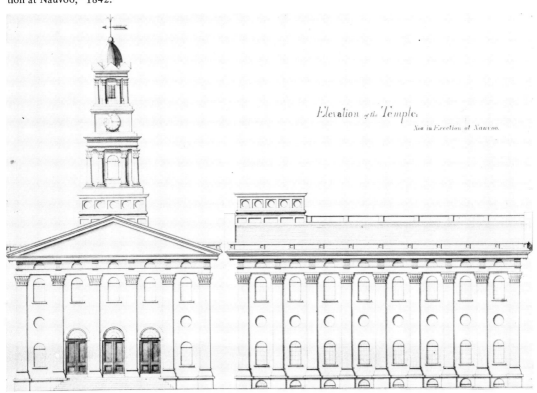

Elevation of the Temple,
Now in Erection at Nauvoo.

and materials were scarce, and the Temple usually had priority for available supplies. Lucian Woodworth, reportedly an English "Gentile,"[45] is cited as the Nauvoo House architect, and one thinks of Charles Dickens' character Martin Chuzzlewit, hoping to build his architectural masterpiece in Eden, U.S.A.[46] A single drawing of the building survives, unsigned and undated, showing the south elevation, uninspired Georgian (Fig. 5.16). Curiously, circles alternate with stars as triglyph ornament, perhaps in deference to the lively "Mormon order" evolving for the Temple. A painting of the structure reveals that only one story above the basement was completed (Fig. 5.17).

Located on the highest point of land in Nauvoo, the Nauvoo Temple dominated the city's site just as it dominated its economy and activity. It was begun in April, 1841, and dedicated on May 1, 1846. Several studies have been made of the Temple's design and construction; but its plan and sections remain subjects for conjecture, and the history of the building process has not been fully documented.[47] The Temple can be understood only in the context of the larger city building process of which it was a part.

Mormon history prior to Nauvoo included the collapse of the Mormon economy in Kirtland, Ohio, in 1837. This financial debacle was caused partly by the expense of the first Mormon Temple (Fig. 5.18), constructed between 1833 and 1836 at a cost estimated to be between forty and seventy thousand dollars.[48] Asher Benjamin's *Country Builder's Assistant* actually provided much of the architectural inspiration for this building,[49] but uniquely Mormon features included four sets of three-tiered pulpits (Figs. 5.19, 5.20) to accommodate numerous priesthood officers; two assembly halls,

instead of one hall with a balcony, in the nave; and an arrangement of canvas curtains subdividing the assembly halls into small sections, useful for the theatrical revelation of visionary experiences and for the arrangement of meetings on a more intimate scale. This building first expresses the vitality and exuberance which was to mark all Mormon monumental architecture in the nineteenth century, but its program was modest in comparison to the structure proposed for Nauvoo, which was ten times more expensive than the Kirtland Temple.

Construction of the Nauvoo Temple involved hundreds of laborers for about five years. Residents of the city were asked to contribute 10 percent of their income or to work one day in ten on the Temple; some were "called" for full-time efforts. Limestone quarries near the city supplied the stone, while timber was floated downriver from Wisconsin logging camps or "pineries" established for this purpose. A single delivery in 1842 was described as nearly one acre on water.[50]

While Nauvoo residents struggled to gather materials for the building, the official Temple architect, William Weeks, was straining to develop his architectural skills. A portfolio of drawings, preserved in the Church Historian's office in Salt Lake City, reveals various hands at work on the Temple's design.[51] A drawing signed "J. McC., Isle of Man, Sept. 1842" suggests that the *parti* was not Weeks' own (Fig. 5.21). Joseph Smith claimed a primary role in the design himself. When Weeks argued against round windows to light the Elders' offices as violating "all the known rules of architecture," Smith responded:

I told him I would have the circles, if he had to make the Temple ten feet higher than it was originally calculated; that one light at the center of each circular window would be sufficient to light the whole room; that when the whole building was thus illuminated, the effect would be remarkably grand. "I wish you to carry out my designs, I have seen in vision the splendid appearance of that building illuminated, and will have it built according to the pattern shown me."[52]

Whether Smith's "vision" was the "J. McC." elevation is uncertain. The other drawings, signed by Weeks, show his crude but steady development of an original "Mormon order" from the Corinthian capitals he copied (Figs. 5.22, 5.23, 5.24, 5.25, 5.26). The formal basis of the new order was suns, moons, and stars, following a Biblical description of celestial glories and rewards.[53] A contemporary observer reported in the St. Louis *Gazette* that "the effect of this image (the Mormon order) is semi-solemn, semi-laughable, and certainly, more than semi-singular."[54] Its vigor and unconventionality remain tremendously appealing.

Mormon rites developed much of their form in Nauvoo, taking on the esoteric symbolism of Masonry (Fig. 5.27), which seems to have inspired bizarre, dramatic rituals for the Nauvoo Masonic Lodge (Fig. 5.28) and for the new Temple.[55] Among the unusual features of the building were a basement with a font where church members underwent proxy baptisms by immersion to save the souls of the dead (Fig. 5.29). The font followed descriptions of a "molten sea" in Solomon's Temple of Jerusalem and was supported on twelve statues of oxen, larger than life size. The main and second assembly floors (Figs. 5.30, 5.31) resembled those of the Kirtland Temple, and included swing seats in the pews so that the congregation could face the pulpits of either the Melchizedek or Aaronic priesthood. In between these two floors were the priesthoods's offices, long and narrow, lit by the contested circular windows. On the top floor was a council chamber surrounded by smaller rooms and offices where every door boasted an outsize lock. Above the council chamber was a promenade which overlooked the town and offered a splendid view of the Mississippi. An octagonal tower contained at least three additional levels, offering an even more spectacular view at the summit. Two daguerrotypes and a contemporary print show competent construction and suggest that the building was a success in terms of conception, siting, and overall massing (Figs. 5.32, 5.33, 5.34).

Jerusalem: The Consequences

The Nauvoo Temple was intended to ensure its builders' salvation, by establishing Nauvoo as a New Jerusalem where Mormons, as a chosen people, could take refuge from the terrors of the Second Coming and reign as "Saints" with Christ. In an emotional, rather than a spiritual sense, the building did function as an instrument of salvation.

After Joseph Smith's death in 1844, grief and confusion overwhelmed the citizens of Nauvoo. Brigham Young succeeded in uniting Nauvoo with a strong plea that the Temple be completed as quickly as possible, both as a monument to Joseph Smith and as the fulfillment of a sacred pledge to build a new Jerusalem. The Temple became the unchallenged center of Nauvoo. Constant baptisms for the dead were conducted as its walls rose. In this ritual, all Mormons were called upon to undergo vicarious baptism for long dead relatives and friends to promote salvation through the Mormon faith.

5.22 Early sketches of sun capitals, with suns emerging
from Corinthian foliage, by William Weeks.

5.23 Sketch of pilasters with crescent moon bases, by
William Weeks.

5.24 West elevation, Nauvoo Temple, sketch by William Weeks.

5.25 West elevation, Nauvoo Temple, alternative sketch by William Weeks.

5.26 "Semi-solemn, semi-laughable, and, certainly, more than semi-singular," sun capital, Nauvoo Temple.

5.27 Masonic symbols, including suns, moons, stars, single eye, and font with oxen.

5.28 Sketch for Masonic Hall, Nauvoo, (Fig. 5.15), possibly by William Weeks, showing single eye in pediment.

5.29 Sketch of baptismal font, basement level, Nauvoo
Temple, by Henry Lewis.

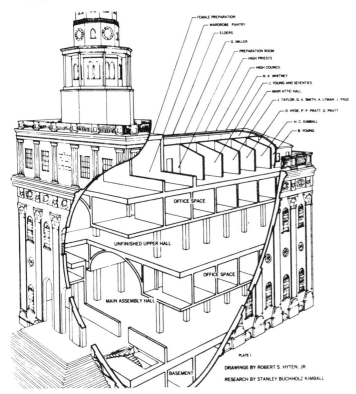

FEMALE PREPARATION
WARDROBE PANTRY
ELDERS
G. MILLER
PREPARATION ROOM
HIGH PRIESTS
HIGH COUNCIL
N. K. WHITNEY
J. YOUNG AND SEVENTIES
MAIN ATTIC HALL
J. TAYLOR, G. A. SMITH, A. LYMAN, J. PAGE
O. HYDE, P. P. PRATT, G. PRATT
H. C. KIMBALL
B. YOUNG

OFFICE SPACE

UNFINISHED UPPER HALL

OFFICE SPACE

MAIN ASSEMBLY HALL

PLATE I.

BASEMENT

DRAWINGS BY ROBERT S. HYTEN, JR

RESEARCH BY STANLEY BUCHHOLZ KIMBALL

5.30 Isometric drawing, Nauvoo Temple, by Robert
Hytten.

Jerusalem: The Cult Center

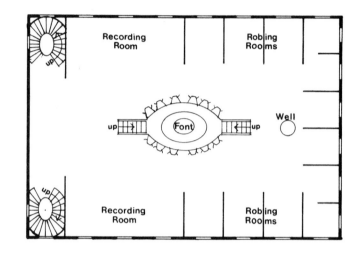

Basement

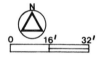

N

0   16'   32'

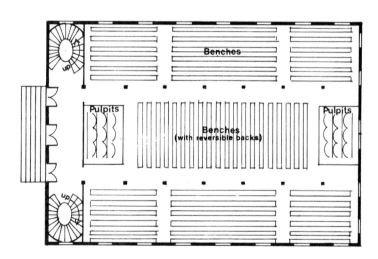

First

5.31 Conjectural plans, Nauvoo Temple.

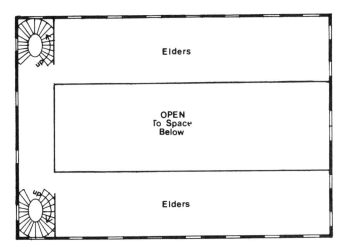

First Floor Mezzanine

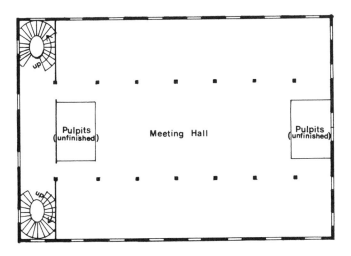

Second

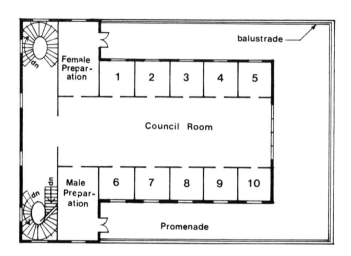

Third

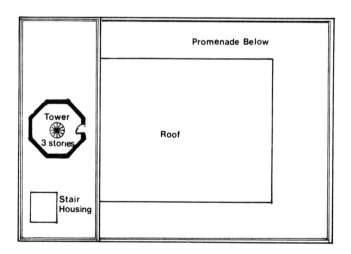

Roof

5.31, continued. Key for third floor: 1, Elders; 2, High
Priests; 3, Miller; 4, High Council; 5, Whitney; 6, J.
Young and Seventies; 7, Taylor, Lyman, Smith, Page;
8, Hyde, P. Pratt, G. Pratt; 9, Kimball; 10, B. Young.

5.32 Daguerrotype, Nauvoo Temple, ca. 1846-1848.

5.33 "Every day is seen, phoenix-like, the ponderous
fronts of new and extensive buildings . . . peering above
the roofs of the more humble ones," Temple dominating
a daguerrotype of Nauvoo, ca. 1845.

5.34 "Persecution and Expulsion of the Mormons
from the City of Nauvoo, Ill., Sept. 1846," by C.C.A.
Christensen, showing the rear of the temple.

This practice of remembrance of the dead, which was first initiated by Joseph Smith, served to dramatize the crises of bereavement and reorganization which the members experienced after Smith's own death in Nauvoo.[56] While baptisms took place in the basement, wagons for the journey west were under construction in the second floor assembly room, so the Temple housed both rituals and activities linking past, present, and future. Throughout their time in Nauvoo the Mormons had stressed their uniqueness, often at the expense of credibility. Finishing the building of the Temple, all participated in the work, proving that they were able to deliver what they had promised themselves and God.

The strategy of creating social change through the development of a model community was imaginable in early nineteenth century America only because the continent itself was unimaginable, a spatial vacuum. But in a settled area, a successful and thriving communitarian settlement with the potential of infinite expansion threatened neighbors who wished to retain an independent life style. Each time their expansiveness had created hostility, the Saints had been forced to abandon settlements in Independence, Far West, Kirtland, and Nauvoo.

Heading west, leading the longest Mormon migration, Brigham Young ignored the attractiveness of California and Oregon, and led the Mormons to the arid Great Basin, the largest unsettled region on the continent. Here, in the isolation of the desert, no eccentric monuments were needed to assert the distinctiveness of the community. The geography of the region demanded cooperative endeavor in irrigation and farming for survival; dissidents could not afford to lose access to land, and more important, water. The Temple, which had been the focal point of communal life in Nauvoo, now shared priority with irrigation ditches, fences, and town centers in Utah, as major cooperative design and building projects.

Salt Lake City was founded in 1847 as the center of a region 1,000 miles long and 800 miles wide. By 1880, 400 new communities had been founded there, following a regional master plan which fixed the sizes of cities, towns, and villages. As railroads came west, the boundaries of the Mormon kingdom of Deseret had to be negotiated with the United States government, and the compromise was the State of Utah. Non-Mormon or "Gentile" settlers eventually came to play an important part in Utah's development. But Deseret was a communitarian dream come true.

Settlement policies reflected the lessons learned in Nauvoo. All water, timber, and mineral resources were considered common property. Speculation was forbidden and land was divided into equal parcels assigned to newcomers. The design of both cities and towns was influenced by the "Plat of the City of Zion," with church buildings, schools, and a community center occupying a central position. The basic residential unit of all these communities was the privately owned family homestead, arranged in the distinctive pattern of square blocks divided into four lots which was developed in Nauvoo.[57] It still prevails in rural Utah villages (Fig. 5.35).

The domestic stepped-gable vernacular style was not developed in Utah, perhaps because water-soluble adobe did not lend itself to gables. Some house plans reflected the practice of polygamy; stylistic eclecticism was the rule, as John Taylor ordered his congregation to "improve your dwelling houses. If you cannot find the style of house to suit you, go off to other places until you do find one, and then come back and build a better one."[58]

In both cities and towns the Mormon Church successfully appropriated all of the symbolic power of "home" and "hometown" to reinforce its religious authority. Like Joseph Smith, Brigham Young was fond of instructing his people to invest their efforts in developing their physical environment:

Let the people build good houses, plant good vineyards and orchards, make good roads, build beautiful cities in which may be found magnificent edifices for the convenience of the public, handsome streets skirted with shade trees,

fountains of water, crystal streams, and every tree, shrub and flower that will flourish and grow in this climate, to make our mountain home a paradise . . . enjoying it all with thankful hearts, saying constantly, "Not mine but thy will be done, O Father."[59]

Pollution became for him a symbol of sin: "Keep your valley pure, keep our towns as pure as you possibly can, keep your hearts pure," he exhorted.[60] Again and again he and his successors emphasized that a paradisiacal landscape and fine buildings were signs of inner spirituality which would be recognized at the Second Coming.

Seeking perfection in small details of the environment enables all Mormons to participate in creating earthly paradise. Popular Mormon magazines give advice about house plans, paint colors (never white), and landscaping, developing an image of a desirable environment and life style which reflects the faith.[61] A contemporary proselytizing pamphlet offers the story of a day in the life of a typical Mormon family.[62] The man of the house, an accountant, helps fellow members of the Mormon priesthood pour concrete sidewalks for their church center. Women, alas, are home making refreshments. A banker and a laborer are members of the work party, demonstrating that care of the communal environment transcends class divisions and reinforces shared religious conviction.

Such participation in improving the communal environment is far more important to Mormons than creating monumental architecture. Brigham Young did claim that God revealed to him the plan of the Salt Lake Temple (Fig. 5.36), drawn by Truman Angell, Sr., in 1854, but construction proceeded slowly over forty years so that the economy would not be disrupted by vast expense as in Kirtland and Nauvoo. The Temple facade includes round windows similar to the ones Smith envisioned, as well as more conservative renderings of the suns, moons, and stars initiated in Nauvoo (Fig. 5.37), so that stylistic continuity has been retained, but it seems likely that the function of the Nauvoo Temple as a focus for collective grief in 1845-1846 changed the role of the temple in the Mormon religion. Although the Kirtland and Nauvoo Temples were designed as places of assembly, Nauvoo became a monument in the funerary sense, a tomb. The Salt Lake Temple and three others built in Utah are not used for regular worship, but serve as massive architectural monuments to the past, present, and future church, where special "Temple work" linked with genealogy takes place.

Despite the fact that Salt Lake City is now an American capitalist metropolis, Mormons remain involved with the physical environment on both practical and symbolic levels, a pattern of involvement which is typically communitarian. They have resolved the dilemma of authoritative versus participatory processes by combining divinely sanctioned plans for the towns and the Temple with general involvement in planting, building, and perfecting the environment. The tension between communal and private territory lessened with the creation of defined town centers to balance private homesteads. The conflict between unique and replicable plans ended when the Temple became a place of occasional, rather than frequent, worship, and Mormons in every new community were no longer exhorted to extravagant expenditures on construction. An image of Eden, the participatory, private, replicable city, is no longer in direct conflict with an image of Jerusalem, an authoritative, communal, unique city.

The Mormons, over half a century, discovered how to integrate vernacular and monumental styles, secular and religious elements of community building. Their history holds general lessons for any community group hoping to use environmental design to support a new social order.

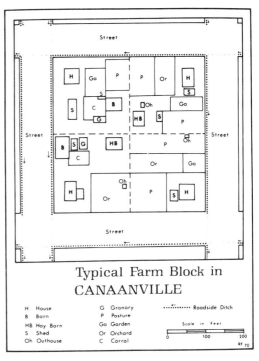

5.35 The "Plat of the City of Zion," repeated in the Great Basin: "Typical Farm Block in Canaanville," drawn by Richard V. Francaviglia.

5.36 Mormon Temple, Salt Lake City.

5.37 Sun and star emblems, detail of 5.36.

1 This area was also a fertile field for the Shakers, the Fourierists, and the Oneida Perfectionists, as Whitney Cross has shown in *The Burned-over District: The Social and Intellectual History of Enthusiastic Religion in Western New York, 1800-1850*, Ithaca, 1950.

2 Thomas F. O'Dea, *The Mormons*, Chicago, 1957. Chapter 1 includes background material on the Seekers, the Shakers, and the Jerusalem community.

Many questions about the relationship between Shaker and Mormon doctrine could be explored. Both groups were fascinated by the symbolism of the Jerusalem temple, as were contemporary Freemasons. Both organized their spiritual hierarchies into three ascending levels. (Arthur Bestor called this to my attention.) Both were concerned with imminent divine visitants to their earthly communities. At least one Shaker, Lemon Copley, joined the Mormons, and in 1831, Smith sent Copley plus Sidney Rigdon and Parley Pratt as missionaries to the Shakers, equipped with the revelation, "The Son of man cometh not in the form of a woman." Joseph Smith, *The Book of Doctrine and Covenants*, 65, Mar. 1831.

3 Raymond Lifchez, "Inspired Planning: Mormon and American Fourierist Communities in the Nineteenth Century," unpublished M.C.P. thesis, University of California, Berkeley, 1972.

4 Smith, *Doctrine and Covenants*, 42, Feb. 1831.

5 O'Dea, *The Mormons*, p. 197. This is the point at which most historians cease to count the Mormons as communitarian socialists. Because their strategy of developing a model community remains based on a communitarian plan, largely unchanged after the proclamation of 1841, I have chosen to pursue the history of design further, as a comparison to other communities which retained a socialist economy.

6 On the role of women, see editorials in *The Wasp*, (Nauvoo, Ill.) Apr. 30, 1842, and June 11, 1842.

7 Feramorz Young Fox, "Notes Concerning Joseph Smith's Plat of Zion City," mimeo, LDS Church Historian's Office, Salt Lake City, p. 3. Fox corrects mistaken versions of the plat published elsewhere.

8 Lowry Nelson, in *The Mormon Village*, Salt Lake City, 1952, p. 15, compares the Mormon farm village to the prevailing American pattern of scattered homesteads and judges it a "social invention" fulfilling the need of a chosen people to prepare a physical location for Christ's second coming.

Page Smith, in *As A City upon a Hill: The Town in American History*, New York, 1966, p. 25, suggests the precedent of New England covenant communities established by the Puritans. These villages were similar in terms of general social goals, but organized with a concern for topography totally absent in Joseph Smith's thinking. Feramorz Fox, in "The Mormon Land System: A Study of the Settlement and Utilization of Land under the Direction of the Mormon Church," unpublished Ph.D. thesis, Northwestern University, 1932, pp. 151-152, disallows the Puritan precedent entirely because of discrepancies in the sizes of Puritan and Mormon land holdings.

Charles Sellers cites the advantages of "safety in numbers" but stresses that "the dominant reason that the Mormons lived in towns was that they had faith in Joseph Smith's rules of order," and makes no further attempt to probe the sources of Smith's inspiration, in "Early Mormon Community Planning," *Journal of the American Institute of Planners*, 28 (Feb. 1962), 25.

9 A curious coincidence: Joseph Smith's wife, Emma Hale, was from Harmony, Pennsylvania, but a different Harmony, in the northeastern part of the state. Rigdon lived in Pittsburgh, close to the Rappist communities of Harmony and Economy.

10 Excellent photographs of the architecture of Harmony and Economy, Pennsylvania, are presented by Charles Stotz in *The Early Architecture of Western Pennsylvania*, New York, 1936, a study which unfortunately includes no town plans. Karl Arndt's chapter, "A Model Town on the Frontier," in *George Rapp's Harmony Society (1785-1847)*, Philadelphia, 1965, draws from the observations of John Melish, who visited Harmony in 1811 and published his *Travels in the United States of America*.

11 The Harmonists designed garden mazes with sacred symbolism described in Chapter 2. Gustavus Hills's 1842 map of Nauvoo shows a radial garden configuration in front of the Nauvoo Temple, but this was probably never executed.

12 Fox, "Notes," pp. 1-3.

13 Polygamy does not explain family sizes of this magnitude. Polygamy was not instituted until the 1840s in Nauvoo. Polygamous men probably did not comprise more than 15-20 percent of church members and the average size of an extended family was 8 to 10, according to O'Dea, *The Mormons*, p. 246.

14 Warren Abner Jennings, "Zion is Fled: The Expulsion of the Mormons from Jackson County, Missouri," unpublished Ph.D. dissertation, University of Florida, 1962, p. 61.

15 *Times and Seasons* (Nauvoo, Ill.), 3 (1842), p. 937. The author regrets that the exact date for this issue is lost.

16 John Kirk to Calvin Kirk, Apr. 3, 1853, letterbook copy, Chicago Historical Society.

17 John Warner Barber and Henry Howe, *Our Whole Country*, vol. 2, Cincinnati, 1861, p. 1099.

18 Robert Flanders, *Nauvoo: Kingdom on the Missis-*

sippi, Urbana, 1965, p. 58, gives figures on English converts. Census figures are shown by Rowena Miller, "Map for Nauvoo Restoration, Inc.," Oct. 29, 1964, office of Nauvoo Restoration, Inc., Nauvoo, Ill. I have relied on Flanders for much background material on Nauvoo.

19 Parley Pratt, quoted in Flanders, *Nauvoo*, p. 76.

20 Joseph Smith, *History of the Church of Jesus Christ of Latter-day Saints, Period I, History of Joseph Smith, the Prophet, by Himself*, vol. 5, Salt Lake City, 1912, p. 296.

21 *Times and Seasons*, Jan. 1, 1844, pp. 392-393.

22 Nauvoo *Neighbor*, Oct. 4, 1843.

23 James Greenlaugh, *Narrative of James Greenlaugh, cotton-spinner, Egerton, Bolton-Le-Moors*, Liverpool, 1842. Flanders's *Nauvoo* also includes a chapter on "The Land Business" attempting to sort out a very confusing economic situation.

24 J. B. Jackson, *Landscapes*, Amherst, Mass., 1970, p. 5.

25 *The Wasp*, Apr. 23, 1842.

26 *Times and Seasons*, 1.8 (June 1840). The exact date for this issue has been lost.

27 *The Wasp*, Oct. 1, 1842.

28 Nauvoo *Neighbor*, May 3, 1843.

29 Emily Coburn, journal, cited in Jennings, "Zion is Fled," p. 53.

30 "Horticulture," *Times and Seasons*, Feb. 1, 1842, p. 678.

31 Ibid.

32 *The Wasp*, Apr. 23, 1842.

33 Nauvoo *Neighbor*, May 3, 1843.

34 Nauvoo *Neighbor*, Oct. 23, 1843.

35 Feramorz Young Fox, in "The Mormon Land System," p. 20, gives information on agricultural collectives.

36 Blocks measured 24 rods by 22 rods.

37 Brigham Young, quoted in Richard Francaviglia, "The Mormon Landscape: Existence, Creation, and Perception of a Unique Image in the American West," unpublished Ph.D. dissertation, University of Oregon, 1970, p. 95.

38 T. Edgar Lyon, Nauvoo Restoration, Inc., Salt Lake City, interview with author, Aug. 1972.

39 Irene Hascall to Ashbel Hascall, Nauvoo, Ill., June 2, 1845, MS, Chicago Historical Society.

40 To use the terms of anthropologist Mary Douglas in *Natural Symbols*, New York, 1970, p. viii, I could describe the Mormons as needing to balance grid (the ego-centered activities stemming from private property and private enterprise) against group (the collective activities of the church as a bounded social unit).

41 Joseph Smith, quoted in Flanders, *Nauvoo*, p. 188.

42 Nauvoo *Expositor*, single issue, June 7, 1844.

43 Joseph Smith, *Doctrine and Covenants*, 124, Jan. 19, 1841.

44 *The Wasp*, Oct. 29, 1842.

45 Flanders, *Nauvoo*, p. 182.

46 Charles Dickens, *Martin Chuzzlewit*, London, 1843.

47 The Temple was fired by an arsonist in October 1848. The ruins were leveled by a windstorm in May 1850 and the stones used for the construction of buildings by members of another communitarian group, French Icarians, who purchased land from the departing Mormons. The Icarians had originally planned to remodel the Temple as a phalanstery. The building which they eventually did create from the Temple stones stood until 1972 in Nauvoo, when LDS authorities in Salt Lake City, superintending the work of Nauvoo Restoration, ordered it demolished, an action which certainly contradicts their official commitment to historic preservation.

Works on the Temple include Don F. Colvin, "A Historical Study of the Mormon Temple at Nauvoo, Illinois," unpublished M.A. thesis, Brigham Young University, 1962, which provides useful summaries of the project's importance but no plans. Joseph E. Arrington, "Construction of the Nauvoo Temple," an unpublished four-volume manuscript in the LDS Church Historian's Office, Salt Lake City, is full of interesting sources, but the manuscript itself is extremely disorganized. Virginia Harrington and J. C. Harrington, archaeologists, offer thorough documentation of the basement construction and baptismal font in *Rediscovery of the Nauvoo Temple: Report on the Archaeological Excavations*, Salt Lake City, 1971.

David S. Andrew and Laurel B. Blank, in "The Four Mormon Temples in Utah," *Journal of the Society of Architectural Historians*, 30.1 (Mar. 1971), 51-65, deal with the iconography of Mormon temples and the influence of Freemasonry on Mormon thought. Unfortunately their discussion of Mormon architecture ignores the development of Mormon town planning completely. Their argument that Mormon temples in Utah utilize the Gothic style because they represent an earthly kingdom rather than a heavenly one is based on an elaborate discussion of religion and politics in Nauvoo in 1841-1844. They ignore the text of the

"Plat of the City of Zion," issued in 1833, which provides primary evidence of the Mormon interest in an earthly kingdom a decade earlier.

Hugh W. Nibley, in "The Idea of the Temple in History," makes a rather irrational plea for the architectural uniqueness of the Nauvoo and Salt Lake Temples, p. 247.

48 Mrs. Peter Hitchcock, "Joseph Smith and His Kirtland Temple," *The Historical Society Quarterly*, Lake County, Ohio, 7.4 (Nov. 1965), no paging.

49 Asher Benjamin, *The Country Builder's Assistant*, Greenfield, Mass., 1805, plate 33.

50 *The Wasp*, Oct. 29, 1842.

51 Portfolio filed as William Weeks' architectural drawings, LDS Church Historian's Office, Salt Lake City, Utah.

52 Joseph Smith, *History of the Church*, vol. 6, pp. 196-197.

53 *I Corinthians*, 15:40-42.

54 St. Louis *Gazette*, quoted in the Nauvoo *Neighbor*, June 12, 1844.

55 Unfortunately, secrecy surrounding "temple work" makes information about the plans of Mormon temples and the rites conducted therein hard to find. O'Dea, in *The Mormons*, pp. 60ff., offers some information on rites. Andrews and Blank deal with Masonic symbolism, particularly the possible influences of contemporary Masonic architecture in Philadelphia and Boston, but they ignore the most obvious source, the Masonic Temple built in Nauvoo in 1843-1844 and still standing.

Other useful works include J. M. Roberts, *The Mythology of the Secret Societies*, London, 1973; E. Cecil McGavin, *Mormonism and Masonry*, 4th ed., rev., Salt Lake City, 1956; and Asael Lambert, *Mormonism and Masonry: A Private Notebook*, Salt Lake City, n.d. (1960?), Bancroft Library, University of California, Berkeley. A common handbook such as Z. A. Davis, *The Freemason's Monitor*, Philadelphia, 1843, includes symbolic sun, moon, stars, and beehive on the frontispiece.

56 Peter Marris, *Loss and Change*, London, 1974, discusses grieving and problems of reintegration for the bereaved, making comparisons between individual grief and collective experience of change which I have applied to the Mormons in Nauvoo.

57 Francaviglia, "The Mormon Landscape," p. 23.

58 John Taylor, Oct. 20, 1881, quoted in Francaviglia, "The Mormon Landscape," p. 98. On houses designed for polygamy, there is much disagreement over forms and functions. See Paul Goeldner, "The Architecture of Equal Comforts," *Historic Preservation*, 24 (Jan.-Mar. 1972), 14-17, and also Leon Sidney Pitman, "A Survey of Nineteenth Century Folk Housing in the Mormon Culture Region," Ph.D. dissertation, Louisiana State University, 1973.

59 Brigham Young, Discourse 16, *Discourses of Brigham Young*, ed. John A. Widstoe, Salt Lake City, 1925.

60 Hugh W. Nibley, "Brigham Young on the Environment," in Truman Madsen, ed., *To The Greater Glory of God*, Salt Lake City, 1972, p. 4.

61 Mormon journals examined, 1870 to present, include *Contributor, Improvement Age*, and *Young Women's Journal*.

62 Elder Gordon B. Hinckley, *What of the Mormons?* Salt Lake City, 1971, pp. 15-16.

6 The Architecture of Passional Attraction

Once a man has seen the street-galleries of a Phalanx, he will look upon the most elegant civilized palace as a place of exile, a residence worthy of fools who, after three thousand years of architectural studies, have not yet learned how to build themselves healthy and comfortable lodgings. In civilization we can only conceive of luxury in the simple mode; we have no conception of the compound or collective forms of luxury . . . .

—Charles Fourier, *Traité de l'association domestique-agricole*, 1822 (trans. Jonathan Beecher and Richard Bienvenu)

Detail of 6.11

Shakers and Mormons built for the millennium; Fourierists substituted psychology for religion and tried to construct communities where buildings and landscapes fostered the collective luxury of complete gratification of human passions. The design of the North American Phalanx, the largest of thirty Fourierist communities established in the United States between 1843 and 1858, provided an experimental focus for the psychological and architectural discussion initiated by Charles Fourier in France in 1808. The proponents of phalansterian association comprised the cast of a stock political melodrama: an eccentric genius; sycophantic, ambitious lieutenants; sympathetic, well-to-do intellectual supporters; idealistic, committed recruits. Fourier provided detailed instructions for the design of an ideal community, but his architect created fantastical illustrations in a rather different spirit. Failing to perceive this difference, the patrons of Fourierism in America accepted the architect's grandiose blueprint, while the members of experimental communities took a more practical view. At the North American Phalanx, members built a viable communal dwelling but were criticized because it fell short of their patrons' conception of what a phalanstery should look like. Conflicts over authoritative and participatory processes of design ranged the patrons against the members; struggles over communal and private territory contributed to the schism. When the patrons shifted their support to other experiments favoring authority, privacy, and uniqueness, the members gave in to bitter recriminations about the economic interests which no amount of "passional attraction" could eradicate.

Charles Fourier was born in Besançon in 1772, the son of a prosperous cloth merchant. His property was confiscated in the siege of Lyon during the French Revolution, so at twenty-seven he became a traveling salesman, hypersensitive to the mercenary reality of commercial life. "I have witnessed the infamies of commerce with my own eyes," he wrote, "and I shall not describe them from hearsay as our moralists do."[1] Self-educated and anti-intellectual, Fourier shunned literature but devoured newspapers and was avid for good talk. Waspish, cranky, yet convinced that "passional attraction" could produce a world of peace and harmony, utterly unorthodox yet wonderfully sensible, he spent his life creating and describing his new theory of society. He anticipated Freud's views on sexual repression and Marx's and Engels's criticisms of capitalist society. Probably the first twentieth century thinker to equal the scope of Fourier's ecological concerns was Buckminster Fuller. Fourier would have loved Fuller's idea of creating an *Operating Manual For Spaceship Earth*.

Fourier published the *Théorie des quatre mouvements et des destinées générales* in 1808, his first major description of a human society motivated by twelve basic passions. He envisioned a world where love and work are the joyous occupations of a global network of communities called phalanxes (from the Greek φάλαξ meaning a compact body of troops, a united front). *Le nouveau monde amoureux* and *Le nouveau monde industriel et sociétaire*, completed in 1819 and 1827, elaborated his theories of love and work.[2]

Fourier viewed his own era as the fifth of eight progressive stages of history. He termed it "civilization," a word with very unpleasant connotations in his writings. The individualist and capitalist orientation of "civilization" was to be followed by periods of increasing community and cooperation, titled Guarantism, Simple Association, and Compound Association. In the era of Compound Association or "Harmony," humans could freely indulge what Fourier identified as the twelve basic passions. These were the five luxurious or sensuous passions (sight, sound, smell, touch, and taste), the four affective or group passions (friendship, love, familism, and ambition), and the three distributive passions (the cabalist, seeking intrigue; the butterfly, seeking variety; and the composite, seeking synthesis). Fourier asserted that passional life in Harmony would be superior to any previous form. He guaranteed all citizens a minimum income and a minimum sexual life, but ignored questions of class conflict, believing that "passional attraction" would obviate the need for struggle between rich and poor.

When all the world had attained Compound Association, the earth would become a paradisiacal environment for human habitation. As one of his followers described it:

... There will be no more wars. Industrial armies will be organized to work under general plans, for the reclamation of the earth's waste places, such as irrigation of deserts and reclothing them with verdure; the drainage of marshes and subjecting them to culture and forestry. These measures will eradicate some of the permanent scourges we are afflicted with, as cholera, plague, typhus, yellow fever, etc.

These legions of industry—armies of construction—would also steadily push cultivation toward the poles, and by planting belts of timber about the globe, protect the people and their crops and cattle. This will enlarge the area of production and in some degree modify climates.

Another unitary labor will be a comprehensive system for improving the means of travel and transportation by water and rail, to promote commerce and the free intercommunication of all peoples. By these means man is to fulfil his function of overseer of the globe, and to improve and maintain in its best condition every part of it.[3]

The Phalanx

The unit of organization in Harmony was to be the phalanx, approximately sixteen hundred people, six thousand acres of land, an industrial and agricultural community in a rural setting (Figs. 6.1, 6.2). Such units would be grouped in countries, states, and nations to cover the globe. Fourier devoted much care to describing the physical arrangements of the phalanx which would bring people together for the purposes of passional attraction. He had an intuitive understanding of the concept of sociopetal spaces, those which encourage stable human relationships, and he employed it in explaining both the buildings and the landscape of Harmony.

The main building of each phalanx was called the phalanstery. Its plan included a series of landscaped courtyards enclosed by wings of dwellings emanating from a central block. All parts of the building were to be connected by interior streets, eighteen or twenty-four feet wide, three stories high, called street galleries or "galleries of association." In plan these galleries recall *traboules*, interior passages between houses which were common in the silk workers' district of Lyon, as well as the commercial arcades of Paris, which are usually cited as Fourier's source of inspiration.[4] Both the courtyards and the galleries were designed to encourage spontaneous meetings, or passional associations, which would occur along the routes joining dwellings, meeting rooms, and workplaces. A system of "compound progression" regulated room sizes so that the habitations of rich and poor would be intermingled throughout the building, theoretically providing an egalitarian, random distribution of spontaneous meetings. Elegant workplaces were considered essential to create "attractive industry," in order that all Harmonians, rich and poor, would find work appealing.

The siting of the phalanstery and the distribution of activities within it received careful attention. The center was for quiet activities. One wing was used to segregate noisy activities and another to provide a visitors' hotel. The storehouses, granaries, and stables were to be located opposite the main dwelling to create a grand square for parades and assemblies. In addition to providing for public pomp and pageantry, Fourier attended to the personal needs of his Harmonians. Children and elderly people would be housed on the mezzanine, away from the promiscuous activities of the galleries of association on the second floor. Dining rooms on the second floor were to be served by raising the tables through trap doors from the kitchens below. During banquets these activities could expand into the adjacent galleries. Widths of structural bays for dwelling accommodations were calculated with concern for both views and plumbing. Heating and ventilation were to be of the most modern type available. Such details fill chapter after chapter.

Fourier's loving concern for the sociopetal possibilities of the built environment has rarely been understood or appreciated.[5] Around 1830 a young and ambitious graduate of the prestigious Ecole Polytechnique, Victor Considérant, became an ardent disciple of Fourier. Considérant seems to have been a skillful political promoter with an imperious manner and little or no visual imagination. His training and inclinations led him to define the role of architecture as "the art around which all others are grouped as the vassals around their suzerain . . . . Architecture is the pivotal art, the art which summarizes all the others, and which, therefore, gives a summary of society itself—Architecture writes history."[6]

Considérant's overbearing view of the architect as a designer and human activities as passive material to be shaped by design had been shared by many earlier utopian architects. Despite his bravado, Considérant was unable to make any contribution to the history of ideal city design; his work was utterly devoid of inspiration. He determined the sizes of the phalanstery buildings—twenty-two hundred feet of length for the main facade!—and then wrapped Fourier's plans and sections in symmetrical, uniform, rigid, neoclassical facades reminiscent of the Palace of Versailles.[7] Considérant's "Sketch of a Phalanx" (Fig. 6.2), in its symmetry, rigidity, and grandiose scale, represents the architectural antithesis of Fourier's desire for an environment which would stimulate all kinds of personal exploration, growth, and change. Unfortunately, Considérant's sketch became the visual symbol of Fourier's proposals, adorning title pages, calling cards, and benefit programs. Later designers such as Charles Daubigny produced more pleasing, varied interpretations of Fourier's plans (Fig. 6.3), but Considérant, as Fourier's chief lieutenant, gave prominence to his own architectural work.

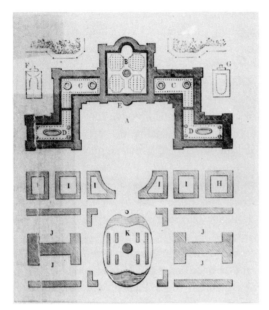

6.1 Plan of phalanstery and rural buildings, Victor Considérant, 1848. *A*, main square for parades and center of phalanstery; *B*, winter garden, planted with trees, surrounded by hothouses; *C, D*, interior courtyards, with trees, fountains; *E*, main entrance, grand staircase, tower of order; *F*, theater; *G*, church; *H, I*, large workshops, stores, granaries, sheds; *J*, stables, cart sheds, and rural buildings; *K*, dovecotes. These plans were first made known to Phalanx members in slightly simplified versions published by Albert Brisbane in 1843.

6.2 Perspective sketch of a phalanstery, Victor Considérant, 1848. "It is too beautiful not to be truth itself, the social destiny of man, the will of God on earth."

6.3 "View of a Phalanx, a French village designed according to social theory of Charles Fourier," Charles Daubigny, ca. 1848. Fourier is shown sitting on a bench in the foreground. "Little hordes" of children advance up the hill; refreshment pavilions for field workers are in left foreground.

When sceptics noted that Considérant's designs might, perhaps, be a bit "too beautiful," he offered the rejoinder: "It is too beautiful not to be truth itself, the social destiny of man, the will of God on earth."[8]

The Phalansterian Landscape

Considérant had little interest in landscape design; his phalanx simply floats on the paper. Fourier, in contrast, viewed the natural and built environments as inseparable. As a child and as an adult, he filled his personal rooms with potted plants of various colors and sizes.[9] A natural bent for geography led him to collect atlases and develop a true love of land, its contours and vegetation. Both botany and geography led him to seek sociopetal approaches to landscape design and site planning in Harmony.

Fourier specified that the ideal phalanx was to be located in a picturesque, varied location, "... provided with a fine stream of water ... intersected by hills ... adapted to varied cultivation ... contiguous with a forest...."[10] What interested him most was the possibility for the spatial distribution of varied productive activities to encourage communal contacts. Beauty alone was not enough justification for concern with landscape, for he viewed gardens in "civilization" as "bodies without souls, as we see no groups of workmen employed in them."[11]

Cultivation of the landscape could take one of three forms—simple, mixed, or compound—according to the level of a society's development. He gave illustrations: simple cultivation would be unrelieved acres of wheat fields; mixed cultivation would occur where soil changes or geography created broken, picturesque combinations of planting; compound or "interlaced" cultivation was the intricate cre-

ation of a number of work groups, who would study the soil and the microclimate, then extend lines of planting and detached plots out from a central area of cultivation.[12] The interlaced type of cultivation permitted the most advantageous utilization of varied terrain, but its main object was social, "to bring different groups together on the same grounds, so as not to leave a group isolated in its work, although the work is not continued for more than two hours."[13] As gardens extended into orchards and orchards into gardens, workers could meet and develop "passional attraction" for each other. Refreshment pavilions provided additional meeting places.

Fourier's belief in the potential pleasure and pageantry of work underlies this account of the ideal landscape in Harmony:

... The gray frocks of the ploughmen, the blue spotted ones of a group of mowers, will be set off by borders, girdles and distinctive ornaments of their Series [work groups]; the wagons and harnesses can also be neatly ornamented, and the ornaments so arranged as not to be exposed to dirt ... in a beautiful valley, all these groups in activity, shaded by colored awnings, working in scattered companies, marching to the sound of instruments and singing in chorus as they change the location of their work ... the domain studded with bowers and pavilions with their colonnades and spires ... the domain covered with its beds of flowers and vegetables and its fields of grain....[14]

In this effusive, pastoral description, Fourier's ideas about passional attraction, or people's involvement in each other and in their work, find an environmental expression which is not distorted by an inappropriate, rigid architecture.

The phalanx depends on carefully designed and cultivated landscapes as well as on sociopetal buildings to stimulate community members, and recalls the Shakers' use of both landscape and buildings at Hancock to reflect their community organization. Fourier would certainly have understood and sympathized with the Shaker vision of a society as a "living building," since he believed that all labor such as construction or planting crops gave expression to human passions and led to communal harmony. Some of Fourier's followers, Considérant in particular, expected Fourierist buildings or landscapes to create instant community, without consideration of how the buildings were built or the landscapes were cultivated, but Fourier himself was most concerned with the processes by which people would shape their surroundings.

From Theory to Experiment

Fourier claimed that he desired a practical test of his ideas by the establishment of a model phalanx which would demonstrate the superiority of phalansterian life. He set the conditions for an experiment very high—sixteen hundred people and $400,000, which he described as necessary for a balance of passions and the establishment of "attractive industry." But he allowed that a small beginning might be made with as few as four hundred people.[15] After two decades of circulating copies of his books to the rich and influential of Paris, he died in 1837, unsatisfied. Although his ideas were tested, in some form, in European experiments launched by aristocrats and factory owners seeking new ways of dealing with their serfs or workers,[16] it was chiefly in the United States that his ideas received a popular hearing.

Albert Brisbane, the son of a well-to-do land speculator from Batavia, New York, the "burned-over" district where millennial religion flourished, studied with Fourier in the course of an extended tour of Europe and returned to the United States to become the leading American propagandist of Fourierism. Brisbane translated some of Fourier's work and tried unsuccessfully to publish it, until someone introduced him to Horace Greeley, editor of the new New York *Tribune*. Greeley's response to Fourier and Brisbane was immediately favorable, probably the reaction of a perceptive editor confronted with a manuscript perfectly suited to the intellectual and political climate of the early 1840s.

Greeley gave Brisbane a front page column in the *Tribune*, titled "Association," where he expounded Fourier's ideas, first weekly, then semiweekly, then daily. Beginning in 1842, Brisbane reached an extremely wide audience. He intrigued New England Transcendentalists such as George Ripley and William Henry Channing, already involved in building an idealistic community at Brook Farm. He reached urban businessmen and artisans, as well as rural farmers who read the *Tribune*'s lengthy agricultural columns. In 1843 and 1844 the Boston and Philadelphia Unions of Associationists were meeting; by 1846 they had formed a national organization.

Others gathered to denounce the group they called "Furyites." Horatio Greenough protested the regularity of life in a planned community: "I hate thy straight lines, and thy arrangements for the elbows, and thy lid that fits over all, with the screws ready in thy hand. . . . The measure which thou hast scientifically taken of me is my measure now, perhaps . . . but I feel that I am destined to outgrow thy feet and inches hereafter...."[17] Donald McLaren, author of "Boa Constrictor, or Fourier Association Self-Exposed," objected to the economic basis of Association: "No! ye men of the Tribune! ... American industry, the sprightly robust nursling of civilization in this Western world, will never be decoyed from the fostering care of its fond and generous nurse...."[18] A debate was joined which occupied American intellectual and political circles for twenty years and was cut off only by the advent of Civil War.

In October 1842, Brisbane announced in the *Tribune* that he wanted contributions to finance the establishment of an experimental community. In 1843 he published *A Concise Exposition of the Doctrine of Association, or Plan for the Re-organization of Society*, in which he defined his tactics: "The whole question of effecting a Social Reform may be reduced to the establishment of one Association, which will serve as a model for, and induce the rapid establishment of others."[19] The extent of Brisbane's ambition to change the world manifested itself in the name he chose for the hypothetical model community, the North American Phalanx. Although Brisbane desired one experiment on a grand scale, his proselytizing launched about thirty experimental communities, none commanding the extensive resources of capital and labor which Fourier had specified for a test of his theories.

Brisbane gathered both potential financial supporters for his cause and converts who were willing to live in the new community, but the political attitudes and "passional attractions" of these two groups diverged from the start. The expositors and patrons preached the gospel of Fourier in grandiose generalities, labeling "civilized" urban life Hell and life in the Model Association Heaven,[20] all with fervor befitting revivalist circuit riders. Those most receptive to the communitarian call tended to be without education or substantial funds, small business owners and urban working people like Fourier himself, who chafed at the inequities of daily life enough to commit themselves to drastic changes. At first these proselytes accepted Fourierism just as the expositors presented it, but when they joined in establishing experimental communities their thinking inevitably was changed by the pressure of practical constraints and experience of Association.

For the patrons, it was always a case of "us" and "them." Brisbane, who published copious and detailed instructions on how to organize and run a model community, had no taste for such a life in practice, not even for the role of commander general: "Had I been called upon to become the originator and manager of one of them, I should have declined, knowing myself wanting in the knowledge and preparation indispensable for such an undertaking."[21] Marcus Spring of New York and James T. Fisher of Boston, wealthy merchants involved in the Associationist cause, exchanged letters in 1848 describing some recruits as passive "good ground" for the ideological seed they wished to plant.[22] The *Tribune* approved of some as belonging to "the better class of mechanics."[23] Although the intellectual luminaries of the Fourierist movement did gather at Brook Farm, in West Roxbury, Massachusetts, and at the Raritan Bay Union, in Eagleswood, New Jersey, these communities were exclusive and never intended to become economically self-sufficient. More typical were the twenty-odd communities formed by idealistic readers of the *Tribune* who hoped to offset their lack of financial backing by their determination to make a living by farming and light industry.

The sixty founders of the North American Phalanx came from Albany, New York. Among them were a morocco manufacturer, an agent for the Erie Canal, a homeopathic doctor, a grocer, a shoe store proprietor, a shoemaker, a leather store proprietor, a druggist, a coachmaker, a coal dealer, a stove dealer, a lawyer, a painter, the owner of a small steamship line, the part-owner of a tobacco company, a blacksmith, a carpenter, a wood turner, a silver plater, a mason, a hatmaker, and their fam-

ilies.[24] Probably most of them were feeling the economic squeeze following the Panic of 1837, for their collective resources amounted only to about $7,000, which they used as the down payment and working capital for a 673-acre farm in Colt's Neck, New Jersey. They adopted Brisbane's hypothetical name, "North American Phalanx," before Brisbane realized the limits of their finances, and although he protested, they would not relinquish it. Reluctantly he and the coterie of Fourierists centered in New York gave the group from Albany their provisional support, although at some future date they hoped to establish a larger and more "scientific" experimental community. Because of the publicity surrounding the name, and, eventually, because the Phalanx existed for thirteen years, John Humphrey Noyes, in his *History of American Socialisms*, judged that "this was the test experiment on which Fourierism practically staked its all in this country."[25]

To sympathize with the complexity of political, social, and economic structures which the North American Phalanx adopted (Fig. 6.4), seemingly quite pointless for the administration of a New Jersey farm, one must recognize both the practical and the naïve elements of their idealism. Although the members lacked the prescribed resources for a full-scale experiment, they agreed that it was crucial to add their experience to Fourier's ideas in order to unite theory and practice. Charles Sears, the group's chief apologist, explained that ". . . while we would not in the slightest oppose a scientific organization upon a large scale, it is our preference to pursue a more progressive mode, to make a more immediately practical and controllable attempt."[26] The members commenced building new social, economic, and political institutions with the ambition to cre-

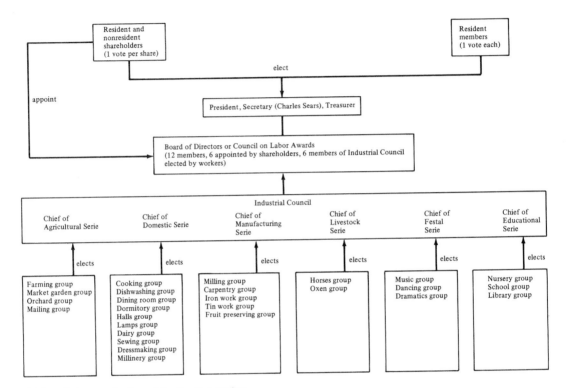

Resident and
nonresident
shareholders
(1 vote per share)

Resident
members
(1 vote each)

elect

appoint

President, Secretary (Charles Sears), Treasurer

Board of Directors or Council on Labor Awards
(12 members, 6 appointed by shareholders, 6 members of Industrial Council
elected by workers)

Industrial Council

| Chief of Agricultural Serie | Chief of Domestic Serie | Chief of Manufacturing Serie | Chief of Livestock Serie | Chief of Festal Serie | Chief of Educational Serie |

elects · elects · elects · elects · elects · elects

Farming group
Market garden group
Orchard group
Mailing group

Cooking group
Dishwashing group
Dining room group
Dormitory group
Halls group
Lamps group
Dairy group
Sewing group
Dressmaking group
Millinery group

Milling group
Carpentry group
Iron work group
Tin work group
Fruit preserving group

Horses group
Oxen group

Music group
Dancing group
Dramatics group

Nursery group
School group
Library group

6.4 Fourierist organization of the North American
Phalanx, constitution of 1849.

ate "a complete commonwealth, embracing all the interests of the state, differing only in magnitude."[27] Given these goals, it is no surprise that a member recalled that "their days were spent in labor and their nights in legislation for the first five years of their existence."[28]

Unlike most sectarian communitarian groups, the Phalanx members adopted no unusual social or religious practices. Resident membership varied between 100 and 120. Both single people and families lived in the community; families retained care of their own children, although a nursery and day care center freed parents for work. Feminist issues were supported more in theory than in practice. Women, who had voting rights in the government of the community from the start, were not made directors until after 1853. The Phalanx was assertively nonsectarian, although clearly Christian. Evening meetings were held to provide opportunities for general participation in the social and political affairs of the community, but although members developed their self-critical spirit, institutions such as the Oneida Community's "mutual criticism" were never established to regulate personal relationships.

Environmental design serves to emphasize the difficulties of the Phalanx's development. Of all American experimental communities, only the followers of Robert Owen and Charles Fourier began with complete, detailed plans for physical design. Because Owen chose to purchase a town built by the Harmony Society, New Harmony, Indiana, design was not a major practical concern for his group. In contrast, the members of the North American Phalanx found that the ideal image of a Phalanx, described by Fourier, sketched by Considérant, and envisioned by the American promoters, was an onus they never escaped. In terms of both landscape and buildings, the promoters' tendency to focus on the ideal obscured the community's tangible environmental achievements.

Landscape Design

The earliest descriptions of the Phalanx domain (Fig. 6.5), dating from the time of its purchase in 1843, echo the demands of Fourier and Brisbane for variety and fertility. The New York *Tribune* of September 5, 1843, mentions the "mildness and salubrity of the climate," the "invigorating atmosphere" of the ocean nine miles distant, the benefit of distance in shielding the site from strong winds, "excellent meadows," "a good water power . . . [available] at a moderate expense."[29] Five months later the *Tribune* reports "inexhaustible marl beds," "good timber," "warm and mellow soil."[30] A *Tribune* reporter visiting in October 1844 admitted that the soil between Red Bank and the Phalanx was somewhat sandy but averred that upon crossing a bridge and reaching the domain, he saw that "the soil assumed a very different appearance, being of a rich brown color, indicating fertility and strength." In the same romantic vein he describes approaching the

6.5 Site plan, North American Phalanx, ca. 1854.

dwellings with "bursting wild grapes clustering the whole length of our path." The land is "beautifully undulating" with "romantic dells, rocky glens" and "fine little streams." However, even this exaggerated picturesqueness will improve in the future: "The Domain . . . will be expanded to three miles square when they get funds enough—that being the space which Fourier required for forests, parks, and all other purposes of an Association."[31]

An expert observer unprejudiced in favor of Fourierism, Frederick Law Olmsted, author and scientific farmer, later the designer of New York's Central Park, wrote about the land more objectively:

There are six hundred acres of land in the domain of the Association, most of it of the ordinary quality of "Jersey land." . . . Two beds of (marl) . . . of superior quality are on the property. A stream of water running through it gives a small milling-power. The nearest tidewater is five miles distant, where steamboat communication may be had daily, but at irregular hours, with New York, a poor sandy road to be travelled over in between. The land cost twenty-five dollars an acre, and I believe I have stated all the material advantages of the location. . . .[32]

Examination of a site plan of the domain, prepared when the property was for sale in 1855 (Fig. 6.6), reveals that the community developed its estate in accordance with good land-use planning and farming practices. The Smith and Van Mater farm buildings they had purchased were adapted and extended as residential centers (Fig. 6.7). The Seristery, a new brick building used for fruit preserving, was located near existing barns (Fig. 6.8). A sawmill, gristmill, and workshops were located on Trout Brook, near the main road through the prop-

erty. Natural woodlands were left surrounding the domain; cleared areas were planted in patterns which suggest a tentative attempt to establish Fourier's interlaced system of cultivation. In 1844 they requested agricultural advice from the Shakers; in 1845 the horticulturalist E.N. Kellogg joined the group.[33] By June 1848 their orchards included 6,700 trees; their nursery, 4,800.[34] James J. Mapes, editor of *The Working Farmer*, visited and praised their experimental fields in 1849.[35] Other visitors reported that their fruits and vegetables sold at premium prices in New York because of their high quality and honest weight.[36]

The landscape design which the community undertook included the development of pleasant walks and bowers in the woods adorned with rustic seats. Around 1850, Trout Brook was dammed to create a small lake in front of the dwellings. Flower gardens and shade trees were planted. Three French immigrants laid out a more formal garden.[37] Despite these genuine accomplishments, thirteen years is little time for creating paradisiacal surroundings, and the domain never measured up to Fourier's glowing descriptions of the landscape in Harmony.

Building the Phalanstery:
Authority versus Participation

Victor Considérant stated that "architecture writes history." The development of buildings on the domain is the history of a struggle between the authoritarian promoters of Fourierism and the members of the community. The promoters followed Considérant and wished to hire outside laborers to erect an enormous edifice which they believed would in itself create a community. The members living on the domain wished to build up their community by participating in the design and construction of a small-

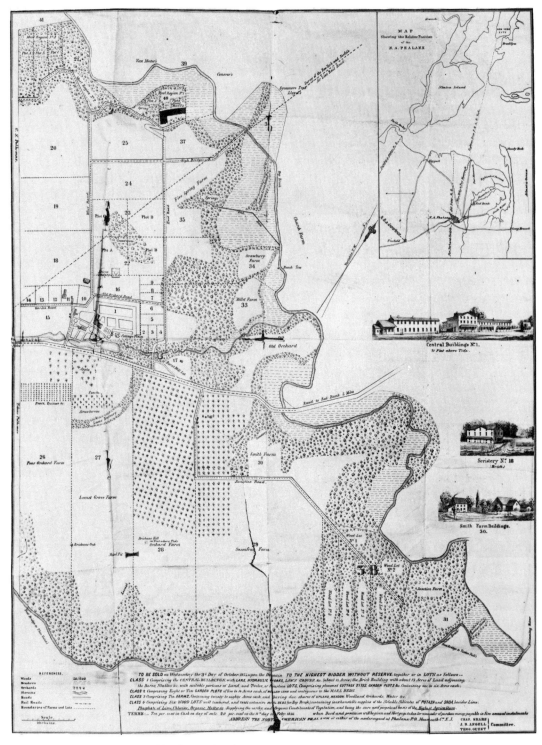

6.6 "Map of the Domain of the North American Phalanx," divided into farms and lots for sale, 1855.
Shows meadows and orchards, Brisbane Hill in lower
center; marl pits to north; transport to New York as
inset.

6.7 Smith Farm Buildings, used as the Phalanx school, constructed before 1843.

6.8 Seristery, workshop of the Fruit Preserving Group of the Manufacturing Serie, 1850, brick.

er communal dwelling over several years' time.

In September 1843, an advance party from Albany arrived in Monmouth County to take possession of the domain. They occupied to overflowing the Van Mater and Smith homesteads and began work on a communal dwelling (Figs. 6.9, 6.10) which was designed to include twelve suites for families, each with a parlor and one or two bedrooms, interconnecting doors allowing some flexibility of suite arrangements, although members requested door locks for their rooms early in 1844.[38] The plans were competently drawn, probably by David and Ogden Flansburgh, carpenters hired in Albany and sent to head the Phalanx's construction efforts.[39]

In October 1844, as this slow and practical process of construction was proceeding, a *Tribune* reporter dismissed these achievements rather lightly:

The buildings of the Phalanx are all temporary and will be superseded in due time by a grand Phalanstery which will furnish accommodations for two thousand persons, with dining halls, concert rooms &c., besides a wing for manufactories and workshops. The distance from one wing to another of a full-sized phalanstery would be half a mile. . . .[40]

The July 1847 issue of *The Harbinger* carried an article by a *Tribune* reporter discussing plans for an ideal phalanstery and mentioning Brisbane Hill as the appropriate site on the domain for such an edifice.[41] A watercolor rendering of the domain (Fig. 6.11) shows communards gazing at Brisbane Hill, turning their backs on the existing buildings.

The movers behind the grand Phalanstery plans declared themselves in February 1848 by establishing the Phalansterian Realization Fund

Society. The members included Horace Greeley, Marcus Spring, James T. Fisher, Edmund Giles, Edmund Tweedy, and James Kay. With Brisbane these men had attempted to dissuade the Phalanx members from commencing their experiment in 1843. But five years had not enabled them to sponsor anything more "scientific," so they decided to make do with the North American as the object of their benefactions. The patrons demanded a monument for their money, however, a communal version of the palace of Versailles envisaged by Considérant.

Greeley and Brisbane had published schematic plans for a "Grand Unitary Edifice" in the *Tribune* as early as 1842.[42] Within seven years James Kay, head of the Philadelphia Unitary Building Association, was promoting more detailed plans with a staggered, three-tiered, columniated facade, adorned with decorative ironwork balconies (Fig. 6.12).[43] And Marcus Spring and James Fisher, the wealthy merchants, were exchanging letters about various brickmaking machines to use clay from the domain to make bricks for a palatial structure.[44] This group had a clear goal: they pledged to lend the Phalanx $35,000 over a five-year period if they would use the funds for a "Grand Unitary Edifice."[45]

The Phalanx members were dubious of the value of such an enormous monument. They believed that their community had to develop slowly and cohesively; that they needed to "dispossess ourselves of old forms, and build up within ourselves first the new institutions, before we give them outward expression."[46] They felt that the residents of a community should determine its building program, and that the buildings could never precede the community's development. E. N. Kellogg expressed the

6.9 Central buildings on the Phalanx domain, including, left to right, communal dwelling, 1844; Phalanstery, 1849-1852; and cottage built by Marcus Spring, 1852. Frame construction.

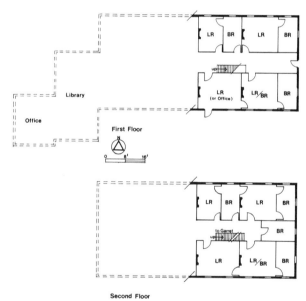

6.10 Communal dwelling, 1844, schematic plans of existing part of structure (now relocated near barns).

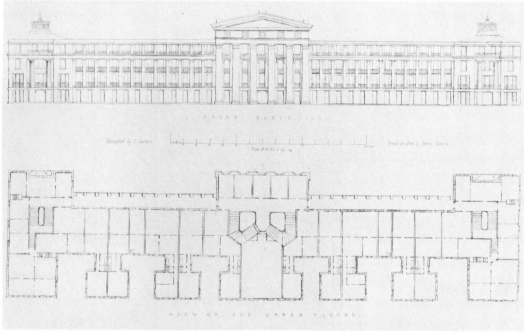

6.11 Communards gazing at Brisbane Hill, proposed site of a grand phalanstery, watercolor by Thomas W. Whitley, 1852, showing barns, communal dwellings, and Smith Farm buildings in center. Foreground shows communards and stones engraved with names of American Fourierists, Brisbane, Greely (*sic*), Channing, Ripley, and Dana, as well as Fourier and Lazarus, a physician.

6.12 "Grand Unitary Edifice," with three tiers of galleries, designed by James Sartain, Philadelphia, 1849.

The Architecture of Passional Attraction   166

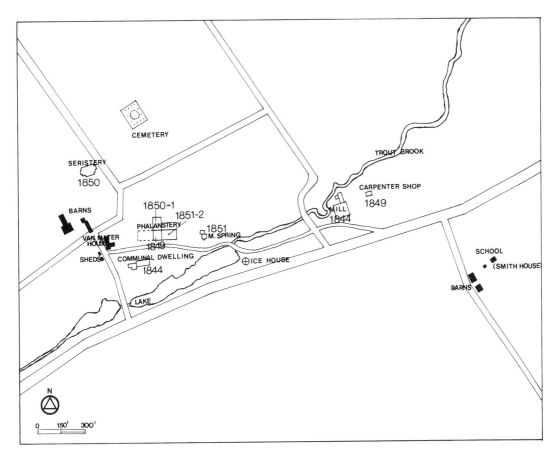

6.13 Diagram of central portion of Phalanx site, in
1854. Buildings existing before 1843 are shaded.

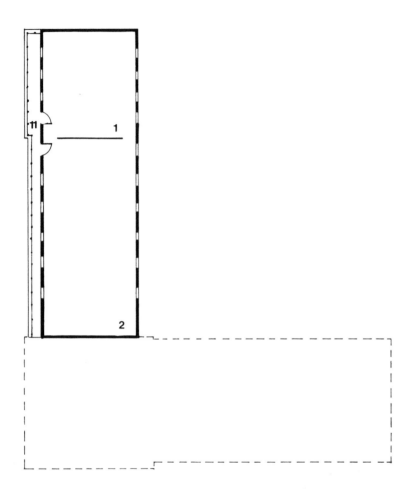

Basement

0   16'   32'

6.14 Schematic plans, North American Phalanstery, 1849-1852, shown here and on following pages. Meeting places ranged in size from the parlors to the dining hall. 1, laundry; 2, dairy; 3, kitchen, 4, stage; 5, dining hall; 6, library; 7, parlor; 8, office; 9, living room; 10, bedroom; 11, gallery; 12, balcony; 13, loft for sleeping.

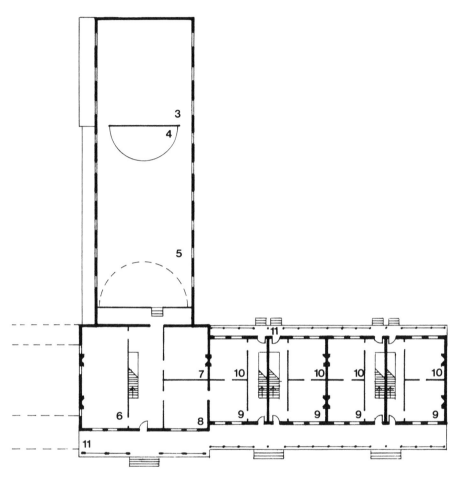

First

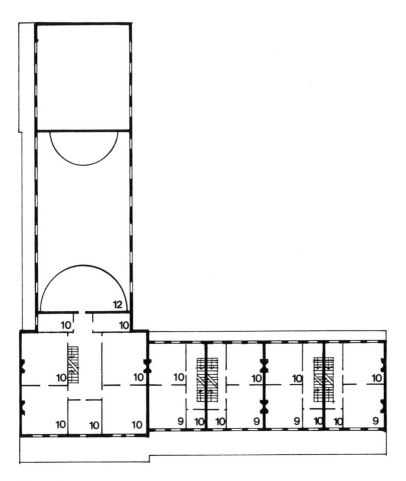

Second

6.14, continued

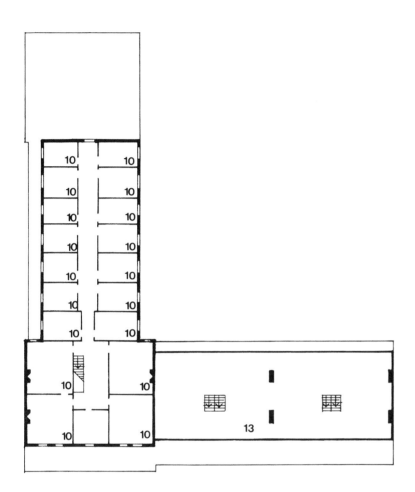

Third

members' uncertainty about launching an over-ambitious building program: "We do not know the site, nor the style in which five hundred people would wish to build. We could not prepare plans and ought not to commence an edifice until we are strong enough. . . ."[47] Edmund Tweedy replied for the Phalansterian Realization Fund Society, dismissing this objection with characteristic, patronizing arrogance; he thought that building an edifice with public rooms was simply the equivalent of building shops for workmen.[48] Tweedy provoked a unanimous vote of the Phalanx's Executive Council: "That the interests of this Association will not be best promoted by the appropriation . . . proposed by the New York Phalansterian Realization Fund Society."[49]

As the Phalanx members proved resistant to the Society's desire for a grand structure, the proffered benefaction shrank. A first installment of $7,000 was reduced to $6,000 and then to $4,900. With difficulty a compromise was reached which allowed the Phalanx to spend $1,400 on land improvements, $1,500 on its mill, and $2,000 for the construction of the first wing of a new dwelling.[50] The patrons' dreams of a building on Brisbane Hill with a facade half a mile long had been countered effectively by the members' more practical and comprehensive views of environmental design. The patrons' goal of a monumental edifice also seems to have been compromised by the members' decision to construct the new dwelling themselves, resisting the patrons' pressure to offer the job to "civilization" at the lowest bid.

John B. Coleman, chief of the Carpenters' Group, was delegated to solicit members' suggestions about the new dwelling, draw the necessary plans, make estimates of construction costs, and supervise construction. The members agreed upon a simple design for a frame building to be constructed in at least four stages (Figs. 6.13, 6.14). Its gradual development required that it be closely related to existing dwellings and facilities. Like the Van Mater homestead and the first communal dwelling, built in 1843-1844, the new Phalanstery was to be oriented north-south. A central block, containing some communal rooms and some dwelling spaces, was to be extended north in a wing for the dining room and kitchen, east and west in dwelling wings.[51]

Community and Privacy

Given all of the idealistic assumptions about the design of a monumental structure which the members had to combat, their decisions show a remarkable mixture of economic practicality and social sophistication. They recognized that the most important and original aspects of Fourier's environmental thinking were his suggestions about using built form to bring members of the community together in varied social encounters. They emphasized the importance of circulation spaces, gave special attention to threshold spaces, and assured that a variety of spatial experiences, intimate and grand, communal and private, would exist in their new Phalanstery. Halls were broad and generous. "Galleries of association" lined two facades; small back stoops for apartments dotted a third facade (Fig. 6.15). The scale of meeting places ranged from a parlor fifteen feet square to the dining hall, two stories high, seventy by twenty-nine feet.

Despite the grandiose and rigid prototypes advocated by Considérant and by James Kay, the Phalanx members chose to expand upon local models of residential construction rather than imitate European civic buildings. One likely prototype for the Phalanstery was the structure erected at Brook Farm in West Roxbury, Massachusetts, which burned in 1845, just before completion. *The Harbinger* described this building as

. . . wood, one hundred and seventy-five feet long, three stories high, with attics divided into pleasant and convenient rooms for single persons. The second and third stories were divided into fourteen houses, independent of each other, with a parlor and three sleeping-rooms in each, connected by piazzas which ran the whole length of the building on both stories. The basement contained a large and commodious kitchen, a dining-hall capable of seating from three to four-hundred persons, two public saloons, and a spacious hall or lecture-room.[52]

Both the Brook Farm structure and the "Long House" erected by Fourierists at Ripon, Wisconsin (Fig. 6.16) in 1844-1845 emphasized good planning, sound detailing, and modern mechanical equipment as more important than architectural ornament. Their goals were comfort and convenience, represented at the North American Phalanx by louvred French doors opening onto shady porches, central steam heating, and gaslight (Fig. 6.17).

At the Phalanx, the need to provide some private areas was met with a variety of accommodations, available at different rentals, which revealed the group's uncertainty about finding a single architectural solution to suit both members and the occasional resident patron. Suites for families had been established in the 1843-1844 communal dwelling and more suites with one or two bedrooms plus individual rooms and dormitories were provided in the new dwelling.[53] Anyone who sought more privacy was allowed to design and build a cottage, either an addition to the 1844 dwelling or an independent structure located on the "Cottage Plain" east of the new Phalanstery. Marcus Spring, a summer resident patron, chose to build such a cottage (Fig. 6.18) in 1852, and his desire for privacy first isolated him from this community and later led him to an even more extreme construction at the Eagleswood community.

Private spaces varied in kind and quantity, but communal spaces in the Phalanstery compensated for some crowding by creating an appropriate setting for an organized, dignified, and joyful communal life. The entrance hall delighted members and visitors with wallpaper bordered and patterned with sylvan scenes. Balustrades and woodwork showed careful design and construction. The dining hall, also used for meetings, theatrical performances, dances, and lectures, was lit by three chandeliers and adorned with paintings of historical scenes, portraits, busts, and a mural of an ideal phalanstery entitled "The Great Joy."[54] A semicircular balcony used by musicians sheltered the entrance area; a semicircular stage projected from the opposite wall, beneath the mural. Behind and below the dining hall was a kitchen, dairy, and laundry room complex outfitted with steam-powered appliances.

Amid these tangible achievements, one wonders at the presence of the mural of "The Great Joy." Was it an emblem of unrealistic future plans for development? Or a concession to the goals of the patrons which the members did not share? On May 6, 1851, a banquet was held at the Phalanx to celebrate the completion of the second stage of the community's building program, and the opening of the new dining hall. Upon such an occasion one would expect communal self-congratulation, and this sentiment does seem to have animated the members. A patron, James T. Fisher, was visiting from Boston, however, and his preoccupations were of a different nature—the verso of his banquet menu, found among his collected papers, bears a sketch of a gigantic phalanstery.[55]

Unique Versus Replicable Plans

By 1856 the North American Phalanx was dissolved, the domain sold at auction. The conflict between the patrons' ideal of a unique building and the members' practical progress in construction, seen in the debates about the plan of the Phalanstery and epitomized in the sketch made by Fisher during the banquet in 1851, continued for four difficult years in various forms. The members never faced the problem of duplicating their model community, because its life span was too short, but they were working to create a replicable model. Their materials were straightforward; their plans, flexible. Building by accretion, they adopted certain guiding principles and then developed each new section of their dwelling according to their needs, year by year. This approach would have perhaps developed into an "intentional vernacular" style with more time. In contrast to the efforts of the members to develop a replicable community, the patrons of the Phalanx kept pressing for uniqueness, and became involved in the founding of two new communities.

Marcus Spring, perhaps desiring more authority, and certainly wanting more privacy, decided to establish a community called the Raritan Bay Union at Eagleswood, New Jersey. In this experiment a collective economy was abandoned for the principle of "every tub left to stand on its own bottom."[56] Spring's first act was to spend $40,000 on the erection of a large stone phalanstery (Figs. 6.19, 6.20) sited across a substantial lawn from a large private dwelling

for himself and his family. Just as Charles Dickens was unwilling to sit in a Shaker chair, so Spring seems to have feared the "architecture of passional attraction." The tableau of his private residence confronting the group's collective residence (Fig. 6.21) would seem ludicrous were it not for the fact that the Raritan Bay Union attracted a number of Phalanx members in addition to the "writers, artists, and people of means and leisure" who completed the group. The community lasted no more than two or three years, since the members had little taste for anything besides the country house fun of socializing and politicking. Sarah Grimké, a feminist and abolitionist, made a typical complaint—she felt that she and her sister, Angelina, were no more fit to wait on tables than Angelina's husband, abolitionist Theodore Weld, was suited to dig potatoes.[57]

During the summer of 1853, when this elite community was gathered at Eagleswood, Albert Brisbane and Victor Considérant were traveling on horseback through the vast reaches of northern Texas, making plans for the largest, most grandiose Fourierist community conceivable. According to the bulletin of the Texas Emigration Union, circulated in Europe, "They were delighted beyond all measure with this country, which more than met their most sanguine expectations. In local advantages, in fertility of soil, in beauty of scenery, they pronounced it unrivalled. Here they felt was the place, before all others, to plant the seeds of a new social order."[58] The rhetoric has a familiar ring. Ten years earlier Brisbane had made a similar trip with Allen Warden of Albany to inspect possible sites for the North American, and ten years earlier he had delivered similar, glowing reports of a unique domain.

Circumstances in Texas actually were not in

6.15 North American Phalanstery, ca. 1900, after use
as a commune, boardinghouse, and apartment house.

6.16 Communal dwelling, Wisconsin Phalanx, Ripon, Wisconsin, 1844-1845, photograph showing entrances to suites. First and second floor galleries have been removed.

6.17 Doors to family suites and shuttered French windows opening onto gallery (now removed), south facade of east wing, North American Phalanx.

6.18 Cottage built by Marcus Spring, on Phalanx site, 1852.

6.19 For some Fourierists, building an edifice with
public rooms was simply the equivalent of building
shops for workmen: Raritan Bay Union, Eagleswood,
New Jersey, phalanstery commissioned by Marcus
Spring, ca. 1853, photographed in 1938 after long use
as school and then as an industrial building.

6.20 The Phalansterian Realization Fund Society always wanted a monument for its money: central doorway, Raritan Bay Union Phalanstery.

6.21 A ludicrous confrontation expressing the conflict between private and communal territory: the private residence of Marcus Spring facing the communal dwelling of the Raritan Bay Union.

the least propitious. The government of Texas refused Considérant a land grant,[59] so he went ahead and purchased land from a speculator who sold scattered sections, a standard policy to raise the value of lots retained by the speculator. A domain three miles square could never have developed there, but elaborate plans were circulated for the city of Réunion (Fig. 6.22) and American and European colonists came by the dozen. By July 1856, Considérant, who ran the colony as a dictator, sniffed failure in the air—colonists living in rude log cabins, no industry, no grand edifice. In the middle of one night he disappeared and was next seen in Paris, writing pamphlets about the failings of human nature.[60]

Together Eagleswood and Réunion attracted some thirty-five of the Phalanx's one hundred and twenty members. The rest remained committed, but misfortunes weakened their sense of purpose. The year 1853 was a bad one for agriculture. In 1854, a fire destroyed the gristmill, sawmill, blacksmith shop, tinsmith shop, and offices. This was a depression year, and the insurance company holding a policy on the mill declared bankruptcy and could not meet the Phalanx claim.

The destruction of the mill revived a debate which had preoccupied members for several years previous to the fire, concerning whether or not the mill's location on the domain, five miles from Red Bank and ten miles from Keyport (Olmsted's acute observation of ten years earlier) was the optimal location for their nascent industry. Some members favored keeping industry on the domain for the sake of having physically bounded and coherent community territory, others were willing to move the mill to Red Bank in the hope of increased business. Debates lasted six months but generated no

agreement, since both factions were unwilling to borrow heavily to finance the alternative proposed by the other. On February 13, 1855, the community voted to dissolve.

The actual dissolution of the North American Phalanx provoked many evaluations of its achievements and failures. Of all nineteenth century communitarian settlements in the United States, it offered the most congenial, appealing life style, one which found ready acceptance among contemporary visitors and is still attractive to communards today. A good spirit prevailed among members at work and at the daily communal meals. Guests remarked upon the genial sociability, the excellence of the food (everything the "best of its kind"),[61] the comfort of the dwellings. Observers came expecting to find themselves surrounded by sectarians, eccentrics, fanatics—and left amazed. The only distinguishing characteristic which Frederick Law Olmsted could discern was lack of "disagreeable self-consciousness," which prompted him to say that he would choose to send an adolescent son to the Phalanx for four years rather than to Harvard or Yale.[62] A correspondent from *Life Illustrated* also remarked on the lack of "personal eccentricity which is popularly supposed to characterize 'world menders' in general and the disciples of Fourier in particular."[63] He wondered how, given the members' easy, tolerant manner, the Phalanx experiment had "held its place for twelve years in the midst of a social order against which its very existence has been a continual protest."[64]

The struggle to foster sociability and simultaneously challenge the existing economic and social order ultimately took its toll. During the thirteen years of its existence the experiment polarized the views of supporters of Fourierism. The patrons of the experiment, who refused to transcend an authoritarian, visionary ideal, avoided major changes in their own financial position and life style, preferring theory to practice. The members identified their common economic interests more and more clearly, resenting the interference of patrons whose lives and fortunes were not at stake in the day-to-day operations of the community. One member remarked, sarcastically, "It is a misfortune that some of our wealthy and able Phalansterians cannot find a large and prosperous Phalanx already established. They seem to be in too easy circumstances to go and make one themselves."[65] Or, as another communard, an outsider, put it more succinctly: "Association is a great school for Communism."[66]

Despite their introduction to aspects of economic conflict which Fourier had passed over too lightly, the patrons chose to remain oblivious, and continued to support new schemes for establishing unique communities. Eagleswood and Réunion displayed the patrons' true commitment to the early stages of communitarian idealism and revealed their inability to stick with a single experiment and offer intellectual and financial support during hard times as well as good times. The members were little wiser, for although some of them purchased small farms and remained in the Colt's Neck area, quite a few joined new communitarian ventures, some financed by other capitalists. Alcander Longley set up a Phalanx at Sparta Township in Indiana in 1858, later joined the Icarian Community in Iowa, and published the *Phalansterian Record* in Cincinnati and *The Altruist* in Saint Louis, which helped to launch a number of new communities in Missouri. In 1909, at the age of seventy-seven, Longley was still actively involved in the planning of underfinanced communitarian ventures.[67] Charles

Sears's career was similar. He joined a Fourierist community in Silkville, Kansas, between 1870 and 1884, and continued to write about communitarian socialism during his entire lifetime.[68]

It took the objectivity of a different community to profit from the experiences of the Phalanx and apply those lessons to the work of shaping another experiment. The Oneida Community had access to the records of A.J. Macdonald, a traveling journalist who had visited the Phalanx three times, and they also had the notes of Erastus Hamilton, one of their leaders who interviewed a survivor of the Phalanx experiment in 1868.[69] The group at Oneida took the risk of locating their industries away from their domain, close to transportation and water power, a decision which helped establish the profitability of their industries. They also learned much from Fourier and the North American Phalanx about the design of a communal dwelling. They chose to emphasize sociopetal spaces in relation to their sexual practice of "complex marriage" and built at a much slower pace than the Phalanx: thirteen years of planning, gathering resources and members; twelve years of developing their domain and industries before commencing a permanent communal dwelling; and eighteen years of planning and construction before their dwelling was complete.

Besides the Oneidans, many other groups continued to be fascinated by Fourier's proposals for passional attraction and its architectural expression. A "familistère" was built by the industrialist Jean-Baptiste Godin at Guise, France, beginning in 1859; some of his supporters, including Marie Howland, then worked on designs for Albert Kimsey Owen's Topolobampo community in Mexico, in 1881.[70] An extraordinarily elaborate "Social Palace" was designed for a community at Fountaingrove, California, in 1894-1895. As late as 1934, the New-llano community created a phalanstery-type communal dwelling in Louisiana. If one lesson encapsulates the North American Phalanx's experience, it was that the creation of a more humane environment depends more on economic and social practice than architectural theory. The ideal develops from the real; there are no architectural shortcuts to Harmony.

6.22 "Plan of lands belonging to the Europeo-American Colonization Society in the County of Dallas, Texas," including "Plan of Building Lots and Gardens in Réunion," the colony organized by Victor Considérant in 1854. Shaded areas are colony lands, which do not adjoin.

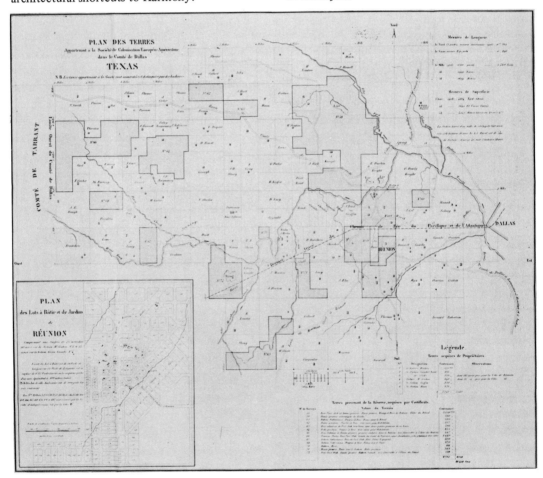

1 Charles Fourier, *Le nouveau monde industriel et so-ciétaire* quoted in Frank E. Manuel, *The Prophets of Paris*, Cambridge, Mass., 1962, p. 200.

2 *Le nouveau monde amoureux* proved far too un-orthodox for publication and remained part of a series of unpublished notebooks until the 1967 edition of Fourier's *Oeuvres complètes* was issued. Because of the fragmentary nature of individual publications is-sued during Fourier's lifetime and the repetitious com-plexity of the *Oeuvres*, *The Utopian Vision of Charles Fourier*, selected texts edited, translated, and intro-duced by Jonathan Beecher and Richard Bienvenu, Boston, 1971, is the best available English source of his writings.

3 Charles Sears, *The North American Phalanx: An His-torical and Descriptive Sketch*, Prescott, Wis., 1886, pp. 2-3. This is his paraphrase of Brisbane's translation of Fourier. These memoirs are dated Silkville, Kansas, May 10, 1879.

4 See note 7.

5 Le Corbusier's careful study of Fourier and his in-corporation of many Fourierist ideas in his Unité d'Habitation in Marseilles is a major tribute to his in-fluence. See Peter Serenyi, "Le Corbusier, Fourier, and the Monastery of Ema," *Art Bulletin*, 49.4 (Dec. 1967), 277-286.

6 Considérant, *Description du phalanstère et considé-rations sociales sur l'architectonique*, Paris, 1848, p. 38, my translation.

7 See Walter Benjamin, *Charles Baudelaire: A Lyric Poet in the Era of High Capitalism*, tr. Harry Zohn, London, 1973, pp. 158-160. Helen Rosenau compares the Phalanx to the Palais-Royal in Paris, where shop-ping arcades and apartment houses were developed around three sides of the palace garden in 1780. This garden was a gathering place for wealthy Parisians, and then, during the Revolution, an open-air club adjoin-ing gambling tables and a house of prostitution in the palace. For descriptions of other squares in Paris, see *The Ideal City in Its Architectural Evolution*, Boston, 1959, p. 134; Leonardo Benevolo, *The Origins of Modern Town Planning*, Cambridge, Mass., 1967, p. 12.

8 Considérant, *Description*, p. 11, my translation.

9 Beecher and Bienvenu, *Utopian Vision*, p. 4.

10 Charles Fourier, *Selected Works*, tr. Julia Franklin, London, 1902, pp. 137-138.

11 Fourier as paraphrased by Albert Brisbane, *The So-cial Destiny of Man*, Philadelphia, 1840, p. 386.

12 Ibid., pp. 376-377.

13 Ibid., p. 379.

14 Ibid., pp. 386-387.

15 Beecher and Bienvenu, *Utopian Vision*, p. 240.

16 Benevolo, *Origins*, pp. 56-75; Beecher and Bien-venu, *Utopian Vision*, pp. 65-67, although their de-scriptions of American Fourierism are not accurate and cast some doubt on their reports of European ex-periments.

17 Horatio Greenough, "Fourier et Hoc Genus Omne," *The Crayon*, 34 (June 13, 1855), 371-372.

18 Donald C. McLaren, *Boa Constrictor, or Fourier Association Self-Exposed*, Rochester, New York, 1844, p. 8.

19 Albert Brisbane, *A Concise Exposition of the Doc-trine of Association, or Plan for a Re-organization of Society*, New York, 1843, pp. 73-74.

20 *The Phalanx* (London, England) 1 (Apr. 3, 1841), frontispiece.

21 Redelia Brisbane, *Albert Brisbane, A Mental Biog-raphy*, Boston, 1893, p. 218.

22 Marcus Spring to James T. Fisher, Mar. 16, 1848, Fisher papers, Massachusetts Historical Society.

23 New York *Tribune*, May 23, 1843, quoted in Her-man Belz, "The North American Phalanx: Experiment in Socialism," *Proceedings of the New Jersey Histori-cal Society*, 81.4 (Oct. 1963), 227.

24 Ibid., p. 227, note 45. Sears's "Historical and De-scriptive Sketch," (reminiscences of 1879) reports an average membership of about 150; this figure is prob-ably high. Belz describes the sixty members who joined in 1843: "Out of twenty-eight cases where oc-cupation could be ascertained, a middle-class back-ground appeared in nineteen and an artisan or work-ing-class background appeared in nine instances. The leadership of the Phalanx seems to have been largely middle-class." Applications for membership in 1848-1849, reveal almost an equal split between classes; by 1854-1855 there were more work-ing-class applications. Most applicants came from the urban areas of the Northeast. Few farmers applied, al-though farming was the leading occupation.

25 John Humphrey Noyes, *History of American So-cialisms* (1870), New York, 1966, p. 449.

26 Charles Sears, "A History of the First Nine Years of the North American Phalanx, Written . . . at the Re-quest of Macdonald; dated December 1852," quoted in Noyes, p. 458.

27 Sears, "Historical and Descriptive Sketch," p. 8. Economic organization of the Phalanx was based upon two principles: labor was classified as necessary, use-ful, or agreeable (with a descending level of remunera-

tion); remuneration was given, not only for active labor, but also for the use of capital and the use of skill, in the ratio 5:4:3. Labor depended on the distribution of all able-bodied workers (including children) into six "series": agricultural, livestock, mechanical, domestic, educational, and festal. Workers could choose which serie and group they wished to work with.

Between 1844 and 1849 the Phalanx's income was derived from the Agricultural Serie. In 1845 the manufacture of mustard began on a small scale. After 1849 commercial milling of hominy became an important source of income. In the 1850s the community developed fruit-preserving techniques and established the first commercial cannery in New Jersey. The leading mechanical pursuit was carpentry, and the labor was applied to the Phalanx buildings.

28 "A Week in the Phalanstery," part 1, *Life Illustrated*, Aug. 11, 1855.

29 New York *Tribune*, Sept. 5, 1843.

30 New York *Tribune*, Feb. 1, 1844.

31 New York *Tribune*, Oct. 23, 1844.

32 Frederick Law Olmsted ("An American Farmer"), "The Phalanstery and the Phalansterians," New York *Tribune*, July 24, 1852.

33 Eric Schirber, "The North American Phalanx, 1843-1855," unpublished paper, Department of History, Princeton University, 1972, p. 76. This is the best existing historical study of the Phalanx, and I have relied on it for background material.

34 North American Phalanx, "Proceedings," June 1848, Monmouth County Historical Association Library (MCHAL), Freehold, N.J.

35 Schirber, "North American Phalanx," p. 115.

36 Kalikst Wolski, "A Visit to the North American Phalanx," tr. Marion M. Coleman, *Proceedings of the New Jersey Historical Society*, 83.3 (July 1965), 157. Wolski, a Polish engineer, visited in 1852.

37 Julia Bucklin Giles, "Address to the Monmouth County Historical Association on the North American Phalanx," MS, n.d. (1922?), MCHAL, Freehold, N.J., p. 14.

38 Schirber, "North American Phalanx," p. 64.

39 Ibid., p. 55. Other construction workers included John M. Drew, Albert Hinkley, and W.J. Parmenter, according to North American Phalanx, "Proceedings," Jan 1848-Jan. 1849. All were members.

40 New York *Tribune*, Oct. 1, 1844.

41 N. C. Neidhart, article in *The Harbinger*, July 4, 1847, quoted in Noyes, p. 473.

42 New York *Tribune*, Aug. 13, 1842.

43 *Constitution of the Philadelphia Unitary Building Association*, Philadelphia, 1849.

44 Marcus Spring to James T. Fisher, March 16, 1848, Fisher papers, Massachusetts Historical Society.

45 North American Phalanx, "Minutes" (MCHAL), Feb. 18, 1848.

46 Charles Sears, *Exposé of the Conditions and Progress of the North American Phalanx*, New York, 1853, p. 21. This pamphlet includes financial data for 1844 to 1853.

47 North American Phalanx, "Minutes," May 21, 1848.

48 North American Phalanx, "Minutes," June 4, 1848.

49 Ibid.

50 Ibid.

51 The west wing was never built, probably because of financial losses in 1853.

52 *The Harbinger*, Mar. 3, 1846, quoted by Noyes, *History of American Socialisms*, p. 554.

53 Nathan C. Meeker, in the New York *Tribune*, noted the acoustical problems of adjoining suites in a unitary dwelling (quoted in Noyes, *History of American Socialisms*, p. 506). Dwelling rentals were calculated as 10 percent of the construction cost per year, according to *Life Illustrated*, Aug. 11, 1855.

54 Fredricka Bremer, *The Homes of the New World*, tr. Mary Howitt, New York, 1853. She describes the new phalanstery as the "Little Joy," p. 613. Accounts of her two visits to the Phalanx are included on pp. 76-84, 611-624.

55 Fisher Papers, Massachusetts Historical Society.

56 Noyes, *History of American Socialisms*, p. 48.

57 Maud Honeyman Greene, "Raritan Bay Union, Eagleswood, New Jersey," *Proceedings of the New Jersey Historical Society*, 67.260 (Jan. 1950), 18.

58 Texas Emigration Union, *Bulletin*, Fisher Papers, Massachusetts Historical Society.

59 William and Margaret Hammond, *La Réunion: A French Settlement in Texas*, Dallas, 1958, p. 73. Basically the proslavery government did not want an antislavery, prosocialist community in its midst, and Considérant's willingness to be "neutral" on the slave issue did no good.

60 Ibid., p. 109.

61 *Life Illustrated*, Aug. 18, 1855.

62 Olmsted, "The Phalanstery."

63 *Life Illustrated*, Aug. 11, 1855; ibid., Aug. 18, 1855.

64 *Life Illustrated*, Aug. 18, 1855.

65 Alcander Longley to James T. Fisher, January 22, 1858, Fisher Papers, Massachusetts Historical Society.

66 Noyes, *History of American Socialisms*, p. 290.

67 Arthur Bestor, *Backwoods Utopias: The Sectarian Origins and the Owenite Phase of Communitarian Socialism in America: 1663-1829*, 2d enl. ed., Philadelphia, 1970, p. 56.

68 Letters from Charles Sears and Elijah Grant in the Elijah Grant papers at the University of Chicago Library trace the lives of several Phalanx members after 1856. Grant tried to recruit many of them for his Silkville, Kansas, community.

69 A. J. Macdonald, "Materials for a history of communities," MSS, Beineke Library, Yale University, New Haven, Conn. Accounts of three visits made by Macdonald to the Phalanx. Macdonald's work was incomplete when he died; John Humphrey Noyes incorporated it in his *History of American Socialisms*. Noyes includes an account of Erastus Hamilton's talk with a surviving member of the Phalanx, pp. 508-511.

70 See Marie Howland, *The Familistère* (former title, *Papa's Own Girl*, 1873), Philadelphia, 1974; also Ray Reynolds, *Cat's Paw Utopia*, El Cajon, Calif., 1973.

7 The Architecture of Complex Marriage

Communism in our society has made itself a house.

—John Humphrey Noyes, dedicating the new Oneida Mansion House, February 27, 1862

7.1 A group of Oneida Perfectionists, John Humphrey
Noyes in right foreground, ca. 1863.

Glance at a photograph of the assembled members of the Oneida Community (Fig. 7.1) and you will intuit the charisma of the leader who dominated the community's history, John Humphrey Noyes. Born in Putney, Vermont, in 1811, Noyes studied theology at Andover Seminary and at Yale, where he adopted a heresy known as Perfectionism and developed a sensational preaching style which ran to such exhortations as "The truth is a living thing and loves to be hugged."[1] In 1834 Noyes announced that God demanded the progressive development of a millennial kingdom on earth, recalling similar pronouncements made in 1773 by Ann Lee, leader of the Shakers, and in 1830 by Joseph Smith, the Mormon prophet. Noyes converted his mother, two of his five sisters, and one of his two brothers. Between 1836 and 1847 others joined them in Putney to establish a small community seeking what they called a "sociology," or communal life style, appropriate to their theology of Perfectionism. They studied the Bible as well as the Fourierist journal, *The Harbinger*, published at Brook Farm, and any other communitarian publications they could secure.

The Perfectionists gave the name "Bible Communism" to their new "sociology." In addition to asserting their belief in common ownership of property, they developed two communal practices called "mutual criticism" and "complex marriage." Mutual criticism required a member to appear before a committee of older members who evaluated his or her personal strengths and weaknesses. Occasionally a person was called before the whole membership for criticism. Unlike the Shakers, whose creed demanded immediate perfection, or the Fourierists, whose theory of history allowed them a gradual approach to "Harmony," the Perfec-

tionists accepted individual human failings but expected to eliminate them through the application of collective insight. Just as they believed mutual criticism could cure spiritual failings, so they assumed it could heal sickness, and, for that matter, modify their landscape and climate. Whatever problems they identified, God would help to solve.

Complex marriage derived from Noyes's prediction that in heaven there would be no marriage, but a divine "feast" at which every "dish" is free to every guest.[2] All members believed themselves united in a group marriage. Men and women could seek each others' company to engage in *coitus reservatus*, but individuals were encouraged to "keep in circulation"[3] and avoid exclusive personal attachments which might overshadow group feeling. Members' letters convey the mixture of prudery, piety, and sensuality which permeated this Victorian sexual revolution. One woman criticized a man for praising a particular woman: "I hope you will have grace to keep personal feelings out of your intimacy and endeavor to make her love for you a means of increasing her love for Christ and Mr. Noyes."[4] Another exulted, "I invite Christ to be my lover."[5] A few years later, the same woman confided in a more yearning tone:

Seymour, I *do* get *real hungry* sometimes to see you. . . . I hope you will not make too much of what has been said about Mr. T. and myself . . . we have had quite a pleasant time in loveing [*sic*] but now his heart seems turned in another direction. Florilla is the object of attraction now and vica [*sic*] versa all right the hearts of men and womin [*sic*] are in the hands of the Lord.[6]

Her sexual unorthodoxy, justified by Christian mottoes, is still too daring for words: another letter discussing her love affairs is marked "read and rub out."[7]

When the members of the Perfectionist community began to test their radical ideas by living communally and practicing complex marriage, their more conservative neighbors ran them out of Putney. By the end of 1848 a group of about fifty men, women, and children had gathered at Oneida, in the "burned-over" district of central New York State, where a few converts to Perfectionism owned farms. The new arrivals purchased one hundred and sixty acres of additional land to launch a model community. The community spread out as it gained new members, establishing a branch commune in Brooklyn, New York, in 1849, for publishing and business purposes, and, in the next few years, establishing small branches in Wallingford, Connecticut; Newark, New Jersey; Putney and Cambridge, Vermont; and Manlius, New York, where some converts owned property. Eventually all of these communities were disbanded, except for Wallingford.[8] Oneida was always the center of the Perfectionists' activities, the model estate which they hoped would enshrine communism and complex marriage and convert the rest of the world.

The Perfectionists' community building efforts were fueled by a potent combination of holy optimism and mundane tenacity derived from their religious beliefs. Since they held no orthodox religious services, their evening meetings mixed Noyes's "Home Talks" with plans for community development. In many ways community organization took the place of religious ritual, a common occurrence in nonsectarian communities, but an unusual abdication of authority for a religious group. Some participants reported that time counted for little compared to the group process. "Unity is the essential thing," wrote one of the members, ". . . business success and all other good things will follow."[9] Although group decisions were taken according to the "law of love" in open meetings, small committees carried out administrative functions (Fig. 7.2). Despite rhetorical support for women's right to equal jobs and education, and women's adoption of trousers under short dresses and of short hair, women rarely spoke in meetings and were usually relegated to women's committees concerned with domestic affairs. According to a law of "ascending fellowship" younger members were bound to follow the guidance of older ones, in political as well as sexual matters.[10] At the top of the pyramid was John Humphrey Noyes, who exercised unchallenged authority, personally introduced many girls and women to complex marriage, and refused to submit to mutual criticism unless it were administered by Saint Paul himself. His son, Theodore, commented that the only person he ever saw Noyes treat as an equal was Elder Frederick Evans, head of the Shaker community at New Lebanon.[11]

Convinced that "in due time the interior life which is given us will ultimately have the means of clothing itself in fitting forms of external excellence and beauty,"[12] the Perfectionists looked to their physical environment to provide tangible evidence of their success at every stage of community development. They found the ideas of Horatio Greenough most congenial,[13] for he led them to declare that true beauty would result when every communal function had a corresponding physical form. They asked themselves how to create "a Community architecture—a style of building which shall be adapted to the character of our institution, and

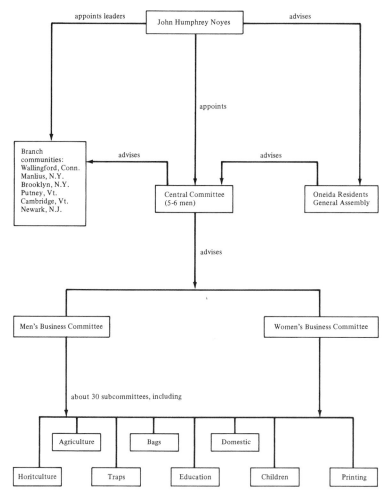

7.2 Working out the "law of love": Perfectionist organization, Oneida Community.

which shall represent in some degree the spirit by which we are actuated."[14] They also wondered, "In what manner should Communism work out its ideal in respect to land culture? and wherein should it diverge from the ordinary system of agriculture?"[15] Although the Oneidans were somewhat reluctant to admit Fourier's influence on them,[16] building for complex marriage can be seen as a very literal version of building for "passional attraction." They substituted for the facade of Versailles and the "galleries of association" the facade of a Victorian country house and the corridors, bedrooms, and sitting rooms designed to facilitate complex marriage. They produced a structure with a conventional bourgeois, exterior form concealing an unusual arrangement of interior spaces suited to their sexual revolution.

Eventually the Perfectionists built the community of their dreams with the profits from their business enterprises, only to find that the world could not be converted to Perfectionism by the establishment of a single working model of a Perfectionist utopia. Thousands of visitors[17] came to Oneida to view the wondrous community, but most could not accept economic communism and institutionalized cohabitation. In the 1870s some sanctimonious preachers launched crusades against the community, which was already threatened by internal struggles over Noyes's succession. In 1879 legal action under an immorality law was threatened, and Noyes fled to Canada. The Perfectionists then decided to abandon communism and group marriage, formed a joint-stock corporation to manage their business enterprises, and officially rejoined the larger society. Noyes concluded, with characteristic optimism: "We made a raid into an unknown country, charted it, and returned without the loss of a single man, woman, or child."[18] The process of charting and the new topography represent the subject of this chapter, the design of Oneida.

The community's earliest visions of the environmental perfection of a beautiful plantation flourished amid mystical explanations of the significant location of their domain and unfulfilled hopes for fecundity which God would bestow upon their soil. Several editions of the community's *Handbook* claim that Oneida is located at the center of a circle formed around three of the boundary points of New York State, New York City, Niagara Falls, and Rouse's Point (this explanation omits mention of the southwestern corner of the state, which would shift the center), and they feature a map (Fig. 7.3) to illustrate this significance.[19]

In this "unique" location they planned to "convert our entire domain into a garden," and to make horticulture their subsistence, rather than agriculture. Members exhorted each other "not to talk about *the farm* any more, but the *garden.*"[20] One member wrote:

I believe we are destined in the future to carry fruit culture to a development and perfection that the world has no conception of. Will not the refined life of the resurrection work through us to the outward world? . . . Christ is master of the elements, he marshals the winds in their season, he maketh the trees to blossom, and the fruit to unfold. . . . Will he not come and live with us, and surround us with a genial climate, outwardly as well as inwardly?[21]

The *Horticulturalist* for November 1864 compliments the Oneida community on its fine fruits, an eventual horticultural success probably due to Henry Thacker, a landscape gardener from Owasco Lake, New York, who joined the community in 1853.[22] He strove to improve the productivity of the community's fields and orchards with scientific methods, although he also warned the members that the climate was far from Edenic and did not favor fruit. When they had some successes, most community members gave Thacker less credit than their spiritual life, reiterating their belief that "love is a better element for anything to grow in than selfishness."[23] As they saw it, horticulture was simply "applying our system of criticism and self-improvement to the land."[24]

After their first eight to ten years at Oneida, when the motto "Horticulture our subsistence" had proved a pastoral fancy, the community turned to commerce and manufacturing. Their vision of an ideal environment began to reflect the ideas of Robert Owen and Charles Fourier about model industrial communities. Views of the main dwellings published in community reports in 1852, 1863, and 1870 reveal a changing physical image (Figs. 7.4, 7.5, 7.6). A picturesque frame house built into the side of a hill, surrounded by trees and arbors, is replaced by massive brick buildings with facades of an urban character. The foreground includes figures as well as foliage in the later sketches.

The final site plan of the community (Fig. 7.7) represents a synthesis of phalanstery plans by Charles Fourier, first published in the United States by Albert Brisbane in 1840,[25] and designs by Robert Owen for "Villages of Unity and Mutual Cooperation." They never adopted Fourier's plan for "interlaced cultivation," preferring to emphasize picturesque landscaping made fashionable by Davis, Downing, and Olmsted. The Mansion House dominates their domain, sited on high ground and symmetrically placed in a bend of the Oneida Creek. It includes both housing and institutional uses and encloses a landscaped courtyard. The main access road separates the Mansion House from barns and service buildings clustered across the road, an important Fourierist

7.3 "The center of the Empire State," map showing
Oneida Community. *C*, Central R.R.; *M*, Midland
R.R.; and circle which does not circumscribe the state
of New York.

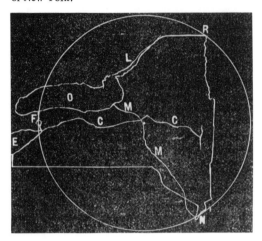

7.4 First Mansion House, view from the southeast,
1852.

7.5 First Mansion House, Children's House, and
Second Mansion House, view from the northeast, ca.
1863.

7.6 First Mansion House, Second Mansion House (including second Children's House), and Tontine, view
from the northeast, 1870.

7.7 Oneida Community, site plan, ca. 1870.

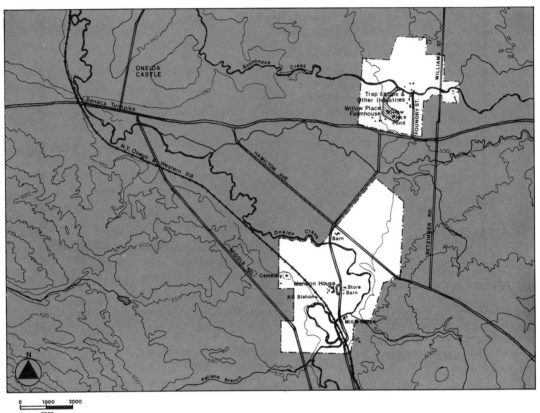

7.8 Fourierist influence in the street gallery: plan for wing for Oneida Community Mansion, 1877, by Lewis W. Leeds.

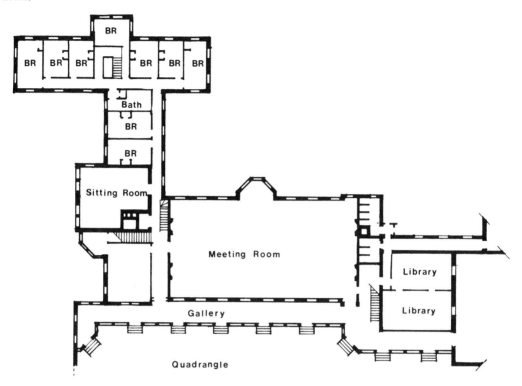

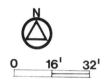

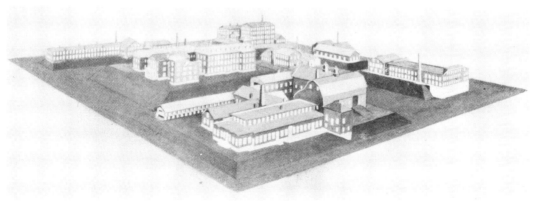

7.9 Wooden model of Oneida Community dwellings and workshops, by Ethelbert Pitt, 1901.

pattern, but major industries are located at a distance, as Owen recommended. There is evidence, however, that the community hoped to develop their Mansion to include the street galleries and courtyards which Fourier recommended. The design for a new wing, developed in July 1877, includes a bedroom section which closes the original courtyard and two projections which imply a plan for two additional courtyards to the north and west (Fig. 7.8). A glassed-in exterior corridor on the ground floor shows the direct influence of Fourier's designs. Unfortunately the wing was built in truncated form without the gallery and completed only three years before the community's dissolution in 1881.

Evidence of the importance of a strong overall environmental image to the members of the Oneida Community, their need for a "true object" upon which they could "fix their desires," abounds in the community publications.[26] Every *Annual Report* and *Handbook* carries illustrations and detailed inventories of the main buildings with descriptions of the principal rooms and the activities conducted within them. The *Circular*, the *Daily Journal*, and the *American Socialist* swell with personal rhapsodies about furniture, buildings, and land cultivation. One fervent author produced two articles praising a single room.[27] Detailed reports on topics such as "The O.C. Laundry" or "An Inside View of the Tontine" were common.[28] From these articles a community argot can be gleaned: many spaces had special names, such as the "Court" (a junction of corridors), "Ultima Thule" (a remote bedroom wing), the "West Avenue" (a corridor) or the "Circularium" (an old mill used as offices for the *Oneida Circular* and various community industries).[29] Records of the physical results of their endeavors were accompanied by detailed accounts of the design process, including the names of the members involved in design or construction activities and the general debates that took place in the community before certain plans were approved.

The members' strong sense of themselves and their domain was also expressed in terms of the physical breadth of their estate, which they never tired of viewing. Frequently members ascended the two towers of the Mansion House,[30] which enabled them to survey their domain. Often visitors were taken on this trip as well, to see what the community *Handbook* described as "a landscape of unspeakable beauty . . . spread before us . . . the lawn with its neatly trimmed paths, the flower gardens with their brilliant colors, and the rustic seats and arbors . . . beyond are the orchards and the vineyards. . . . The Community home farm extends for half a mile in most directions . . . and towards the northeast . . . over a mile."[31]

Even after the community's dissolution, the influence of its physical image lingered in the minds of former members. One man continued to write articles about the process of constructing community buildings over thirty years after the breakup.[32] Another former member, Ethelbert Pitt, made a scale model of the community (Fig. 7.9) for an exhibition in Buffalo in 1901. He included all of the community's red brick buildings mounted on a flat rectangle, an abstract platform for the Perfectionists' economic and architectural achievements, devoid of reference to existing topography or location. It is reminiscent of Robert Owen's model of a new community for New Harmony, Indiana, displayed in 1825 to assure viewers of the genius of his physical plan at a time when his community did not exist.[33]

The Oneidans' theology of Perfectionism and their "sociology" of Bible Communism made somewhat conflicting demands in terms of design. As Perfectionists they required an adaptable environment which could be "perfected." As Bible Communists they required a well-defined environment which could regulate collective activity. Perfectionism found expression in inventions, in cultivation of the landscape, and in adaptation of the buildings. At the same time Bible Communism found expression in the sociopetal and sociofugal structuring of the collective dwelling through circulation spaces and viewing points arranged to foster or prevent small group meetings.

Some of these approaches to design were undoubtedly borrowed from other communities: what the Oneidans learned from the Fourierists about using circulation spaces to bring people together was balanced by what they learned from the Shakers about using spaces to keep people apart. As the Oneidans became more and more skillful and sophisticated builders, they were able to use participatory design to enliven some aspects of authoritarian government, just as they used repressive design to restrain some aspects of complex marriage. Building ultimately became an essential symbolic activity for the community, as it was for the Shakers, but the forms encouraging spatial constraint and release were fully built, rather than partly built and partly imaginary. Ultimately the Oneidans came close to having too many contradictions embodied in the form of their Mansion House. The Perfectionists did manage to retain their unique balance of authoritative and participatory design at Oneida; but to do so it was necessary to close their branch communities and become so introverted that replicating the Oneida model was unthinkable. Noyes had

the last word on this as everything else: "...We consider it our business not to proselyte mankind by superficial efforts, but to present a working model of communism, and leave its effect on others to the silent action of truth and the Providence of God."[34] This "working model" is very like Owen's and Fourier's mechanical "patent office" models; a closer look at Perfectionist design at Oneida reveals the dominance of this image.

Perfectionism and Inventions

Emphasis on inventions in the community derived from two sources: the Perfectionists' economic need to find novel or technically ingenious products to manufacture, and their psychological need to believe that they were not only superior to the rest of the world, but unique. The means they developed to foster inventiveness among the members were a high level of education, group support for unusual ideas, and rotation of jobs to encourage recognition of analogous design problems.[35]

At Oneida members young and old were encouraged to pursue a variety of intellectual interests ranging from classical Greek to biology. The community library contained 3,581 volumes in 1871 and subscribed to over 140 periodicals.[36] Group support for inventiveness began about 1854 when John Humphrey Noyes announced that the community could not provide for itself economically through horticulture, and members began to invent products which could be manufactured and sold. Noyes himself devised a design for a traveling lunch bag (Fig. 7.10); the horticulturalists, with the help of a visitor from the North American Phalanx,[37] began to work out methods of fruit preservation; another member, Charles Ellis, made rustic lawn furniture. Most successful was

Sewell Newhouse, whose previous design for an animal trap was developed into a full line which was marketed nationally to provide the main source of community income for many years.[38] In addition, the foundry which furnished equipment for the trap shop helped to launch the establishment of silk thread manufacture, in 1866, and silverware manufacture, begun in 1877 at a branch community in Wallingford, Connecticut, which remains a successful enterprise a century later.[39]

The Perfectionists' emphasis on inventiveness did not stop when their economic security was assured. Members were encouraged to design or perfect all manner of domestic items. Improvements in clothing, furniture, tools, all were lauded as great discoveries by the editors of the community journals. The women, fed up with high-heeled, high-laced boots, invented what they called the "Final Shoe" (Fig. 7.10). A lazy-susan dining table (Fig. 7.10) was produced for the communal dining room. An improved mop wringer, an improved washing machine, and an institutional potato peeler were devised by carpenters working in the kitchen and laundry, examples of the benefits of the community's employment policy, which provided for job rotation every few months in order that techniques learned in one community enterprise could be applied to problems encountered in another.[40]

This love for domestic conveniences extended beyond their own inventions to the latest in construction techniques or mechanical equipment. Central steam heating, installed in 1869, caused almost hysterical excitement: "Goodbye wood sheds, good-bye stoves, good-bye coal scuttles, good-bye pokers, good-bye ash-sifters, good-bye stove dust and good-bye coal gas! Hail to the one-fire millennium!"[41] The latest models of steam baths and earth closets were subjects for great rejoicing in the 1870s.[42]

Perfecting the Landscape

Next to household inventions, the landscape was the most accessible area for members' participation in design. Long after the original fervor of the community to develop its domain as a paradisiacal garden had abated, the members continued to develop their estate. They stated that they hoped to demonstrate that a fine estate was not a capitalist treasure but a natural commodity within the reach of a community of modest means.[43] They also hoped to encourage both individual and collective expression through landscape design, or "earth sculpture," as they called it.[44]

Their concerns included both the practical and the decorative aspects of site planning. They arranged orchards and vineyards on the western hillsides of their domain, fields on the alluvial land next to the Oneida Creek, and fifty acres of gardens near the Mansion House. To any scientific farmer who wished to join them, they advertised themselves as possessing a good agricultural library, thoroughbred stock, and well-equipped, convenient farm buildings.[45] Their general knowledge about landscaping is manifested in the *Circular* articles which discuss the work of Capability Brown and Andrew Jackson Downing, praise important projects such as Olmsted's plan for New York's Central Park, and reflect in their titles local concerns such as the "Improvement of Meadows," and "Trees on the O.C. Lawn" (this last article listing varieties according to both English and Latin names).[46] The level of community participation in landscape activities was high. Under the direction of Henry Thacker and "E. B.," a group of ardent amateurs laid out the grounds around the Mansion House with hedges, clumps of trees, shaded walks, a summerhouse, a formal garden, and an "avenue of elms," all recorded on an 1869 map entitled "Buildings and Southern Grounds," which shows every tree and shrub (Fig. 7.11).

Underlying all their landscaping activities was the sense that their landscape should change as their communal requirements changed. An entry in the *Daily Journal* for July 9, 1866, confirms the group's interest in letting the definition of communal functions guide their aesthetic choices:

S.W.N. is this morning engaged in cutting a direct path from the main entry of the New House to the office door of the Store, intersecting the oval green in front of the portico. A kind of contest has been going on in the minds of a good many between the taste that preferred to keep the oval intact and the necessity that demanded the path; but it may be assumed as a safe principle that beauty and utility are never truly antagonistic. At some future time the paths and grass plots may be entirely re-arranged in conformity with new requirements and new ideas.[47]

This incident and the writer's comments epitomize the adaptation which characterized the Perfectionists' process of design. A member who sensed an ongoing communal requirement for a path was allowed to alter a regular geometrical form which had been imposed on the landscape. The active process of "perfecting" was preferred to the static state of perfection; the possibility of a new design seduced the Perfectionists away from the one they had already created.

Perfecting Communal Buildings

Adaptation was the sign of a "live Communi-

ty"[48] to the Perfectionists, manifested in their dwellings and their workplaces, as well as in their landscape. In 1847, when members of the Putney community arrived at Oneida to settle their land, they found two small farmhouses, two log cabins, and a shed. By 1848 they needed additional dwelling space and began to build the first Mansion House (Fig. 7.12), a frame structure which has been described by Harriet Worden, the daughter of community members. Additions were made in 1849, 1850, and 1851, with concurrent changes in uses of spaces and arrangement of interior partitions. Worden recounts the joke of a workman that "the community folks should hang their partitions on hinges and set their buildings on castors, they change so often," but she asserts proudly that changeability "shows the disposition of the community as a whole"[49] to seek the best spatial organization possible with limited means. George E. Cragin, a member, offers a similar description of the "Old Mill Garret" constructed in 1850, which served as a granary, rustic seat factory, dormitory, broom factory, sawmill, silk spinning factory, tin can factory, and storage shed.[50]

After the first hectic decade at Oneida, adaptation was confined to the large-span work spaces. These were contained in the Tontine, built in 1863, which served the community as kitchen, dining rooms, carpenter's shop, trap shop, printing office, bag shop, fruit preserving establishment, and laundry[51] and housed the early activities of the silk industry as well. The changes over time which marked the development of the community's social and dwelling areas were of a different order. The community's population living at Oneida stabilized at about two hundred in 1855. A master plan integrated the development of new facilities with

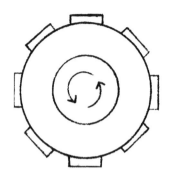

7.10 Perfectionist inventions: Travelers' lunch bag, 1865; the "final shoe," 1869; and lazy susan dining table.

7.11 "Love is a better element for anything to grow in than selfishness": landscape plan of southern grounds of Oneida Community, 1869, showing formal garden (faintly), variegated planting, and oval drive, Mansion House at upper right, railroad station at lower left.

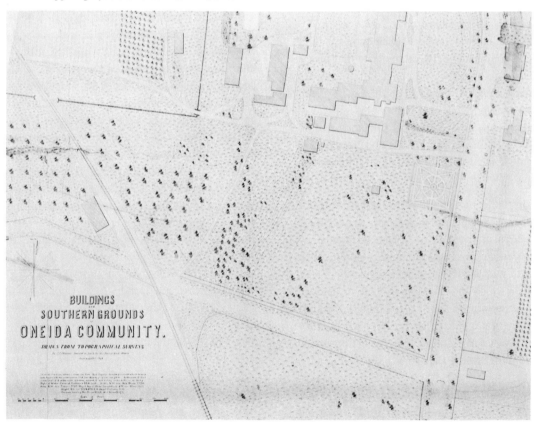

BUILDINGS
AND
SOUTHERN GROUNDS
ONEIDA COMMUNITY.

DRAWN FROM TOPOGRAPHICAL SURVEYS

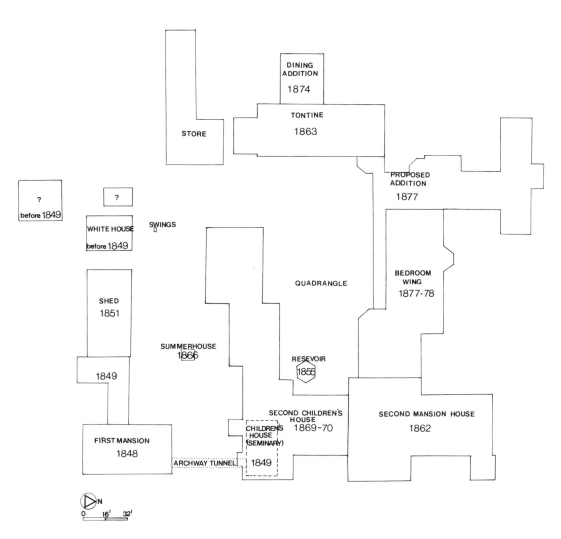

DINING
ADDITION

1874

TONTINE

1863

STORE

PROPOSED
ADDITION

1877

?

before 1849

?

SWINGS

WHITE HOUSE

before 1849

BEDROOM
WING

1877-78

QUADRANGLE

SHED

1851

SUMMERHOUSE

1866

RESEVOIR

1856

1849

SECOND CHILDREN'S
HOUSE

1869-70

SECOND MANSION HOUSE

1862

CHILDREN'S
HOUSE
(SEMINARY)

1849

FIRST MANSION

1848

ARCHWAY TUNNEL

N

0   16'   32'

7.12 Diagram of Oneida Community building sequence, 1848-1878.

the gradual replacement of old ones. Carefully designed additions required few changes in the interior plans of existing buildings.

Although a diagrammatic plan of the second Mansion House was published in the *Circular* on September 5, 1861, showing only the wing built in 1861-1862, two rendered elevations (Figs. 7.13, 7.14) show both this wing and part of the 1869-1870 wing, suggesting that the two segments were conceived at the same time. A mansard roof was employed to add an extra habitable story to the 1869-1870 wing, indicating self-conscious willingness to mix architectural styles. This is substantiated by the admission that "in a structure that grows up by gradual accretion like our Community homes, we do not look for the architectural purity and precision which would belong to a statehouse or a church. Our eye is rather pleased, and our interest piqued by noticing the evidences of time, and the successive stages of progress that have passed over the work."[52]

The Mansion thus became an architectural record of community development: new wings symbolized new eras. The wing of 1861-1862 represented industrial prosperity and the regularization of complex marriage; the wing of 1869-1870, called the "Children's House," represented the end of a ban on childbearing and the beginning of "stirpiculture," an experiment in eugenics; the wing of 1877-1878, designed by an outside architect, represented re-engagement with the outside world and resultant controversies over "worldliness" leading to the breakup. The aesthetic appeal of the completed structure lies in the lively proliferation of motifs developed with uniform use of materials—red brick walls, white wooden trim, and patterned slate roofs. Both the community's builders and their hired architect, Lewis W. Leeds of New York, who designed a final dwelling wing in 1877, contributed diverse elements in the construction of the various segments of the building. Despite the variety of facade treatments, coherent exterior massing allows the building to dominate the landscape (Fig. 7.15) while an interior courtyard called the Quadrangle (Figs. 7.16, 7.17) offers the contrast of landscaped space defined by the building. Since community members had done most of the Mansion House construction themselves, their buildings offered them an architectural survey of the "evidences of time," the "successive stages of progress" which Perfectionist labor had brought about.

7.13 East elevation of Second Mansion House, water-color rendering by Erastus H. Hamilton, 1861.

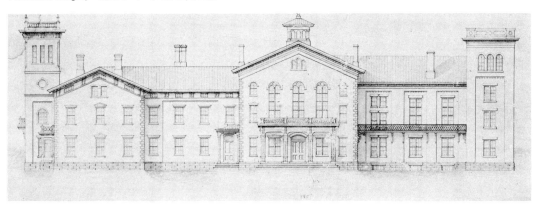

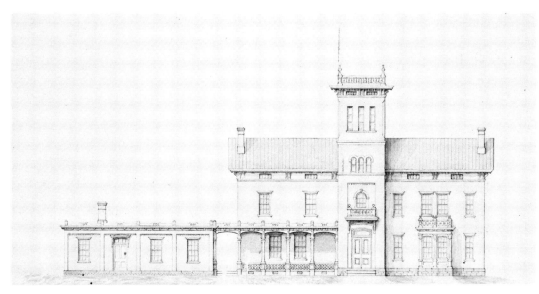

7.14 Second Mansion House, south elevation.

7.16 Aerial view, Second Mansion House, ca. 1960.

7.17. Perfectionists in the Quadrangle, ca. 1875. Erastus Hamilton is the gray-bearded man at left of seated group. Women are attired in Bloomer dresses; ivy-covered mount is a water storage tank; rustic wooden seat is a community product.

7.15 "Yet by patience, forbearing one with another and submitting one to another, the final result satisfied everyone": Second Mansion House, view from the southeast.

Just as the community satisfied the spiritual requirements of Perfectionism through collective design activities—inventions, cultivation of the landscape, and the adaptation of buildings—so it satisfied the social demands of Bible Communism through calculated arrangements of interior spaces. The sociopetal and sociofugal qualities of spaces, the qualities of encouraging or discouraging personal interactions, were concepts intuitively understood and used by the community to achieve the complex balance between community and privacy which their sexual practices required. This environmental manipulation was achieved over time. Fifteen years of experience enabled the community to progress from constant and perhaps disorganized adaptation of its first Mansion House to planned development of its second Mansion House; in the same manner, fifteen to twenty years of experience allowed the community to cease seeking new spatial "inventions" and develop proven patterns of organization which fostered a sense of "home" and regulated the flow of communal and private activities.

The Oneida Community's *Annual Report* of 1849 describes the development of its first "Tent Room," an improvised combination of bedrooms and a sitting room (Fig. 7.18) which was the most unusual feature of its first Mansion House:

. . . As the first winter drew near and the finishing of the house lingered, it became evident that this intention must be abandoned unless some new method of constructing dormitories, more expeditious than the usual one, could be devised.

One half of the third story, i.e., a space of 35 feet by 30, was finished as a single apartment. Within this apartment, twelve tents (each about 7 feet by 8, large enough for a bed and all the other apparatus necessary for a dormitory) were erected against the walls of the room to form a hollow square. The tents were made of cotton cloth, supported on upright wooden frames about seven feet high, and open at the top. The space between the tops of the tents and the ceiling of the room (about 2 feet) gave free circulation to air and light. The interior of the hollow square, a space about 18 feet by 14, became a comfortable sitting room for the occupants of the tents. One large stove in the center of this room was found sufficient to warm the twelve rooms around it and two reflectors suspended in the same apartment gave light enough for all ordinary purposes to the whole.[53]

Although their neighbors were scandalized by these flimsy and unconventional bedroom arrangements, the residents were pleased: "Much might be said of the increased sociality of the Tent Room, as compared to the cold isolation of the ordinary apartments. . . . The reunions here, for study, conversation, and music, form a constant social element, both improving and delightful."[54]

Earlier the Perfectionists had asked themselves what might be the elements of a "community architecture." In the Tent Room they found an answer on an intimate scale, as in its courtyard analog they were able to develop a suitable plan for the extensive wings of the community mansion.

Although the invention of the Tent Room pleased its occupants and a second version was included in the 1851 wing of the first mansion, for a time the community continued to seek novel forms of spatial organization. In 1856 plans for a second Mansion House were discussed at evening meetings. The alternatives proposed seem to be derived from Joseph Paxton's Crystal Palace and Orson Squire Fowler's octagonal houses, from Andrew Jackson Downing's manuals on country houses, and Catharine Beecher's works on domestic interiors, from Hudson River steamboats and grand hotels, as well as from the inspiration of the Tent Room.[55]

The debates about the design of the new mansion were described in the *Circular*:

What constitutes the truest ideal of a Community dwelling? Several of our thinkers have accordingly set themselves to work to devise plans for a building which shall be in all respects adapted to a Community like ours; and the result has been, that for a week past, the Association has been regaled with a series of evening lectures, showing the working of different minds on the same subject, and affording us at once a pleasing and profitable entertainment.

Several prefer the octagonal form of building; and one proposes a house 150 feet in diameter, two stories in height above the basement—the center of the building to be occupied by a room 90 feet in diameter, extending to the roof, and surmounted by a dome of the same size; the remainder, consisting of an outside rim of thirty feet wide, surrounding this central room, to be occupied above by tent rooms for sleeping, and below by business rooms, &c., &c.,—the basement to be divided into a kitchen, dining-room, washing and ironing apartments, &c. This plan is quite magnificent, but objections are made on account of its impracticality. . . .

Another proposed a rectangular building of about 80 by 100 feet, with a court in the center, surrounded on three sides, and opening to the south. A fourth thinks the general plan of our present dwelling very convenient, and proposes a modification and enlargement of the same, with a new arrangement of inside details. Another advocates the octagonal form, but with the limitation of 100 feet diameter, and a central room of 52 feet diameter, extending three stories, or thirty feet to the roof, and lighted by a dome of the same size—the surrounding periphery or rim of 24 feet, being divided in the two upper stories into a double tier of state-rooms similar to those on board steamboats, and supplied with berths, or beds, at the option of the occupants.[56]

These schemes suggest amateurs' untrained imaginations at work. Although the community numbered an architect, Erastus Hamilton, among its members, he encouraged wide-ranging discussion as the best means of generating a good plan. Hamilton, converted by Noyes at a convention in Genoa, New York, in September 1847,[57] joined the community with his family the following spring, in time to become chief of the construction of the first Mansion. Probably he devised the Tent Room, but he seems to have demanded very little personal recognition for his work. He described the design of the second Mansion House as a collective endeavor resolved through the patient pursual of consensus:

When we built our new house, how many were the different minds about material, location, plan! How were our feelings wrought up! Party-spirit ran high. There was the stone party, the brick party, and the concrete-wall party. Yet by patience, forbearing one with another and submitting one to another, the final result satisfied every one.[58]

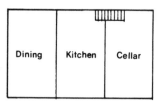

First

7.18 "Much might be said of the increased sociality of the Tent Room, as compared to the cold isolation of ordinary apartments . . . ": First Mansion House, diagram showing Tent Room, ca. 1848.

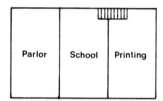

Second

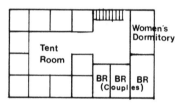

Third

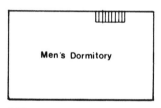

Attic

0   16'   32'

7.19 Second Mansion House, 1861-1878, schematic plans, opposite and on following pages. 1, Office, cloakroom; 2, reception room; 3, library; 4, lower sitting room; 5, single bedroom; 6, shared bedroom(?); 7, bathroom; 8, lounge or workshop(?); 9, workshop; 10, dining room; 11, dining addition; 12, balcony of hall; 13, west sitting room (drawing room); 14, home parlor (south sitting room); 15, nursery kitchen; 16, balcony of upper sitting room; 17, nursery; 18, "hub"; 19, south tower; 20, children's parlor (east room); 21, west avenue; 22, ground corridor; 23, porch; 24, north tower; 25, hall; 26, stage; 27, upper sitting room.

The Architecture of Complex Marriage   208

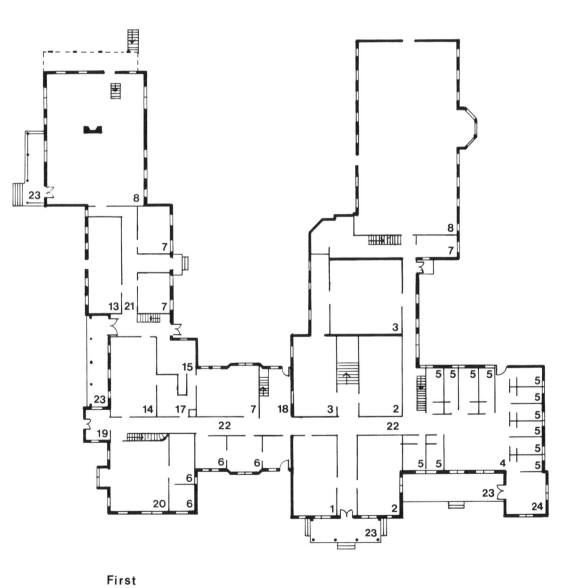

First

0　　16'　　32'

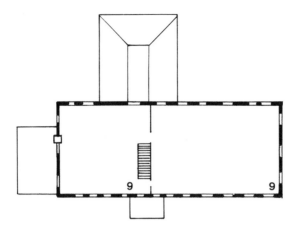

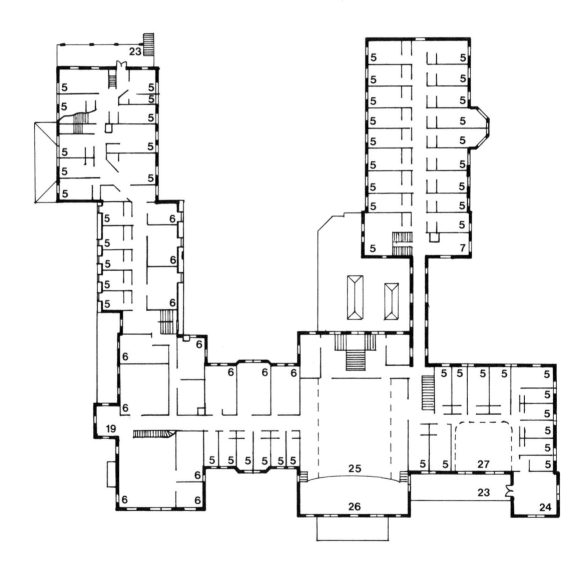

Second

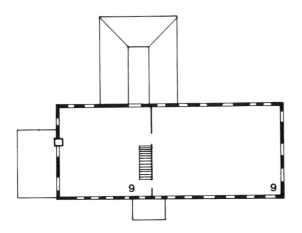

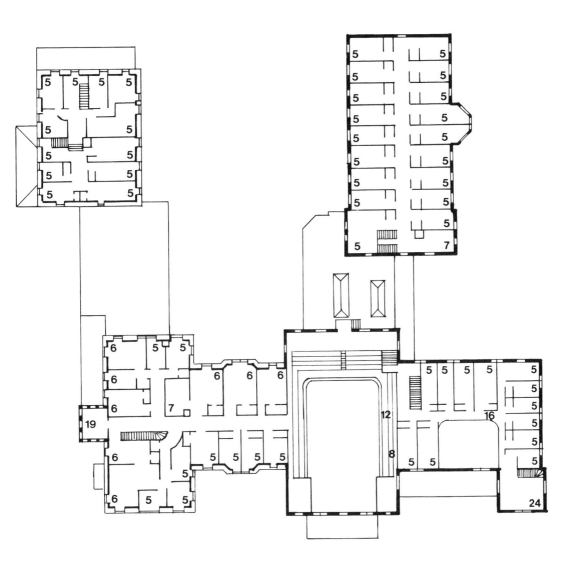

Third

Ultimately the community decided in favor of a new structure (Fig. 7.19) organized much the same way as its first Mansion House, which is original in plan and section but owes much to Downing in elevation (Fig. 7.20). Communal facilities were placed in prominent positions on the first and second floors. Sitting rooms open to major circulation routes and surrounded by small bedrooms (the basic Tent Room pattern) defined neighborhoods within the bedroom wings.

Several principles of Bible Communism were incorporated in the design of the sitting rooms and bedrooms. The casual encounters essential to the increased sociability which had been prized in the Tent Room were fostered by circulation spaces passing through areas of communal activity. The presence of communal activities outside bedroom doors obviated the possibility of loneliness for residents and at the same time decreased the possibility of exclusive relationships. The required variety of complex marriage was enforced by surveillance of bedroom doors from the sitting rooms (Fig. 7.21). Familial or sexual attachments could be easily discovered and discouraged. The bedrooms themselves were designed to preclude the association of exclusive small groups. Although Oneida was unique among nineteenth century communities in providing private rooms for many of its adult members,[59] the community insisted that these spaces not be used as sitting rooms.[60] The plan by Lewis W. Leeds for a typical bedroom in the 1877 wing (Fig. 7.22) shows a space seven and one half feet wide and fifteen and one half feet deep, which would have been furnished with a closet, a work table, a bed, and two chairs,[61] a space much less conducive to entertainment of visitors than a square room of similar area.

Although sitting rooms of various sizes were scattered throughout the Mansion House, the most important and most elaborate was the Upper Sitting Room (Fig. 7.23), a two-story version which owed its unusual cross-section to John Humphrey Noyes's fascination with the grand decks of Hudson River steamboats.[62] The addition of a second level enriched the sitting room's activities by doubling the possibilities for circulation and observation. The two bedroom levels were connected with the two levels of the adjoining hall. A member remarked that the Upper Sitting Room "is the room of all others in which the true home feeling finds the freest play,"[63] perhaps because it provided the fullest architectural development of the balance between community and privacy crucial to Bible Communism.

The Upper Sitting Room was the Oneida Community's most distinctive architectural composition, but many other Mansion House spaces were conceived in terms of the community's desire to foster specific patterns of communal interaction. The building encouraged various types of social contact through a variety of spaces and a number of sequences of spatial expansion and contraction.

A quick tour of some of the Mansion's meeting places would begin with the Hall (Fig. 7.24) which housed gatherings of the entire community every evening. Two hundred or more members sat at small tables on the main floor or crowded into the balconies to plan, criticize, design, sing, act, or sermonize. The community dining room (Fig. 7.25) was designed to permit only random contacts since seating was determined by place in the serving line, in order to associate "old and young, male and female, in a good and wholesome manner," and "to diffuse a spirit of politeness and sociability not other-

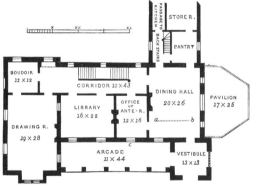

7.20 "Southern Villa–Romanesque Style," perspective sketch and plan of principal floor, by Andrew Jackson Downing, 1850.

EASY
INVOLVEMENT

0   4'   8'

CONSTANT
SURVEILLANCE

7.21 Diagram of easy involvement and constant surveillance, Second Mansion House.

7.22 Typical narrow bedroom plan, 1877 wing of Second Mansion House, by Lewis W. Leeds.

7.23 ". . . The room of all others in which the true home feeling finds the freest play," Upper Sitting Room, Second Mansion House, during the "Children's Hour," 1870.

7.24 A theatrical performance in the Hall, Second Mansion House, 1870. This is the room where evening meetings were held to determine community design policy.

Complex Marriage, Community, and Privacy   215

7.25 Community members at dinner in the main dining room, Second Mansion House.

7.26 "All are well-informed": members in the library,
Second Mansion House, 1870.

wise attainable."[64] The library (Fig. 7.26) encouraged private study in a communal space. The "Court," a central hallway, sheltered unstructured activities and meetings, related to the circulation paths which crossed there. Corinna Noyes describes the Court as a well-defined place because of its clutter, including the stairs to the cellar and the Turkish bath, an umbrella cupboard, a drinking fountain, stacks of buckets for the home fire department, a large bulletin board which was considered "an important family institution," a combination thermometer/barometer "visited regularly by certain statistically minded people," and a large interior window opening into the adjacent library which delighted the children, who were not allowed into the library alone.[65] The nursery kitchen (Fig. 7.27) provided more structured opportunities for casual meetings. Here the members chose to retain a stove after they had central heating in the Mansion, for a specific heat source would gather members. They wrote, "If we have a general rendezvous, here it is. . . . If you wish to see the greatest number of persons in the shortest space of time, just take a seat. . . ."[66]

To describe and define the spaces within their Mansion so carefully and precisely, the Perfectionists needed to be extremely aware of the nuances of psychological responses evoked by such stimuli as the size of tables, personal distances in meeting rooms, the warmth of a stove, or the provision of unstructured activities in waiting areas.[67] This is the tone of Fourier's prescriptions for the phalanstery, the architecture of "passional attraction" translated from speculation to reality. The Oneidans' skill as environmental psychologists was unexcelled among communitarians. The Shakers' use of posture and distancing regulations, if more thorough, was decidedly less appealing.

Guiding the reader on a brief tour of some of the more prominent or characteristic spaces in the Mansion House is possible because the Perfectionists and their supporters often advanced a catalogue of their tangible physical achievements to counter the world's dismissal of them as fools, sexual deviants, or religious fanatics.[68] These defensive arguments provide much information about their physical environment, but obscure their design process by emphasizing its products. An evaluation of the community's contribution to environmental design depends on appreciation of their collective skills in both defining and creating a coherent physical environment, skills which transcend the accumulation of land or the erection of buildings.

Their first achievement was the definition of an image of community which was meaningful to all members. They spent ten years developing religious, social, and economic principles by which they chose to live; taking all of these into account they began to establish an attitude toward their environment. They commenced with a pious and mystical idea of a horticultural paradise, a naïve conception of Eden on earth, which they soon modified to a practical plan for the development of residential, agricultural, and industrial activities. Borrowing from whatever sources they found useful, they devised their own sensible site plan, which was collectively accepted in group discussions. This collective acceptance was reinforced by emphasis on the visual reality of the community's domain—its landscape, buildings, and boundaries—and through the verbal catalogues of its physical attributes found in community publications.

Their second achievement was designing and building the unified community which they had imagined for themselves. By stimulating inventiveness on the part of members and harnessing the results, they established a secure economic basis for their building program. They welcomed both individual and group efforts toward environmental perfection as expressive of their millennial religion. Certain areas were identified as appropriate for either decorative or functional improvement—household objects, the landscape, communal buildings. Although adaptation was extremely important to them ("the fundamental law of nature in all structure,"[69] they called it) they understood the uses of fixed physical form in reinforcing the social design of Bible Communism. The unique qualities of certain ritual spaces were recognized and heightened; the effective force of circulation paths in promoting communal interaction was recognized and exploited. A rhythm of diverse spatial sequences was developed which had well-understood psychological equivalents; varied environmental settings accommodated the meaningful communal events in members' lives, from the intimacy of complex marriage, to the casual friendliness of a "sit-down chat,"[70] to the ceremony of evening meetings with "Home Talks" by John Humphrey Noyes (Figs. 7.27, 7.28).

The activities of planning, design, and construction were constantly occurring on different scales. It is especially important to note that the community's achievements could not have resulted from the work of a single designer at one time—they represent the results of over thirty years of patient collective experimentation. Unlike the various groups of Fourierists, who were caught between their allegiances to the ideal and the real, the Oneidans were united in their devotion to perfecting practical things. They were fascinated by the design process as it applied to mechanical inventions and described

this process in an article entitled "Principles of Beauty":

If we compare the form of a newly-invented machine with the perfected type of the same instrument, we observe as we trace it through the phases of improvement, how weight is shaken off where strength is less needed, how functions are made to approach without impeding each other, how the straight becomes curved and the curve is straightened, till the straggling and cumbersome machine becomes the compact, effective, and beautiful engine.[71]

The Perfectionists defined their lives in terms of the perfection of the environment; it is tempting to term their collective home a machine for communal living.

7.27 "... If we have a general rendezvous, here it is ... if you wish to see the greatest number of persons in the shortest space of time, just take a seat ... ": "pocket kitchen" or nursery kitchen.

7.28 Varied scales accommodated the meaningful communal events in members' lives, from the casual friendliness of a "sit-down chat," to the ceremony of evening meetings: the Hall.

The Architecture of Complex Marriage   220

1 Maren Lockwood Carden, *Oneida: Utopian Community to Modern Corporation*, Baltimore, 1969, p. 56. Carden's book and comments by Robert Fogarty, Kathleen Zimmerlin, and Mary Lou Welby provided background for me.

2 Carden, *Oneida*, p. 8. Also see Henry Seymour, *The Oneida Community: A Dialogue*, n.p., n.d. [1885], p. 16.

3 Pierrepont B. Noyes, *My Father's House: An Oneida Boyhood*, New York, 1937, p. 39.

4 Charlotte Augusta Miller to Seymour W. Nash, Wallingford, Conn., Dec. 16, 1863, in the Evan Rupert Nash Family Papers, Stanford University Library, Palo Alto, Calif.

5 Sarah B. Nash to Seymour W. Nash, Wallingford, Conn., May 18, 1854, Nash Papers.

6 Sarah B. Nash to Seymour W. Nash, Wallingford, Conn., June 19, 1859, Nash Papers.

7 Sarah B. Nash to Seymour W. Nash, Wallingford, Conn., June 25, 1859, Nash Papers.

8 A substantial dwelling was built at Wallingford in 1876. See "Early Site of Masonic Home Occupied By Strange People," *The Connecticut Square and Compasses*, Jan. 1958, pp. 7ff, for photograph.

9 Erastus Hamilton, letter dated New York, Mar. 31, 1868, published in the *Oneida Circular*, Apr. 13, 1868, reprinted in John Humphrey Noyes, *History of American Socialisms* (1870), New York, 1966, p. 509.

10 Carden, in *Oneida*, p. 49, discusses women's roles. She mentions that Noyes considered women inferior to men, p. 67. For the law of "ascending fellowship," see ibid., p. 88. Economic equality was extended only to members: over 200 outside workers were employed by the Community in 1875, according to Carden, p. 42.

11 Pierrepont B. Noyes, *My Father's House*, p. 266.

12 *Oneida Circular*, Oct. 28, 1855. Many of these unsigned *Oneida Circular* articles resemble Noyes's own style, possibly emulated by other authors.

13 "Principles of Beauty," *Oneida Circular*, Nov. 9, 1853, pp. 411-412.

14 "Community Architecture," *Oneida Circular*, Nov. 6, 1856, p. 166.

15 "Community Agriculture," *Oneida Circular*, Jan. 8, 1857, p. 202.

16 On their interest in Fourier: "We differ widely from him on the most essential points. . . . He relies on *attraction*. . . . Our motive power is faith. . . . We expect, however, to learn many things about externals from Fourier." *Bible Communism: A Compilation from the Annual Reports and Other Publications of the Oneida Association and its Branches*, Brooklyn, N.Y., 1853, pp. 7-8. I found a copy of a Fourierist lithograph of "Harmony" in the Mansion House attic in 1971.

17 The *Oneida Circular*, September 26, 1870, reports over 1,000 visitors during the previous week. The *Oneida Circular*, October 14, 1872, reports 3,699 registered guests for that year, and estimates twice as many unregistered guests. Members feared "the hotel feeling" but did nothing to limit the numbers of visitors, in part because serving them meals was profitable.

18 John Humphrey Noyes, quoted by Constance Robertson, in *Oneida Community: An Autobiography 1851-1876*, Syracuse, 1970, p. 26. See also Constance Robertson, *Oneida Community: The Breakup, 1876-1881*, Syracuse, 1972, for a full account of dissolution.

19 *Handbook of the Oneida Community*, Oneida, N.Y., 1871, p. 2.

20 "Attractive Industry," *The Free Church Circular*, Oneida Reserve, N.Y., 4 (Apr. 25, 1851), 138. Note the term borrowed from Fourier, "attractive industry."

21 "T.L.P.," "Fruit Growing at Oneida," *Oneida Circular*, Oct. 16, 1856, p. 155. Fourier, who dreamed of armies of conservation workers and planned for a better climate under the Divine Social Code, may have inspired this faith.

22 The *Horticulturist* notice is cited in the *Oneida Circular*, Nov. 14, 1864. On Thacker, see G.E.C. (George E. Cragin), "Trap Making on Oneida Creek," part 1, *The Quadrangle*, 4.4 (Apr. 1913), 1-2, and also the *Oneida Circular*, Sept. 24, 1853, p. 358.

23 *Oneida Circular*, Oct. 10, 1882.

24 "Attractive Industry," p. 138.

25 Albert Brisbane, *Social Destiny of Man*, Philadelphia, 1840, frontispiece.

26 *Oneida Circular*, Jan. 8, 1857, p. 202.

27 "H. M. L.," "The Upper Sitting Room," *Oneida Circular*, Jan. 11, 1869; Jan. 18, 1869, pp. 341, 347.

28 "The O.C. Laundry," *Oneida Circular*, May 8, 1871, p. 144. "An Inside View of the Tontine," *Oneida Circular*, Mar. 8, 1875, p. 78. The Tontine was a kitchen and workshop building named after a Boston hotel, according to William Alfred Hinds, "Album," MS and photographs, Oneida Community Historical Committee.

29 Their concern with names seemed to reach a pitch in the discussion of a title for their second Mansion

House: "In many ways we are moved to thankfulness for the success we have had in the erection of our new dwelling. It beautifies the grounds, it will be a comfortable and attractive house, it will afford opportunity for the fuller development of many elements of Community life. . . . But what shall we call the new dwelling? . . . We need a name that shall be somewhat suggestive of the Life which it shall infold. If we were Fourierists we should call it the Phalanstery. We are not a Phalanx, but a Community. How would Communistery do? Or Koinonistery, from the Greek *Koinonia*—fellowship, communion? Or Koinonia Hall? What shall it be?" *Oneida Circular*, Oct. 3, 1861, p. 139.

30 A third tower was projected (but not built) in the 1877 design for a new wing.

31 *Handbook of the Oneida Community*, 1871, p. 10. Complementary to the members' happy consciousness of the physical world of their own domain was their anxious concern about "the outside." The community owned only a few sets of women's traveling clothes (as opposed to the bloomer dresses worn at Oneida) and these were assigned to members who had permission to leave the domain, usually granted for visits to branch communities, or business trips. When a member returned from the outside world, he or she was subjected to the purifying rituals of a community steam bath and a bout of mutual criticism.

Rather contrary to this insularity is the expansive concern for regional planning, expressed by Noyes in the *Daily Journal*: "Let our interest in beautiful surroundings by no means be confined to our own domain; but, on the contrary, wherever we go in this wide world, let us do all we can to stimulate the love of improvement and beauty in our neighbors . . . I want to see this whole valley of several thousand acres all under the highest cultivation." (July 16, 1866, pp. 47-48.)

Perhaps he had an eye to acquiring his neighbors' property. Between 1863 and 1869 the community purchased additional land on the Sconondoa Creek, as documented in "Map No. 1" of "Big 4" land purchases, Collection of Oneida, Ltd.

32 G. E. C. (George E. Cragin), "The Indian Saw Mill," *The Quadrangle*, 4.3 (Mar. 1913), 7-9; "When We Made Brick," 6.12 (Dec. [1913]), 9-10; "Water Supply At Kenwood, 1848-1911," 4.5 (May 1913), 9-12; also by Cragin, signed "Jorg-ee," "The Old Mill Garret," 7.9 (Sept. 1914), 1-2; and, signed "An Old Boy," "The First Children's House," 6.12 (Dec. [1913]), 10-12.

33 Figure 2.6.

34 *The Oneida Community: A Familiar Exposition of its Ideas and Practical Life, in a Conversation with a Visitor*, Wallingford, Conn., 1865, p. 19.

35 J. J. Gordon, *Synectics*, New York, 1966, is a modern treatise on group creativity which reiterates these ideas.

36 *Handbook of the Oneida Community*, 1871, p. 9.

37 Mr. Gray, in 1853, according to the *Oneida Circular*, September 16, 1872, p. 302.

38 Cragin, "Trap Making," discusses this in detail.

39 *Oneida Circular*, Sept. 26, 1870, p. 223.

40 *Oneida Circular*, Aug. 2, 1869.

41 *Oneida Circular*, Feb. 14, 1870, p. 380.

42 *Oneida Circular*, July 15, 1872, p. 227, describes Moule's system of earth closets. "The O. C. Turkish Bath" is described in the *Oneida Circular*, Jan. 27, 1876, p. 28.

43 "E. B.," "Researches in Landscape Gardening, No. 1," (of 7), *Oneida Circular*, Mar. 20, 1862, p. 24.

44 Ibid.

45 *The Oneida Community: A Familiar Exposition*, p. 20.

46 Capability Brown, Andrew Jackson Downing, and Frederick Law Olmsted are discussed by "E. B." in "Researches in Landscape Architecture No. 3," *Oneida Circular*, Apr. 3, 1862. "City Gardens," *Oneida Circular*, July 6, 1853, p. 266, offers a view of urbanism: cities need parks because there are too many small pieces of private property. Communists unite their lawns and thus parks are an inherent feature of their communities. See also Henry Thacker, "Improvement of Meadows," *Oneida Circular*, Nov. 9, 1869, p. 271, and "Trees on the O. C. Lawn," *Oneida Circular*, Sept. 26, 1870.

47 *Daily Journal*, July 9, 1866, pp. 23-24. "S. W. N." may be Seymour W. Nash.

48 *Oneida Circular*, June 28, 1869, pp. 119.

49 Harriet Worden, *Old Mansion House Memories*, Kenwood, N. Y., 1950, pp. 23-24.

50 Cragin, "The Old Mill Garret."

51 *Oneida Circular*, June 28, 1869, p. 119.

52 *Oneida Circular*, Feb. 22, 1869, p. 391.

53 Oneida Association, *First Annual Report*, Oneida Reserve, N. Y., 1849, p. 57.

54 *Oneida Circular*, Apr. 25, 1852. "Social" sometimes meant sexual to Oneidans, as in "social intercourse." Here the meaning is not clear.

55 "Community Architecture," p. 166, mentions the St. Nicholas Hotel in New York as an example of the

world's "community" mansions. This was a common theme in Fourierist writings. The Crystal Palace is discussed in *The Free Church Circular* (Oneida Reserve, N. Y.), 4 (Apr. 16, 1851), pp. 120-126. See also Orson Squire Fowler, *A Home For All*, New York, 1848. The Oneidans shared Fowler's passion for phrenology, which may have led them to his architecture. Other sources were Andrew Jackson Downing, *The Architecture of Country Houses*, New York, 1850, and also Catharine Esther Beecher and Harriet Beecher Stowe, *The American Woman's Home*, New York, 1869. Beecher recommends Lewis W. Leeds's innovations in ventilation, which may have led to his commission to design the 1877 wing of the Mansion. Another important source may have been Alexander Davis's Llewellyn Park, New Jersey, suburb, designed for the Perfectionist businessman Llewellyn Haskell, beginning in 1853.

56 "Community Architecture," p. 166.

57 Oneida Association, *First Annual Report*, pp. 3-4, p. 57. Pierrepont Noyes suggests that Hamilton practiced in Syracuse before joining, *My Father's House*, p. 36.

58 Hamilton, quoted in John Humphrey Noyes, *History of American Socialisms*, p. 509.

59 *The Oneida Community: A Familiar Exposition*, p. 13.

60 Pierrepont Noyes, *My Father's House*, p. 39.

61 *Oneida Circular*, Oct. 10, 1870.

62 *Handbook of the Oneida Community*, 1871, p. 8.

63 *Oneida Circular*, Jan. 6, 1868.

64 Robertson, *Autobiography*, p. 100.

65 Corinna Ackley Noyes, *The Days of My Youth*, Kenwood, N. Y., 1960, p. 66.

66 *Oneida Circular*, Feb. 21, 1871.

67 For contemporary discussions of such issues, see Robert Sommer, *Personal Space*, Englewood Cliffs, N. J., 1969, and Erving Goffman, *Behavior in Public Places*, New York, 1963.

68 See their own *Handbooks*, as opposed to outsiders' evaluations such as Isaac G. Reed, Jr., "The Oneida Community of Free Lovers," *Frank Leslie's Illustrated Newspaper*, Apr. 9, 1870, pp. 54-55, and Apr. 25, 1870, pp. 38-40.

69 "Principles of Beauty," p. 412.

70 Corinna Noyes, *The Days of My Youth*, p. 66.

71 "Principles of Beauty," p. 412.

8 Communes within Communes

We are a church all the time, even in our homes.

—Amana saying, 1908

8.1 Amana colonists, 1902.

The True Inspiration Congregations of Amana, Iowa, built more than most communitarian groups, but they lacked the fervent sectarian enthusiasm for building characteristic of the Shakers, Mormons, or Perfectionists. Between 1843 and 1862 they founded thirteen American communities, seven of them sustained as communistic villages until 1932. Sexually, socially, and environmentally they chose a middle road, subordinating family and property to church and community. Compared with the eccentricities of celibate groups or the poignant crises of free love communities, the religious and social practices of Amana communards may seem stolid (Fig. 8.1). Environmental design is still an interesting aspect of Inspirationist history: families occupied suites within communal houses grouped in neighborhoods served by communal kitchens, a complex pattern repeated in seven adjacent but separate villages on their Iowa domain.

Their network of communal houses, kitchens, and villages was a distinct alternative to the large communal dwellings of the Shakers, Fourierists, and Oneidans, or the single-family dwellings of the Mormons. It anticipated, in fully developed form, the "cooperative housekeeping" which the Union Colonists talked of in 1869, and the "Next Step" for socialist women which Alice Constance Austin proposed at Llano del Rio in 1918. Despite a grim domestic regimen featuring dark clothes, daily church, and a diet of potatoes and sauerkraut, the Inspirationists' approach to domestic environments was a unique and viable one. Their gradual development of communal networks relied on pious pragmatism rather than millennial or communist conviction. In contrast to Shaker architecture, based on sexual oppositions, and Fourierist architecture, based on "passional at-traction," Inspirationist architecture relied on compromise, but what it lacked in emotive power it made up for in sound common sense.

As a pietist response to the official Lutheran Church in Germany, Johann Friedrich Rock and Eberhard Ludwig Gruber initiated the "New Spiritual Economy" or True Inspiration Congregations about 1714. They celebrated the writings of the prophets and the apostles as earlier "inspired" ones or instruments (*Werkzeuge*). Their own utterances and sayings, such as the "Twenty-four Rules for Godliness and Holy Conduct," or the "Twenty-one Rules for the Examination of Our Daily Lives," still provide the main spiritual guide for Inspirationist believers.[1] About 1818 Barbara Heinemann, a former woolen mill worker and domestic servant of Leitersweiler, Germany, and Christian Metz, a cabinetmaker of Ronneburg, started an Inspirationist revival as *Werkzeuge*. As their congregations grew, any persecuted Inspirationist believers were urged to group together in settlements. Around 1830 the group leased first, a medieval cloister at Marienborn, then one at Arnsberg, and then a convent at Engelthal. At the same time that they began to live in these old monastic environments and farm communally, they leased the buildings of the Herrnhaag, which had been designed and built a century earlier by the Moravian Brethren for communal living. For those industrial workers converted to the faith, a cloth factory was established by the wealthier Inspirationist believers. Thus three principles of their later communistic economy were established in their earliest cooperative settlements in Germany: division of the believers into village groupings; communal development of land in each village; and provision of industrial work to complement agriculture.

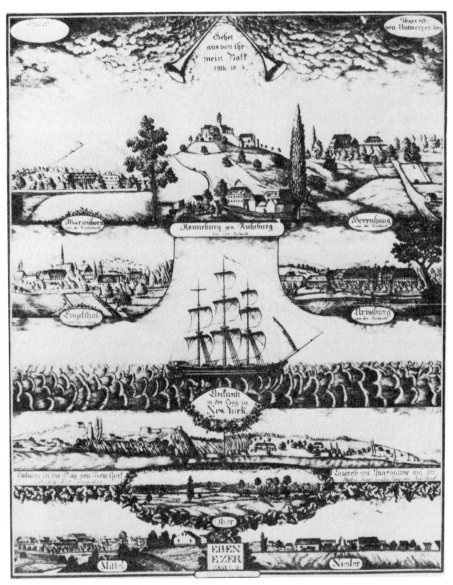

8.2 Three principles were established in their earliest
cooperative settlements in Germany: division of the
believers into village groupings; communal development of land in each village; and provision of industrial work to complement agriculture. Lithograph by
Joseph Prestele, ca. 1850, showing Ronneburg, Marienborn, Engelthal, Herrnhaag, and Arnsberg, above ships
which carried Inspirationists to New York, on their
way to settling Ober, Mittel, and Nieder Ebenezer.

A lithograph by Joseph Prestele (Fig. 8.2) showing Ronneburg, Marienborn, Arnsberg, Engelthal, and Herrnhaag, above Upper, Middle, and Lower Ebenezer, depicts the migration of over eight hundred Inspirationists to the New World beginning in 1842. They followed the lead of the Moravians, who had preceded them at Herrnhaag and had established communities in North Carolina, Pennsylvania, and New Jersey; also the example of the Harmonists, millennial communists organized in Württemberg, who established their first community in Pennsylvania in 1805; and the Separatists, from Württemberg as well, who settled Zoar, Ohio, in 1817.[2] In northwestern New York State the Inspirationists built four villages on 5,000 acres of land purchased from the Seneca Indians. They acquired additional land when they converted the residents of two other established villages in Canada, renamed Kenneberg and Canada Ebenezer. They set up a woolen mill with machinery brought from Germany, but despite their economic success, encroaching Buffalo residents precipitated a second westward migration.[3] Between 1855 and 1865 the group sold its Ebenezer land to individual settlers. Traveling with machinery from their German factory and timber from their Canadian lands, they moved to Iowa County, Iowa, establishing seven villages within an agricultural and industrial territory of forty square miles. This case study will be concerned chiefly with the patterns of building in Iowa, although the community's years of experience in Germany and in New York contributed to the vernacular style so distinctive there.

The orderly migrations of the Inspirationists were based on piety, since the ultimate source of both religious and practical authority was revelation, the thousands of "inspirations" received by Christian Metz and Barbara Heinemann. The Inspirationist system of government is shown in Fig. 8.3. The *Werkzeug* conveyed messages to an elected council of thirteen elders who exercised religious and civil authority over the community as a whole. Committees of elders in each village (each elder appointed for life by the *Werkzeug* or the council) ran the affairs of each village.[4] With the exception of Barbara Heinemann, disqualified as a *Werkzeug* between 1823 and 1849 because she chose to marry, women held no positions of authority in the community. Only widows and single women over thirty voted in the annual meeting of members along with the men. Like Joseph Smith at Nauvoo or John Humphrey Noyes at Oneida, Christian Metz played the role of a wise but an authoritarian father, one who knew what was best for his flock. This restrained both men and women from active discussion of community issues. The transition from temporary to permanent communism between 1850 and 1854 was perhaps the one hotly debated issue, but Metz dealt with it by offering repeated revelations from the Lord that communism was necessary for religious survival, and the wealthier members of the group were ultimately persuaded.

The economic organization of the Inspirationists, as an extension of theocratic government, exhibited both the virtues and faults of their authoritarian structure. The community prospered at first, because of good management and the security of collective organization in farming a new territory. The youngest members, however, grew up accustomed to prosperity and

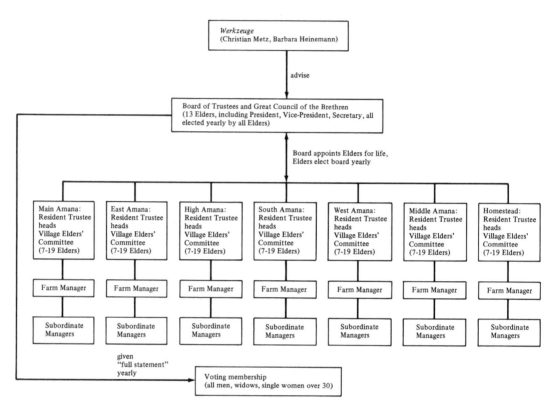

Werkzeuge
(Christian Metz, Barbara Heinemann)

advise

Board of Trustees and Great Council of the Brethren
(13 Elders, including President, Vice-President, Secretary, all
elected yearly by all Elders)

Board appoints Elders for life,
Elders elect board yearly

Main Amana:
Resident Trustee
heads
Village Elders'
Committee
(7-19 Elders)

East Amana:
Resident Trustee
heads
Village Elders'
Committee
(7-19 Elders)

High Amana:
Resident Trustee
heads
Village Elders'
Committee
(7-19 Elders)

South Amana:
Resident Trustee
heads
Village Elders'
Committee
(7-19 Elders)

West Amana:
Resident Trustee
heads
Village Elders'
Committee
(7-19 Elders)

Middle Amana:
Resident Trustee
heads
Village Elders'
Committee
(7-19 Elders)

Homestead:
Resident Trustee
heads
Village Elders'
Committee
(7-19 Elders)

Farm Manager

Farm Manager

Farm Manager

Farm Manager

Farm Manager

Farm Manager

Farm Manager

Subordinate
Managers

Subordinate
Managers

Subordinate
Managers

Subordinate
Managers

Subordinate
Managers

Subordinate
Managers

Subordinate
Managers

given
"full statement"
yearly

Voting membership
(all men, widows, single women over 30)

8.3 Inspirationist organization at Amana.

to having decisions made for them. There was no collective process developed to encourage individual initiative and energy. To make sure the farm work was done, outside laborers were hired, who were reported to be half again as productive as the Inspirationists, who frequently stopped work for meals or church. Women's labor was never used effectively because of sex role stereotypes. As time passed, Inspirationists seem to have concentrated their individual energies on decorating their own homes, and tending their private gardens for personal revenue. Like the Mormons and the Union Colonists, they busied themselves with the processes of life they could control, and the collective grew weaker and weaker, until the "Great Change" in 1932 instituted individual ownership of houses, land, and shares in the Amana corporation.

Like their government and economic organization, social organization among the Inspirationists evolved in Germany and Ebenezer before their arrival in Iowa. A conflict between sexuality and asceticism tormented some of the Inspirationist leaders, since one of Gruber's most esteemed "Rules for the Examination of Our Daily Lives" suggested that men should "Fly from the society of women-kind as much as possible, as a very highly dangerous magnet and magical fire."[5] The source of sexual temptation was always seen as female, which established religious justification for the male chauvinist tone for the community. Since celibacy would have restricted the Congregations' growth, marriage was permitted, at twenty-four for a man and twenty for a woman. During the prescribed one- or two-year engagement, the parties would be separated in different villages, to test the tie. Newly married couples and new mothers were demoted to the lowliest status in

the church which ranked its congregations as first, second, and third, and ranked members within congregations by the position of the benches they were allowed to occupy. Newly marrieds might not get housing promptly assigned. Pregnant women were encouraged to conceal themselves; elders who conceived children might have to resign.[6] Thus marriage was subordinated to neighborhood structure, defined in terms of separate villages and communal housing neighborhoods within them, as well as to the church.

The theocratic hierarchy of the community defined Amana's environmental design as well as its economy and social structure. Environmental design was undertaken in an authoritarian but competent manner, with Metz and Heinemann guiding the elders, who directed the masons and carpenters in each village. No participation or inventiveness was encouraged from the general membership. The justification for this authoritarian approach was not the "God has designed it" argument used by so many sectarian leaders, but rather the belief that the members should concern themselves with spiritual rather than worldly cares. In contrast to the Shakers, Mormons, and Oneidans, the Inspirationists believed in an otherworldly heaven rather than a paradise on earth. Planning and building on earth, therefore, were not related to their religious aspirations and could serve no proselytizing purpose. These activities became reflections of pragmatic rather than millennial communism, instruments of religious cohesion and control. The next sections describe the Inspirationists' skill in planning and building, particularly their solutions to the dilemmas of community and privacy, uniqueness and replicability. Their failure to come to terms with the problems of authority and participation undermined their successful resolution of the other dilemmas, however, and a process of disintegration began which is still continuing in the name of individual participation.

Land Use

With the theocratic approaches to environmental design they had established in Ebenezer, the Inspirationists conquered their Iowa territory between 1855 and 1865. Their choice of land and their plans for its use reveal the sagacity characteristic of successful communitarian settlements' land use. Their first purchase included about 3,000 acres of government land and perhaps the same amount of private land, which they added to continually until an unbroken tract totaling 25,659 acres (in 1932) was assembled. In the valley of the Iowa River they acquired fertile soil, stone and timber for building, water power for their mills. Six villages were sited on both sides of the river valley to command the farmland and to allow easy transport between town centers. When railroads entered their county, the society purchased additional land in order to acquire two shipping points on their domain.

In contrast to the Fourierists, who hoped to achieve "passional attraction" by intermingling 1,600 people at work and at home in one phalanstery, the Inspirationists hoped to achieve economic and social control by dividing a population of about that size into seven distinct villages. The smallest of these villages was about the size of the North American Phalanx or the Oneida Community (150 to 200 people); the largest, over 600. The Shakers also divided their communities into isolated subgroups, "families" strung out along their farmland, but the average Shaker family was a smaller group (30 to 100 people) defined by the spiritual rank of its members. Shaker communities reputedly owned four times the amount of land controlled by Amana,[7] but this was divided among their scattered communities, some of which lacked the labor force to farm it. The Amana site plan (Fig. 8.4), drawn at a scale comparable to the plans of the other communities, indicates how large a region was developed in Iowa, and consolidated by the establishment of a civil township roughly equivalent to the community's borders.

Amana was not only the largest but also the most systematically developed communitarian site. A survey of the Amana domain made in 1932 reported 10,626 acres of farmland, 6,373 of open pasture, 8,137 of timber, and about 520 of town sites.[8] Each of the villages had a farm manager responsible for the cultivation of the lands allotted to the village (Fig. 8.5). The communards' crops and yields seem to have been similar to those of their Iowa neighbors— corn, oats, wheat, hay, and potatoes predominated.[9] Good harvests were celebrated by processions of flower-decked horses and wagons through the villages. The community does not seem to have experimented much in agriculture or horticulture. The kitchen house gardens of two or three acres cared for by the women were particularly productive (Figs. 8.6, 8.7).

Every yard in the villages was highly cultivated, however, and all of the houses had trellises mounted a few inches off the facades which were covered with grapevines. Many had special planters for flowers built into the foundation walls.[10] A visitor reported seeing more flowers in Amana than over the entire journey from Chicago to Amana, noting that "vegetables, trees, and fruit bearing bushes are intermingled with flowers, with here and there a tiny lawn interspersed, all the ground beautifully cared for ... no unutilized land."[11]

Despite this interest in horticulture, Amana residents were wary of too much aesthetic concern with landscaping. Barbara Heinemann had delivered a stinging revelation against the "pleasures of the eye ... a mark of worldliness," in 1880:

See to it that all trees not bearing fruit be removed from the house, for they belong to the pleasures of the eye. You indeed have the opportunity to plant a fruit tree instead, in which the Lord and all sensible people take pleasure.[12]

When William Alfred Hinds of the Oneida Community visited Amana, he rather naïvely applied his own community's interest in picturesque landscaping to the Inspirationists' domain. He criticized "rough board fences and untidy sidewalks" and proposed that each village should have "a public park, beautiful with ornamental shade trees, winding paths, grottos and fountains, flower-gardens, and play-grounds."[13] Obviously this was more in the spirit of Downing or Olmsted than Inspirationist discipline. It is surprising that flowers survived Heinemann's call to asceticism unless they retained some Edenic symbolism. Evergreen trees surrounding the communal cemeteries were also undisturbed, and flowers and the evergreens remain the distinctive elements in the Amana landscape offering the "pleasures of the eye" (Fig. 8.8).

As a complement to agriculture, each village also developed crafts and industries. A blacksmith's shop, a cabinetmaker's shop, a general store, post office, bakery, dairy, wine cellar, and sawmill operated in most of the villages. The major industries were the mills in Amana and Middle Amana where woolen cloth was woven or cotton cloth dyed and printed as calico. A canal several miles long was designed and dug by the colonists between 1863 and 1866 to provide additional waterpower at these locations. Observers viewing the mills reported that labor-saving inventions seem to have been in use, but not patented.[14] Very comfortable en-

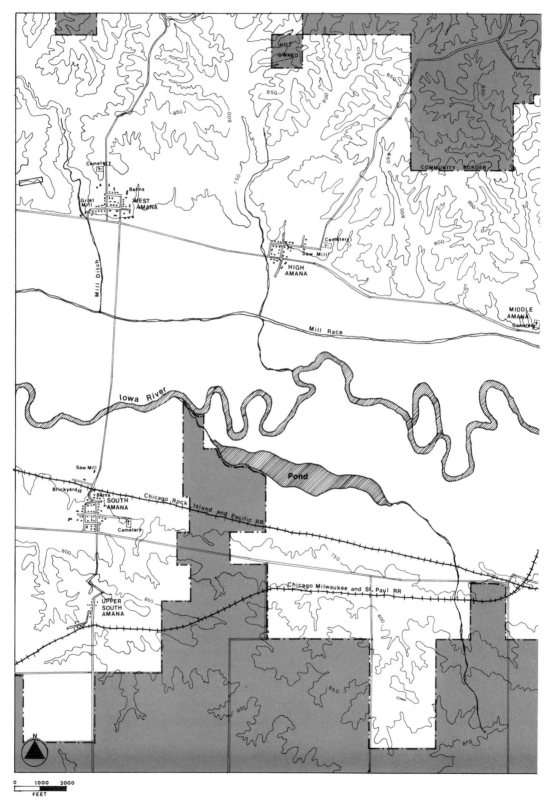

NOT
OWNED

850

850

800

750

COMMUNITY BORDER

650

800

850

Cemetery

Barns

Grist
Mill

WEST
AMANA

Mill Ditch

Cemetery

Saw Mill

HIGH
AMANA

MIDDLE
AMANA

Cemetery

Mill Race

Iowa River

Pond

Saw Mill

Brickyard

Barns

SOUTH
AMANA

Chicago Rock Island and Pacific RR

Cemetery

800

750

Chicago Milwaukee and St. Paul RR

UPPER
SOUTH
AMANA

850

800

850

850

850

N

0   1000   2000
FEET

8.4 Site plan, Amana Community, ca. 1880.

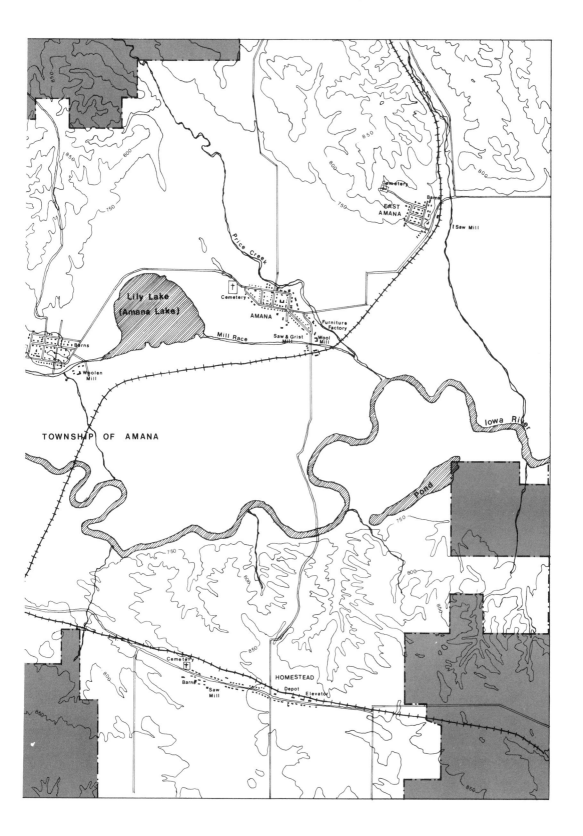

Communal Territory 233

8.5 Amana Community, land use, 1936.

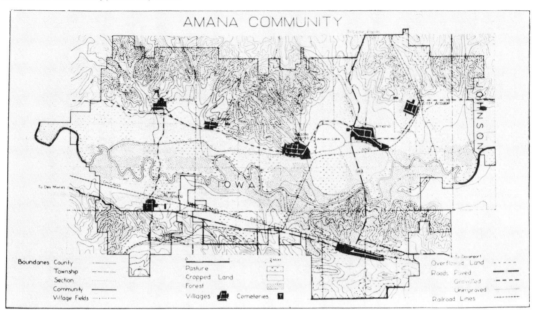

8.6 Former kitchen house, garden, and "foot street," 1973.

8.7 "Vegetables, trees, and fruit bearing bushes are
intermingled with flowers, with here and there a tiny
lawn interspersed, all the ground beautifully cared
for . . . ": Amana women working in a kitchen house
garden, 1932.

8.8 Communal cemetery with identical grave markers,
surrounded by evergreens, Amana, 1971.

Communal Territory   235

8.9 Middle Ebenezer and Lower Ebenezer, New York,
plans showing perimeter streets used as detours to
keep outsiders from entering the villages.

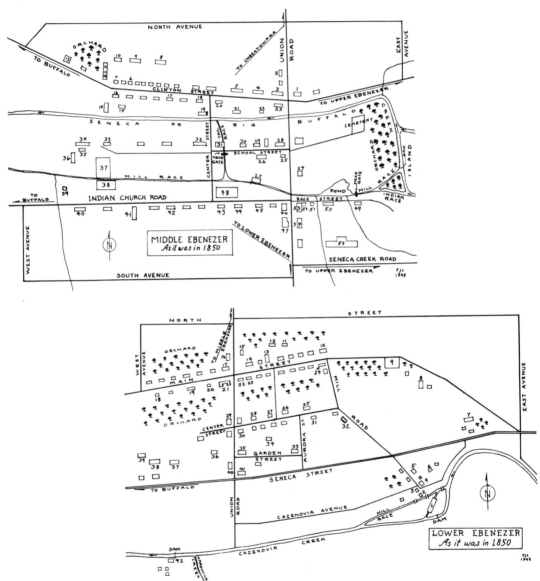

vironments seem to have been provided for the workers—cushioned seats were available so the operatives could sit, vases of flowers brightened the interiors, and tables for coffee breaks or lunch were placed in alcoves with cabinets of cutlery and china. Lest this seem like an overly glowing report, one visitor commented that in 1902 the regular schedule was ten hours per day, and in the busy season increased to thirteen and a half.[15]

Borders

Aside from retaining their German language in America, the Inspirationists at Amana do not seem to have taken too many steps to isolate themselves, since visitors frequently patronized their gristmills and sawmills and traded for their products, while hired laborers and even passing hoboes were housed at the borders of the villages. There is some evidence that around the turn of the century visitors were a nuisance— reportedly 1,200 per year in Main Amana in 1908.[16] Earlier Barbara Heinemann had proclaimed, "Thou shouldst erect a partition wall that the ungodly may no longer visit the community."[17] Raised street crossings in the various villages did have the effect of discouraging strangers with automobiles, but these were lowered about 1918.[18] In Ebenezer arrangements to prevent worldly traffic through the villages seem to have been quite elaborate (Fig. 8.9). An observer noted the presence of north, south, east, and west roads skirting the perimeter of each village, and the presence of gates at strategic entrances to the densely settled parts of the Inspirationists' territory, concluding that:

We might think that there was really no reason for these streets, inasmuch as there were no houses on them. . . . Obviously they were de-

tours . . . to keep out the offensive rubberneck tourist, and to check any influence the "world" might exert by the dress, and equippage, and manners of outsiders passing through.[19]

In contrast to this sheltered existence at Ebenezer, one reporter describes the young people of Homestead or South Amana in the early twentieth century: longing for a more exciting life, gathered at the railroad depots on the evenings when they had nothing else to do.[20] Were they hoping for glimpses of the dress and manners of "worldly" passengers on the trains passing through?

Borders between villages seem to have been defined as carefully as those of the larger domain. The land was divided into seven parcels corresponding to the separate villages established within it, and except for the biennial Love Feast (*Liebesmahl*), permission was necessary to visit an adjoining village for reasons other than work. Because each village was fairly self-sufficient, with craft shops, a dairy, and a bakery, trading between villages was minimized. Elders of the Great Council held their meetings in each of the different villages in rotation, but Shambaugh reported so little interchange between ordinary members that they claimed to be able to detect another member's home village through his or her dialect.[21]

Block and Path Systems

Many outsiders who visited the Amana villages described the towns as oriented around one "straggling street," the German *Strassendorf*.[22] One can contend that the residents viewed their villages differently, focusing their attention on the interiors of the blocks rather than on the streets, in accordance with the community's overall attitude stressing design as internal order rather than external display. Thus an observer with traditional ideas of streets would look down the main street of an Amana village and perceive a line of houses (Fig. 8.10). But Amana residents would concentrate on the interiors of the blocks, where a network of "foot streets" joined the houses with communal kitchen houses, turning each interior area into an active pedestrian space (Fig. 8.11).

The four Inspirationist towns at Ebenezer show the period of transition from linear village plans to internal block arrangements. Upper Ebenezer, built in 1843, is a strictly linear town, but Middle Ebenezer and Lower Ebenezer, built in 1842 and 1843 respectively, show a number of cross streets. (New Ebenezer, built in 1852, reverts to the strictly linear arrangement, but it was a factory site with few activities.) The churches and kitchen houses in Ebenezer do not seem to have been placed in any regular configuration. In this context it is important that the villages were quite isolated and perimeter roads kept outside traffic away from the settlements.

In Iowa the situation seems to have changed over time. Perimeter roads were not designed around the villages, and perhaps the inward turning block structure was established to compensate for them. Amana and West Amana, the first two settlements built by the Inspirationists in 1855 and 1856, show linear streets, although the block structure is regularized and developed off to one side. South, High, and East Amana, built in 1856, 1857, and 1860, show the typical block structure. Middle Amana, planned in 1862, the only village for which an original plat exists, was clearly conceived of as six blocks. Two exceptions exist, both railroad depots. Homestead was organized by other settlers and then purchased by the Inspirationists in 1861;

its plan is linear, severely constrained by the railroad. "Upper" South Amana is a linear afterthought to South Amana, an extension of one of the streets from South Amana to the railroad line, where a depot and hotel were established.

The structure of the inward-turning blocks which developed in all of the Amana villages except Homestead is shown most clearly in the plans of Main Amana and South Amana (Figs. 8.12, 8.13). In both cases six or seven residences and kitchen houses surround the block where the main church is located. The only access to the church is by the foot streets penetrating the center; the only access to the schools, which are located in side blocks, is by foot street; the same is true for the South Amana kindergarten. Thus the residences and kitchen houses surround and protect the communal institutions, and these centers of communal activity guarantee that the interiors of the blocks will be lively places, conducive to casual meetings. Despite Amana's change to a system of private property and corporate enterprise, the communal path systems still exist, now as concrete sidewalks rather than rough plank walks. They serve as excellent places for children to play, as well as for adults to meet their neighbors.[23] They foster the same sort of casual meetings as Fourier's street galleries and landscaped courtyards, lacking only the weather protection of the galleries.

8.10 Outsiders often saw Amana villages as one "straggling street": Main Amana, undated photograph.

8.11 Amana block, 1971.

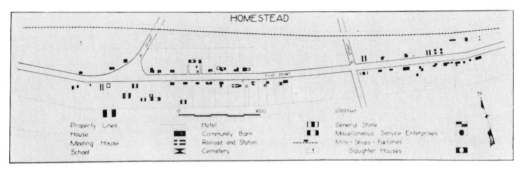

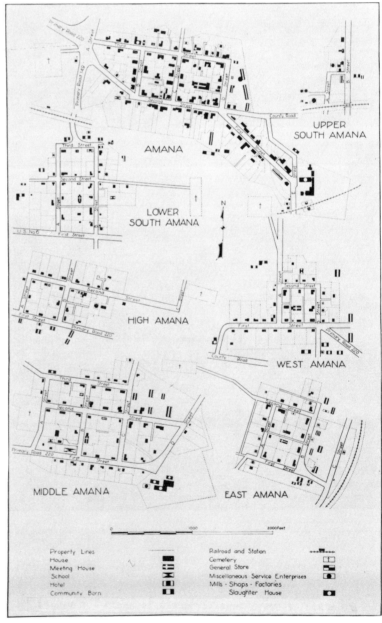

Communes within Communes   240

8.12 Perhaps the inward turning block structure was established to compensate for the lack of perimeter roads: Amana villages, town plans, 1936.

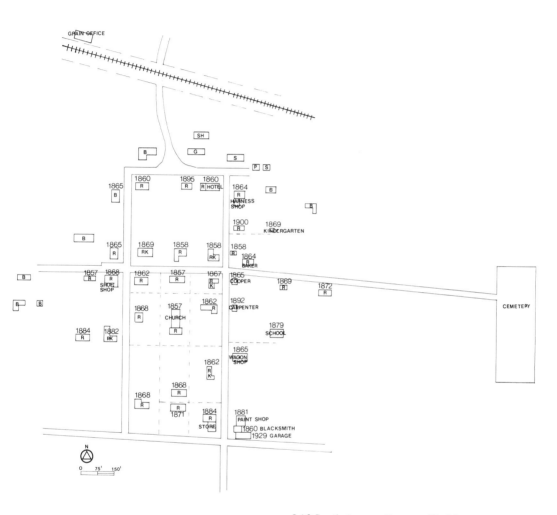

8.13 South Amana, diagram of building uses and dates of construction, 1932. Church, school, and kindergarten are reached by "foot streets," which foster the same sort of casual meetings as Fourier's street galleries and landscaped courtyards were designed to. Foot streets shown as dotted lines. *R*, communal residence; *K*, kitchen house; *B*, barn; *G*, granary; *S* shed; *H*, hired men's houses; *P*, post office.

Churches

Community for Amana residents was officially defined in terms of religion: "We are a church all the time, even in our homes," they said. [24] Amana residents attended church and prayer meetings more often than any other group discussed in these case studies, perhaps eleven times a week. Stone or brick churches in the villages resembled elongated houses, with one or two elders' residences built at the ends (Figs. 8.14, 8.15, 8.16). Villages had one or two churches, each with one to four meeting rooms, filled twice a week for simultaneous services for the separate classes. The largest meeting room in the main church of a village was used for general meetings of all ranks, which took place once a week; rooms in the neighborhood kitchen houses were used for daily prayer gatherings.

The Amana meetinghouse rooms were as severe as Shaker meeting rooms, but less beautifully finished and colored. Benches and floors were plain, scrubbed wood; walls were whitewashed light blue; a small table and benches for the presiding elders faced the congregation (Fig. 8.17). Worship consisted of long readings from the Bible and the testimonies of the *Werkzeuge*, and the singing of a few hymns. Although the community members came together frequently in the churches, sociability was not encouraged. Men and women sat on opposite sides of the room; women left the meeting before the men and dispersed immediately. Only one note of levity can be introduced in a description of the churches—the village wine cellar, from which each Inspirationist was assigned a yearly ration of homemade wine, was located in the basement of the church, just below the meeting rooms. This no doubt allowed the elder in residence to supervise the supply, but it seems an incongruous mixed use.

Kitchen Houses

Amana had fifty-two kitchen houses which have been called "the dynamic centers of the villages."[25] In appearance the kitchen houses resembled the ordinary residences, with larger extensions at the rear, which were the kitchens (Figs. 8.6, 8.18, 8.19). The second floors of the houses served as the kitchen bosses' (*Kuchenbas*) living quarters; the first floors, as communal dining rooms where thirty to fifty people came for three to five daily meals and evening prayer meetings. The provision of so many meals provoked a visitor to comment that "the constant coming and going gives one the idea that life is a continual scramble for something to eat."[26] Men and women downed the starchy fare at separate tables, and all observed silence. The main meals were eaten "rapidly, but with decorum," timed at fifteen minutes to half an hour.[27] Festivities at Amana, while somewhat muted, seem to have been most often celebrated at the kitchen houses. For weddings, fancy cakes and wine were served in the bride's kitchen house. At the *Liebesmahl* long services were interrupted with a special kitchen house meal. Even the solemn *Unterredung*, a yearly general confession which members seem to have dreaded, was accompanied by special meals for visiting elders at the kitchen houses.

Besides being centers for celebrations, the kitchen houses were sociable places to work. Eight or ten women under the direction of the *Kuchenbas* were responsible for cooking, setting tables, cultivating the kitchen house garden, and preserving their surplus produce. Wagons from the bakery, the dairy, and the slaughterhouse brought news as well as bread, milk, and meat to the kitchen house workers. One woman from Homestead claimed that her family depended on the kitchen house "for the only social life we knew, for snatches of gossip and legitimate news, and just ordinary companionship."[28]

Work at the kitchen houses seems to have been slow—day care was provided so that almost all women who did not have children under two years of age could be assigned to kitchen or garden work.[29] Labor-saving devices were not common in the kitchens (Fig. 8.19), so the Inspirationists do not seem to have used communal cooking to take advantage of either mechanization or economies of scale to free women's time. Work was strictly sex segregated, and whatever time the women did not spend at the kitchen house was spent in private housework, laundry, or sewing. Whatever their inefficiencies, throughout the society's history the kitchen houses were a bulwark of collective living. They were initiated in Ebenezer, and their breakdown preceded the dissolution of the communistic society and its replacement with a corporation. Shortly before 1932, when more and more Inspirationists took away food in baskets to be reheated on kerosene stoves for family meals at home, the communal dining rooms served only bachelors and hired hands. Their decline is often cited as a clear indicator of the lack of communal spirit in this period.[30]

Communal Dwellings

Complementing the Amana kitchen houses were the communal houses without kitchens where most of the Inspirationists lived (Figs. 8.10, 8.20). Some bachelors were housed in larger hotels, but most members lived in the typical two-story houses of unpainted wood, brick, or sandstone. The most common plan had a center hall, with two two-room suites on each floor. Some side hall plan houses were built as well. (Fig. 8.21 shows the standard

plan and Fig. 8.22 one of the many variations.)

It is not at all clear why the Inspirationists chose to build dozens of traditional single-family houses divided into suites, rather than erect a few communal residences on the scale of Shaker or Fourierist dwellings. One must also ask why the communal houses in Amana were often mistaken for single-family houses. The astute observer of many communities, Charles Nordhoff, wrote of Amana: "each family has its own house."[31] Was he encouraged in this mistaken interpretation by the Inspirationists, whose "Amana Heim" Museum is today presented as a single-family dwelling?

Possibly the Inspirationists' experience in Ebenezer led them to de-emphasize communality. The immigrants must have decided to abandon the monastic arrangements they had occupied on lease in Germany and follow single-family prototypes in building houses. Then, three or four families were assigned to each house, and the kitchen house system was developed, in order to give food and shelter to large groups of new arrivals. At some point during the 1840s, their first decade in America, the Inspirationists must have become aware of the furor that "unitary dwellings" could create. Most observers assumed that such arrangements implied free love and lax morals on the part of the inhabitants— even the celibate Shakers were presented with this accusation. So perhaps the Inspirationists made two decisions: one was to keep their houses as communal dwellings, because it was convenient; the other was to let outsiders assume that they saw single-family dwellings, rather than communal dwellings, because it would create less trouble. This may have been made easier by the association of certain families with certain houses over time. Elders retained the power of assigning members to living space. Nearly everyone was related, and any system of priorities for close relatives would create what appeared to be extended families or families with cousins as lodgers, very common arrangements in the rest of nineteenth century America.

Other communitarian groups experimented with an intermediate size of communal dwelling, striving for something midway between the unitary dwellings which Fourier proposed to encompass whole communities, and the single-family houses which groups like the Mormons and the Union Colonists developed as symbols of family stability and sources of financial investment in the community. A Moravian plan for Salem, North Carolina, drawn in 1765, shows uniform two-family houses, but most Moravian communities seem to have been built with a mixture of one-family houses and dormitories for single members.[32] The Harmonists tried various arrangements in the three towns they built before 1825. Harmony, Pennsylvania, was a town of single-family houses, but the group then gave up marriage for celibacy, and the towns of New Harmony, Indiana, and Economy, Pennsylvania (Fig. 8.23) include dormitories for single members and, apparently, houses with kitchens accommodating a communal family of about eight or ten members, some married and some single, which seem to be a close equivalent to the Amana arrangements.[33] French Icarian socialists in Nauvoo, Illinois, built wooden apartment houses (Fig. 8.24) about 1848 which resemble the Amana houses, but were more crowded. With eight rooms, they accommodated one family per room. One central dining hall served everyone at mealtimes.[34] Swedish Jansenists in Bishop Hill, Illinois, built between 1849 and 1851

what might have been the largest of all communal dwellings, "Big Brick," which included ninety-six one-room apartments. They seem to have had second thoughts and concentrated on building smaller communal dwellings between 1850 and 1860, creating two smaller dwellings (Fig. 8.25) with one- and two-room suites, still in use as apartments in 1947.[35]

All these dwellings are cited with a note of caution, since information on numbers of rooms and residents in communal dwellings is notoriously inaccurate and contradictory. What these examples do establish is that the small communal houses at Amana represented an important middle range of communitarian designs emphasized in Illinois and Iowa. When very large communal dwellings proved either too regimented or too unwieldy, and when the private home proved too much associated with private property, what many groups turned to was a compromise in the size of the dwelling which balanced community and privacy. Amana colonists seem to have achieved this balance and maintained it better than any other group.

How much privacy did the Inspirationists have in their homes? Inside the communally owned and built dwellings, private suites of two or more rooms were assigned to the members by the elders. Accounts of how much space members were given vary from the upper estimate of a private bedroom and sitting room for each person, plus a family sitting room, to a minimum of two rooms for a newly married couple.[36] One account of a Homestead family in the early twentieth century suggests extra space: the quarters for a mother and two children included a parlor used only on very rare occasions; a combination sitting room-dining room equipped with sink, kerosene stove, and table; and three bedrooms. Privacy did not en-

8.14 As many as eleven religious services were held per week: exterior of Inspirationist church, with attached residences, Main Amana, 1875.

8.15 Interior view of Inspirationist Church, Main Amana, 1875.

8.16 Inspirationist Church, Main Amana, 1971.

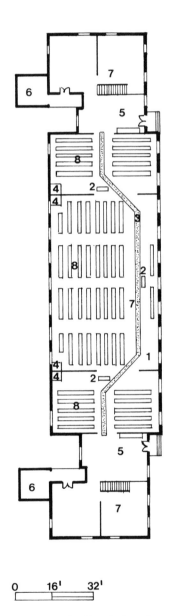

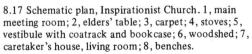

8.17 Schematic plan, Inspirationist Church. 1, main meeting room; 2, elders' table; 3, carpet; 4, stoves; 5, vestibule with coatrack and bookcase; 6, woodshed; 7, caretaker's house, living room; 8, benches.

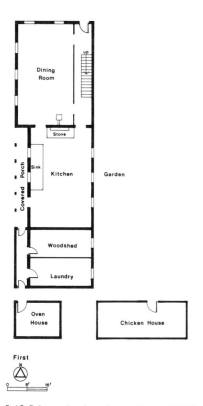

8.19 Inspirationists do not seem to have taken advantage of mechanization or economies of scale to free women's time: interior of Homestead kitchen house, showing sink at rear, brick stove at left, undated photograph.

8.18 Schematic plan of main floor of kitchen house. Kitchen boss lived above.

8.20 Typical frame and stone houses, Amana.

8.21 Schematic plan of typical Amana center hall house, which could have accommodated four families in two-room suites.

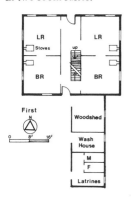

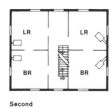

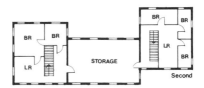

8.22 Schematic plan of Dr. Charles F. Noe House, Main Amana, showing three to five family suites, with a shared storage attic.

8.23 Dwellings built in New Harmony, Indiana, after 1824, left, communal house, right, bachelors' dormitory.

Community and Privacy   249

8.24 Communal houses with one-room apartments,
Icarian Community, Nauvoo, Illinois, ca. 1848.

8.25 Communal apartment house, with one- and two-
room apartments, Bishop Hill, Illinois, 1850-1860.

sue, however; the children's grandfather, an elder, lived on the floor below them, and fear of his disapproval caused the children to tiptoe about at play.[37] In a community where religious standing was so important, and religious censure so public, many adult residents must have felt constrained by their relatives' or neighbors' closeness as well.

Whether or not residents had enough privacy, the communal houses provided scope for private property. The suites in the houses were finished in light blue whitewash, and heated with iron stoves like the churches. All other interior decoration was up to the members, and all furnishings were private property, acquired as inheritances or gifts or purchased with the yearly cash allowance given to each member or with the proceeds from the private gardens and vines outside the houses. German heirlooms were highly prized. Most windows had "long, light colored calico curtains, . . . held back by tin clasps."[38] Pictures were forbidden; only religious images and mottoes in illuminated script (resembling the more austere Shaker spirit drawings) were permitted. The floors were covered with rag carpets tacked down in strips, and removed for twice-yearly cleanings. Amana horsehair mattresses seem to have been designed with the same cleanings in mind, in three sections for easy removal.[39] The overall appearance of the Amana apartments seems to have been clean and moderately comfortable; neither as spare as the Shakers' rooms nor as bourgeois as the Oneidans'. They were all fairly similar in quality, and any departure from traditional patterns of furnishing—such as one woman's attempt to purchase a bathtub with savings accumulated over years—would be met with reproof of worldliness by the elders.[40]

Replicable Buildings

Just as Inspirationist discipline maintained uniform domestic interiors, so it produced similar buildings in every village, but the approach to building was flexible enough to vary with local site conditions and materials. Less is known about the development of the design process among the Inspirationists than other groups, since only one drawn building plan exists. Probably centralized control was exercised more at Amana than among the Mormons or the Shakers. Only few general decisions were made by revelation, and there was no equivalent to the "Millennial Laws" or the "Plat of the City of Zion." The degree of consistency in Amana building measurements and detailing suggests that where revelation left off, the elders took up, perhaps with diagrams similar to those carried by traveling Shaker builders. The tradition may have been oral rather than written, however, as an old carpenter in Amana reports that he never worked from a plan but knows that houses were constructed with sixteen-foot bays, and halls eight feet wide.[41] Whatever the methods of transmitting their traditions, the Inspirationists in Amana developed an intentional vernacular style of building, based on the requirements of their communal program.

Perhaps the most striking feature of Amana's vernacular is the lack of various distinctive formal types besides the basic dwelling. Kitchen houses are dwellings with large additions at the rear; churches resemble dwellings stretched a few extra bays in length; stores and mills are similar to the churches; only barns are different (Figs. 8.26, 8.27, 8.28, 8.29). A uniform two-story scale prevails throughout the villages, broken only by factory smokestacks and the occasional fire tower or windmill (Fig. 8.30). The choice of similar structures to house most functions supports adaptation and mixed uses: residences are combined with churches, schoolhouses, kitchens, and workshops of all kinds. The lack of signs identifying activities adds to the impression of overall uniformity, and while visitors might complain of not being able to find places, this did not trouble the residents.[42]

The Inspirationists' standardized approach to building form was contradicted somewhat by their willingness to use whatever material was at hand: wood, locally made brick, or locally quarried sandstone. Materials varied slightly according to function, for there are many residences constructed entirely of unpainted wood (thought to be an economy since trees and labor were plentiful, and capital to buy paint was scarce), but few factories and no churches were built only of wood. Community records show that over half of the buildings constructed between 1855 and 1932 were adapted or enlarged at some later date, and it is common to find two or more materials used in such structures.[43] Detailing depended more upon building material than building function. Prominent keystones are used in some masonry arches, and dentil cornices and lintels are used in some brick structures, without distinction between factories, houses, and churches. A brick church looks more like a brick factory than a stone church; a stone church most closely resembles a stone residence or store.

Comparison between Inspirationist and Shaker uses of materials is revealing. The Shakers also based their vernacular style on residential prototypes which they enlarged and extended to meet various needs. But the Shakers exploited differences of materials, color, scale, and texture to distinguish functions. At Hancock, the large brick dwelling gains in contrast to the small frame meetinghouse, painted white, or a frame shop building, painted tan. These distinctions are then heightened by the Shakers' meticulous detailing; a shop stair is less elaborately finished than a dwelling stair, reinforcing the functional distinctions of building shape, color, and placement. The Shakers despised "architecture" as unnecessary aesthetic striving, but every nail, every board, every building, had its exact place in the Shaker world. Even a casual visitor could perceive this order, if not the concept of the Shaker society as a "living building" which lay behind it.

Like the Shakers, the Inspirationists averred that they were not interested in "architecture" but, unlike them, they were content to press for a rather stolid sameness in building. Weathered wood, brick, and sandstone form motley, earthcolored villages, restrained into orderly patterns by the uniformity of building heights and sizes and the regularity of block and path networks. They demonstrate competence rather than transcendent craft, but powerful competence, unusual in rural America. Perhaps the calculated but aesthetically unselfconscious solidity of their town plans and typical buildings could be faulted as a bit smug: in building, as in all their worldly activities, they succeeded, not by brilliant inspiration, but by eliminating mistakes.

Avoiding Uniqueness

For the Inspirationists, design was always a matter of internal order rather than external proselytizing. They did not need to use their model community as a tangible demonstration of visual uniqueness to advertise their religious doctrines, because they were not looking for recruits or admirers. In their unconcern for their public image, they resemble some socialist countries more than other nineteenth century socialist experiments.

Despite their unconcern with visual uniqueness, the Inspirationists produced the best-planned communistic settlement of their era. Developing their region as seven separate villages rather than launching seven isolated experiments, or one large experiment, helped to ensure that their economic base was diverse. Building small communal houses, and neighborhoods grouped around communal kitchen houses, helped to consolidate both privacy and community for residents. The innovative networks of "foot streets" linked private and communal territory effectively. All of this organization had a certain beauty—green fields, rolling terrain, and masses of flowers make Amana villages lovely places to be in the summer—but the planning achievements appeal more to the intellect than to the eyes. The arrangement of residential accommodation and circulation conveys a feeling of solidarity but lacks the imaginative appeal of a Shaker dwelling or a phalanstery.

Considering the communitarian goal of duplicating successful experiments, one can suggest that the Inspirationists did not recognize the full extent of their accomplishments, that they developed a replicable system but failed to try to reproduce it across the nation. (They did give advice and aid to the Hutterian Brethren, who are now the largest communitarian group in existence, with some 21,000 members in over 200 communities.)[44] It is probably more accurate to say that the Inspirationists recognized their own limitations and did not try to exceed them. The system of religious authority which restrained members from making mistakes in planning and design also kept them from active participation. This lack of participation is what ultimately destroyed the balance between community and privacy: community was perceived as too rigid, authoritarian, and boring. Without a communal ideology which incorporated participation, like the Shakers' involvement in a "living building" or the Oneidans' espousal of Perfectionism, members never had the pleasure of inventing a window latch, making a "spirit drawing," or redesigning the communal landscape to suit their personal vision. Religious authority was overtaxed, personal expression was suppressed, and any attempt to launch new experiments would only have quickened the ultimate dissolution.

The current residents of the Amana villages still harbor an unmet need for participation in design. The distinctive character of the domain has been based on a collective tradition involving residential prototypes, local materials, and consistent, plain detailing. The whole environment is much more than the sum of its parts. The network of communes with communal villages, within the larger communist (but not communal) domain, is fascinating because the systems of sharing are complex and the environmental structure supports the subtleties of the collective organization. However, the appeal of the Amana environment has always been underrated by observers used to the monuments, fetishes, and personal territory of capitalist society.

Now it seems that Amana residents themselves have come to undervalue their collective heritage. The "Great Change" of 1932 gave individuals their own houses and shares of stock in the Amana corporation; current prosperity results from corporate success with tourism as much as with wool and refrigerators. Individual remodelings and renovations reflect both prosperity and the long stifled desire for personal expression. Brick houses flash decorative aluminum screen doors, stone houses receive additions sheathed in blue aluminium siding (the old indifference to materials); restaurants in the old kitchen houses acquire plastic paneled interiors and neon signs; ornamental ducks and wheelbarrows sit on the lawns. Each building so transformed is subtracted from the village, set apart from the tight network of original houses, churches, mills, and barns. Because Amana's architecture lacks symbolic display it is especially vulnerable to this crass remodeling: demolition would almost be kinder. A flood of tourist pamphlets discussing the community's "unique collective organization" accompanies the steady erosion of the unique collective environment. Although some residents remember the society before 1932, and most are the descendants of members, none seem to recognize history repeating itself. Just as a need to participate in decisions changed the balance between communal and private territory in 1932, so the same need to participate in design is destroying the balance between unique and replicable buildings today.

8.26 Stores and mills are similar to the churches and the dwellings: general store and warehouse, Homestead, ca. 1870.

8.27 Warehouses, Homestead, ca. 1870, showing arched lintels.

8.28 Woolen mill, Amana, 1908.

8.29 Woolen mill and canal, Amana, 1974.

8.30 Weathered wood, brick, and sandstone form motley, earth-colored villages, restrained into orderly patterns by the uniformity of building heights and sizes:
view of Amana, 1875.

Notes to Chapter Eight

1 These precepts are listed in Bertha M. H. Shambaugh, *Amana That Was and Amana That Is*, (1932), New York, 1971, pp. 234-242, 243-244. The first part of this book is the major history of the community written in 1908 which I have used for general background information in this chapter.

2 Although these groups of German immigrants are usually considered communitarian socialists, their strategies differed from those of the great number of millennial or socialist communities. They limited proselytizing by retaining their native language, an aid to the isolation of their model communities, but a severe restriction on the audiences they could reach. The Moravians, Separatists, and Inspirationists also limited their commitment to socialism, espousing it only as a support for religious organization adopted during periods of hardship and transition.

The interconnections between these groups need elucidating. The Zoar community had a strong link with Ebenezer because Christian Metz recruited Carl Meyer, a Zoar Separatist, to become his leading legal and business adviser. See Francis Alan Duval, "Christian Metz, German-American Religious Leader and Pioneer," unpublished Ph.D. dissertation, Department of German, State University of Iowa, 1948, pp. 90-147.

3 Duval covers this period thoroughly. The Oneida Community also purchased former Indian land. Neither group had much compassion for the displaced Indians. Perhaps the Inspirationists moved west to get away from the "burned-over district," where the Shakers, Mormons, Fourierists, Oneidans, and other groups had all established settlements, as well as to move away from the "worldly" citizens of Buffalo.

4 Barbara S. Yambura, with Eunice W. Bodine, *A Change and A Parting: My Story of Amana*, Ames, Iowa, 1960, suggests the existence of a hereditary elite among the elders, who often chose their sons to succeed them or sent them for rare outside education as doctors or pharmacists (p. 144). Some families even considered the children of others within the commune not "good enough" for marriage (p. 176). This may have reflected the original class structure in Germany, when businessmen, factory workers, and farmers joined the church.

5 Shambaugh, *Amana*, p. 244. Metz had a daughter by a woman he did not marry who died in childbirth, so his guilt may have been a source of his later moralizing on marriage. See Yambura, *A Change*, p. 170.

6 Yambura, *A Change*, pp. 174-175. This is the only extensive account of daily life in Amana written by a resident which I have been able to locate.

7 Charles Nordhoff, *The Communistic Societies of the United States* (1875), New York, 1966, p. 117.

8 H. Guy Roberts and Tom White, surveyors, letter to Charles R. Fischer, State Securities Department, Des Moines, Feb. 23, 1932. Shambaugh gives slightly different figures for 1908, p. 85.

9 Darrell H. Davis, "Amana: A Study of Occupance," *Economic Geography*, 12.3 (July 1936), 223.

10 Ruth Geraldine Snyder, "The Arts and Crafts of the Amana Society," unpublished M.A. thesis, Department of Fine Arts, State University of Iowa, 1949, p. 23.

11 Richard T. Ely, "Study of Religious Communism," *Harper's Magazine* 105 (Oct. 1902), 659-668, reprinted in *The Palimpsest*, 52.4 (Apr. 1971), 193-194. He also admired the "school forest" cultivated by the children, and commented on the profusion of birdhouses, still a feature in the Amana landscape.

12 Shambaugh, *Amana* p. 89. The Shakers did not allow flowers at all. In most aspects of design the Inspirationists were less rigid than the Shakers. This is the one example of lack of discipline which works in their favor aesthetically.

13 William Alfred Hinds, *American Communities*, Chicago, 1902, p. 280.

14 Shambaugh, *Amana*, p. 157.

15 Ely, "Religious Communism," p. 185. He saw no flowers in the factories.

16 Shambaugh, *Amana*, p. 91.

17 Ibid., p. 325, n. 184. This must have been before 1883. In 1875 Nordhoff reported that farmers from the surrounding area coming to sell wool in Amana would bring their families and be welcomed at "the little inn" (*Communistic Societies*, p. 405).

18 Millard Millburn Rice, "Eighty-Nine Years of Collective Living," *Harper's Magazine*, 177 (Oct. 1938), 522-527, reprinted in *The Palimpsest*, 52.4 (Apr. 1971), 205.

19 Frank J. Lankes, *The Ebenezer Community of True Inspiration*, Gardenville, N. Y., 1949, pp. 95-96.

20 "How It Was in the Community Kitchen," published by Marie's Gift Shop, Middle Amana, Iowa, n.d. (1973?), p. 17.

21 Shambaugh, *Amana*, p. 318, n. 142.

22 Nordhoff, *Communistic Societies*, p. 32; Davis, "Amana: A Study of Occupance," p. 226.

23 During my visits to Amana, I noticed a difference in sociability (or protectiveness). On the streets, I was just another tourist, but on the foot streets inside each block, residents greeted me and chatted about what I was doing.

24 Shambaugh, *Amana*, p. 272. On the number and location of services, see p. 269 and p. 413.

25 Yambura, *A Change*, p. 79. There were fifty-two kitchens at the peak of population, about 1890, according to Shambaugh, *Amana*, p. 411.

26 Lulu MacClure, "Life in Amana" (ca. 1885), *The Palimpsest*, 52.4 (Apr. 1971), 221.

27 Nordhoff, *Communistic Societies*, p. 33; "How It Was In the Community Kitchen," p. 7.

28 Yambura, *A Change*, p. 79. Also see "How It Was In the Community Kitchen."

29 The nursery was a small, one-room frame building in each village where two to four women tended a dozen children one to five years old. Lulu MacClure described one as furnished with "a chair, two tiny tables, high-backed benches, a wire screened stove, . . . a good Dutch cradle, wide enough to make six children comfortable" (p. 220). Outside was a wide porch with benches, a large grape arbor, and, in its shade, a great sand pile. The Museum of Amana History has a display reconstructing this scene.

30 Yambura, *A Change*, p. 7.

31 Nordhoff, *Communistic Societies*, p. 30. At another point in his chapter (p. 32) he says, "Each family has a house for itself, though when a young couple marry they commonly go to live with the parents of one or the other for some years."

32 John W. Reps, *The Making of Urban America*, Princeton, 1965, p. 451; also see W.J. Murtagh, *Moravian Architecture and Town Planning*, Chapel Hill, N.C., 1967.

33 John W. Larner, "Nails and Sundrie Medicines," *Western Pennsylvania Historical Magazine*, 45.2 (June 1962), 115-138; and 45.3 (Sept. 1962), 209-227.

34 "Icarian Influence on Temple Square," Nauvoo (Ill.) *Independent*, Apr. 5, 1972, p. 8.

35 Delmar LeRoy Nordquist, "The Development of An Immigrant Community in Architecture, Arts and Crafts," unpublished M.A. thesis, Department of Art, State University of Iowa, 1947, p. 33.

36 Nordhoff, *Communistic Societies*, p. 33, writes that they "have often a bed in what New-Englanders would call the parlor." Shambaugh produces both the most generous and most minimal estimates, pp. 125-127. As families grew, so did space allocations, which should explain most of the contradictions in estimates.

37 Yambura, *A Change*, p. 45.

38 MacClure, "Life in Amana," p. 215.

39 Yambura, *A Change*, p. 122.

40 Ibid., pp. 234-240.

41 Peter Marris, interview with Dan Turner, Main Amana, April 16, 1974.

42 MacClure, "Life in Amana," p. 216.

43 Amana Society, "Village Appraisals," 2 vols., held by the Amana Society's main office, Amana, Iowa.

44 John A. Hostetler, *Hutterite Society*, Baltimore, 1975.

9 The Disintegration of Association

... The highest ambition of a family should be to have a comfortable, and, if possible, an elegant home, surrounded by orchards and ornamental grounds, on lands of its own.

—Nathan Meeker, addressing residents of Greeley, Colorado, 1870

9.1 Union Colony members posed in front of the colony headquarters, 1870.

The Shakers were described as unnatural, the Oneidans as immoral, and the Mormons as peculiar, but the members of Union Colony Number 1 received more praise than abuse from their contemporaries (Fig. 9.1). The town which they founded in 1869, Greeley, Colorado, is today a stock-raising, farming, and university center of 40,000 people. Yet despite steady growth, Greeley is a rather disappointing communitarian experiment, for within four years of its founding the colonists had abandoned most of their communal institutions and created a town indistinguishable from dozens of others in the region. Greeley demonstrates how easily communitarian idealism could disintegrate through too much emphasis on privacy and private property. Or, to put it another way, Greeley's history helps to clarify the relationship of communitarian settlements to other American frontier towns, since the colony came closer and closer to the norm as each communal institution was discarded.

The founder of Greeley had visited the Shakers, Mormons, Fourierists, and Oneidans before planning the Union Colony, and he drew from these experiments Fourierist vagueness about economic "Association" and Mormon idealization of the single-family home, two of the weakest features of these four communal systems. Members of the Union Colony wanted community, but they were unwilling to adopt any religious, social, or economic practice which threatened the family or individual initiative. They sought a rational, voluntary, cooperative community, without much understanding of economic planning or environmental design, and after a frantic year of town building, they discovered, with some dismay, that communal life had been sacrificed for economic growth. Greeley's ambivalence about privacy and property reflected the confusion of all communitarians after the Civil War, when idealists increasingly sought literary solace, the evolutionary, costless socialism of William Dean Howells's *Altrurian Romances* or Edward Bellamy's *Looking Backward*. Greeley's leader, Nathan Meeker, encompassed in his own life this attenuation of communitarian idealism and, characteristically, he was always more at ease writing about ideal communities than organizing them.

Nathan Cook Meeker was born in Euclid, Ohio, in 1817, and seems to have been a wanderer from his late teens, writing poetry, working as a journalist in New Orleans and New York, teaching in Allentown, Pennsylvania, and Orange, New Jersey. In 1844 he married Arvilla Delight Smith, and they joined the Trumbull Phalanx, a Fourierist community of about 200 people in Braceville, Ohio. Life in this Association seemed a great social undertaking, which Meeker described with a metaphor of exploration:

. . . a few caravels have adventured across the unknown ocean, and are now, at the dawn of a new day, drawing nigh unto strange shores, covered with green, and loading the breeze with the fragrance of unseen flowers.[1]

Communal life at Trumbull was conducted in temporary communal dwellings, but he expected that the future phalanstery, "the magnificent palace of the Combined Order, will equally shame the temples of antiquity and the card-houses of modern days."[2] Within three years Trumbull's members had abandoned their experiment, discouraged by sickness and lack of resources. Meeker's considered view of this commune was bitter: some members shirked work; others conspired for power. "Here," he declared, "I *learned how much cooperation people would bear.*"[3] Meeker also seems to have developed an aversion to the Trumbull Phalanx's communal housing, for in later life he shunned the Fourierist view that the collective dwelling could foster a strong sense of community and insisted that family dwellings must be the basis of the community design.

Following the dissolution of the Trumbull Phalanx in 1847, Meeker exercised his social idealism in fiction. In "The Adventures of Captain Armstrong," an unpublished novel, he described a South Pacific island where natives designed successful communitarian settlements.[4] From fiction he turned to journalism again, writing for the Cleveland *Plain Dealer*, and then for the New York *Tribune*, first as a war correspondent, then as agricultural editor. "Reform" subjects made his reputation: an analysis of the dissolution of the North American Phalanx and a glowing series on the Oneida Community were followed by pieces on such subjects as workers' control in Troy, New York, and model tenement houses suitable for cooperative housekeeping in Boston.[5] As one of the leading American writers on community, Meeker was sent to Utah in 1869 to do a series of articles on Mormon towns in the Great Basin. Snowstorms kept him from Salt Lake City, but he saw a great deal of Colorado in the company of two railroad land agents and returned to New York with a vision of founding a communitarian settlement in the West.[6]

Meeker used his journalistic reputation to launch his proposal for "A Western Colony," published in the *Tribune* in December 1869. Five thousand letters of inquiry resulted.[7] An organizational meeting was held and an executive committee empowered to choose a specific location in Colorado, write a constitution, and handle the colony's financial affairs (Fig. 9.2). Some 442 members joined immediately, perhaps one-half farmers, one-third artisans, and the remainder small business owners, many of them residing in counties where successful communistic settlements existed.[8] It is difficult to guess how much economic cooperation or social cohesion the members expected from Meeker's new community, since anyone who paid a $155 membership fee was admitted, but a communal budget of over $100,000 promised to provide substantial collectively owned improvements. Although Meeker proposed that the colony should emphasize cooperative industry and cooperative housekeeping, he promised to allow private property and to keep the nuclear family intact. Collective land purchase, irrigation, and fencing (Fig. 9.3) were organized to support individual ownership of residential, business, and farm land. This program was much like the Mormon arrangements in Salt Lake City, but it lacked religious sanctions to enforce cooperation. Like the North American and Trumbull Phalanxes, it was to be a Christian but nonsectarian community. Temperance was the only official doctrine; Greeley became the third temperance town in the United States, following the example of Vineland, New Jersey, and Evanston, Illinois.

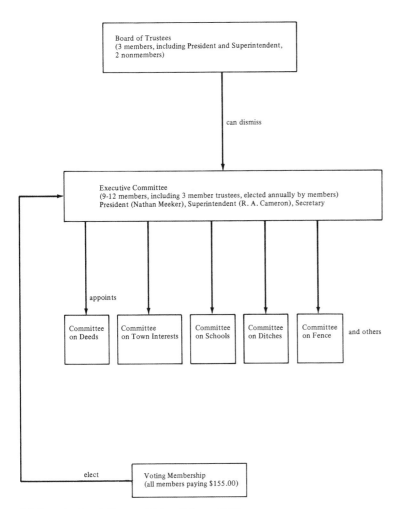

9.2 Organizational diagram, Union Colony, 1870.

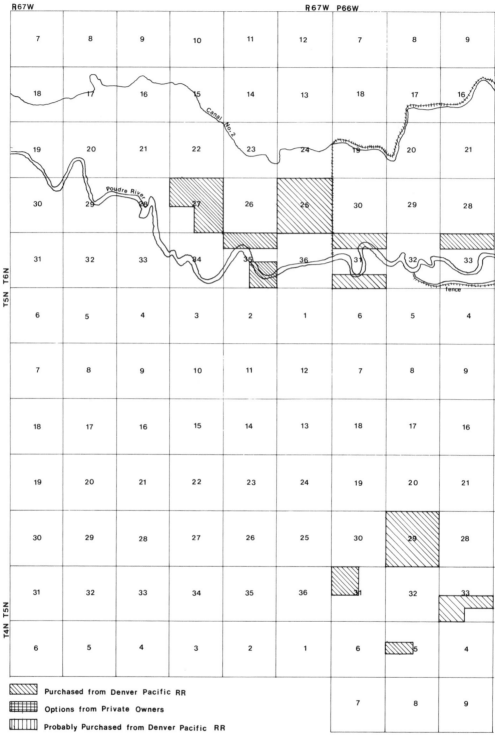

9.3 Collective land purchase, irrigation and fencing supported individual land ownership: diagram of land ownership showing canals, land purchased from Denver Pacific Railroad, land held on option from private buyers. Even-numbered sections were homestead land, some of which was held on option by colonists.

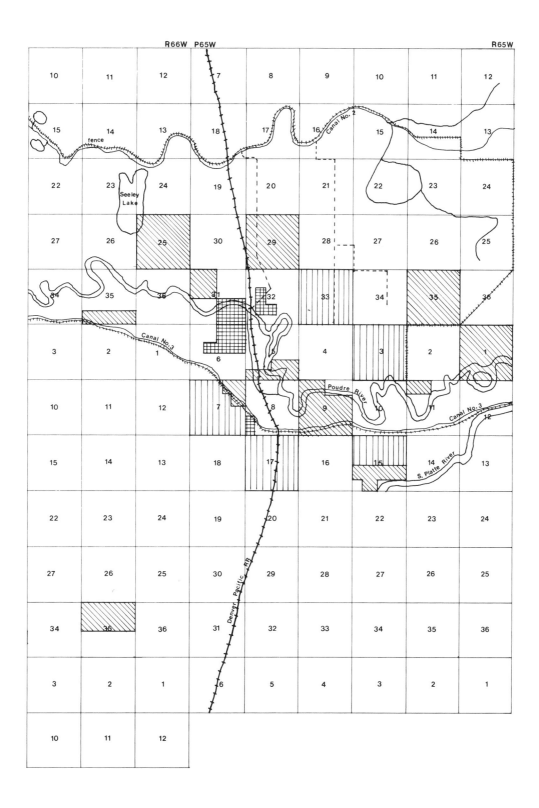

The Disintegration of Association   265

The Rocky Mountains of Colorado were grand and romantic, with what one Greeley writer described as "parti-colored rocks . . . [appearing] as if all the paint shops in the universe had emptied upon the massive mountains,"[9] but the flat land to the east was commonly known as "The Great American Desert." Meeker borrowed the vocabulary of geologists and irrigation engineers to persuade colonists that what was called desert would make ideal farmland. He began by arguing that the fertile soil of the midwestern prairies was simply the residue of the better soil in Colorado:

. . . mountains once stood upon this
ground . . . by glacial and other powerful
action . . . the lighter material was born away
from this great storehouse of fertility far east-
ward, forming the soil of the great Prairie
States.[10]

Of course the Colorado soil needed irrigation, but Meeker argued that "irrigation is preferable to rain. . . . Production will be greater here than anywhere else,"[11] following William Byers, chief promoter of railroad lands in Colorado, who described the land as "a savings bank crammed with riches since Noah's flood—and therefore ready to honor drafts for an unlimited amount; for irrigated land never wears out. . . ."[12] Biblical sanction for the process of irrigation was inferred by irrelevant Edenic reference:

That a country where irrigation is a necessity, is
favorable to health and human development,
would seem evident from the fact that the first
human pair precious in the sight of their Cre-
ator—were placed in the garden of Eden, which
was watered by a river.[13]

And Meeker described the town of Greeley, seen from the mountains, as a garden in miniature, "the lots being beds, and the streets, paths; even though it is only 90 days since a plow turned the first furrow."[14]

9.4 Conjectural site plan, Union Colony, 1871, showing approximate community boundary.

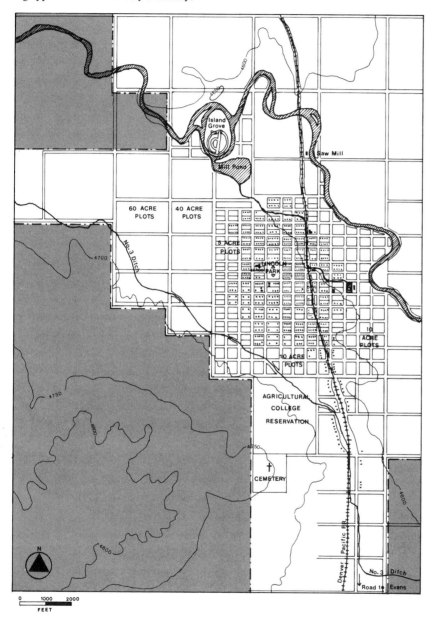

9.5 It resembled a land speculator's map, marking
anonymous plots to be sold to anonymous buyers:
town plan, Greeley, 1871.

9.6 "Village Improvement from the Foundations,"
view across Lincoln Park and Luna Lake, 1870.

9.7 Lincoln Park, ca. 1871, with newly planted trees,
Luna Lake on left, Baptist Church on right.

Edenic Rhetoric   269

If the Union Colonists' idealism about the fertility of their soil and the possibilities for irrigation was unbounded, idealism about their town plan was lacking. During the single public meeting which was held to discuss the town's layout, Meeker proposed Northampton, Massachusetts, his mother's home, as a model, while Horace Greeley recommended Londonderry, New Hampshire.[15] Although they wished to cluster dwellings in the manner of Puritan or Mormon villages, neither appreciated complex land allocation according to topography in New England Puritan settlements. Meeker also praised Salt Lake City as a "model for those who would build towns,"[16] but he seems to have admired Mormon grids and irrigation systems without any understanding of the Mormon residential styles, neighborhood patterns, or communal buildings discussed in Chapter 5.

An unimaginative grid (Figs. 9.4, 9.5) was laid out for Greeley, with the east-west streets named for trees and the north-south streets named for famous men. Lincoln Park, a rectangle ornamented with moon-shaped and ear-shaped artificial lakes named Luna and Auricular, was to be complemented by double rows of shade trees lining every street (Figs. 9.6, 9.7). A picturesque park called "Island Grove" was sited north of the town. According to one resident's reminiscences, Greeley offered "village improvement from the foundations," referring to popular tree-planting "village improvement" campaigns.[17] Unlike the community plans developed by the Shakers, Fourierists, Oneidans, and Inspirationists, the Greeley plan lacked communal territory. More than anything else it resembled a land speculator's map, marking anonymous plots to be sold to anonymous buyers.

Outside the town of Greeley, the Union Colony promised to provide irrigated farmland suitable for growing wheat, sugar beets, and potatoes, among other crops. The organizers promised water from the Cache la Poudre River to irrigate all plots, based on an estimate of $20,000 needed for four canals to serve 112,000 acres, which were either owned outright or under option.[18] When the first canal (Fig. 9.8) was opened, water was described as "dancing through the flumes like a ministering angel, scattering blessings all along its path."[19] Despite this angelic vision, most of the crops were lost for lack of water. After several unsuccessful attempts to bring water through canals which were too small or inadequately graded, the wealthier farmers and outside investors joined forces to raise over $400,000 to build adequate canals. The original estimate was only 5 percent of the total cost. Greeley colonists took the lead in introducing irrigation to other Colorado communities, and some of them developed inventions which contributed to the irrigation technology of the time. However, the small farmers of the Union Colony were forced to abandon their hopes of a cooperative water supply, and many of them chose to sell out and move elsewhere because of the high cost of water in Greeley.

The Union Colonists also underestimated the problems of collective fencing. When members of the Colony's locating committee first saw the Greeley site, it was a field where two hundred head of cattle were grazing, and this pastoral touch encouraged them to purchase it. But as soon as farmers began to cultivate the prairie, they had to contend with hungry range cattle who attempted to devour their crops. Unlike other communitarians, the Union Colonists never wished to emphasize their separation

9.8 Water danced through the flumes "like a ministering angel": first water from Number 3 Ditch, Greeley, 1870.

from their neighbors, but the easiest way to keep the cattle out seemed to be to fence the colony in. Work on a colony fence began in 1871 under divine sanction invoked by a journalist: "Heaven itself is fenced, and no anti-fence man can ever enter there."[20] It promised visual uniqueness as well as security, since Meeker claimed that there was no other fence "enclosing so many pieces of land owned by different persons anywhere else in the world."[21] Thirty-three-foot horizontal posts, seven-foot vertical posts, and iron wire were used, at a staggering cost of about $400 per mile. The fence extended approximately forty miles but was never finished because the Union Colony ran out of money. A group of farmers purchased it from the colony in 1874; most Greeley farmers had switched over to individual barbed wire fences by 1890.

Compared with irrigation ditches and the colony fence, shade and fruit trees were a relatively small item in the colony budget, but even this contribution to an Edenic landscape met with disaster. Seedlings were purchased in Illinois and transported to the site in the spring of 1870, where they withered for lack of water. They were revived and planted in midsummer; then they either died in the winter or were consumed by a plague of grasshoppers which descended the following spring. Some colonists persisted in planting more trees, and eventually had better luck, but Greeley's self-chosen title of "Garden City" was not won without a sruggle.

The farmers of Greeley formed a faction to agitate for colony funds to be spent on ditches and fences. Those who came to start businesses hoped that colony funds would be spent on incentives to build up industry in the town. Inducements to capitalists were first advertised in 1869 and 1870, when the colony feared a lack of resources. "Friendly" capitalists were invited to purchase vacant homestead land surrounding the colony, but even a promise of 50 percent interest produced no volunteers.[22] Colonists then offered suitable sites free of rent to mills, factories, and a large hotel.[23] For the hotel bonus, stone, concrete, or brick construction of at least ninety rooms was stipulated, a gigantic size in line with the optimistic prediction of a total population of 100,000 by 1880. There were no takers. To entice the S. S. Kennedy Company to settle in Greeley, the colony spent $10,000 to develop a millrace in 1871, which flooded so much land that many settlers had to be relocated at additional expense. The colony's Executive Committee also used its power to build public buildings to help private investors. A temporary Union Colony headquarters was erected in 1870 with 50 percent colony capital. In 1872, upon refund of the loan plus interest, the builder was full owner of the largest building in town, on a centrally located plot.

In contrast to the leaders' concern for major investors, there was no financial support for the "Co-operative Stock and Dairy Association." Although this was the largest collective enterprise undertaken by community members, it was undersubscribed and lost most of its cattle in the harsh winter of 1871-1872. Plans for building a cooperative laundry and bakery were never pursued, perhaps because of the inherent challenge they presented to domestic organization. Meeker attempted to guide economic planning through editorials in the Greeley *Tribune*, but his writing reflected total inability to perceive conflicts of interest. He held the Associationist view, first advanced by Fourier, that capitalists could easily be converted to cooperation once they had joined the community, but incentives to capitalists, plus poor management of collective resources, undermined the prospects of economic cooperation in Greeley. Meeker thought that cooperation would produce vast profits because it represented a rational evolution of capitalism. Unlike the Shakers, who believed communism and capitalism were antithetical, like heaven and hell, and set to work to develop a communistic economy, Meeker and the Union Colonists just waited for the rational, moral system of cooperation to take hold. And waited. . . .

Idealism frustrated in communal planning, irrigation, and industries was channeled into the construction of over 300 single-family homes in the colony's first year. The notice announcing the foundation of the colony stated that ". . . happiness, wealth, and the glory of the state spring from the family" and went on to exhort prospective members to "labor with the best efforts life and strength can give to make the home comfortable, to beautify and adorn it, and to supply it with whatever will make it attractive and loved."[24] In his "Prospectus" for the Greeley *Tribune*, Meeker repeated these sentiments: ". . . The highest ambition of a family should be to have a comfortable, and if possible, an elegant home, surrounded by orchards and ornamental grounds, on lands of its own."[25] He sounds like Catharine Beecher, advocating the model family commonwealth as the "Heaven-devised unit of the family state," or Brigham Young, encouraging Mormons to labor so that "angels may delight to come and visit" their habitations.[26] A model communal home like the North American Phalanstery or the Oneida Mansion House might be sufficient to absorb its members' collective idealism, but model single-family homes always produced isolation, even when they were ideologically tied to communal goals like the Mormon religious kingdom.

Although Meeker himself had been a homeless man, a wanderer most of his life who had uprooted his own wife and children to preach domesticity in Greeley, he attempted to set an example for the other Union Colonists by constructing a substantial adobe house for his family. Perhaps he was imitating Mormon domestic architecture without knowing exactly how it had evolved as a millennial religious symbol. Some colonists lived in shanties and others gathered in a communal dwelling named the "Hotel de Comfort" during the first months of settlement (Figs. 9.9, 9.10), but Meeker constantly chided them all and encouraged them to build houses. In one editorial he reproved "our young men" living in "Bachelor's Hall" for their lack of refinement;[27] in another, he praised the "educated mechanics" of Greeley as those "who know quite well what a nice house should be and who are able and anxious of themselves to build it."[28] In addition to building his own house (Figs. 9.11, 9.12), Meeker planned to build a model furnished cottage to rent to invalids, and if the model, with "all the comforts of one's own home,"[29] proved to be a success, he envisioned a rest cure industry flourishing in Greeley.

This emphasis on single-family homes and domestic life can be viewed as a shortsighted call for financial and emotional investment in the colony. The colony's rules provided that residence lots must be improved within one year, or the members would not be issued deeds to the land. A few colonists tried to pass muster with shanties or claim jumpers' houses on wheels, but the houseproud outnumbered the shiftless. Idealism about the family home was fervent and overlooked the isolation of women. Thus the deliberate exclusion of women from Mormon communal life was repeated in an unconscious way in Greeley. Meeker claimed to support women's efforts to learn typesetting, agricultural skills, and public speaking. The colonists were quite familiar with collective cooking, cleaning, and child care, which the Shakers, the Oneidans, and the Fourierists adopted in order to change women's roles within their communities. Meeker had written an article in praise of various proposals for cooperative industries run by women, but private male chauvinism contradicted his published support for cooperative housekeeping: "...A woman is weak unless she can have a comfortable house; and a man is not only weak but untidy unless he has a housekeeper."[30] His promise to preserve the nuclear family in Greeley led him to approve the domestic isolation of women: women showed themselves little in public during the first year of the colony's existence, and Meeker proudly reported that they were struggling to make their dress neat and their homes elegant.[31]

9.9 Main Street, Greeley, 1870.

9.10 "Hotel de Comfort," structure moved to Greeley from Cheyenne, Wyoming, by rail in 1870, for use as a communal dwelling. Later it was called "The Tabernacle" and used for colony meetings and religious services. It then became a school, and finally, in 1880, at the time of this sketch, was used as a livery stable.

9.11 "The highest ambition of a family should be to
have a comfortable, and if possible, an elegant home":
sod house, Greeley.

9.12 Nathan Meeker House, adobe, Greeley, 1870.

As soon as their town plan had been laid out and residential lots assigned, the thousand-odd residents of the Union Colony behaved as if there were very few collective decisions to be made about communal and private territory, since their communal institutions were voluntary ones. During the first year of the community's existence, members were constantly active in colony meetings, religious services, lyceum discussions, and Farmers' Club meetings. These voluntary institutions sustained the communal life, in place of communal work, but their meeting places were temporary ones. The community did erect a large school in 1873, but its use was mainly for classes (Fig. 9.13). The lack of communal space was especially serious because casual sociability in the semipublic spaces such as offices and shops was discouraged in favor of domesticity.

Meeker hoped to establish a Union Church in Greeley, with a minister who preached about cooperation, but soon after arriving in Greeley members of various sects demanded different ministers. The colony then donated land to five congregations, and two of them built churches and all appointed clergy by 1872 (Fig. 9.14). Religious jealousies destroyed Greeley's two lyceums, which met weekly for political, scientific, or philosophical debates, because some ministers felt that the lyceums infringed upon doctrinal subjects and asked their parishioners not to attend. The lyceums lasted until 1873 or 1874, about as long as the Farmers' Club, which sponsored lectures and discussions and supported the allocation of colony money to communal ditches and communal fences, but dissolved when some farmers went bankrupt and others joined the Grange.

It is tempting to speculate that the lyceums and the Farmers' Club might have flourished if

they had had adequate communal meeting space. Secret societies such as the Odd Fellows, the Grand Army of the Republic, the Freemasons, the Good Templars, the Knights of Pythias, and the Ancient Order of United Workmen replaced the lyceums, and the Grange replaced the Farmers' Club. The first three of these groups had built a large communal meeting hall on land which had been donated to them by the colony in 1871; the Grange also established a permanent hall.

In contrast to the secret societies, the colony had deliberately refused to create any permanent gathering places. The colony office was cramped and temporary, and the "Hotel de Comfort" was used as a boardinghouse and a school as well as for public meetings. Only the Greeley parks, the public schools, and the public reading room were planned as permanent communal facilities, and their uses were obviously limited. Meeker was complacent about the lack of space for social meetings and casual contacts. In 1870 he wrote an article called "Lounging Places" which rejects the Colony office (too small), the bank (privacy enforced), the Greeley Hotel (too many guests), the printing office (too noisy), and the barber shop (haircuts enforced). Meeker's conclusion is to recommend HOME: "the best place in town or in the world and it ought to be patronized more."[32]

Looking at the commercial and residential buildings which were erected in Greeley, one finds small frame and brick stores (Figs. 9.15, 9.16), then larger brick business blocks (Figs. 9.17, 9.18, 9.19) in the central area, all completely separated from the frame houses in the residential areas. There was no close integration of workshops and residences as at Amana or Nauvoo, and there were no neighborhood services, since the town plan marked some lots as commercial, others as residential, and emphasized these divisions. Individuals built what they liked, free from restrictions about materials or styles, unaided by design guidelines like the "Plat of the City of Zion" or the Millennial Laws. Most of the construction was done by residents and the town's forty-odd carpenters; absentee architects sent plans for the school and at least one church. Commercial and domestic building budgets and styles reflected competition for social status; straggling blocks of unrelated buildings were the result. During the first years of feverish building activity, residents may have felt united in their struggle to build up the town, but when building stopped and they had time to step back and survey the results, they found that they hadn't built in unison at all (Fig. 9.20).

The environment reflected, quite accurately, the social structure Meeker described in 1870: an emerging class system within the colony, a hierarchy of "educated mechanics," farmers, "well-educated" farmers, teachers and agents, politicians, ministers, and professionals. He commented that "a silent and unconscious struggle" was going on between the politicians and the educated industrial class but failed to commit himself, saying vaguely that ". . . if the politicians lose their power, and a more practical class succeed them a great change will have taken place."[33] The struggle was resolved by the Union Colony's incompetence in collective irrigation, incompletion of collective fencing, support of private industry, inattention to cooperative industry, and obsession with private houses. In June 1871 the colonists voted to replace the Union Colony's officers with an elected town government. A month later, land sales were open to the general public. Less prosperous colonists were bought out by the wealthier ones, and it became clearer and clearer that the community would be a "success," for only the "successful" could afford to remain.

9.13 Meeker Public School, 1873, W. J. H. Nichols,
architect.

9.14 Methodist Church, Greeley, 1871.

9.15 Individuals built what they liked, free from restrictions, unaided by design guidelines: E. C. Monk, Groceries, Drygoods, Boots and Shoes, Eighth Street, Greeley, 1870.

9.16 Greeley House, the first hotel, set up in a frame structure moved from Evans, Colorado, and other early commercial buildings, around 1871.

9.17 Oasis Hotel, Greeley, 1882.

9.18 Park Place, Greeley, 1886.

9.19 Greeley Opera House Building, 1886.

9.20 The town developed a hodgepodge of symbolic
religious architecture, a rambling business district, and
hundreds of houses and shacks, before everyone recognized that the colony had been successfully "boomed"
into a city which was not in any way a commune:
bird's eye view, Greeley, 1882.

The Union Colonists may have seemed insufferably superior to their Colorado neighbors, with their concern for temperance, moral character, and elegant homes, but they were not interested in being unique. In environmental design, as in social structure, the colony selected undemanding solutions which neither compelled imitation nor offered obstacles to duplication. Greeley lacked both distinctive vernacular building and distinctive monumental building. It could be reproduced, but reproduction became rather meaningless in communitarian terms.

Meeker had predicted that "in the success of this colony a model will be presented for settling the remainder of the vast territory of our country,"[34] and Horace Greeley had given his benediction, "I believe there ought to be not only one but a thousand colonies."[35] No one could have agreed more than the railroad land agents who had sold the colonists their land. They were the active proselytizers, outsiders who made use of the communitarian ideal to promote more colonies formed on the model of Greeley's "success."

Because the colony site was so isolated, the railroad formed its main link with the outside world. Beginning in 1870 the Union Colonists had looked to the Denver Pacific Railroad as the audience for their success or failure in the same way that other colonies looked to their neighbors. The colonists sited their first headquarters where it could be seen from passing trains, and they insisted that enough money be spent on the building to make a good impression on rail travelers.[36] The first instance of a zoning problem in Greeley was a complaint against a blacksmith shop located too close to the railroad depot.[37] And when the Union Colony's first annual report was prepared, the members distributed it on trains crossing the Plains.[38]

When the railroad land agents needed help to launch new colonies, some Union Colonists like General Robert A. Cameron were hired to help out. He promoted the Fountain Colony at Colorado Springs, the Chicago-Colorado Colony at Longmont, and Union Colony Number 2 at Fort Collins.[39] Some of these ventures attempted some cooperative development like Greeley. Others were launched by unscrupulous speculators who simply found it convenient to adopt the term "colony" as an inducement to settlers. Imitations of Greeley were still being promoted in the 1890s. Their communal institutions were based on Greeley's assumption that anyone would be glad to have more community if they didn't have to give up property or privacy to achieve it.

Perhaps the history of Greeley seems anticlimactic after Hancock, Nauvoo, Phalanx, Oneida, and Amana, but it reflects a period of anticlimax. The Union Colony combines concentrated, nonsectarian, communitarian idealism, in its most popular, pre-Civil War, Fourierist form, with equally idealistic respect for the sanctity of the nuclear family. Nathan Meeker's writing anticipates the spirit of Howells, Bellamy, and Gronlund, the literary Christian socialism which demands no struggle and no compromises, which evolves gradually and painlessly, on paper. The Union Colony translates this spirit into town planning, and the result is an average American town with a single idealistic episode in its early history.

Meeker once made the cynical proclamation that the only way to make sure that people would exert themselves in a cooperative enterprise was to make them responsible for their own financial success or failure within the cooperative framework.[40] As the idealist and polemicist who kept everyone else in Greeley active, he himself fared badly in business: his nursery was ruined by drought and grasshoppers; his real estate venture was criticized as a conflict of interests; his paper, the Greeley *Tribune*, was beset by rivals; his "Co-operative Stock and Dairy Association" failed during a hard winter; his plan to build invalid cottages on town land was postponed indefinitely for lack of capital.

Pressed by creditors in 1878, Meeker accepted a post as government agent among the Ute Indians. The Utes became for Meeker a new communitarian venture. He may have known of Christian Priber, who attempted to establish a communistic settlement called Paradise among the Cherokee in 1736.[41] More likely, he was inspired by the hero of his own utopian novel, Captain Armstrong, who was alleged to have taught South Pacific savages "all the arts and industries of modern civilization without its vices."[42] Meeker recruited idealistic young men from Greeley as assistants, but all found the process of persuading a tribe of intrepid hunters to take up agriculture rather discouraging. A crisis developed in 1879. Meeker was impatient to plant a demonstration field and plowed up a Ute corral and pasture, an important communal territory. He summoned military support, and the Indians reacted angrily to this invasion of their territory. The Utes set fire to the agency, shot Meeker and his aides, mutilated Meeker, and took the women as prisoners. In a final ironic scene, one of the Ute leaders regaled Meeker's captured wife and daughter with passages quoted verbatim from Meeker's many solemn articles on the Indians and their "uncivilized" ways, articles in which his perennial optimism was tinged with racism and bitterness.[43]

He died as he lived, an idealistic writer for whom words were always more real than actions, compromise was unthinkable, and class struggle, unnecessary. At the Trumbull Phalanx he had asked, "Are men forever to be such consummate fools as to neglect even the colossal profits of Association?"[44] At the end of his life he was still asking the same question, equating "colossal profits" with cooperation, never understanding that sacrifice is half of sharing. The Union Colony advertised collective religion, industries, irrigation, fences, and housekeeping, but members were unwilling to give up existing faiths, personal capital, or Edenic myths for these collective ideals. The town developed a hodgepodge of symbolic religious architecture, a rambling business district, and hundreds of houses and shacks before everyone recognized that the colony had been successfully "boomed" and "puffed" into a city which was not in any way a commune. Present-day Greeley (Fig. 9.21) retains something of the original colonists' obliviousness to environmental contradictions, for despite a welter of neon, motels, and parking lots, they haven't yet cut down all of the Union Colony trees to widen the streets, and residents optimistically advertise their town as the "Garden City of the West."

9.21 "The Garden City of the West," Greeley, 1972.

1 Nathan C. Meeker, letter dated Aug. 10, 1844, reprinted in John Humphrey Noyes, *History of American Socialisms* (1870), New York, 1966, p. 332. In this same letter he describes the Trumbull Union Church, similar to the church he endeavored to organize in Greeley.

2 Ibid., p. 330.

3 David Boyd, *A History: Greeley and the Union Colony of Colorado*, Greeley, Colo., 1890, pp. 12-13. This is the major historical work dealing with the colony's affairs which I have relied upon for general background. The author was a colonist and provides the most complete published biography of Meeker. A manuscript biography dictated by Arvilla Delight Meeker is held by the Bancroft Library, University of California, Berkeley.

4 Boyd, *A History*, p. 15. I can find no trace of this novel, which Meeker's son, Ralph, described to Boyd.

5 On the North American Phalanx, "Post Mortem and Requiem, by an old Fourierist," New York *Tribune*, Nov. 3, 1856, in Noyes, pp. 499-507; on Oneida, an article from the New York *Tribune*, May 1, 1867, is quoted in *Handbook of the Oneida Community*, Wallingford, Conn., 1867, pp. 4-5; on the Mormons, "Salt Lake City, The Mormon Capital," in the New York *Tribune*, Apr. 1, 1870, and other articles in the *Daily Colorado Tribune*, Feb. 20, 1870, and the *Desert Evening News*, Feb. 28, 1870.
See also "Co-operation: How It Works in Troy," New York *Tribune*, Feb. 2, (1869?), undated clipping in Greeley Municipal Museum; and "Co-operation: Model Tenement Houses and Co-operative Housekeeping," New York *Tribune*, semiweekly, Aug. 31, 1869.
For his fiction, see Nathan C. Meeker, *Life in the West*, or *Stories of the Mississippi Valley*, New York, 1868. The publisher is Samuel R. Wells, who also issued a great variety of phrenological materials. The stories are much better than some of Meeker's righteous or sentimental journalism would suggest, especially "Going to Be a Mormon."

6 Railroads were granted a government subsidy of twenty square miles of land for every mile of track they laid, and they organized agencies, such as the National Land Company, to find buyers. The railroad agents advertised heavily in eastern papers and owned some western papers. Horace Greeley was probably friendly to these agents as *Tribune* advertisers and may have sent Meeker out to do a public relations piece. Hubert Howe Bancroft, in his *Works*, vol. 25, *The History of Nevada, Colorado, and Wyoming, 1540-1880*, San Francisco, 1890, refers to this possibility obliquely, on page 12.

7 Nathan C. Meeker, "A Western Colony," New York *Tribune*, Dec. 4, 1869. Replies are cited in "The Lo-

cating Committee Returns East," *Daily Colorado Tribune*, Feb. 21, 1870, p. 1. This paper tended to optimistic estimates, but other sources for earlier dates suggest this figure is accurate. Some of the letters of inquiry are held by the State Historical Society of Colorado in Denver.

8 "Applications for Membership in the Union Colony of Colorado from those who answered Nathan C. Meeker's 'Western Colony' in the New York *Tribune*, December 1869," folder of completed forms, Greeley Municipal Museum. Many applicants came from the "burned-over district" of upper New York State, and others resided in the area of the Washentaw and Trumbull Phalanxes, Oneida, New York; Zoar, Ohio; Bishop Hill, Illinois; and Nauvoo, Illinois. A majority of applicants declared that their savings ranged from $1000 to $5000, which, if true, would make them considerably more prosperous than the members of most other communitarian groups.

9 "The Union Colony," Greeley *Tribune*, Illustrated Extra, July 1880, p. 2.

10 Nathan C. Meeker, "Union Colony: Small Farms and Large Profits," New York *Tribune*, Sept. 18, 1870.

11 Ibid.

12 William Byers, quoting Colorado Territorial Governor McCook, in Boyd, *A History*, p. 157.

13 Nathan C. Meeker, "The Union Colony," *Daily Rocky Mountain News*, Jan. 19, 1870, p. 1, reprinted in James F. Willard, ed., *The Union Colony at Greeley, Colorado, 1869-1871*, University of Colorado Historical Collections, Colony Series, vol. 1, Boulder, 1918, p. 232.

14 Nathan C. Meeker, "Commencing Anew," New York *Tribune*, July 10, 1870. Given all this traditional Edenic imagery, it is surprising not to find the popular argument that "rain follows the plow" advanced in Greeley. For a discussion of the belief that cultivation could change climatic conditions, see Henry Nash Smith, *Virgin Land*, New York, 1957, chapter on "The Garden and the Desert."

15 See Meeker, "A Western Colony," for his suggestions, and "Minutes," *Proceedings of the Union Colony Association*, Dec. 24, 1869, reprinted in Willard, *The Union Colony*, pp. 1-12, for other colonists' proposals of New Braunfels, Texas, and Painesville, Ohio, as models.

16 Nathan C. Meeker, "Salt Lake City," New York *Tribune*, April 1, 1870.

17 "Village Improvement from the Foundations," an unsigned, undated MS in the Greeley Municipal Museum. The author seems to have firsthand knowledge

of early town planning meetings and is perhaps Ralph Meeker or Nathan Meeker.

18 Boyd, *A History*, pp. 59-61, contains detailed accounts of irrigation estimates and results. The following discussion is based on his analysis.

19 [William E. Pabor], *First Annual Report of the Union Colony of Colorado, Including a History of the Town of Greeley*, New York, 1871.

20 "H" [Chauncey L. Hall], "From Our Travelling Correspondent," *Daily Colorado Tribune*, Oct. 20, 1870, p. 2, reprinted in Willard, *The Union Colony*, p. 289.

21 Nathan C. Meeker, "Fence Building," Greeley *Tribune*, Apr. 12, 1871, p. 2.

22 Willard, *The Union Colony*, p. 232, and "Minutes," Jan. 3, 1870.

23 "Minutes," Mar. 5, 1870, pp. 12-13.

24 Meeker, "A Western Colony."

25 Nathan C. Meeker, "Prospectus," Greeley *Tribune*, Nov. 16, 1870, p. 3.

26 See Chapter 2, n. 30; Chapter 5, n. 37.

27 Nathan C. Meeker, "Our Young Men," Greeley *Tribune*, Dec. 7, 1870, p. 2.

28 Nathan C. Meeker, "What Kind of People We Have," Greeley *Tribune*, Nov. 23, 1870, p. 3.

29 Meeker, "Union Colony: Small Farms and Large Profits."

30 Meeker, "What Kind of People We Have," p. 312; see also "Cooperative Housekeeping," parts 1-5, *The Atlantic Monthly*, 39 (Nov. 1868-Mar. 1869) and Melusina Fay Peirce, *Co-operative Housekeeping; How Not to Do It, and How to Do It, A Study in Sociology*, Boston, 1894.

31 Meeker, "What Kind of People We Have," p. 311.

32 Nathan C. Meeker, "Lounging Places," Greeley *Tribune*, Dec. 28, 1870.

33 Meeker, "What Kind of People We Have," p. 310.

34 Meeker, "A Western Colony."

35 "Minutes," reprinted in Willard, *The Union Colony*, p. 6.

36 "Minutes," May 13, 1870, ibid., p. 24.

37 "Minutes," Sept. 15, 1870, ibid., p. 75.

38 Pabor, "First Annual Report"; "Minutes," Apr. 15, 1871, reprinted in Willard, *The Union Colony*, p. 109.

39 For a history of other colonization attempts in Colorado, see James F. Willard and Colin B. Goodykoontz, eds., *Experiments in Colorado Colonization, 1869-1872*, University of Colorado Historical Collections, vol. 3, Boulder, 1926. See also Chapter 10, n. 8.

40 Nathan C. Meeker, "Co-operation," Greeley *Tribune*, Jan. 18, 1871.

41 On Priber, see Arthur E. Bestor, *Backwoods Utopias: The Sectarian Origins and the Owenite Phase of Communitarian Socialism in America, 1663-1829*, 2d enl. ed., Philadelphia, 1970, p. 36.

42 Boyd, *A History*, p. 15.

43 Ibid., pp. 358-359.

44 Meeker, letter dated August 10, 1844, quoted in Noyes, *History of American Socialisms*, p. 332.

10 Feminism and Eclecticism

The Socialist City should be beautiful, of course; it should be constructed on a definite plan, each feature having a vital relation to and complementing each other feature, thus illustrating in a concrete way the solidarity of the community; it should emphasize the fundamental principle of equal opportunity for all; and it should be the last word in the application of scientific discovery to the problems of everyday life, putting every labor saving device at the service of every citizen.

—Alice Constance Austin, October 1916

10.1 A group of members, Llano del Rio, Christmas, 1914.

If Greeley represents a decline in idealism about the communal environment, Llano del Rio could be described as an extreme attenuation. The community was launched in California in 1914 and moved to Louisiana in 1917, surviving for twenty-four years, always on the verge of financial collapse, never solvent enough to build very much. Its history of factional disputes is a dreary one, enlivened by two episodes of architectural interest. In California, Alice Constance Austin, a feminist and self-trained architect, led the community in criticizing the ways in which the political problems of women were reinforced by the design of traditional dwellings. Under her leadership the group developed a model single-family home which they believed would suit an egalitarian society, one which offers significant contrast to dwellings discussed in the previous case studies. In Louisiana, colonists wanted to build model family homes, but when pressed for funds, they erected four different communal dwellings, turning the site into a veritable museum of communal building types, including a combination shop and dormitory, a phalanstery, two cruciform nurseries, and one big house. Quite unconsciously, Llano members created a tableau of architectural indecision which summarized over a hundred years of communal building.

When Job Harriman was defeated as the Socialist Party and Labor Party candidate for mayor of Los Angeles in 1910, he suggested that his supporters organize an alternative socialist town in the Antelope Valley north of the city. Born in rural Indiana in 1861, Harriman had trained for the ministry before attending law school in Colorado Springs, a town organized ten years earlier as the Fountain Colony of Colorado in imitation of Greeley. Harriman then moved to California, where he became involved in communities based upon the ideas of Edward Bellamy and William Dean Howells, novelists who portrayed the evolution of socialist society as a rational, nonviolent process which involved few or no changes in the role of the nuclear family and the private home. Bellamy's Boston in the year 2000 is a vague "White City" where consumer goods are delivered to every home through pneumatic tubes.[1] Howells's Altruria is a country of single-family homes where the inhabitants "do not think it well that people should be away from their homes very long or very often";[2] and Altrurian colonists believed in "the sacredness of the home" as a "foundation stone of the community," sentiments very similar to those of Nathan Meeker.[3]

Harriman recruited Alice Constance Austin, a self-trained architect who shared his reverence for the family home but hoped to reorganize cooking and laundry as communal activities. Harriman also enlisted a banker, labor leaders, a journalist, and a membership director to implement his plan for an alternative town:

... We will build a city and make homes for
many a homeless family. We will show the
world a trick they do not know, which is how
to live without war or interest on money or

rent on land or profiteering in any manner.[4]

He called himself a Marxist but argued that seeing socialism in practice was more persuasive than reading *Capital*. Some 900 members (Fig. 10.1) joined the community; they were described by a visitor in 1917 as "men and women of intelligence and common sense ... substantial persons who had banded themselves together to attempt to work out a community life that was without a capitalist and where the fruits of toil went ... to the laborer."[5] Urban workers and small business owners were joined by a substantial number of farmers. A quarter were Californians; most came from west of the Rockies. Almost all were American born, white, and Protestant. In return for a membership fee of $1,000 each family was to receive a house, and men would be employed in community industries at a fixed rate per day. No economic equality was granted to women, who were assigned to domestic work or handicrafts at less than men's wages.

Just as at the North American Phalanx, conflict developed at Llano between the nonresident directors and the resident members, who believed they could run the colony more democratically and more efficiently. Government by the directors and a board of industrial managers (similar to the "serial" organization of Fourierist communities) was supplemented with a board of commissioners elected by the resident members (Fig. 10.2).[6]

The colony's industries proliferated in much the same way as its organs of government, with new efforts established which overlapped and challenged previously established ones. Thus the community described itself in April 1917 as including

shoeshop, laundry, cannery, garage, machine shop, blacksmith shop, rug works, planing mill, paintshop, lime kiln, sawmill, dairy, cabinet shop, brickyard, flour mill, bakery, fish hatchery, barber shop, commissary, print shop, cleaning and dyeing plant, nursery, rabbitry, poultry yards, hog raising, vinegar works, bakery, photographic studio, drafting studio and art studio,[7]

while failing to mention that many members were picking fruit on neighboring farms as day laborers, because many of the industries were small or unprofitable.

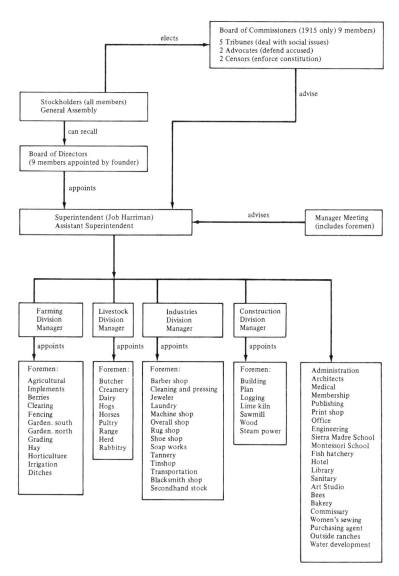

Board of Commissioners (1915 only) 9 members)

5 Tribunes (deal with social issues)
2 Advocates (defend accused)
2 Censors (enforce constitution)

elects

advise

Stockholders (all members)
General Assembly

can recall

Board of Directors
(9 members appointed by founder)

appoints

Superintendent (Job Harriman)
Assistant Superintendent

advises

Manager Meeting
(includes foremen)

Farming Division Manager	Livestock Division Manager	Industries Division Manager	Construction Division Manager	
appoints	appoints	appoints	appoints	

Foremen:	Foremen:	Foremen:	Foremen:	Administration
Agricultural Implements	Butcher	Barber shop	Building	Architects
Berries	Creamery	Cleaning and pressing	Plan	Medical
Clearing	Dairy	Jeweler	Logging	Membership
Fencing	Hogs	Laundry	Lime kiln	Publishing
Garden. south	Horses	Machine shop	Sawmill	Print shop
Garden. north	Pultry	Overall shop	Wood	Office
Grading	Range	Rug shop	Steam power	Engineering
Hay	Herd	Shoe shop		Sierra Madre School
Horticulture	Rabbitry	Soap works		Montessori School
Irrigation		Tannery		Fish hatchery
Ditches		Tinshop		Hotel
		Transportation		Library
		Blacksmith shop		Sanitary
		Secondhand stock		Art Studio
				Bees
				Bakery
				Commissary
				Women's sewing
				Purchasing agent
				Outside ranches
				Water development

10.2 Organizational diagram based on constitution of
March 1917, Llano del Rio.

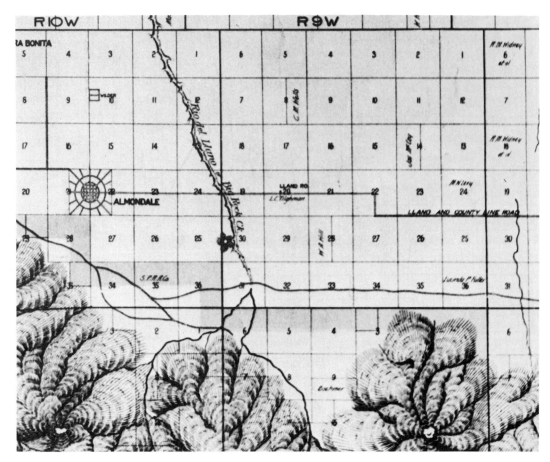

10.3 Detail of Los Angeles County Map, 1898, showing Almondale, a "Sunset Colony" for raising almonds; the Tighlman Ranch, which became the central section of the Llano del Rio community; and the "Rio del Llano."

The Llano organizers chose a site adjoining the Mohave Desert, ninety miles by road from Los Angeles and twenty miles from Palmdale, the nearest railroad depot. The area they selected had first been settled in the early 1890's as Almondale, a "Sunset Colony" organized in Chicago by *Farm, Field and Fireside* magazine in emulation of "the great Horace Greeley in his New York *Tribune*, Greeley Colorado colonization enterprise."[8] Since the Chicago organizers had promised their colonists irrigated land to produce an almond crop, they excavated a tunnel approximately three quarters of a mile long for this purpose before going bankrupt. Their unusual radial town plan remained unrealized when residents dispersed after three years (Fig. 10.3).

Unmindful of the downfall of Almondale, the Llano organizers planned to develop the desert until it was as "green as the map of Ireland."[9] They talked of a "white city," "unique and beautiful,"[10] an agricultural and industrial community of six thousand residents, "far removed from the hurly-burly of the artificial cities, in God's open country, right on the land."[11] Ultimately they owned or controlled about 2,000 acres, chiefly desert land, some in the foothills of the mountains. Thirty picturesque acres at Jackson's Lake were designated as the community's "resort." Views of snow-capped peaks tended to inspire colonists to rhapsodize about their scenery, and views of the colony from the peaks were colored by desert sunsets, but the colony site itself was cold in winter, hot in summer, arid, and flat. Furthermore, the parcels owned by the community were not contiguous, since the organizers had purchased land in scattered locations on the east side of the Big Rock Irrigation District

(Fig. 10.4) in an attempt to gain control of adequate water.[12]

Despite problems of internal and external transportation and irrigation, Llano's organizers celebrated the advantages of their environment in their publications, *Western Comrade* and *Llano Colonist*. First the productive possibilities were overpraised: "Once this rich plain—which in its dry state is valueless—is touched by water and the plow, a veritable gold mine of virgin strength is tapped. This land will yield its wealth of fruit and grain, beef, wool."[13] Houses, barns, workshops were "to be completed within a week," month after month. A prodigious amount of building was accomplished (Figs. 10.5, 10.6) but the colony journals always promised even more. Every single piece of equipment was inventoried, again and again, as if the catalog were a holy litany promising success: "19 wagons, 16 plows, 3 buggies . . . 3 trucks, 4 autos . . . 5 barber chairs . . . 2 pianos . . . 3 bath tubs, 12 lavatories, 5 sinks. . . ."[14] Despite the obvious lack of plumbing fixtures, Llano claimed to be the "cleanest, most sanitary village in California."[15]

Predictions for the distant future were effusive. Llano was becoming the "metropolis of Antelope Valley."[16] "Llano is a spot of destiny."[17] And they cared for "not Llano alone, but Llano repeated, multiplied, the Llano idea carried irresistibly throughout the west, conquering prejudice, spreading hope, extending the cooperative idea."[18]

While the *Western Comrade* advertised bliss and comfort, colonists complained of inadequate housing (Fig. 10.7). The community's first dwellings (Fig. 10.8) were tents and adobes, uncomfortable in damp winter weather

10.4 Land Status Map, Big Rock Creek Irrigation District, 1917, showing scattered Llano del Rio holdings.

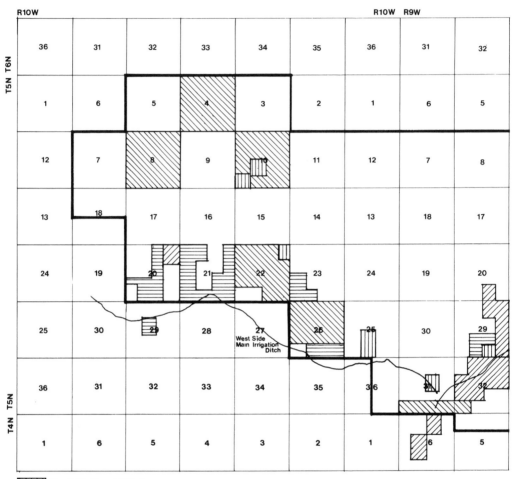

Deeded to Llano del Rio Co.

Tax title held by Llano del Rio Co.

Decreed out of Big Rock Creek Irrigation District

Patented previous to Big Rock Creek Irrigation District

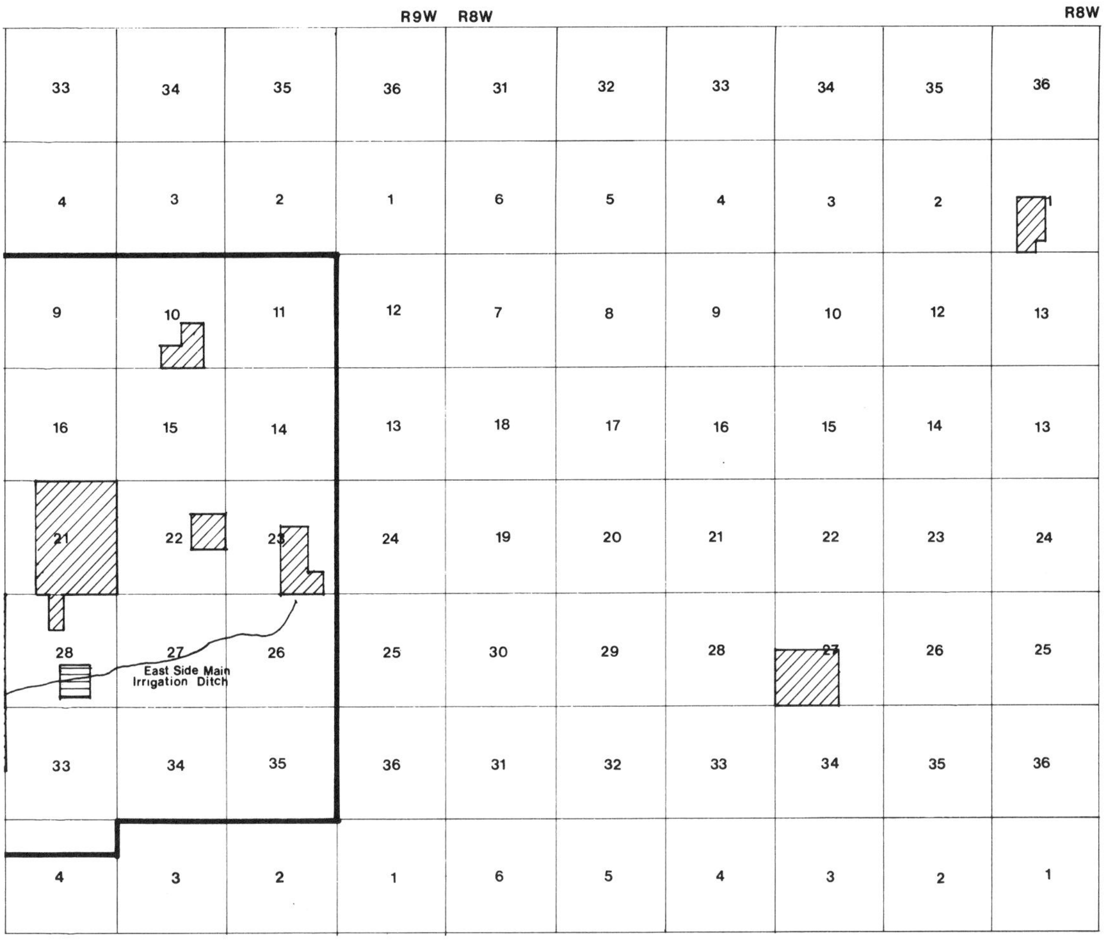
R9W
R8W
R8W
East Side Main
Irrigation Ditch

10.5 "The metropolis of the Antelope Valley," a
"spot of destiny," conjectural site plan, Llano del Rio,
ca. 1917.

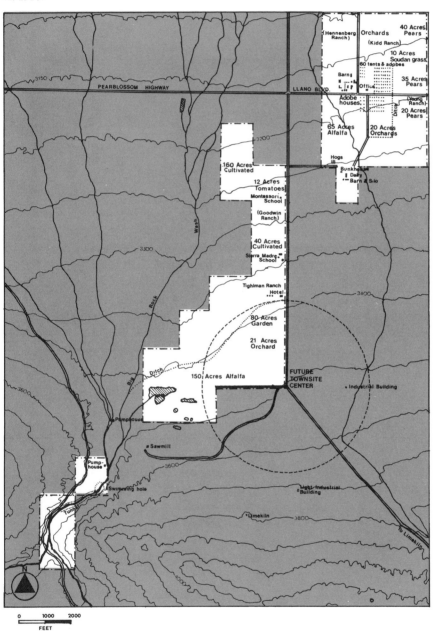

10.6 Dormitory and hotel, Llano del Rio, 1915-1917.
General assembly meetings took place in the hotel
dining room.

10.7 Llano adobe houses, 1915.

10.8 Exterior of a Llano home, adobe, 1916.

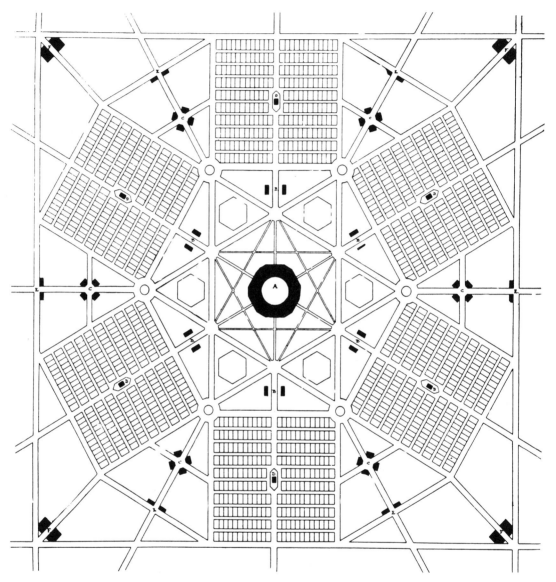

10.9 Leonard A. Cooke, plan for the city of Llano,
1915. *A*, civic center; *B*, schools; *C*, stores and hotels;
D, clubhouses; *E*, garages; *F*, industrial and business
sites.

but praised by "Doc" Robert K. Williams, a Fresno chiropractor, who wrote articles about Llano's "snow-white" tents and "snug" adobe houses.[19] Houses were cramped, according to the Elkins family: "The kitchen is too small and too low, no air at all, seven in the family and its an awful small place not quite (six) feet high. . . ."[20] Construction crews did poor work, according to Josephine Miller, who protested that her abode house should not be built without a foundation.[21] One member was lucky enough to be given a frame house, then found that it was boards without battens, so that flies rushed in.[22] Williams' soothing injunction that building teams should construct other members' houses as if they were building their own was of no avail.[23] Every family was engaged in the struggle for shelter, and the community managers did not hesitate to threaten dissident members with eviction as a disciplinary sanction. Vociferous complainants were threatened: construction of their houses was delayed indefinitely or they were housed "across the wash" with the other dissidents, a move which aggravated factionalism in the community.[24]

One member defended the authoritarian style of the nonresident directors in planning and constructing the community:

. . . Our job was to get some shelter erected and keep the food supply coming. . . . We were a buying club, a building club, a road making club . . . running like a circus with twenty rings . . . those who could do anything at all had to step in and do it, regardless of constitutions, Rochdale principles, union rules, IWW theories, Socialist theories, and even the Ten Commandments.[25]

Perhaps the authoritarian style of decision mak-

ing would have been accepted if the site had been a better one. Dry seasons were disastrous, local officials blocked construction of a dam, and the soil proved generally poor, problems which preceded the colony's move to Louisiana after its self-styled "socialist" banker foreclosed the group's mortgages.

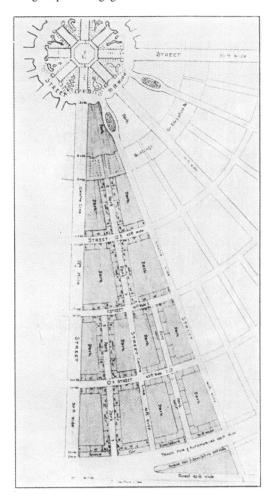

10.10 Plan of a sector of the Llano townsite, showing community center, parks, educational buildings, streets with row houses, "track for automobiles," and "stands for spectators," by Alice Constance Austin, ca. 1916.

At the same time that design and construction proceeded in a rather highhanded manner at Llano del Rio, members participated in extended discussions of the architecture of the ideal Socialist City led by Alice Constance Austin. Perhaps debate over future alternatives proved useful in deflecting conflict over the authoritarian tactics of the directors. It was unfortunate that just as members developed a radical approach to dwelling design, the community foundered financially and no new homes were constructed.

Alice Constance Austin assumed the role of city planner and architect for Llano del Rio between 1915 and 1917, bringing architectural drawings and models to the weekly Llano General Assembly for discussion, teaching in the colony's Sierra Madre Industrial School, and writing a series of articles on "Building a Socialist City" for the *Western Comrade*. She was not a member of the community but, according to one member, offered her services in the hope of seeing a lifelong dream fulfilled.[26] Another member characterized Austin as an upper-class radical, the daughter of a railroad executive. She read George Pullman's propaganda on model towns at the Chicago Columbian Exposition in 1893, and then educated herself to become the designer of a model town which would be owned and run by workers.[27]

Leonard A. Cooke drew up a preliminary site plan for Llano (Fig. 10.9) in 1915. Austin's plan was less grandiose than Cooke's, but while his plan was designed for arid land, which the community owned and occupied, hers was prepared for a better site not included in their land holdings (Fig. 10.10).[28] Austin seems to have absorbed most of her town planning theory from Ebenezer Howard, author of *To-Morrow: A Peaceful Path to Real Reform*, published in London in 1898 and reissued in 1902 under its well-known title, *Garden Cities of To-Morrow* (Fig. 10.11). Austin's debt to Howard is reflected in the organization of the city and its central buildings as well as in the graphic presentation of these ideas, but her approach to dwelling design was distinctively feminist and Californian.

Howard outlined the economic and social structure of a town of 30,000 inhabitants housed on 1,000 acres surrounded by a "green belt" of allotment gardens and farms. His civic buildings were set in parkland, ringed by a "Crystal Palace" which served as a pedestrian shopping arcade and winter garden. A radial street system culminated in a ring railway line. Austin accommodated 10,000 people on 640 acres, the square mile area common to many ideal communities planned for the United States. A green belt of unspecified size was to surround the town. Her civic center (Fig. 10.12) recalls Howard's "Crystal Palace," with eight "rectangular halls, like factories, with sides almost wholly of glass,"[29] leading to a glass-domed assembly hall.

Howard's diagram included six major "boulevards," twelve "roads," and eighteen "streets." Austin provided more vehicular circulation but reduced street width (50 feet versus 120 feet) because she placed all business traffic underground. A complex infrastructure of railway tunnels housed utilities, central heating, commercial deliveries, and deliveries from the central kitchen. Perhaps this infrastructure owes something to her family's railroad interests; perhaps it is based on Bellamy's descriptions of pneumatic deliveries in *Looking Backward*. Howard proposed external transportation in the form of railway lines; Austin allowed each family an automobile and housed them in communal garages. Perhaps Austin's most memorable transit innovation is whimsical: the ring road around the city doubles as a drag strip with stands for spectators on both sides.[30]

Austin's housing designs, like the infrastructure of her town plan, expressed her concern with the organization of domestic work and its implications for the role of women. She rejected the idea of large combined households of the sort established by the Shakers, Fourierists, and Oneidans. She does not seem to have known about the communal houses of intermediate size supported by kitchen houses which were developed at Amana, probably because the Inspirationists never publicized their plans. It is quite likely that she knew of various programs for cooperative housekeeping or removing the housework from the house, since she argued that if washing was sent out, cooking could be also.

Dissatisfaction with the role of women in a sexist society motivated Austin more than a desire to emulate other communes' household arrangements. Like Charles Fourier, she had nothing but scorn for the dwellings of "civilization." She maintained that the traditional home functioned as a Procrustean bed to which "each feminine personality must be made to conform by whatever maiming or fatal spiritual or intellectual oppression." She reminded members that despite being "drilled from babyhood to isolation in the home and conformity," women are as individual in their tastes and abilities as men. In her Socialist City, with labor saving devices in the home and central laundries and kitchens, a woman would be "relieved of the thankless and unending drudgery of an inconceivably stupid and inefficient system, by which her labors are confiscated. . . ."[31]

Charlotte Perkins Gilman raged over this "confiscation" in *The Home* and suggested careers for women; in spite of her criticism of the socialization and economic exploitation of women, Constance Austin offered not careers but domestic life for the socialist woman, who would inhabit ". . . a peaceful and beautiful environment in which she will have leisure to pursue her duties as wife and mother, which are now usually neglected in the overwhelming press of cooking and cleaning. . . ."[32] Her program is therefore a synthesis of the domestic efficiencies proposed by Catharine Beecher, who wished to "redeem" women's profession as homemakers, and the collective economies proposed by those communitarians who organized communal work to lighten women's labor. Single and childless, like Beecher, Austin neglected the needs of single adults and idealized motherhood. Her plans do not include any version of the communal hotel accommodations and communal child care which were actually available at Llano del Rio. Although these omissions narrow the scope of her vision of a better future for women, her designs for the individual homes were excellent. Her plans were presented as early as September 1915, when one member sketched a typical house in a letter to her daughter (Fig. 10.13). A scale model of the design was on view when the community celebrated May Day in 1916 (Fig. 10.14).

Living in southern California, Austin perhaps had some knowledge of the innovative workers' housing which Irving Gill had built near San Diego in 1910, the Lewis Court in Sierra Madre (Fig. 10.15). Gill surrounded a square site with small concrete houses connected by open porticos which presented a solid wall to the street and completely enclosed a large communal garden. Austin's scheme was larger and more complex. She included continuous street facades and communal gardens like those designed by Gill, but she also developed private patio areas enclosed by the houses and separated from the communal gardens (Figs. 10.16, 10.17). She wished to promote privacy and discourage quarrels between neighbors; she also intended to make family child care easier, since the private patio could be supervised from every room in the house.

Austin's architectural details make the houses good places for people: she provided sleeping porches to take advantage of the mild climate and Llano's wonderful mountain views (Fig. 10.18); built-in furniture, including roll-away beds (which could be "swung at a touch"); awnings for the porch in case of rain; seats and plants on the roof parapets; "wide, easy stairs" with window seats at the landings; heated tile floors; and French windows with decorated frames to eliminate fussy draperies. All of her proposed interiors seem natural, comfortable, and handsome. The influence of William Morris and the arts and crafts movement are apparent in her assumptions that Llano's furniture should be crafted in local workshops: window frames "delicately carved in low relief on wood or stone, or painted in subdued designs" are proposed as the basis of a whole new art industry at Llano.[33]

Austin set forth four criteria for her Socialist City: beauty, illustration of the solidarity of the community, illustration of equal opportunities for all, and employment of labor saving devices. Most of these criteria reflect the three dilemmas faced by all communitarian settlements: balancing authority and participation in design, communal and private territory, unique and replicable plans.

Charles Nordhoff once observed that communards "do not speak much of the beautiful with a big *B*," but by defining beauty as "fitness" to the climate and to a "certain psychic quality, the purpose for which the town exists,"[34] Austin established a communal aesthetic based upon choice and participation of the users in design. She presented alternative facade treatments (Fig. 10.19) of her basic house plan, offering members the aesthetic pleasure and variety of designing "decorative schemes of different kinds."[35] She believed that "the private garden will offer unlimited opportunity for the owner to exercise his taste and originality,"[36] just as the small neighborhood parks would offer the possibilities of red, green, or blue color schemes, flowers or vegetables in ribbons, fountains and recreational facilities. She believed that "new types of architecture should arise under fundamentally new conditions of living"[37] and suggested that special land be reserved for members' architectural experiments. She hoped that socialists would give vent to their "aggressively original nature," and she was not about to preempt the pleasures of such an enterprise.

She balanced her emphasis on participation in design for individuals and small groups, with a demand for communal unity and authority. She declared that the political results of "allowing each person to build to suit his own fancy" were inappropriate in the Socialist City. She wished "construction on a definite plan, each feature having a vital relation to and complementing each other feature, thus illustrating in a concrete way the solidarity of the community."[38] Only if land and dwellings were owned and developed collectively could the full range of community services be provided: utilities, heating, food, and laundry.

Her definition of equality of opportunity depended on a balance of private and communal features: equal housing; more or less equal ac-

10.11 "Ward and Centre, Garden-City, A Diagram Only. Plan must depend on site selected," showing garden, civic buildings, central park, Crystal Palace, Grand Avenue, exterior ring of factories, allotment gardens and dairy farms, Ebenezer Howard, 1902.

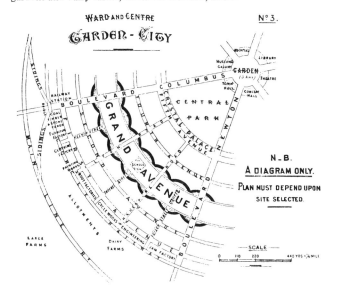

10.12 "Civic Center," by Alice Constance Austin, published in 1935, designed before 1916.

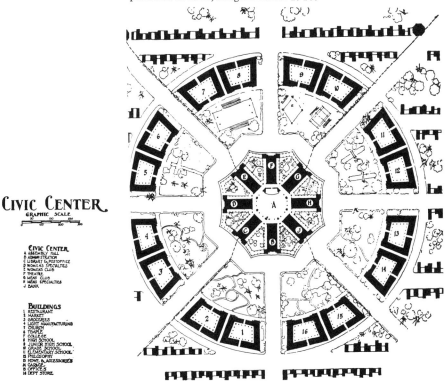

10.13 Sketches by Josephine Miller of designs presented by Alice Constance Austin, 1915. *A*, schoolhouse facade; *B*, schoolhouse from the side; *C*, courtyard houses, showing party walls darkened.

A

B

C

10.14 Alice Constance Austin showing model of house and renderings of civic center and school to Llano colonists, May 1, 1916.

10.15 Workers' housing, Lewis Courts, Sierra Madre, by Irving Gill, 1910. Although it was designed for workers, the client who commissioned it found it elegant enough to charge middle class rents.

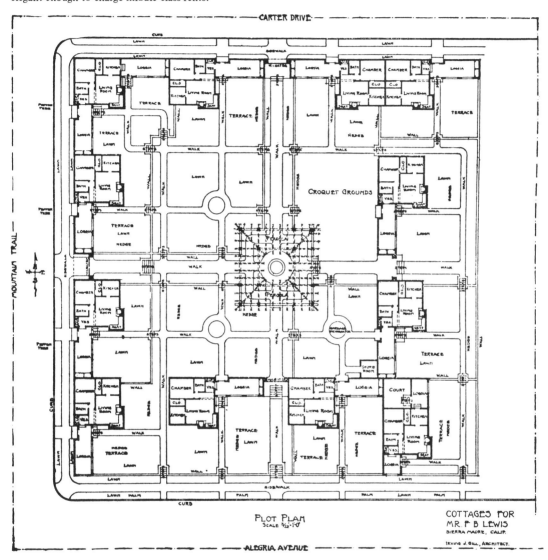

10.16 Axonometric drawing of patio houses, showing
garages in front, distribution tunnels below, sleeping
porches on second story, gardens enclosed and behind
houses, by Alice Constance Austin, published in 1935,
designed before 1916.

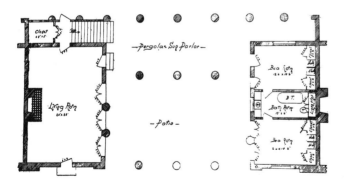

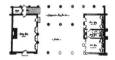

10.17 "Permanent Residence for Llano del Rio," by
Alice Constance Austin, ca. 1915, main floor, showing
living room, patio, pergola or sun parlor, bedrooms,
and bathroom. Smaller version shows plan at scale
of other dwelling plans in Chapters 4-10.

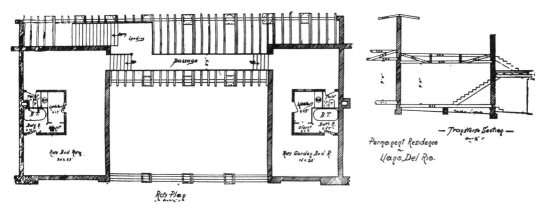

10.18 Roof plan, showing roof bedrooms and baths, and connecting passage.

10.19 "Alternative Elevations for Park Front," Italian and Pueblo, by Alice Constance Austin. Colonists were invited to produce additional plans.

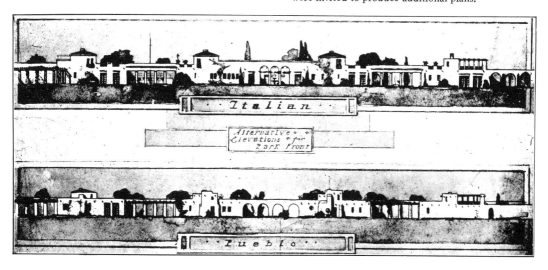

cess to community facilities (no house is more than half a mile from the community center); and a car for every family. The final criterion for the Socialist City, that it "should be the last word in the application of scientific discovery to the problems of everyday life, putting every labor saving device at the service of every citizen,"[39] recalls the desire for visible uniqueness typical of all communitarian experiments. Of course, if an automobile, as a symbol of equal opportunity and the "last word in scientific discovery," were provided for every family, Austin's tiny "parkways" would become inadequate, generous parks would become parking lots, and the whole question of community boundaries would have to be reevaluated.

Aside from this problematic provision for private cars (perhaps more justifiable in 1916 than it would be today), Austin's design allowed for both communal and private territory, unique and replicable plans. The houses she proposed were to be personalized and distinct, adapted to specific sites, yet quite simple and easily duplicated. She had the basic elements of an "intentional vernacular" worked out, and presented them articulately and persuasively. In Austin's proposals for the Socialist City one can find serious obstacles to realization: she planned large parks and gardens, knowing that the community did not have an adequate water supply, and she designed the extensive communal infrastructure knowing Llano lacked capital. She was very practical, however, when she planned thick-walled courtyard houses for the desert climate and took advantage of the socialist context to eliminate large kitchens in residential construction. As a design synthesis, incorporating the best of Ebenezer Howard, Irving Gill, William Morris, Catharine Beecher, and Charlotte Perkins Gilman, her work is unique in American architectural history.

Reactions to her plans among members of the community varied. One member recorded his favorable comments on what he called the Austin City Plan and the Austin House Plan, describing the designer as second only to Job Harriman in guiding Llano's exploration of socialist ideals.[40] Another's comments were negative. A woman described one of Austin's school designs as a "jail school house" and criticized the housing:

... The only yard there is to be is between your kitchen and bedrooms or however it is planned. There will be no place for clothes line, wood shed etc. as there is no back yard. I think it perfectly hideous but she has made Harriman think it perfect. . . .[41]

Austin, for her part, was modest about her successes and dealt gently with individual objections: ". . . Some blocks in the city will be cut up into front and back yards for the benefit of the conventionally minded. Every type of mind should be free to express itself in the Socialist City."[42] Unfortunately the community's financial condition worsened as the housing plans developed, and by the fall of 1917 it was clear that Llano's California land would not be developed as an ideal Socialist City.

After the colony's move from Llano del Rio to Louisiana, Constance Austin set up an architectural office in Los Angeles and reworked her Llano designs to appeal to other potential clients. She stressed her design's adaptability to many sites, climates, and economic systems, arguing that the uniformly sized socialist patio house could expand or contract, even to the point of allowing a palace to be built side by side with a cottage.[43] In *The Next Step: How to Plan for Beauty, Comfort and Peace with*

Great Savings Effected by the Reduction of Waste, published in 1935, she abandoned socialism so far as to write about the problems of the real estate developer and the difficulties of accommodating domestic servants, but she died with her plans unrealized by either socialist or capitalist financing. Because her houses were designed to reorganize "women's work," they represent a level of innovation which has still not been achieved in American residential construction today.

Late in 1917 Llano del Rio rallied its most stalwart members, packed up movable property, and chartered a train for Stables, Louisiana, where the members took over another unpromising site, an old lumbering town which they renamed Newllano. The group was saddled with debts but put a brave face on the move, chronicling the adventures of "Louisiana-ing Un-de-Luxe" in the *Western Comrade*.[44] Job Harriman grew ill with worry; George T. Pickett replaced him as leader in 1920.

The colony cherished one hope of progressing beyond subsistence farming: the discovery of oil on the property. All trial wells were dry. A few branch farms were established in New Mexico, Arkansas, and Louisiana, but most of them seem to have drained rather than augmented the colony's finances. Another source of income was government aid for experimental agricultural cooperatives, but this was never substantial. Commonwealth College and several socialist publications established themselves at the colony and gained for it a measure of renown in leftist political circles. The Depression years provided an influx of new members, but subsistence living subdued even the most enthusiastic communards. By 1938 the community dissolved amid factional fights and legal battles which are still continuing among former members.

Under Austin's guidance, Llano colonists in California had thought of themselves as building a city of single-family homes populated by a relatively anonymous group of 900 members. Llano in Louisiana included about 40 members in 1919 and 167 in 1921, and reached a maximum of about 500 in 1930. They never had any financial hope of building an ideal city, although in 1927 Ebenezer Howard, Austin's mentor, visited them and encouraged them to try to do so. The community officially maintained that single-family homes should form the basis of the community, and a 1923 plan shows "Pine Court," "Rose Court," and "Oak Grove," all divided into single-family lots. However, poverty and the large numbers of bachelors in the community dictated the construction of communal dwellings. A brick building which served as store, workshop, and bachelors' lodging was constructed between 1918 and 1920 (Fig. 10.20). During the same period a large concrete shed was remodeled into a communal dance hall and assembly hall to continue a tradition of community dances established in California. Communal buildings were also provided for children, following the precedent of the Sierra Madre Industrial School at Llano in California, which had housed forty teenagers. In Newllano, two communal residences for boys and girls were constructed before 1923 (Figs. 10.21, 10.22). Perhaps Austin's design for a town center was a prototype for their cruciform plans with extended bedroom wings and central play areas. In 1924 the colony's young people constructed a large communal house, the "Kid Kolony," at a site two miles from Newllano (Fig. 10.23). The largest communal dwelling, constructed in 1934 to house the influx of new members seeking economic refuge during the Depression, resembled a Fourierist phalanstery with open galleries and interconnected one-, two-, or three-room suites (Figs. 10.24, 10.25, 10.26). Residents took their meals at a communal dining hall called "the hotel."

With these five communal dwellings and a number of private houses scattered on the domain, Newllano was never a coherent environment, just as Llano del Rio had never been more than a few barns and farmhouses, one clubhouse, and dozens of tents and adobes. Yet at Llano del Rio people had energetically argued over plans, hauled rock for foundations, and cut timber for framing, hoping to see the Socialist City rising from the desert before their eyes. At Newllano, little energy was spent on discussing what the community's environment should be like. Although they engaged in a number of construction projects between 1918 and 1937, few of them were consistent with the 1923 plan for the community's growth. Their buildings included every possible communitarian approach—from tents, to suburban houses, to small communes within the commune, to a gigantic phalanstery. Unconsciously they created a fantastic museum reviewing a century of styles in communal housing (Fig. 10.27).

Perhaps Richard Ridgeway, an elderly member, best described the jumbled Newllano environment:

Unless you are patient and humble, our unpaved streets and sidewalks, our unpainted houses, our patched clothes and plain food will discourage you. . . . The real, worthwhile things of Llano, being psychological, are modest and unobstructive, and have to be coaxed, courted, and cajoled in order to be seen.[45]

Contrast this with the architectonic bombast of a colony advertisement soliciting contributions:

Can You Build?

After Every Whirlwind of Revolution
Comes the Task of the Builders!

Today: Ahead of the Revolution,
Integral Co-operation is
Building, NOW, the Impregnable
Breastwork, the Llano Co-operative
Colonies!

Before Your Very Eyes, Individualism
Disintegrates! The Palaces of the
Profiteers Crumble and Fall Apart!
. . . .
Be one of the Master Builders!
Spread the Cement of
Co-operation![46]

The image of Llano colonists as "master
builders" offers a faint echo of the Shakers' triumphant hymn calling their members to form a
"living building." The Shakers believed that the
United States was the "new earth" prophesied
by John the Evangelist, and that their role was
to "redeem the earth," to create the "new heav-
en" which fulfilled the prophesy. They danced
and designed and built with fierce energy.
Llano colonists, over a century and a half later,
retained only the vaguest outlines of a national
communitarian strategy, and their expectations
were passive ones. As the Shakers set out to
"redeem the earth," so the Llano colonists expected the earth to redeem them. They thought
the Big Rock Creek would turn the California
desert into flourishing orchards; they hoped
cutover Louisiana timberland would gush forth
oil to make them rich. Such fantasies reached
manic heights; one optimist envisioned gas sta-
tions along the highways of America as the economic basis of a national Llano network.

Whether they dreamed of agricultural estates
or oil strikes, infrastructures or dwellings, the
group never understood the relationship between organizing themselves and organizing
their living environment, the relationship which
the Shakers had articulated so completely.
Newllano, with its shanties and socialist college,
its phalanstery and its Kid Kolony, was the result of members' haphazardly building anything
they could think of to prop up the "impregnable breastwork" of socialism. Of course the palaces of the profiteers have not crumbled of
their own accord. And Llano's master builders
always mixed their own cement of cooperation a bit too thin.

10.20 Lodging house and industrial building, New-llano, ca. 1918-1920.

10.21 Communal dwelling for children, Newllano, ca.
1918-1923.

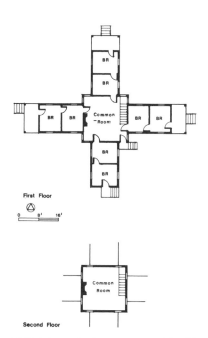

10.22 Schematic plans, communal dwelling for children, Newllano.

10.23 "Kid Kolony," communal dwelling for adolescents, Newllano, under construction, 1924.

10.24 "Unless you are patient and humble . . . our unpainted houses, our patched clothes and plain food will discourage you. . . ." Communal apartment house, Newllano, 1934, view from northeast.

10.25 Interior courtyard, communal apartment house, 1934, view from south, showing open galleries.

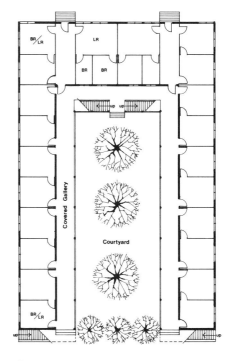

10.26 Schematic plan, communal apartment house, Newllano, 1934.

10.27 Site plan, Newllano, ca. 1937, showing single family houses, oil well, hospital, old hotel, children's dormitories, apartment house, and a variety of other communal and industrial buildings.

1 Edward Bellamy, *Looking Backward: 2000-1887* (1887), Boston, 1926.

2 William Dean Howells, *A Traveller from Altruria* (1894), New York, 1968, p. 141.

3 Christopher Oakes, "Altruia, California, 1894-1896, A Communitarian Study," unpublished paper, University of California, Berkeley, 1973, p. 5.

4 Gentry Purviance McCorkle, notes from unpublished memoir, "Wayside Memories of a Tennessee Rebel," n.d. [1962], p. 5, Huntington Library, San Marino, Calif. Also see Mellie Miller Calvert, "The Llano del Rio Cooperative Colony," MS, Huntington Library, San Marino, Calif., n.d. (1962-1969?). Both accounts suggest that McCorkle was a sharp operator who used the colony's funds to speculate in land and then foreclosed mortgages he held himself and took over the best parcels.

5 A[rchie] R[oy] Clifton, "History of the Communistic Colony Llano del Rio," *Annual Publications,* Historical Society of Southern California, 11.1 (1918), 80-90. Clifton surveyed members on June 26, 1917, and compiled a list of members' former occupations:

transportation	6
professional	15
printing	5
clerical	10
mining	8
manufacturing	18
business	73
building	13
farming	104

Members were asked to fill out a questionnaire on their politics. See "Application for Membership in the Llano del Rio Co-operative Colony," California Historical Society, San Francisco. McCorkle describes the installment plan financing: "Many skilled workmen in Los Angeles were out of work and were glad to join with us. A suspended member would pay $10.00 down and $10.00 a month. These installment payments pretty soon were $800.00 a month" (pp. 8-9).

6 In 1915 the majority of commissioners were members of the Welfare League, or "Brush Gang," which met secretly (in the sage brush) to discuss reforms. They demanded that nonresident directors move to the colony and that a complete audit of the community finances be made public, since they suspected, quite correctly, that the directors' socialist idealism was subordinated to a fever for acquiring land. The directors responded by expelling the dissidents, justifying their position as "good business" and defending the development of socialism according to what they described as the ruthless but effective techniques of successful capitalism. *Western Comrade,* 3.6 (Oct. 1915), 20. Also see Frank Miller to Mellie Miller Calvert, Llano, Calif., Dec. 3, 1915; Welfare League of the Llano Colony, memo to the directorate, mimeo, Dec. 3, 1915, and "Declaration of Purpose," mimeo, n.d., Huntington Library, San Marino, Calif.; and deed records, Los Angeles County.

7 "The Gateway to Freedom," *Western Comrade,* 4.12 (Apr. 1917), 2.

8 *Sunset Colonies: Fair Oaks and Olive Park in the Heart of California,* Farm, Field and Fireside and Western Rural Colony Department, Chicago, 1894, p. 1.

9 John Dequer, "Llano del Rio," *Western Comrade,* 3.8 (Dec. 1915), 25.

10 James R. Nickum, "Impressions of Llano del Rio Co-operative Colony," *Western Comrade,* 2.1 (Nov. 1914), 27-28.

11 Harvey Armstrong, "Fellowship in Work," *Western Comrade,* 3.1 (May 1915), 20.

12 McCorkle, p. 8. Control of an adequate water supply provoked debate between environmental goals and socialist methods. Recruits from the Young People's Socialist League of Los Angeles established residence on the first tracts of land purchased for the colony, in order to pack the voting lists of the Big Rock Creek Irrigation District. They then voted the landowners on the west side of the creek out of the district. Purviance McCorkle recounts that a warden sent to enforce this decision was thrown in the Big Rock Creek by five west-side ranchers. Ten Llano supporters then dunked the west siders. This maneuver and resultant hostility could explain why Llano was stripped and vandalized when most residents left in 1917.

13 Dequer, "Llano del Rio," p. 25.

14 H. M. Wood and J. E. Wallace, "Survey and Inventory," September 15, 1915, mimeo, Huntington Library, San Marino, California, repeated with variations in *Western Comrade* articles.

15 *Western Comrade,* 3.4 (Aug. 1915), 14.

16 "Llano Colony's Progress Rapid," *Western Comrade,* 3.4 (Aug. 1915), 11.

17 "What Are Assets?" *Western Comrade,* 5.5 (Sept. 1917).

18 "Llano Colony Adds 2750 Acres to Its Holdings," *Western Comrade,* 5.1 (May 1917), 16-17.

19 R. K. Williams, "Colony Celebrates Anniversary," *Western Comrade,* 3.1 (May 1915), 18. See also a complaint, George Heffner, memo to Franklin Wolfe,

Llano, Calif., Apr. 18, 1915, p. 2. Huntington Library, San Marino, Calif.

20 M[eyer] Elkins, memo to Llano del Rio Board of Commissioners, n.d. (1915), Huntington Library, San Marino, Calif.

21 Josephine Miller to Mellie Miller Calvert, Llano, Calif., Nov. 14, 1915, Huntington Library, San Marino, Calif.

22 Jose Mauricio to Llano Board of Commissioners, n.d. (1915), Huntington Library, San Marino, Calif.

23 R. K. Williams, "Enthusiasm Rules Llano," *Western Comrade*, 1 (1914), 29.

24 Josephine Miller to Mellie Miller Calvert, Llano, Calif., Oct. 3, 1915, Huntington Library, San Marino, Calif.

25 Walter Millsap, transcript of interviews with Abe Hoffman for UCLA Oral History Project, July 15, 1962, UCLA Library, Los Angeles, p. 66.

26 Josephine Miller to Mellie Miller Calvert, Llano, Calif., Sept. 11, 1915, Huntington Library, San Marino, Calif. Austin was born ca. 1865 and died in Los Angeles, ca. 1935. She lived in Santa Barbara, California, in a house she designed herself. I have not been able to find much further biographical information.

27 Millsap transcript, pp. 50-51.

28 Cooke's plan was sited on the approximate location of the existing settlement, section 21, Twp. 5N, Range 9W. Austin's plan was prepared for higher land with better access to water, but the community owned only a portion of her site in section 32, Twp. 5N, Range 9W.
Leonard A. Cooke traded 200 acres of land for a directorship in the colony in 1915. He joined the Royal Lancashires, British Army, in a defense construction job in 1916. Other Llano designers include William Braun, mentioned in Williams, "Enthusiasm Rules Llano," p. 19, and "Angell," mentioned by R. K. Williams in "A Trip Over the Llano," *Western Comrade*, 5.3 (June-July 1916), 12.

29 Alice Constance Austin, *The Next Step*, Los Angeles, 1935, p. 45.

30 John Reps, *The Making of Urban America*, Princeton, 1964, p. 406, gives an account of a race on a circular boulevard in Corona, California, in 1913 which may have inspired Austin's design for the Llano del Rio race course or drag strip.

31 Austin, *The Next Step*, p. 63. On Peirce, see Chapter 9, note 30. See also Ebenezer Howard, *Domestic Industry as It Might Be*, London, 1906.

32 Alice Constance Austin, "The Socialist City," *West-

ern Comrade*, 5.2 (June 1917), 26. See also Charlotte Perkins Gilman, *The Home: Its Work and Influence*, New York, 1902.

33 Austin, "The Socialist City," June 1917, p. 26.

34 Ibid., p. 14, and "The Socialist City," *Western Comrade*, 4.11 (Mar. 1917), 28.

35 Charles Nordhoff, *The Communistic Societies of the United States* (1875), New York, 1966, p. 399; Alice Constance Austin, "Building a Socialist City," *Western Comrade*, 4.6 (Oct. 1916), 17.

36 Austin, "The Socialist City," Jan. 1917, p. 26.

37 Austin, "Building a Socialist City," Oct. 1916, p. 17.

38 Ibid.

39 Ibid.

40 Millsap transcript, p. 47, pp. 51-52.

41 Josephine Miller, Sept. 11, 1915.

42 Austin, "The Socialist City," Jan. 1917, p. 26.

43 Austin, *The Next Step*, p. 23. See also Walter Millsap, "The History of United Cooperative Industries," mimeo, August 1966, p. 2, California Historical Society, San Francisco.

44 R. K. Williams, "Louisiana-ing Un-de-Luxe," *Western Comrade*, 5.6-8 (Jan.-Feb. 1918), 37.

45 Richard Ridgway, "Llano's Whole-Souled Ones Or What It Is All About," *Voice of the Self-Employed*, 1.4 (Apr.-May 1934), 3.

46 *Llano Colonist*, Feb. 11, 1933, p. 6.

III Learning from Utopia

11 Edge City, Heart City, Drop City: Communal Building Today

We have built us a dome on our beautiful plantation
And we all have one home and one family relation.

—Oneida song, 1870s

We built a big dome (a domelette next to what we're into now) out of rubber hose, wooden dowels, and this enormous yellow parachute, under which we would gather in circles and search for our center. By dope or by grope . . . we began to discover it . . . heart city.

—Hugh Romney describing the Hog Farm, 1967-1968

"Monogram of Political Economy," frontispiece from
T. Wharton Collens, *Eden of Labor*, 1876, showing the
"natural value" of rural life expropriated by four
urban capitalists.

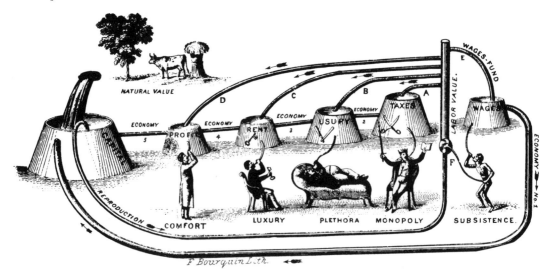

Communal excitement of the past decade seems to have surpassed the peak of nineteenth century fervor when Brisbane was calling out to all "Social Architects" from the front page of the New York *Tribune* and Emerson claimed that every man had a draft of a new community in his pocket. Just as no complete catalog of nineteenth century experiments has been made, so no full communal census exists at present, but one current study reports the establishment of at least one thousand contemporary communes.[1] Their stances are as diverse as their predecessors'. They describe themselves as Jesus freaks and atheists, revolutionaries and apolitical types, hip and straight, puritan and promiscuous, feminist and male chauvinist, urban and rural, technologically primitive and sophisticated. One typology sorts out communes according to purpose: retreat (dropping out and getting away); missionary (implementing an ideology and converting people); or domestic (setting up a household).[2] All three categories would have to be subdivided into urban and rural examples, and many communes' activities spread into all of these areas, or develop from one orientation to another. Generalizations about the movement are difficult to support, partly because current communes are still in early years of development, but a few points of comparison with their predecessors seem clear.

A rather large proportion of nineteenth century communards were relatively poor people, farmers and artisans, some immigrants, some native born, all hoping that collective organization could help them achieve a comfortable life style, even, in some cases, an explicitly middle-class life style. Many historic communards believed that a successful model community would inspire widespread imitation during a period of national expansion, just because of the similarity of their goals with those of the rest of society. In contrast, most contemporary communards come from comfortable, suburban, middle-class backgrounds, which they explicitly reject in favor of a more "natural" or a more "responsible" life style. Few contemporary groups describe themselves as creating models to be duplicated. Many see the commune as a group isolated from the larger society, which they perceive is collapsing and therefore irrelevant. In 1854 Victor Considérant predicted that the Fourierists would create the "nucleus of a new society" in the virgin soils of the frontier. Many of today's communards, if they described themselves as a "nucleus" at all, would tend to agree with Paul Goodman's prediction of "Rural Life, 1984" when communes will function as monasteries did in the Middle Ages, communities preserving humanistic culture when cities become unlivable.[3] The doomsaying tone is simultaneously self-mocking and serious; they dare not predict their own survival without questioning that possibility for the rest of the world.

In some ways the historic communitarian tradition is very much part of the contemporary movement: the Hutterians and the Bruderhof provide the example of communal life maintained for many generations; although there are few Shakers living, one of the most influential leaders of the Lama Foundation, a large commune in New Mexico, was raised in a Shaker community. A few groups revere communal history—the Twin Oaks community in Virginia has named some of its buildings for famous historic communes. Other groups reject communitarian history completely, or, like Project One in San Francisco, develop their own eccentric explanations why historic groups have "failed" but contemporary ones will "succeed." The purpose of this chapter is not to attempt any complete analysis of contemporary groups, but to review communal symbols—the garden, machine, and model home—and communal dilemmas—authoritative versus participatory processes, communal versus private territory, and unique versus replicable plans—in order to ask where contemporary groups stand.

The gardens, the machine, and the model home continue to fascinate communards as symbols of nature, technology, and self, just as they did in the last century, but interpretations have changed with the times. The Garden of Eden is not a frequent reference point now. Although one California commune, Morning Star Ranch, explicitly identified original sin as cutting up and selling the American land,[4] everyone wants to escape the guilt of an American Adam or an American Eve. There is emphasis on the whole world, rather than the New World, expressed in the *Whole Earth Catalog*, the *Mother Earth News*, and the commune-launched "Earth People's Park." The suggestion that Americans have cut up Mother Earth, with her "sweet flowing breast," has certain overtones of family discord, hatred for powerful, paternalistic authority figures, all expressed in a sentimental (Oedipal?) union with the land. American Indian tribes, ignored by historic communards, are revered by many communes today for their respectful relation to land and nature. Group names like New Buffalo in New Mexico and Laughing Coyote in Colorado reflect this idealization; Marge Piercy's novel, *Dance the Eagle to Sleep*, tells of revolutionary communards organized as Indian tribes; an issue of *The Modern Utopian* magazine offers a "tribal cluster pattern" of land use to allocate 20 million acres in "Earth World."[5] Communes in the eastern part of the United States seem less involved in Edenic parallels or Indian culture than their Western counterparts, but Ray Mungo provides an alternative vision of a paradisiacal landscape now lost to us. He prefaces a brief account of *Total Loss Farm* in New England with a literary pilgrimage on the Concord and Merrimack rivers, traversed by Thoreau when they were in more pristine condition.[6]

If the literal identification of communal sites with earthly paradise has ended, desire to redeem the earth by improving the land has vastly increased. Contemporary groups continue the historic communal traditions of careful land use and good farming practices, but some of the techniques have changed. Organic farming and ecology demand that some "scientific" historic practices, such as the use of chemical fertilizers, be avoided. As a result, communal farms are not nearly as profitable, compared with noncommunal farms, as they were a century ago. Self-sufficiency implies a more complex cycle of consumption and reuse than such groups as the Shakers or the Inspirationists put into effect, so the careful recycling of waste has taken on added importance for contemporary communes, whether they are urban or rural. "Ecotecture," a combination of ecology and architecture, describes an approach to building that uses natural or recycled materials, developing wind and solar technology for domestic power and heating.[7] There is little or no interest in symbolic or picturesque landscaping in contemporary communes, perhaps because it seems luxurious, perhaps because the fashion has passed in the larger society for such displays.

The locational conflict between city and country has been much intensified since historic communes settled into the agrarian "middle landscape," siting themselves further westward in each decade. Contemporary communes have been established simultaneously all over the United States, but like the "burned-over district" of New York, special centers of excitement now are northern California, Oregon, the Southwest, and New England. Just as their predecessors did, contemporary groups often settle on poor land which is all they can afford: vacant land, arid and infertile, like Greeley,

Colorado, or Llano del Rio, California; abandoned farms; derelict urban space such as abandoned city center warehouses or decrepit, "funky" nineteenth century houses in older sections of the cities.

Some communes—perhaps half?—are city centered and of these many are determined to remain in the city. Project One is located in an old warehouse in San Francisco; Synanon, in San Francisco and Oakland warehouses; a Marxist law commune, in old courtyard housing in Los Angeles; Project Place, in an old Boston school. All of these groups consider themselves resource communes, with schools, a drug addiction program, legal aid, a dropout center keeping residents tied to the physical centers of existing society.

Aside from these "missionary" urban communes, many other domestic urban communes are relatively transient, lasting a few years, with a mixture of students and other members trying out communal life styles before making a commitment to a commune just outside the city or even a more isolated rural commune. A Berkeley communard described the three stages of transition many communards experience as "Fat City," "Edge City," and "Real City," steps reminiscent of the Shaker converts' gradual indoctrination through private property, cooperation, and communism. Fat City is middle-class America, dedicated to needless consumption and exploitation: "I am Fat City, it is my life, my childhood and my adolescence. It has pampered me, fed me, taught me, and surrounded me." It is the suburb which "instead of synthesizing the best of both an urban and a rural life has denied itself the quality of either in exchange for the material benefits of both." Edge City is the tentative attempt to make a communal life within the metropolitan territory

11.1 Images of garden and machine: a model industrial
community set in a pastoral landscape, sketch after a
design by Robert Owen, 1834. Classical detailing cannot dull the impact of smokestacks.

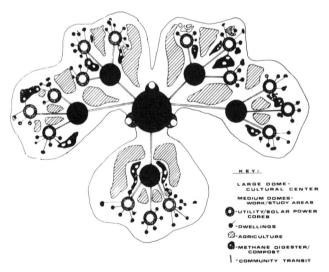

KEY:

LARGE DOME -
CULTURAL CENTER

MEDIUM DOMES -
WORK/STUDY AREAS

-UTILITY/SOLAR POWER
CORES

-DWELLINGS

-AGRICULTURE

-METHANE DIGESTER/
COMPOST

-COMMUNITY TRANSIT

11.2 High tech and no tech side by side, the same in-
congruities as the Owenite plan, in a collage for "Radial Cluster Villages," by the Village of Arts and Ideas,
Berkeley, 1972.

claimed by Fat City. The transition involves inconsistencies since Fat City provides Edge City with surplus materials and its technology. It is in the city or near enough for people to gather materials and recruits. And Real City? This would be "a human and economic system . . . to provide the spontaneity and allowance for individual initiative of an ideal capitalism with a level of security in services of a socialist system."[8] The location of Real City is perhaps as remote as the realization of its prospects.

For most contemporary communes, Edge City is the only viable position, and the likely location is the city or nearby. A Berkeley commune called the Village of Arts and Ideas represents the common struggle of Edge City to transform itself into an ideal, remote, Real City. The urban commune successfully published a book, renovated a house, and experimented in the design of windmills, domes, and inflatable structures. But their hopes for "radial cluster villages" seem reminiscent of Robert Owen's parallelogram and mirror none of their practical ability to get things done (Figs. 11.1, 11.2).[9] The bubble diagram of alternating areas for agriculture and domes, "wilderness" and transit lines, "no tech" and "high tech" side by side, reveals hopeless incompatibilities. It suggests Alice Austin's plan for railway tunnels as infrastructure in Llano del Rio's desert, "garden" city. Historic communes, composed of members with rural backgrounds, like the Shakers and the Inspirationists, had an easier time accepting the limitations of rural life. They began rural and stayed rural, and experienced none of the hesitating steps which some of today's communards must take to establish first a city commune, then one close to the city, then one quite far removed, which is not hopelessly out of touch with reality.

If the move to the country is the point when many urban groups are forced to realize that they like rural talk but can't manage rural living, it is also the main point of technological change, when idealism about "alternative" technologies is put to the test. Communards' idealism about technology has changed drastically since the time when Owen and Fourier proposed their communitarian plans as social "inventions" for mass production. Technology is no longer a synonym for progress but a subject of vast ambivalence in society. Many communards recognize technology as highly ideological and reject what they identify as "corporate technology" in favor of an "alternative technology" they hope to develop. Alternative technology is, however, as much a social invention as anything Owen and Fourier had in mind—it will end the alienation of workers and the wasting of resources. The San Diego New Alchemy Institute defines it broadly: alternative technology should "function most effectively at the lowest levels of society, so that the 'poorest people' should be able to use it; it should be based primarily on ecological and social considerations, rather than those of economic efficiency; it should allow the possible evolution of small, decentralized communities; and it should consume relatively small amounts of resources."[10] Other theorists have different projections for liberatory technology in the future, especially for the potential of miniaturization. Murray Bookchin argues that this is the main thrust of contemporary technical advance, and that for the first time in history the miniature reactors, transistors, and computers exist which can make the communitarian strategy viable.[11] This bears some resemblance to the old communitarian cry for miniaturization in response to urbanization, translated from political to economic terms. Paolo Soleri's proposals for new cities draw a different conclusion from similar optimism about miniaturization, since he proposes to concentrate millions of people in a single megastructure with centralization, rather than decentralization, made possible by miniaturized technology.[12]

All these attitudes toward the uses of technology are a bit abstract—the moment of truth for any rural commune comes when the members have to decide whether to dispense with a telephone, cut off electricity, or refuse town water. It takes a while to learn how to run a generator with wind or to heat with solar energy, although numerous handbooks produced by communal groups help new communes to speed up the processes. Certainly inventiveness is prized among communards as much as ever—to be able to build with salvage, keep old engines running, or get new "alternative" power devices operating. The historic emphasis on advanced mechanical equipment, steam heating, or gaslight is gone. So is emphasis on labor saving devices. Thanks to American fetishes for electric knives and toothbrushes, ten-speed blenders and floor waxes, no one wants to be bogged down with this middle class paraphernalia. The Oneidans, who took so much pride in inventing the forerunners of some of these labor saving devices, were hoping to support a factory and a bourgeois home, and that is what today's communards claim to be fleeing.

Idealism about "alternative" technology suggests some of the "alternative" approaches to the commune as an ideal home, a symbol of the collective self. At least three attitudes can be identified: nostalgic, mobile, and feminist. The bourgeois domesticity of the Oneidans and the Fourierists, the housepride of Nauvoo, Greeley, and Amana are gone, for very few communards want to offer the world a prosperous, fashionable facade. As a prototype the suburban American single-family home is anathema, and inflatables or domes bearing no relationship in massing or plan to traditional houses are popular. Identification with American Indians and oppressed Third World peoples leads to adoption of tepees and yurts. In terms of interior design, plastics and drip-drys are rejected in favor of wood and hand weavings. Old fashioned wood-burning stoves are celebrated; so are log cabins, suggestive of pioneer homesteads (Figs. 11.3, 11.4), and even sod prairie houses have been resurrected. A few communes have remodeled old barns as dwellings, and many have remodeled old houses, describing historic preservation as a form of ecological "recycling."

Opposed to nostalgic identification with the tepee or the pioneer homestead is the communal liking for model, mobile homes. Communal buses, with psychedelically painted and renovated interiors, mock twentieth century mobility by association with hippie domesticity. Often the homestead and the bus complement each other, and groups alternate between them. In 1965 and 1966 Ken Kesey's Merry Pranksters lived on a farm in Oregon and in a warehouse in San Francisco and traveled on "Furthur," a 1947 white bathtub of a bus described by Tom Wolfe in *Electric Kool Aid Acid Test*.[13] Around 1967 some of the Pranksters established the Hog Farm. After two years of

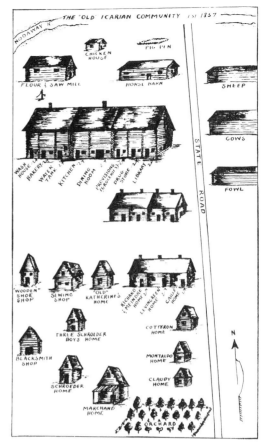

11.3 Log cabins, Icarian community, Corning, Iowa, 1857.

11.4 A model communal home of the nostalgic type: log cabin under construction at the Kingdom of Heaven commune, Taos, New Mexico, 1972.

pig farming they developed a road show of lights, slides, music, and portable domes, transported in a caravan of buses and trucks led by the Road Hog, a manifestation in the Dadaist manner which toured American universities and towns, bringing the zaniest aspects of the commune and drug culture to out-of-the-way places—part community, part circus, and part rock spectacle. Other groups enjoyed this way of life—a group called "The Family" crowded about fifty people into a small school bus before they settled in Taos, New Mexico, in 1968.[14] The Village of Arts and Ideas travels in a van equipped with plexiglass windows and mirrors, to distort the passing landscape, or "alienate alienation" in "Consumerica," as one passenger described it. And, even though vehicles may violate the standard of "alternative technology," they are justified by their missionary spirit and apocalyptic purpose. Here is the Village group stopping for gas:

Floating over the flatlands of Berkeley in the intermedia caravan at sunset. . . . Slowing down on San Pablo for a bit of standard oil. Peter gives Ralph, Judy and I some kind of herb like ginseng root to suck on while we wait. Fill it up with fossil fuels! But wait a minute, that doesn't quite jive right in my mind, I mean how can I forget the Eutopia or Bust! bumper sticker on the back of this old mail truck. I mean come on now what about all this talk about running your car on cow manure or chicken sheeeet man? Its OK though, really I guess everyone inside realized that the old "Fill er up" mantra can only lead to a Bust, sooner or later.[15]

The pioneer homestead and the communal bus often appeal to machismo, and feminist communards have quite different ideas about ideal homes. Feminist visions of the model community are in many ways very close to the ideals of the Shakers, the Fourierists, and the Oneidans, all of whom hoped to improve the role of women by lightening domestic labor in a communal household. Although many of them favored communal housekeeping and child care to give women more free time, with the exception of the Woman's Commonwealth, founded in Belton, Texas, in 1886, historic communards were not separatists. Some contemporary urban, political communes include men and women in groups which are dedicated to abolition of sex-stereotyped work roles, the sharing of housework and child care. For them the commune makes lighter labor possible because all chores are shared. The New City commune in Maine recently attempted to design housing to suit such arrangements. Other groups are interested in providing housing for divorced or separated women discriminated against in the commercial housing market, perhaps through converting existing apartment houses for women and children, with communal kitchens and day care. Groups in New York and San Francisco have worked out such plans.[16] The Women's Building in Los Angeles is an example of a parallel activity—it houses about ten different women's organizations, including the Feminist Studio Workshop, but is not a communal residence.

All of these models of the ideal home—the homestead, the bus, the feminist stronghold—restate the need expressed by John Humphrey Noyes of Oneida to "get beyond the little man and wife circle," to reject the tight nuclear family, stifling or uncaring, to abandon what Philip Slater has describes as our national "pursuit of loneliness" in favor of a voluntary communal commitment.[17] As the communal home becomes a symbol of the communal family and its increased sharing, it is imitated, by psychologists running "growth centers," and by architects and real estate developers who are planning homes, all of whom hope the communal charisma will rub off a bit. "Growth centers" like Esalen in California hope to achieve some of the closeness of a communal household for a few days' time. Architects and architecture students at Berkeley spent a term in 1972 creating "a place in the country," hoping to create a communal solidarity through the building process even though they lived on the site only three days a week. Commercial real estate developers don't want to build communes, but a few of them hope to provide a bit of communal feeling for retirement communities, singles communities, and single-family houses grouped around community centers. A New Hampshire developer reportedly consults his charts of historic and contemporary communal organizations before he approves a new site plan.[18]

Whatever their attractions, growth centers and speculative developers' and architects' designs cannot duplicate the commune as a model home. These schemes presume an outside organization and a transient clientele. The model community, designed, built, and inhabited by its members, reflects their collective identity because of the process they experienced. The dilemmas of authoritarian and participatory processes, communal and private territory, unique and replicable plans, represent the means of reconciling life style and life space, and they must be resolved by residents.

Contemporary communes have much the same struggles over authority as their predecessors, and some communes do demand the absolute obedience enforced by the historic sectarians. Leaders of the Children of God, the Re-Education Foundation, Synanon, Fort Hill, and The Farm hope to have as much power as the Shakers or the Inspirationists to control their membership, and their building processes reflect this desire. At the Fort Hill Community, in Roxbury, Massachusetts, Mel Lyman was recognized as an absolute authority figure. A reporter who visited in 1971 commented on "Mel's master bootcamp building and training plan," put into effect in 1966 when houses were "stripped to the studs and rafters and entirely rebuilt, in some cases stripped and rebuilt again after Mel discovered a 'mistake.' "[19] Similarly, at Synanon, launched in California in 1960, with several branches now operating, Chuck Diederich, the founder, holds absolute authority and many former drug addicts are incorporated into the community through a severely authoritarian process. A San Francisco architect, Bernard Kaplan, has designed Synanon's rehabilitation of a San Francisco warehouse and their new community at Tomales Bay with little evidence of group participation.[20] Perhaps the most authoritarian process of all is taking place at Arcosanti, in Arizona, where architecture students pay tuition to the designer, Paolo Soleri, for the experience of helping to build the ideal city of the future. This is not exactly a commune, although some of the builders do stay on to be part of a community. Reportedly, only Soleri exercises much power in making design decisions. All of these design and building processes launched in hierarchical communities under architects' direction seem quite effective, but, like those historic communes whose designs were said to come from God, one cannot expect much growth, change, or innovation, when "God"— Lyman, Diederich, Soleri—stops giving orders.

Unlike these examples, many communal groups avoid rigid decision-making structures. The Hog Farm developed a game of "God for a day" where members, in alphabetical order, took turns ordering everyone else in the commune to perform their wishes—one asked everyone to build him a stone mountain—a process to help them to discover the meaning of authority and participation, and the "power we have as a group."[21] Although there is less faith in rules, constitutions, or organizational charts, stable communities usually develop all of these as they grow beyond eight or ten people. Participation in planning and building can be an especially valuable tool for small groups exploring the implications of growth, although often it simply reveals disorganization and timidity.

In communities which are using the processes of planning and building to explore ideology, sometimes conflicts are uncovered which cannot be resolved. The Cambridge Institute's New City Project held meetings of several dozen people during 1971 to help to plan a rural socialist city, but when the time came to buy land in the country, some of the participants decided that they would rather plan than build, and formed a "New City Consulting Group" while others organized the commune.[22] The Sunrise Hill Community in Conway, Massachusetts, discovered that their communal building process revealed disparate ideas about participation and privacy:

In the building of this house, at the very outset, some of the lack of unity and coordination among the members was already visible. . . .

Getting all of the people, tools, and materials together at the site, and a clear plan before them was no easy task. . . .

While the building was going on, some members decided they did not—after all—wish to live in a communal building, but preferred a separate shelter for themselves. . . .

Suddenly the new building was not for all but only for some, and the work slowed accordingly. It was no longer a physical meeting ground for everyone in the community, no longer a focus of communal energy and will. . . . *One* shelter had been needed, *three* were begun, and *none* were completed.[23]

At another commune in Bolinas, California, the process of building launched debates about male authority, for the men wanted to get the house done in a hurry to their own design specifications, and the women saw it as "a process to participate in and learn from," although they had few construction skills.[24]

Learning construction skills can be an exciting and valuable part of community building, particularly for urban residents unused to building, and for women, who have been discouraged from acquiring such skills in the outside world. At Twin Oaks in Virginia everyone approached the process of building with trepidation, since only one male member of the community had sufficient confidence to believe that the group could actually erect a building.[25] In time the group came to share his confidence, and they began to hire themselves out as builders of houses for contractors in their town.[26] A woman at Project One in San Francisco reported that construction was important to group cohesion because "just in the act of putting up walls you learn what it is to make a space—you learn what a sound is. . . .[27] The Hog Farm seemed to find that getting volunteers to help them erect their temporary domes began to create a sense of community through participation: "everybody felt responsible. . . . They had helped."[28] Berkeley students building collectively wrote that "lifting a beam or a roof was always a high . . . somehow afterwards it seemed easier to be friends."[29] And one woman commented on her "need to *complete* (by myself) a small detail that is part of a place built by everyone . . . the joy of someone telling me that they like my window . . . feeling the value of my place in the group."[30] These sentiments would have seemed familiar to the Shakers or the Oneida Perfectionists, who were always encouraging members to perfect some part of the communal environment, finding in the building process a way of synthesizing individual and collective idealism. Occasionally participation in building can become an end in itself, if a group substitutes construction work for a more specific shared ideology or mission. More Houses in California organized groups of communards to rehabilitate the houses they lived in, and then sell at a profit, earning their living as they constantly moved on to build again. This is reminiscent of the activities of the Harmony Society, who built four American towns in the nineteenth century, perhaps because the Harmonist leaders could maintain celibate discipline only while members were fully involved in the feverish work of construction.

Contemporary communes wrestle with the problems of defining new conventions of community and privacy, just as their predecessors did, but with less fully developed solutions utilizing boundaries and vantage points, and fewer varieties of communal and private spaces connected by circulation spaces. Many communards have experienced a stage of strong reaction against private property—the "open land" communes in California, Morning Star Ranch and Wheeler's, or Drop City in Trinidad, Colorado—and by refusing to establish their boundaries, these communes became known as "crash pads" for young people on the run from straight society. Most groups tighten their boundaries as they mature, siting themselves at the end of dirt roads, or no roads, with signs asking the world to keep out, except perhaps on visiting days. Symbolic fences are no longer adequate. Many groups refuse to give out their addresses or locations.

Few contemporary groups seek town boundaries to define themselves as geographical and political entities, as Amana did. One new development is the reidentification of some existing towns as communal villages, composed of small communes and sympathetic family households, like Canyon and Bolinas, California. Each communal group regulates its own internal affairs, but all turn out for town projects. A collective boundary is especially important for emphasizing the feeling of closeness. Canyon is a watershed surrounded by forest reserve, and one of the Bolinas communards proposed defining its boundary by limiting the size of sewer pipe to make population growth unfeasible in the future.[31]

Within the communal boundaries, however they are defined, developing adequate communal spaces remains a crucial task. There are fewer religious meeting places because there are fewer sectarian communes today. Emphasis is placed on multiuse dining and meeting spaces less formally defined than the Feast Hall at Harmony or the Hall at Oneida. For many urban groups the need can be met only by tearing down walls of dwellings designed for single families to make communal spaces of adequate size.[32] For other urban groups in warehouses the problem is subdividing large spaces, and somehow softening them, to make them seem convivial, warm places (Fig. 11.5). Rural groups escape these issues, and some have created distinctive single buildings as multipurpose communal centers. Two outstanding examples are the Lama Foundation's adobe buildings in New Mexico and the Oregon Family's circular council house.

The need for private spaces is still debated and no one has developed a clear resolution of the dilemma of communal versus private territory. Some communes have deliberately abolished privacy for everyone, as part of their initiation. The Family justified squeezing about fifty people into a bus and then packing the same number into a four-room house in Taos by saying:

Privacy, or the view that the human needs to be physically and completely alone without anyone else present, has no validity. Privacy is in your head. You can have 'privacy' in a crowded room if you like . . . Maybe you need to be jostled. . . .[33]

The same spirit motivated a Cambridge commune where the members decided to remove the bathroom door, to get over prudishness; a group marriage commune in Connecticut where members decided to abolish private space, to make it easier to rotate bedrooms every night;

and a communal handbook which suggests the removal of all interior walls to facilitate greater communal cohesion.[34]

The belief that violating communards' attitudes toward personal space will create instant communality seems unsophisticated compared to the ways in which the Shakers and the Oneidans prepared their members to accept new definitions of communality. A member of a California commune commented on his experience living with six people in a twelve by twenty-four foot shack: "Communication and openness increased for all of us, but not to the extent that our physical and social contact had increased."[35] Members of his group were not psychologically prepared to accept constant living on top of one another, and they had not the Oneidans' pious justification that living crowded together helped them to learn the virtue of forbearance.

Sociologists who observed rural California communes in 1971 came to the conclusion that a "big house" approach and lack of privacy were typical of the first year only in the groups they studied. Newly formed communes, they argued, need to act out their identity as communes, so they drop their boundaries and stage a scene of "communal life" for all visitors. As soon as a group's coherence is established, the various members may react against this kind of enforced community and withdraw to create individual or family dwellings. For the most part such private dwellings do not contain kitchens or other functional spaces, but are light, playful structures, designed to give some protection from the weather and some privacy in "spiritual matters." These observers reported that the private spaces have an "intimate quality that is extremely uncomfortable when an 'outsider' enters." The interior space usually reflects the

11.5 Turning an urban warehouse into a model communal home means subdividing and softening the vast spaces: plan for warehouse rehabilitation, Synanon, San Francisco, 1972.

11.6 "Blueprint for a Communal Environment," ca. 1969, *The Berkeley Tribe*, plans for rehabilitating Berkeley "tickey tackey" neighborhoods, by closing alternate streets, using land for vegetable gardens, increasing communal circulation on all levels, and combining apartments into larger dwellings with communal living areas and kitchens.

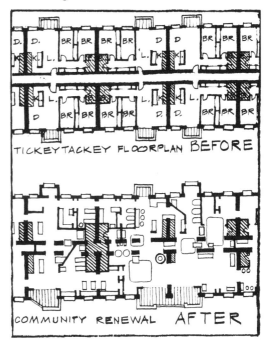

structure without the modification of walls, closets, bureaus, or inside doors. All personal artifacts are immediately visible. Meditation or study is a prominent use of the space, with "skylights, lofts, or small, shrine-like furniture."[36]

This is quite different from Amana or Llano del Rio, where the ideal was to provide conventional family units without kitchens. The equation of private space with self-realization and self-revelation would have seemed wrong to many nineteenth century communes, except perhaps Oneida, where most adults had single rooms. In a way it seems to reflect the culture of suburban America, where young people expect to have their own rooms in family houses. Slightly more structured private dwellings are characteristic of communes where the communards are older and incorporate their families. Libre in Colorado includes family dwellings of various types, many of them domes, located outside of each other's range of sight, to increase privacy.[37] A plan for the Ranchos Colorados commune in Orinda, California, where some of the prospective members were middle aged, shows a ring of private houses, fully equipped with kitchens, around a community center, which is about as private as a commune can get.[38]

The history of communal building recounted here suggests that single-family dwellings are generally a hindrance to communal life, that like the "big house" phase, the "little houses" must be replaced by more complex organization of communal and private territory. The experience of the North American Phalanx, Oneida, and Amana shows that more complex forms are possible. The single-family homes of Greeley offer a warning about the perils of too much privacy which is repeated in one perceptive communard's fear of communes disintegrating into "hippie tract developments."[39] Some few groups do seem to be developing their environments to gradually achieve a better balance. The Twin Oaks community hopes eventually to give every member a private room in a communal building, like Oneida; Birchwood has developed a plan for a series of suites defined by locking and unlocking doors, much like the Phalanx's 1843 communal dwelling, and the Square Pigeon advocates a theory of subneighborhoods within the community which is reminiscent of Oneida's sitting rooms.[40] At Synanon, temporary use of a private room is allowed for those who have demonstrated responsible behavior. Privacy is thus measured in time, and the element of sexual regulation is suggestive of the repressive side of Oneida, effective if not attractive.

A number of communes are aware of the importance of circulation spaces as links between communal and private spaces. The Harrad Commune in Arlington, Massachusetts, identified its most congenial space as a broad landing on the stairs with a radiator underneath, a parallel to the direct heat source in the Oneida Community's "pocket kitchen."[41] The Village of Arts and Ideas modified its Berkeley house by creating a large communal space and then working on circulation spaces, developing better transitions and entrances to private spaces. A commune of Cambridge families connected four attics to provide communal space overhead and private space below, but the acoustical problems were substantial, and they might have done better to link basements or ground floors. No contemporary commune seems to have a theory of design as strong as Fourier's "galleries of association," or a circulation system as intricate as Amana's path networks, although many of the tentative designs may move in these directions, like a Berkeley collective's plan for re-habilitating "tickey tackey" streets (Fig. 11.6). Most groups perceive themselves as committed to flexible spaces and adaptation, but underrate the inflexibility of single family housing and the importance of circulation spaces for stimu-lating activity.

The historic communes' dilemma, in choosing between unique buildings which would distinguish their sites, or replicable but undis-tinguished buildings, was resolved by those groups able to develop what has previously been described as an "intentional vernacular" style of building. Such a style uses local materi-als and a small number of basic building types, adapted to local site conditions, extended or contracted as local programs require. Contem-porary communes are less committed to the strategy of duplicating their communities as models, so many emphasize uniqueness more than replicability. For some, a nose-thumbing, theatrical eccentricity constitutes uniqueness; others hope to persuade the public that their in-novations in building merit imitation, and for them the dilemma still exists.

If the dilemma remains, the areas in which it may be resolved have changed greatly. Very few communes seem interested in claiming unique or central locations for their sites, not wanting to define themselves according to the topog-raphy or the boundaries of an America they re-ject. Uniqueness as a form of building shape is exploited beyond the faint beginnings suggested by Fowler's octagons, used at Modern Times and Hopedale, the round buildings and domes at Point Loma, and others (Fig. 11.7). Buck-minster Fuller's geodesic, in spite of mili-tary exploitation by the Air Force, has inspired the contemporary development of domes and zomes, whose structural innovations have be-come a general communal symbol, although their use is concentrated primarily where the climate permits in the southwest and California (Fig. 11.8). Domes are something different from the habitations of society, where "corners constrict the mind," writes Bill Voyd of Drop City.[42] Other communards decided that they

11.7 One of ten oval houses constructed by a spiritualist community, Spiritual Springs, New York, ca.
1852-1857, and domes of the Temple and the
Homestead, behind round dwellings, Point Loma,
California, ca. 1900.

11.8 "Corners constrict the mind," photograph of
Drop City and instructions for making domes and
"zomes," 1969.

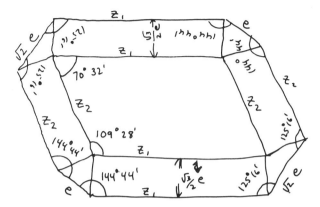

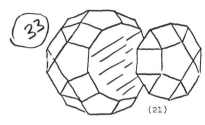

(21)

decagon fusing ring
of the exploded regular
dodecahedron.

Fusing ring of an exploded
rhombic dodecahedron. This ring
cuts behind the diamond where
the zones marked z_1 and z_2 cross.
The ring follows edges except where
it cuts across the two squares
which lie outside the acute angles
of the diamond.

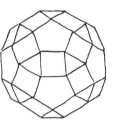

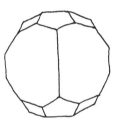

two over lapping rings cut
off of exploded regular dodecahedra

If the dihedral angle between
these two planes were 120°
then three figures cut back
this way could fit as shown
below

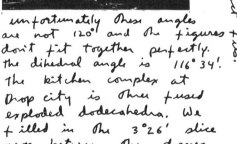

unfortunately these angles
are not 120° and the figures
don't fit together perfectly.
the dihedral angle is 116° 34'.
the kitchen complex at
Drop city is three fused
exploded dodecahedra. We
filled in the 3° 26' slice
gaps between the domes.

When I first discovered that this dihedral angle
was 116° 34' instead of 120° I couldn't accept it.
It seemed so if our universe were flawed. If
the angle were 120° you could pack these together
endlessly in perfect tile.

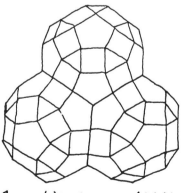

these figures are slightly
distorted to make them meet.

"hate square rooms," and they selected "a design for a hexagonal split level house with pentagonal rooms, an upper and lower deck, and a domed dining tower with a dumbwaiter up the center."[43] Uniqueness sought in terms of color is common; old houses are painted brilliant contrasting colors, especially effective on Victorian gingerbread. Thunder Mountain, Nevada, a religious commune, erected statues and signs visible from the highway reminiscent of the advertising billboard style of Holy City (Figs. 11.9, 11.10). Uniqueness just for the hell of it is boasted: members of the Lewd Commune, a nudist group in Cambridge, Massachusetts, claimed that they developed a unique environment for nudity by keeping the indoor temperature at 78°; people at Project One, located in an old warehouse, joked that they were the only commune with a loading dock.[44]

Perhaps the choice of building materials is the area where most contemporary groups have succeeded in distinguishing themselves. Some groups still rely on adobe, brick, and stone, and may go so far as to be unwilling to live under "anything that has had its molecules rearranged."[45] For many other groups, constructing habitations with any materials they can salvage or scavenge has become a high polemical art. Railroad ties and telephone poles provide supports; old windows offer a variety of outlooks. At the Thunder Mountain Commune in Nevada, a rusted typewriter and an old stove form part of the reinforcing of a wall; massed soda bottles serve as structural window walls. In Canyon, California, one attempt to use salvaged plumbing fixtures developed into a sculptural assemblage of hundreds of water faucets, valves, and pipes, a few of which work. Most famous of all are the car tops chopped into triangles to sheathe domes at Drop City. Most of them were cut for fifteen cents apiece from wrecks in an automobile junkyard, but "Peter Rabbit," a member, claims (with characteristic exhibitionism) that when the group needed one last top he located a new gold Cadillac parked outside a Taos motel, and the "shitmobile turned convertible overnight."[46]

In salvage the communes have found an extremely suggestive approach to both unique and replicable building. The materials have a strong political message, mocking middle America, which produced the original objects for consumption and obsolescence. Builders can identify with squatters in Latin America and Africa, where salvage building is a way of life, and, at the same time, retain ties with the America which surrounds them. As the Oneidans were pleased with the stages of progress revealed in their Mansion House, so communes can find immediate progress in viewing windows, hardware, and junk redeemed from uselessness.

Salvage is an artistic material as well as a political one. Thunder of Thunder Mountain is a sculptor; many Drop City members were New York artists; Hog Farmers worked on graphics in the entertainment industry in Los Angeles. Consciously or not, they are all in the tradition of Kurt Schwitters, the German Dadaist, who extended the techniques of collage to "salvage building" with his first *Merzbau* in Hanover in 1925. Yet for all its uniqueness—the brashness with which salvage buildings confront conventional structures, and the artistic potential of collage—salvage can happen everywhere that communards choose to make a point about building and have enough inventiveness to get the junk to stand up. (Or, if one sees old buses as salvage as well, it can happen as long as communards keep them running.)

Salvage encourages adaptation and perfectionism, the creation of a richer, more developed environment over time. It encourages chance and the *objet trouvé* leading to flexibility in interior design. The Oneidans moved their walls and buildings, to the extent that a workman joked they should be on hinges and castors, but they remained basically conventional buildings. Kaweah's fanciful tents were perhaps more flexible, but this was seen as a temporary solution to their communal housing needs (Fig. 11.11). Some of today's communards are willing to rely on inflatables and collapsibles permanently. The *Mother Earth News* published a design for a living unit with many collapsible elements (Fig. 11.12). The Square Pigeon has built such a communal environment, and the Hog Farm equipped the Road Hog with benches which are also lockers and open out to double bunks. [47] Collapsible furniture suggests economies of space, just as salvage represents economies of materials, reuses which can make an environment richer. Collapsible furniture also implies flexibility. As Andrew Sun and Bruce Hackett put it, "The interplay between structures and people remains informal so that structure seems to support social action rather than define it. . . . It indicates that one is alive in the present and not simply applying solutions arrived at elsewhere to present circumstances."[48]

Salvaged building materials and adaptive techniques help to insure that a commune's building efforts will be unique, but they also lead to a replicable style which can be employed by communal groups sharing a very general ideology. Handbooks on building issued by various communes spread the ideas of domes, salvage, and alternative sources of energy to both communes and individuals. Steve Baer's *Dome Cookbook* from the Lama Foundation instructed people in modeling and building "zomes."[49] *Village One*,

a planning manual developed by the Village of Arts and Ideas, was publicized at various communal design conferences. *The Whole Earth Catalog* led people to books on adobe and rammed earth, as well as manuals on domes, and discussions of environmental psychology like *The Hidden Dimension* and *The Silent Language*.[50] Other popular handbooks are Ken Kern's *The Owner-built Home*, and Art Boericke's *Handmade Houses*, which celebrates some communal and some private constructions.[51] Small magazines carry articles on building and a few films are available, so that information networks surpass anything existing in the nineteenth century.[52]

Despite all this technical and aesthetic literature, there is not much popular writing which links social and political issues to design, as Owen and Fourier attempted to do, or, to a lesser extent, Fowler and Beecher. Paolo Soleri is still working and publishing in the tradition of architects who design ideal cities, but his work frightens more adherents than it attracts with its dystopian scale. Peter Cook and others in the Archigram group publish urban structures and dwellings for 1985, but for all the cleverness of their private graphic and verbal argot, their proposals seem tied to concepts of popular advertising, merchandising, and consumption, which are politically unappealing. [53] Probably the most salutary development among theorists is the appearance of dystopian satire. Successful utopian literature has a timeless interest because of its satirical edge, something utopian architecture has generally lacked. Superstudio of Milan, a collective of young architects, mocks the over-serious visionary architecture of Filarete, Le Corbusier, and Wright in its film script, "Deserti Naturali e Artificiali" (Fig. 11.13) and prods us with the horrors of contemporary urban environments in "Twelve Cautionary Tales."[54] The lack of appeal in current utopian propositions and the success of the dystopians support Goodman's view of "Rural Life, 1984," bringing the cynical, self-mocking spirit full circle. If one perceives American urban environments as windowless, computerized, and daily more unlivable, then what is left but making a very different sort of place in the country? Dystopian, satirical architects serve the commune movement much better than those who are still promising to deliver utopias. In satirizing present tendencies by projecting them into the future, they suggest that everyone should take up the building process herself or himself before it's too late.

In reviewing the achievements of contemporary communes and historic ones in building, it is important to remember their differences in age. Most current attempts are less than ten years old, whereas the historic groups discussed in case studies lasted from thirteen years to more than a century. If current groups sometimes seem clumsy, unrealistic, or naïve, it is as if one looked at Hancock, Massachusetts, in 1792, when converts were crowded into an old farmhouse, and decided that the Shakers were sloppy and disorganized; or looked at Oneida in 1848, when some members were still assigned to rooms as married couples, and decided that the Perfectionists had no clear views on community and privacy. Much of the spirit which animated historic groups still motivates communes today. Oneida's joyful song:

We have built us a dome
On our beautiful plantation
And we all have one home
And one family relation.

is echoed in a member's description of the Hog Farm:

We built a big dome (a domelette next to what we're into now) out of rubber hose, wooden dowels, and this enormous yellow parachute, under which we would gather in circles and search for our center. By dope or by grope . . . we began to discover it . . . heart city.[55]

One finds the same quest for a home, a symbolic communal center, where the communards can create "one family relation," or more succinctly, "heart city." Some contemporary groups will no doubt develop model environments over the next few decades which are as subtly worked out, in terms of personal relationships and environmental structure, as Hancock or Oneida at their height. Others will dedicate themselves to gestures, as some communards always have, but they will be adding to the long history of American communal environments a few new experiments which connect with the mainstream of contemporary arts. The Living Theatre, Neo-Dadaism, Happenings, and Archigram seem somewhat contrived if you are used to communal encounter groups, communal salvage building, and communal buses. When the Hog Farm talks of trying to make the "life show" and the "show show" converge,[56] the work of William Morris and Etienne Cabet, with their literary descriptions of vivid, varied, communal environments, suddenly seems tight and dull, confined to three dimensions rather than four. When the members of Thunder Mountain, with their buildings supported by stoves, Coke bottles, and railroad ties, tell us that American cities, as environmental constructions, are preposterous, the polemic is more devastating than any Owen or Fourier could muster. The artistic unity of the Thunder Mountain buildings comes from profound negation of the bourgeois stereotype of domestic architecture. What Tzara, Schwitters, and Duchamp did for poetry, collage, and painting, some American communards are now doing for architecture. Their processes provide one more way to answer the communitarian anarchist, Murray Bookchin, who asks, "How does the liberated self emerge that is capable of turning time into life, space into community, and human relationships into the marvellous?"[57] But this is a negative, nose-thumbing response which leaves a larger question unanswered: how does one relate communal experience to reconstructing the larger society?

11.9 Visual uniqueness achieved with collage techniques: "The Ideal Station," "Your Friend," "Come Up Here and See Something," communal gas station, Holy City, California, 1918.

11.10 Salvage materials carry an artistic message as
well as a political one: Thunder Mountain, Nevada,
communal building of adobe, salvaged metal, bottles,
and railroad ties, photograph 1972.

11.11 Flexible shelters, tents at Kaweah Colony, town
of Advance, California, July 1889.

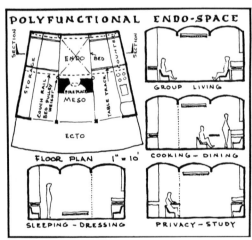

11.12 "The interplay between structures and people
remains informal": "Polyfunctional Endo-Space,"
designed by Ken Kern, 1970.

11.13 If one perceives utopianism as worn out and
urban environments as daily more unlivable, what is
left but making a better place in the country? "Deserti
Naturali e Artificiali" (Natural and artificial deserts),
film storyboard by Superstudio, Milan, 1971.

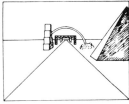

29. UN VIAGGIO IN AUTO IN UN MUSEO DRI-
VE-IN DELL'ARCHITETTURA. Souvenirs di viag-
gio da un viaggio nelle regioni della ragione.
**A CAR JOURNEY TO A DRIVE-IN MUSEUM OF
ARCHITECTURE. Souvenirs from a journey into
the realms of reason.**

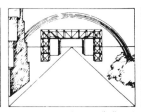

30. Dall'architettura dei monumenti attraverso
l'architettura delle immagini e l'architettura tec-
nomorfa all'architettura della ragione
**From the architecture of monuments through
the architecture of images and technomorphous
architecture to reach the architecture of reason**

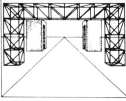

31. (durante il viaggio ci sono apparizioni di
monumenti antichi, arcobaleni e nuvole al neon,
macchine tralicci e statue).
**(throughout the journey there are apparitions of
ancient monuments, rainbows, neon clouds, machines steel framework and statues).**

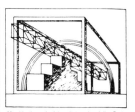

32. L'arrivo trionfale al tempio della Ragion
Pura (scritta: « nella prospettiva storica, la Ra-
gione domina tutto »).
**The triumphant arrival at the temple of Pure
Reason (banner: « in historical perspective, Rea-
son dominates all »).**

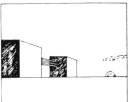

33. COME ILLUMINARE IL DESERTO. Due pri-
smi neri di marmo o cristallo collegati da un
arcobaleno al neon per illuminare la mente,
posti.
**HOW TO ILLUMINATE THE DESERT. Two black
prisms of marble or crystal joined by a neon
rainbow to illuminate the mind, placed...**

34. nei deserti artificiali o interiori. Quando il
sole tramonta i tubi cominciano a brillare a
intermittenza, e nei lampi delle...
**in artificial or interior deserts. When the sun
goes down, the tubes begin to glow intermit-
tently, and in the flashes of...**

35. accensioni appaiono immagini di architettura di sogno, radiosi orizzonti con un fil di
fumo, tempo libero, maisons pour le...
**light images of dream architecture appear, ra-
diant horizons with a wisp of smoke, free time,
maisons pour le...**

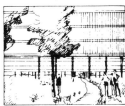

36. week-end, immagini di felicità per mezzo
dell'architettura, costruzioni ariose, città ordi-
nate, spazi verdi...
**week-end, images of happiness through archi-
tecture, airy buildings, ordered cities, green
spaces...**

37. Nella luce che aumenta si vedono i nuovi
monumenti della scienza e della tecnica (Crystal Palace) e le utopie (Falanstery.
**In the growing light, one can see the monu-
ments of science and technology (the Crystal
Palace) and utopias (Falanstery,...**

38. New Harmony, Philadelphia) e le costruzioni eroiche del razionalisr o (Weissenhof, Bauhaus. Ville Radieuse) i cataloghi delle illusioni.
**New Harmony, Philadelphia) and the heroic buil-
dings of the age of rationalism (Weissenhof, Bauhaus, Ville Radieuse): the catalogues of illu-
sions...**

39. e delle utopie. « Il mondo delle idee, delle
credenze, delle fantasie e dei progetti è altret-
tanto reale della realtà - (L. Mumford).
**and utopias. « The world of ideas, of beliefs, of
fantasies and projects is just as real as reality »
(L. Mumford).**

40. I tubi luminosi divengono un arco trionfale e sotto ci passano carovane di nomadi.
impiegati in gita, processioni di pace.
**The glowing tubes become an arch of triumph
under which processions of nomads, white-col-
lar workers on holiday, peace demonstrations,
pass.**

Notes to Chapter Eleven

1 David French and Elena French, "Research on Intentional Communities in the United States: A Brief Report," mimeo, Johnson State College, Johnson, Vt., n.d. (1972?), p. 7, citing Judith Jerome, *Families of Eden*, New York, 1974.

2 Rosabeth Moss Kanter, ed., *Communes: Creating and Managing the Collective Life*, New York, 1973, p. 9.

3 Paul Goodman, *People or Personnel*, New York, 1968, pp. 412-422.

4 Lou Gottlieb, quoted in Stanley Krippner and Don Fersh, "Mystic Communes," *The Modern Utopian*, 4.2 (Spring 1970), unpaged.

5 Marge Piercy, *Dance the Eagle to Sleep*, New York, 1972; Don Benson, "Optimal Size," *The Modern Utopian*, 4.3-4 (Summer-Fall 1970), unpaged.

6 Raymond Mungo, *Total Loss Farm*, New York, 1970.

7 "Ecotecture" was the title of a conference organized at Berkeley in December 1972. "Arcology" is Paolo Soleri's term combining the same words.

8 Doug Dahlin, "Intentional Community," unpublished paper, Department of Architecture, University of California, Berkeley, n.d. (1971?), pp. 6-7, pp. 12-13, p. 23.

9 Village of Arts and Ideas, *Village One*, Berkeley, 1972.

10 New Alchemy Institute, *Bulletin*, quoted in David Dickson, *Alternative Technology and the Politics of Technical Change*, London, 1974, p. 101.

11 Murray Bookchin, *Post-Scarcity Anarchism*, Berkeley, 1971.

12 Paolo Soleri, *Arcology: The City in the Image of Man*, Cambridge, Mass., 1969.

13 Tom Wolfe, *The Electric Kool Aid Acid Test*, New York, 1970.

14 Richard Fairfield, *Communes U.S.A.*, Baltimore, 1972, p. 314.

15 Eric Uddenberg, "Village of Arts and Ideas," unpublished paper, Department of Architecture, University of California, Berkeley, May 1973, unpaged.

16 The experience of Bensalem College in Fordham, New York, reveals that traditional apartment houses resist communal conversions because of their unlit, long corridors, according to Lance Laver and Ira Grossman, "Bensalem College," unpublished paper, Department of Architecture, M.I.T., 1968.

17 Philip Slater, *The Pursuit of Loneliness*, Boston, 1972.

18 "Butter Pecan Builder," *Time*, Jan. 8, 1973, p. 41.

19 David Felton, "The Dangers of Charisma: Mel Lyman and Fort Hill," in Kanter, *Communes*, p. 212. See also *American Avatar*, the Fort Hill publication.

20 Roger Montgomery, "Synanon City," *Architectural Forum*, 133 (Nov. 1970), 52-55. Also see Ellis Kaplan, "Territory and Status–The Uses of Environment within a Communal Society–Synanon," paper delivered at EDRA Conference, EDRA 3/AR8, Jan. 1972, in William Mitchell, ed., *Proceedings*, vol. 1, pp. 13-5-1 to 13-5-4.

21 Hugh Romney, "The Hog Farm," *The Realist*, 86 (Nov.-Dec. 1969), 18.

22 Cambridge Institute, New City Project, "Prospectus," mimeo, Cambridge, Mass., Sept. 8, 1970.

23 Gordon Yaswen, "Sun-Rise Hill," *The Modern Utopian*, 4.3-4 (Summer-Fall 1970), p. 7. (Also reprinted in Kanter, *Communes*.)

24 Dahlin, "Intentional Community," p. 18.

25 *Leaves of Twin Oaks*, 2.22 (Mar. 1973), 6.

26 Kathleen Kinkade, *A Walden Two Experiment*, New York, 1973, p. 95.

27 "Project One," Optic Nerve Videotape, San Francisco, 1972.

28 Romney, "The Hog Farm," p. 23.

29 *Outlaw Builder*, Berkeley, 1972, p. 25.

30 Ibid., p. 27.

31 Steven van der Zee, *Canyon: The Story of the Last Rustic Community in Metropolitan America*, New York, 1972; Bolinas's boundary was discussed at the "Ecotecture" conference in Berkeley, 1972.

32 On conversion of urban dwellings, one very useful manual is Nancy Goodwin, "Halfway Home," unpublished M.Arch. thesis, M.I.T., 1974, a design guide for halfway houses for mental patients which applies also to communal needs.

33 Fairfield, *Communes U.S.A.*, p. 319. Also see Kanter, *Communes*, pp. 430-442.

34 Clem Gorman, *Making Communes*, Bottisham, England, 1972, p. 73.

35 Dahlin, "Intentional Community," p. 22.

36 Bruce Hackett and Andrew Sun, "Communal Architecture and Social Structure," paper delivered at EDRA Conference, EDRA 3/AR8, Jan. 1972, in William Mitchell, ed., *Proceedings*, vol. 1, p. 13-4-4.

37 "Libre," *Architectural Design*, 41 (Dec. 1971), 727-731.

38 New Community I, Planned Unit Development, Orinda, California, "Preliminary Development Plan," November 10, 1971, plan by Douglas Brian Healy, landscape architect.

39 Hackett and Sun, "Communal Architecture," p. 13-4-5.

40 Gorman, *Making Communes*, pp. 71-72.

41 Interview with Harrad Commune, Arlington, Mass., 1969.

42 Bill Voyd, "Drop City," in Paul Oliver, ed., *Shelter and Society*, London, 1969.

43 Dahlin, "Intentional Community," p. 17.

44 Interview with Lewd Commune, Cambridge, Mass., 1969; "Project One," videotape, 1972.

45 Lloyd Kahn, quoted in David Dickson, *Alternative Technology and the Politics of Technical Change*, London, 1974, p. 129.

46 "Peter Rabbit," *Drop City*, New York, 1971, p. 46.

47 Ken Kern, "The Owner-Built Homestead," *The Mother Earth News*, 5 (Sept. 1970), 73; Gorman, *Making Communes*, p. 73; Romney, "The Hog Farm," p. 19.

48 Hackett and Sun, "Communal Architecture," p. 5.

49 Steve Baer, *Dome Cookbook*, Corrales, N.M., 1969.

50 Stuart Brand, ed., *The Whole Earth Catalog* (and supplements), Menlo Park, 1968-1969; Edward T. Hall, *The Hidden Dimension*, Garden City, 1966, and *The Silent Language*, Garden City, 1959.

51 Ken Kern, *The Owner-Built Home*, Oakhurst, Calif., 1970.

52 Art Boericke, *Handmade Houses*, San Francisco, 1973; also see Jan Wampler, "Imprint," *Architecture Plus*, 2 (Aug. 1974), a collection of individualistic, unique houses.

53 Among the journals which communards follow are *Modern Utopian, Green Revolution, Mother Earth News*, and *Communities*. Films include "Peace, Love, Taos, 1970," by the Family, and "Project One" videotape by Optic Nerve.

53 Peter Cook, *Experimental Architecture*, New York, 1970.

54 Superstudio, "Deserti Naturali e Artificiali," *Casabella*, 358 (1971), 18-22; "Twelve Cautionary Tales for Christmas; Premonitions of the Mystical Rebirth of Urbanism," *Architectural Design*, 42 (Dec. 1971), 737-742.

55 Oneida song, quoted in Rosabeth Moss Kanter, *Commitment and Community*, Cambridge, Mass., 1972, p. 9; Romney, "The Hog Farm," p. 18.

56 Romney, "The Hog Farm," p. 18.

57 Bookchin, *Post-Scarcity Anarchism*, p. 54.

12 Premature Truths

By calling everything utopian that goes beyond the present existing order, one sets at rest the anxiety that might arise from the relative utopias that are realizable in another order.

—Karl Mannheim, *Utopia and Ideology*, 1936

Utopias are often only premature truths.

—Lamartine

"Vision of the New Eden," frontispiece from David A. Moore, *The Age of Progress*, 1856, showing a neoclassical palace surrounded by an Edenic garden guarded by two angels.

What is the relevance of communal architecture and planning for a contemporary, largely noncommunal world? How can present-day community groups, architects, planners, and building workers apply the lessons of communal building to the experience of contemporary building projects or the organization of the design and building professions?

In the previous chapters I have used the term "utopia" to refer to an imaginary or experimental scheme for an ideal society, and I have used "ideology" to refer to a body of ideas on which a particular political, economic, or social system, real or ideal, is based. In an extensive discussion of the utopian mentality, Karl Mannheim defines these terms more narrowly. For him, both utopias and ideologies are ideas or values which transcend the existing order, but he limits "utopias" to those ideas which offer revolutionary possibilities, while "ideologies" harmonize with the spirit of the age in a wishful but nonrevolutionary way. Observers who consciously or unconsciously resist revolutionary change will blur the distinctions between utopias and ideologies, regarding them as equally unrealizable. But those who seek change need to recognize and exploit utopias as the "explosive material for bursting the limits of the existing order," which contain "in condensed form the unrealized and the unfulfilled tendencies which represent the needs of each age."[1]

Visionary physical designs can always be made to harmonize with the spirit of society in a wishful but nonrevolutionary way. The history of ideal city design reveals formal solutions consistently appropriated to serve the prevailing economic and social order: fortified, geometrical cities suited Renaissance despots; ideal institutional buildings designed in the nineteenth

century appealed to the organizers of jails, workhouses, and corporate towns. In the twentieth century, the humorless visionary, Le Corbusier, offered society his Radiant City with the slogan, "Architecture or revolution?" Thus, in Mannheim's terms, Le Corbusier defined his own idealistic work as emphatically not utopian, precluding, rather than offering, revolutionary possibilities.

Is it possible to escape the authoritarian stance of planners and architects who propose perfect forms (ideal cities, ideal building types, ideal circulation systems, or ideal "pattern languages") as the expressions of perfectly organized societies? Is it possible to imagine an architecture of liberation, an architecture with revolutionary political implications? Does the experience of historic communal societies offer any more insights than the work of idealistic professionals?

Communal buildings, isolated from their political and environmental context, are often reduced to eccentric artifacts and then equated with architects' ideal designs as impractical follies. Thus single buildings with unusual formal or functional arrangements—the bilateral symmetry of Shaker dwellings, or the "millennial order" of suns, moons, and stars on the Nauvoo Temple—are thought to represent the architecture of historic communal societies. Such buildings are then dismissed as curiosities, with no social or political relevance. The seven preceding case studies show, however, that historic communal societies offer more than odd architecture: they represent a history of organizing and building processes. Here there are "premature truths" to be grasped. Social and economic reorganization must be the basis of any environmental reorganization. A new architecture expressing liberation can come only from a liberated group of people, not from an idealistic architect or planner sitting at a drawing board.

In the preceding cases, I have attempted to describe fully the consistent (or inconsistent) relationships between economic organization, social practice, and building process. Transcending the various outdated millennial religions and utopian socialisms, uniting all the case studies, is the communards' driving desire to shape new communities where landscape, workplaces, and dwellings reflected some egalitarian ideal. In terms of their political development, this effort to organize new communities was perhaps premature. But in terms of design processes, communards discovered some "explosive material for bursting the limits of the existing order," material relevant to all politically committed groups engaged in design.

Despite their spatial and economic limitations, some American communal societies had the resources and the time to create socialist environments more consistent than those created by socialist states. Some communes struggled for decades with all of the hardest design questions. Who decides what dwellings and workplaces will be like? How much space is public? How much is private? How are they connected? How much do groups want their designs to be seen as unique? How much are they models for the rest of society and the world? These are the debates between authoritarian and participatory processes, communal and private territory, unique and replicable plans, which take place in any group attempting to reorganize its environment to reflect greater social and economic equality. Israeli *kibbutzim*, Tanzanian *ujamaa* villages, Chinese communes, and Soviet housing authorities still continue these debates. Although there are no definitive answers, because every group must find a process of design

which reflects its own ongoing search for an appropriate socialist consensus, the Shakers provided a definitive metaphor. The "living building" is an image which links the organizational process to the building process.

Because the lessons of communal building are political and social, more than technical or stylistic, they often apply across the centuries, to rural and urban, primitive and technically sophisticated, agricultural and industrial projects. As the previous chapter suggests, contemporary communes ignore historic communal debates at the peril of repeating their predecessors' mistakes, building in the same tentative ways, reliving the same dilemmas. Larger socialist projects also can benefit from the lessons of the communal experience: *kibbutzim* have repeated some of the arguments made about the Oneida Children's House and the Newllano "Kid Kolony"; Chinese communes have struggled through the same sort of ideological debates about private garden plots as Icaria and Amana; organizers of *ujamaa* villages could study the schemes of land allocation in the farm villages of Amana and Nauvoo; Cuban designers of housing need to understand the strengths and weaknesses of various feminist proposals for collective housekeeping facilities. Not only communes and socialist countries can benefit from the lessons of communal design processes. Any community group which is concerned with using environmental design to support a broader program of social change will have similar questions to resolve—whether they be alternative educational institutions, tenants' collectives, trade unions, neighborhood park committees, or day care organizers. And all of these community groups, if they undertake the design process with a self-conscious desire to further political ends, may generate their own "premature truths" as well.

Reviewing the seven case studies, I believe that a few general principles emerge, as well as some suggestions for the historic preservation of communal projects.

1. Tentative designs representing ongoing collective processes may serve community needs better than finished designs which are the work of only one designer.

In order to use design to explore ideology, define territory, and develop inventiveness, most secular communities need to work with tentative, open-ended plans which reflect varied contributions and interests. Such frameworks invite additions over time and allow the design process to develop along with the political process.

At the scale of the building, a tentative design framework may be a plan for one or more wings of a structure which can grow with the community. The members of the North American Phalanx developed the parts of their phalanstery year by year, framing it in the local style of domestic architecture, revealing in each succeeding wing their convictions about family suites and dormitories. This process allowed community members to be far more consistent in their reconciliation of life space and life style than the members of the Raritan Bay Union, who passively accepted a gigantic brick phalanstery designed by a professional architect and commissioned by a patron who refused to adopt its communal arrangements for his own family. Similarly, the Oneida Perfectionists developed their own formula for housing suited to their sexual practices by experimenting with a temporary "Tent Room," which was refined in later building efforts over the next thirty years. In contrast, the "Social Palace" with "a hundred bowers of love's repose," proposed by a single designer for a community at Fountain-

grove, California, never progressed beyond fanciful plans.

At the scale of the settlement, a tentative design framework can take the form of guidelines or codes for building which are revised over time as the distribution of resources and territory is clarified. The Shakers developed their Millennial Laws to suit larger villages; the Mormons reinterpreted their "Plat of the City of Zion" to accommodate regional development. Just as successful community groups must resist the development of rigid party hierarchies or encumbering bureaucracies, so they must resist rigid or encumbering environments. Like the organizations they shelter, community plans and spaces should be capable of growth and change: the metaphor of the "living building" includes both the organization and its environment.

2. Individual, expressive involvement in construction, landscaping, decorating, and inventions complements collective design frameworks.

The more developed a collective design framework becomes, the more defined areas are needed for individual freedom of expression within it. (This kind of expressive participation is a natural consequence for communities which determine design frameworks by consensus; it is a saving feature for those which develop frameworks more arbitrarily.) In building projects where architects determine every detail, an artificial, formal consistency is achieved at the expense of builders' and users' capacities for self-expression. Politically conscious communities must support and develop these expressive capacities to aid, rather than contradict, the establishment of communal design frameworks and communal territory.

In most successful communes, participation

in construction, landscaping, decorating and inventing was highly developed. In Shaker communities, legendary inventiveness was coupled with meticulous craft, and encouragement for members to create songs and spirit drawings which were metaphors of construction extended the areas of possible self-expression. For the Harmonists, skill and inventiveness in construction helped to obviate possessiveness; for the Oneidans, involvement in landscape design, as well as in industrial design and interior decoration, served a similar function. Of course, individual self-expression without a collective framework could easily become competitive, as housing and commercial construction did in Greeley. The need for self-expression is strong; a collective framework which defines no areas for individual contributions will ultimately be subverted, in the way that Amana residents eventually remodeled their communal houses.

3. Communal territory is not created by taking away private territory.

The experience of all historic and contemporary groups attempting to replace private property and territory with communal property and territory shows nothing so disastrous as forced deprivation of privacy. It is not a means of creating community. Perhaps the Shakers developed the most sophisticated system of initiation to communal territory by letting members gradually proceed from private property to cooperation to communism, moving to neighborhoods closer to the center of their villages with each advance in sharing. This was their indoctrination into the "living building." The contemporary Synanon commune offers a similar process. Newcomers are encouraged to articulate their needs for private space, but more seasoned members take pride in relying less on possessions or personal space to define their position: "Character is the only status."

Community members should be drawn to communal territory by the provision of pleasant, clearly defined places where amenities are concentrated. Communal activities and communal spaces must be developed simultaneously. Even the most basic activities will falter, as in Greeley, without adequate meeting places or workplaces, just as spaces will remain barren without organized activities to fill them. The success of various communal industries may be attributed, in part, to the provision of attractive workplaces which expressed the workers' consciousness that they were the owners and organizers of land, buildings, and resources: Amana's factories were built as well as its churches and equipped with small kitchens and dining areas; meticulous Shaker workshops were fitted with all possible labor saving devices. Fourier's suggestion of refreshment pavilions in the fields would have extended Amana's factory amenities to agricultural workers; Harmonists provided special mobile shelters for their shepherds.

To identify communal territory and locate collective activities, boundaries and vantage points are useful. Roads, gates, fences, landscaping, or distinctive building styles can define the communal territory for members and visitors. Almost all communal groups built towers or established lookouts for a literal overview of their land and activities. By placing communal facilities in central locations surrounded by dwellings, Amana Inspirationists made community territory accessible to members but not outsiders. The fullest exterior identification of communal activities was achieved by the Shakers, who used building form, position, and color to denote various uses.

4. Needs for private territory are not best served by private family houses.

Needs for privacy, expressed by individuals, couples, or families, often can be met best by private spaces within a communal household, large or small. Varied and inventive designs for communal housing which included family apartments, family suites, or individual private rooms have been developed by the North American Phalanx, Oneida, Amana, and Newllano, as well as by some contemporary communes. Their creators accepted the argument, succinctly stated by Charles Fourier and Alice Constance Austin, that even the most elaborate private dwellings lack real luxury, because they are isolated from collective services. Facilities for collective child care, laundry, cooking, and dining can free all members of a community for equal participation in its activities. To ignore the need for such facilities, as the communities at Nauvoo and Greeley chose to, reinforces the problems of sexism and traditional "women's work." Isolated family dwellings often strain the resources of men and women who attempt to share the burden of private child care and housekeeping; they often oppress those women (or men) who must cope with this burden alone.

5. Spaces which link communal and private territory must receive special attention.

Fourier's proposal for street galleries as places of "passional attraction" in the Phalanx was based on his observation of the function of circulation spaces in promoting casual social meetings, and his descriptions of the landscape of "interlaced cultivation" extend this idea to outdoor spaces. Porches and a gallery at the North American Phalanx; corridors, entrance halls, basement tunnels, and sitting rooms at Oneida;

exterior pathways at Amana: all were arranged to provide links between private territory and communal territory. They encouraged spontaneous meetings which nourished a feeling of community among residents, and similar arrangements should be part of any community design.

6. Uniqueness may result from simplification and standardization, rather than complication and expense.

Although extremely eccentric facades were erected at Nauvoo and Holy City by communards who wished to appear unique, the most distinctive approaches to communal building were created by the Shakers and the Amana Inspirationists, groups which developed "intentional vernacular" styles reflecting the unique economic and social structures of their societies. Other communal groups, such as the Oneida Perfectionists and the Llano colonists, evolved distinctive styles of interior design, but favored conventional, bourgeois facades, using eclectic Italianate, French Mansard or Spanish elements.

The Shakers and Inspirationists avoided eccentric display and fashionable eclecticism, in accordance with the belief that ornament was a capitalist luxury in a world where many had no housing. The Shakers created a few standard building types, which they varied for different sites and programs; the Inspirationists used one standard design for domestic, institutional, and factory buildings. Consistent site planning, construction, and detailing make twenty-odd Shaker villages and seven Amana villages easily recognizable. By simplifying every building design and building as solidly as possible, both groups expressed their ascetic communism. The Shakers were more exacting than the Inspirationists, and their architecture is famous for its originality and directness. This is simply the result of the most consistent resolution of life style and life space achieved by any communal group. Its formal rigor depended on the participation of all members of the society in the "living building," manipulating systems of spatial constraint and release which began with body movement and encompassed present and future aspirations, earthly and heavenly space.

Hundreds of communal settlements were constructed in the United States, and dozens remain, often ignored rather than consciously preserved. They are important to our history as consistent environments which reveal idealistic attitudes to land and life. At their best, communes contain imaginative arrangements of communal and private spaces, but whatever their design, these physical remains can reveal the design and building processes which politically idealistic groups undertook, and they should be preserved in ways which emphasize these processes.

A number of small communal dwellings are preserved as historic houses, but this approach isolates residential structures from their social and economic context. A number of sites—including Hancock, Canterbury, Pleasant Hill, Bishop Hill, Nauvoo, Economy, Zoar, New Harmony, and Amana—are preserved as villages or parts of villages. Unfortunately their potential to reveal the consistency of an egalitarian, communal way of life is not fully exploited. One would like to see the communal land returned to its original configuration of fields and gardens, but museums can rarely afford to own and farm the communal land at all. Only Amana retains its original holdings in their full extent. Similarly one would like to view the complete range of communal industries, but dwellings usually receive priority, although curators at Hancock have done an exceptional job of restoring Shaker workshops and barns.

Living reuses of some communal buildings may obscure the original relationship between communal activities and building design, but they serve another purpose: the residents who inhabit these buildings become somewhat more communal in their habits. The result is a kind of transitional architecture useful to a community group seeking a more communal lifestyle. Thus the Oneida Mansion House now functions rather well as an apartment house with many elderly residents who inhabit one- to three-room apartments, and have the use of communal sitting rooms, lounge, theater, library, and dining hall. The North American Phalanx buildings would have made excellent university housing for faculty and students. Unfortunately, consideration of such a renovation was halted when the structure was destroyed by fire in 1972. At Amana, the small communal dwellings and kitchen houses have been converted to single-family dwellings, but the communal facilities remain in the centers of the blocks. One can conceive of turning an American suburban neighborhood back to the Amana model—communalizing land, building kindergartens and schools connected with streets by pedestrian networks, converting one house into a communal kitchen and dining place, perhaps turning other houses into small communes. This would produce very similar results to the Berkeley *Tribe's* proposal for communalizing "Tickey-Tackey," mentioned in the preceding chapter.

Some living reuses are less kind than Oneida's and Amana's: a Moravian building in Hope, New Jersey, has become a drive-in bank; part of a Shaker Village at Enfield, New Hampshire, has been crudely modernized into a Catholic retreat house, religious article shop and parking lot; other Shaker buildings at New Lebanon, and Canaan, New York, have been painted red and white to serve a summer camp, and remodeled with Japanese detailing as a restaurant. Perhaps the Latter-day Saints in Nauvoo have made the greatest mistake as preservationists: they leveled the communal schoolhouse which the Icarian community built in that town in order to give preeminence to the Mormon remains.

When politically self-conscious building processes replace visionary designs as the focus for socialist idealism about the environment, the roles of client, architect, critic, and builder will undergo drastic changes. Communal history suggests some of the possibilities. Groups of clients—who define themselves as communities—will assert themselves politically as communards did, by using design and building processes to express ideology and define territory. Architects who wish to work with such community groups will need skills which support, rather than preempt, group creativity. Straightforward graphics will have to replace esoteric ones; models with movable parts will replace fixed representations of complete designs. As role models, architects will come to admire the teams of Shaker master builders who traveled to building sites carrying some basic framing plans, and then, in collaboration with the local residents and builders, determined the appropriate site and form for a new building and supervised its construction. Or they will adopt the attitude of Erastus Hamilton, the architect at Oneida who attributed the plans of the Mansion House to patience and the willingness to wait for consensus. Any doubts about the abilities of community members to take part in design should be stilled by the memory of Tabitha Babbitt, the Shaker sister who invented a circular saw while working at her spinning wheel, and the dozens of other communitarians whose inventions had architectural applications. Historians will chronicle these new ways of working: the most useful critical works will analyze a community's ability to articulate its goals and organize to achieve them. Individual designs will be dealt with as a contribution to this community process, not as self-justifying works of art.

When clients become politically self-conscious

groups whose identity and activities are heightened by the building process, when architects and historians use their skills to support such groups, what part do builders play? Members of historic communes usually built their own buildings; for them the role of builder implied the role of client as well. To apply this communal assumption to complex, urban societies, one must reorder the pairing of roles. Clients who take on the role of builders can achieve social and environmental consistency; builders who take on the role of clients can exercise social and environmental power.

For the Shakers, the metaphor of the "living building" expressed their efforts to shape the social and economic structure of their community, and the environmental structure, to a millennial ideal. In at least one contemporary urban situation, construction workers have adopted a view of society and its environment as a "living building" they wish to shape, and their efforts deserve brief mention here. In the past few years, several militant unions in Australia[2] have responded to the concerns of ecologists, preservationists, and community groups by refusing to work on projects which the members decide are socially unacceptable. Like communal builders, who are their own clients, these workers do not distinguish between their own needs and those of the people they build for. The builders view themselves as users of the public environment they help to create. When they go on strike out of a sense of responsibility for the consequences of their work, they force other groups to reexamine their roles as well. Community groups must accept responsibility for their goals since they have sanctions to support them; architects must accept responsibility for their designs and cease to design speculative living space or working space which

workers reject as inadequate; critics must accept responsibility for their architectural judgments on social as well as aesthetic grounds. As such social consciousness spreads, design and building processes come closer to communal models, but a survey of such urban efforts to confront the environmental consequences of individualism and economic competition would be the starting point for another book.

Almost two hundred years ago, in the harsh landscape of the New World, refugees from industrial Manchester, England, began to create small, idealistic communities where every building was designed and constructed as a visual statement of the workings of religious communism. They celebrated their achievement with a hymn, exhorting themselves to take pride in what they had made. Their success was shared by other communal groups who attempted to sketch their own "premature truths" in the processes of communal design and building. Politically conscious communities everywhere can still respond to the joy and the hope expressed in the Shaker cry: "Leap and shout, ye living building!"

1 Karl Mannheim, *Ideology and Utopia*, tr. Louis Wirth and Edward Shils, New York, 1936, pp. 192-199.

2 Leonie Sandercock, *Cities for Sale*, Melbourne, Australia, 1975, and Pete Thomas, *Taming the Concrete Jungle: The Builders Labourers' Story*, Sydney, Australia, 1973, offer accounts of these union activities.

Appendix A:
Comparative Chart of Communities

	Hancock	Nauvoo	Phalanx
Dates active	1790-1960	1839-1846	1843-1856
Location	Massachusetts	Illinois	New Jersey
Previous settlements	Yes	Yes	No
Other branches	24, united	Moved to Salt Lake City, branches there	About 30, not united
Population, first year	40	(?) 2,450-5,000	24-112
Maximum population	300	10,000-15,000	112
Maximum acreage	3,500-6,000 (?)	2,000 (20,000 acres disputed)	673
Official religion	United Society of Believers	Church of Jesus Christ of the Latter-day Saints	Christian, nonsectarian
Economic organization	Cooperation leading to total communal ownership and support	Redistribution systems giving way to capitalism with some cooperation	Cooperation; equalized wages
Economic base	Farming, crafts, furniture	Farming, land speculation	Farming, canning, milling
Source of capital	Members	Members and non-resident converts	Members and non-resident stockholders
Sexual organization	Celibacy	Monogamy, some polygamy	Monogamy
Typical unit of adult living space	2-4 people per bedroom, same sex	Double bedroom	Double or single bedroom
Next sizes of units	—	Family house	Family suite or cottage
	Communal "family" dwelling, 30-100 people	Block or crossroads neighborhood	Communal dwelling, under 100 people

Oneida	Amana	Greeley	Llano
1847-1881	1855-1932	1869-1871	1914-1917
New York	Iowa	Colorado	California
Yes	Yes	No	No
At least 6, united	No	Imitations, not united	Moved to Louisiana, branches there
87	572	460	50
205	1,756	1,200	900
654	25,659	60,000	1,990
Perfectionism	True Inspiration Congregations	Christian, at least 5 sects	None
Total communal ownership and support	Total communal ownership and support	Capitalism with some cooperation	Cooperation, equalized wages
Farming, fruit growing, crafts, traps, silk thread, silverware	Farming, woolens, calico printing, furniture	Farming, stock raising, milling	Farming
Members	Members	Members	Members and pledged future members
Group marriage, couples discouraged	Monogamy or celibacy, children discouraged	Monogamy	Monogamy
Single bedroom, some doubles, same sex	Double bedroom or dormitory	Double bedroom or dormitory	Double or single bedroom
Sitting room neighborhood, 14-30 people	Family suite	Family house	Family house or hotel
Communal dwelling, 200 people	Kitchen house neighborhood, 30-50 people	—	—

The chart continues on the next page.

	Hancock	Nauvoo	Phalanx
	—	Ward	—
Largest geographical unit	Village, 300 people	Town, 10,000 people	Community, 112 people
Nongeographical social unit	Community including all branches	Church	Unions of Associationists
Leadership	Prophet and appointed religious leaders	Prophet and appointed religious leaders	Elected president and directors
Religious meetings, all members together	Weekly (village)	1-3 per week	Few or none
Small groups	5-6 per week	None (?)	None
Community business meetings, all members together	None	None	Nightly, then weekly
Role of women (in theory)	Equal	Wives and mothers, plural wives	Should be equalized
Role of women (in practice)	2 women and 2 men in all offices; collective work segregated by sex, domestic and crafts	Isolated domestic work	3 women directors; collective work, usually domestic
Childrearing	Communal (converts and adopted children)	Family	Family plus daycare and school

Oneida	Amana	Greeley	Llano
—	Village, 100-300 people	—	—
Community, 205 people	County, 7 villages, 1,800 people	Town, 1,200 people	Community, 900 people
Community including all branches	—	—	—
Prophet and "leading men"	*Werkzeuge* and appointed elders	Elected president and directors	Elected president and directors
None	2 per week (village), every 2 years (7 villages)	Weekly (then none)	None
None	About 9 per week	None	None
Nightly	1 per year	Weekly, or monthly	1-2 per month
Equal	Spiritually inferior, "dangerous fire"	Should be equalized (?)	Wives and mothers
Collective work, usually domestic, some factory	Collective work, domestic, factory, agricultural	Isolated domestic work, some teachers	Collective work, usually domestic
Communal (stirpiculture)	Family plus daycare and school	Family plus school	Some communal, some family, daycare and school

Appendix B:
List of Communitarian Settlements to 1860

Item numbers are keyed to maps in Fig. 2.1.

1. Plockhoy's Commonwealth, Lewes, Delaware, founded 1663.

2. Labadist Community, Bohemia Manor, Maryland, 1683.

3. Society of the Woman in the Wilderness, near Germantown, Pennsylvania, 1694.

4. Irenia, Plymouth, Pennsylvania, 1697.

5. Ephrata Cloister, Ephrata, Pennsylvania, 1732.

6. General Economy (Moravian Brethren), Bethlehem, Pennsylvania; Nazareth, Pennsylvania; Lititz, Pennsylvania; and Wachovia (or Salem), North Carolina, 1744.

7. Snow Hill Nunnery, Snow Hill, Pennsylvania, ca. 1800.

8. Harmonie Society (Rappites), Harmony, Pennsylvania, 1805.

9. Harmonie Society (Rappites), Harmony, Indiana (later New Harmony), 1814.

10. Society of Separatists, Zoar, Ohio, 1817.

11. Harmonie Society (Rappites), Economy, Pennsylvania, 1824.

12. Shaker Village (United Society of Believers), Mount Lebanon (New Lebanon Township) and Canaan, New York, 1787.

13. Shaker Village, Niskayuna, or Watervliet, Colonie, New York, 1788.

14. Shaker Village, Hancock and West Pittsfield, Massachusetts, 1790.

15. Shaker Village, Enfield, Connecticut, 1790.

16. Shaker Village, Harvard, Massachusetts, 1791.

17. Shaker Village, Tyringham, Massachusetts, 1792.

18. Shaker Village, Canterbury, New Hampshire, 1792.

19. Shaker Village, Enfield, New Hampshire, 1793.

20. Shaker Village, Shirley, Massachusetts, 1793.

21. Shaker Village, Alfred, Maine, 1793.

22. Shaker Village, Sabbathday Lake (or New Gloucester, or Poland Hill), Maine, 1794.

23. Shaker Village, Gorham, Maine, 1794.

24. Shaker Village, Union Village, Ohio, 1805.

25. Shaker Village, Watervliet (or Shakertown), Ohio, 1806.

26. Shaker Village, South Union (or Gasper Springs), Kentucky, 1809.

27. Shaker Village, Pleasant Hill, Kentucky, 1809.

28. Shaker Village, West Union (or Busro), Indiana, 1810.

29. Shaker Village, Savoy, Massachusetts, 1817.

30. Shaker Village, North Union (Shaker Heights), Ohio, 1822.

31. Jerusalem (community of Jemima Wilkinson), New York, 1788.

32. Dorrilites, Leyden, Massachusetts, and Guilford, Vermont, 1798.

33. The Union, Clark's Crossing, New York, 1804.

34. Pilgrims, South Woodstock, Vermont, 1817.

35. Owenites, New Harmony, Indiana, 1825, on site of 9.

36. Yellow Springs Community (Owenites), Yellow Springs, Ohio, 1825.

37. Franklin Community (or Haverstraw Community; Owenites), Haverstraw, New York, 1826.

38. Forestville Community (or Coxsackie Community; Owenites), Lapham's Mills, Coxsackie, New York, 1826.

39. Kendal Community (or Friendly Association for Mutual Interests; Owenites), Kendal, Ohio, 1826.

40. Valley Forge Community (or Friendly Association for Mutual Interests; Owenites), Valley Forge, Pennsylvania, 1826.

41. Blue Spring Community (Owenites), Van Buren, Indiana, 1826.

42. New Philadelphia Society, Phillipsburg (now Monaca), Pennsylvania, 1832.

43. Grand Ecore, Natchitoches Parish, Louisiana, 1834.

44. Germantown, Minden, Louisiana, 1836.

45. Shaker Village, Whitewater, near Hamilton, Ohio, 1825.

46. Shaker Village, Sodus Bay, Sodus, New York, 1826.

47. Shaker Village, Groveland (or Sonyea), Sonyea, New York, 1836.

48. Coal Creek Community and Church of God, Stone Bluff, Indiana, 1825.

49. Nashoba Community, east of Memphis, Tennessee, 1826.

50. The Family, Kirtland, Ohio, 1830.

51. Order of Enoch (Mormons), Independence, Missouri, 1831.

52. Equity, Equity, Ohio. 1835.

53. Community of United Christians, Berea, Ohio, 1836.

54. Brook Farm (independent, then Fourierist), West Roxbury, Massachusetts, 1841.

55. Social Reform Unity (Fourierist), Barrett, Pennsylvania, 1842.

56. Jefferson County Industrial Association (Fourierist), Cold Creek, New York, 1843.

57. Sylvania Association (Fourierist), Darlingville, Pennsylvania, 1843.

58. Morehouse Union (Fourierist), Piseco, New York, 1843.

59. North American Phalanx (Fourierist), Phalanx, New Jersey, 1843.

60. La Grange Phalanx (Fourierist), Mongoquinong, Indiana, 1844.

61. Clarkson Association (Fourierist), Clarkson, New York, 1844.

62. Bloomfield Union Association (Fourierist), North Bloomfield, New York, 1844.

63. LeRaysville Phalanx (Fourierist), LeRaysville, Pennsylvania, 1844.

64. Ohio Phalanx (or American Phalanx; Fourierist), Bell Air, Ohio, 1844.

65. Alphadelphia Phalanx (Fourierist), near Galesburgh, Michigan, 1844.

66. Sodus Bay Phalanx (Fourierist), Sodus, New York, 1844, on site of 46.

67. Mixville Association (Fourierist), Mixville (now Wiscoy), New York, 1844.

68. Ontario Union (or Manchester Union; Fourierist), Bates' Mills, New York, 1844.

69. Clermont Phalanx (Fourierist), Rural and Utopia, Ohio, 1844.

70. Trumbull Phalanx (Fourierist), Phalanx Mills, Ohio, 1844.

71. Wisconsin Phalanx (Fourierist), Ceresco (or Ripon), Wisconsin, 1844.

72. Iowa Pioneer Phalanx (Fourierist), Scott, Iowa, 1844.

73. Philadelphia Industrial Association (Fourierist), Portage (South Bend), Indiana, 1845.

74. Columbian Phalanx (Fourierist), near Zanesville, Ohio, 1845.

75. Canton Phalanx (Fourierist), Canton, Illinois, 1845.

76. Integral Phalanx (Fourierist), Lick Creek (now Loami), Illinois, 1845.

77. Spring Farm Phalanx (Fourierist), 20 miles from Lake Michigan, Sheboygan County, Wisconsin, 1846.

78. Pigeon River Fourier Colony, north of mouth of Pigeon River, Sheboygan County, Wisconsin, 1846 or 1847.

79. Raritan Bay Union (Fourierist), Eagleswood, Perth Amboy, New Jersey, 1853.

80. Réunion (Fourierist), west of Dallas (now Cement City), Texas, 1855.

81. The Fourier Phalanx, Moore's Hill, Sparta, Indiana, 1858.

82. Society of One-Mentians (or Promisewell Community; Owenite), Monroe County, Pennsylvania, 1843.

83. Goose Pond Community (Owenite), Barrett, Pennsylvania, 1843, on site of 55.

84. Colony of Equality (Owenite), Spring Lake Wisconsin, 1843.

85. Hopedale Community (Practical Christians), Hopedale, Massachusetts, 1842.

86. Northampton Association of Education and Industry, Broughton's Meadows (now Florence), Massachusetts, 1842.

87. Marlboro Association, Marlboro, Ohio, 1843.

88. Dr. Abraham Brooke's Experiment, Oakland, Ohio, 1843.

89. Skaneateles Community, Mottville, New York, 1843.

90. Fruitlands, Harvard, Massachusetts, 1843.

91. Congregation of Saints, Lexington, Indiana, 1843.

92. Putney Community (Perfectionist), Putney, Vermont, 1843.

93. Prairie Home Community, West Liberty, Ohio, 1844.

94. Union Home Community, Huntsville (now Trenton), Indiana, 1844.

95. Fruit Hills, Warren County, Ohio, 1845.

96. Grand Prairie Community, Warren County, Indiana, 1845.

97. The Brotherhood, Rural, Ohio, 1847, on part of site of 69.

98. Utopia, Utopia, Ohio, 1847, on part of site of 69.

99. Oneida Community (Perfectionist), Kenwood, New York, 1848.

100. Voree (Mormon), Spring Prairie, Wisconsin, 1848.

(101 is deleted in Bestor's second edition as a duplication.)

102. Wallingford Community (Perfectionist), Wallingford, Connecticut, 1851.

103. Modern Times, Modern Times (now Brentwood), New York, 1851.

104. Mountain Cove Community (Brother-

hood of the New Life), Mountain Cove, Virginia (now West Virginia), 1851.

105. Celesta (Second Adventists), Celesta, Pennsylvania, 1852.

106. Harmonia, Kiantone Springs (Spiritualists' Springs), New York, 1852.

107. Rising Star Association, near Greenville, Ohio, 1853.

108. Preparation (Mormon), Preparation, Iowa, 1853.

109. Grand Prairie Harmonial Institute, sections 5 and 8, Township 23 North, Range 5 West, Warren County, Indiana, 1853.

110. Memnonia Institute, Yellow Springs, Ohio, 1856.

111. Union Grove, Meeker County, Minnesota, 1856.

112. Harmonial Vegetarian Society, Harmony Springs, Arkansas, 1860.

113. Ebenezer Community (Inspirationist), Ebenezer, New York, 1843.

114. Peace-Union, Limestone, Pennsylvania, 1843.

115. Bethel Community, Bethel, Missouri, 1844.

116. Bishop Hill Colony (Jansenist), Bishop Hill, Illinois, 1846.

117. Green Bay (Norwegian Moravian), Green Bay, Wisconsin, 1850.

118. Jasper Colony (Swedenborgian), Jasper, Iowa, 1851.

119. Ephraim (Norwegian Moravian), Ephraim, Wisconsin, 1853.

120. St. Nazianz (Catholic), St. Nazianz, Wisconsin, 1854.

121. Amana Community (Inspirationist), Amana, Iowa, 1855.

122. Aurora Community, Aurora, Oregon, 1856.

123. Teutonia or McKean County Association, Ginalsburg, Pennsylvania, 1842.

124. Bettina, west of Fredericksburg, Texas, 1847.

125. Communia, Communia, Iowa, 1847.

126. Icaria, Fannin County, Texas, 1848.

127. Nauvoo (Icarians), Nauvoo, Illinois, 1849.

128. Oleana, or New Norway, Potter County, Pennsylvania, 1852.

129. Icaria, Corning, Iowa, 1857.

130. Cheltenham (Icarian), Cheltenham, Missouri, 1858.

This catalog is taken from Arthur E. Bestor, *Backwoods Utopias*, "Checklist of Communitarian Experiments," 2d ed., rev. and enl., Philadelphia, 1970. The list does not include the full number of Oneida branch communities or the full number of Moravian communities where the "General Economy" was adopted, perhaps several dozen additional locations. It also excludes Nauvoo, Salt Lake City, and several hundred Mormon settlements in the Great Basin, because their economies were not considered sufficiently "socialist." It excludes the Unitary Home established in New York in the 1850s, probably for the same reason. It was not possible to obtain a similar catalog to bring the maps up to date, although Robert Fogarty of Antioch College has one in process for the period 1861 to 1918 which includes about 150 communities. Wherever I have traveled in the United States, I have heard about additional communities which have not been mentioned in existing catalogs but have left evidence of their existence in anecdotes passed on by members' relatives and descendents.

Bibliography

The best general historical treatments of the communitarian movement are the first two chapters of *Backwoods Utopias: The Sectarian Origins and the Owenite Phase of Communitarian Socialism in America, 1663-1829*, by Arthur E. Bestor, 2d ed., rev. and enl., Philadelphia, 1970, and the communitarian sections of *Socialism and American Life* by Donald Drew Egbert and Stow Persons, Princeton, 1952. Bestor's book includes an extensive bibliographical essay updated to 1969, and Egbert and Persons' work is accompanied by a bibliographical volume by T. D. Seymour Bassett. Other bibliographies include Joseph W. Eaton and Saul M. Katz, *Research Guide on Cooperative Group Farming*, New York, 1942; Helen Jones, "Selected List of References on Communistic Societies," Library of Congress, Division of Bibliography, 1909; and Robert S. Fogarty, "Communal History in America," a bibliography developed for *Choice*, 10.4 (June 1973), pp. 1-8, which is especially useful for communities after 1860. This bibliography will be restricted to source material for the seven case studies, as well as a few general works dealing with utopian thought, communal organization, and the American environment which I have found especially helpful. The notes and lists of illustrations provide further references for all chapters.

The reader approaching communitarian history for the first time can gain an immediate sense of many experiments from John Humphrey Noyes, *History of American Socialisms* (1870), New York, 1966, and from Charles Nordhoff, *The Communistic Societies of the United States* (1875), New York, 1966. Intellectual or experimental precedents for American communities are discussed by Charles Sanford, in *The Quest for Paradise*, Urbana, Ill., 1961; Norman Cohn, *The Pursuit of the Millennium: Revolutionary Millenarians and Mystical Anarchists of the Middle Ages* (1957), London, 1970; and W. H. G. Armytage, *Heavens Below: Utopian Experiments in England, 1560-1960*, Toronto, 1961.

I found Marie Louise Berneri, *A Journey Through Utopia*, Boston, 1950, to be the most helpful of the many reviews of utopian literature. Helen Rosenau, *The Ideal City in its Architectural Evolution*, Boston, 1959, is a well-illustrate˙ discussion of architectural utopias; Anthony Vidler's article, "News from the Realm of Nowhere," *Oppositions*, 1.1 (Sept. 1973), 83-92, offers pointed political criticism of architectural utopianism.

Paul and Percival Goodman's *Communitas: Means of Livelihood and Ways of Life* is well known among architects as a plea for better community design; David Riesman's review of *Communitas*, "Some Observations on Community Plans and Utopia," in *Individualism Reconsidered*, New York, 1955, provides further discussion of how communities should be designed and organized. Thomas A. Reiner, *The Place of the Ideal Community in Urban Planning*, Philadelphia, 1963, includes some comparative drawings of various utopian schemes.

American attitudes toward the natural environment during the eighteenth and nineteenth centuries are most fully conveyed by two literary studies, Leo Marx, *The Machine in the Garden*, Oxford, 1964; and Henry Nash Smith, *Virgin Land*, New York, 1957; as well as Paul Gates, *The Farmer's Age: Agriculture, 1815-1860*, vol. 3, The Economic History of the United States, New York, 1960; and J. B. Jackson, *Landscapes*, Amherst, Mass., 1970, and *American Space*, New York, 1972.

Urban development in nineteenth century America is the subject of Albert Fein, "The American City: The Ideal and the Real," in Edgar Kauffman, ed., *The Rise of An American Architecture*, New York, 1970. Many town plans from the period including some of "Cities of Zion" are published in John Reps, *The Making of Urban America*, Princeton, 1964. Sam B. Warner, in *The Urban Wilderness*, New York, 1973, provides a well-illustrated analysis of American economic history and urban development which is a model for anyone dealing with environmental form and its social and economic contexts.

Issues related to the social concerns of communitarians are dealt with by Clare Cooper, in "House As Symbol of Self," Working Paper no. 120, Institute of Urban and Regional Development, Berkeley, 1971; Rosabeth Moss Kanter, *Commitment and Community: Communes and Utopias in Sociological Perspective*, Cambridge, 1972; and Benjamin Zablocki, *The Joyful Community: An Account of the Bruderhof, A Communal Movement Now in Its Third Generation*, Baltimore, 1972, a perceptive sociological study of a single community. John McKelvie Whitworth, *God's Blueprints: A Sociological Study of Three Utopian Sects*, London, 1974, deals with the impact of religion on communal organization among the Oneidans, Shakers, and Bruderhof. Judith Fryer, "American Eves in American Edens," *The American Scholar*, 43.2 (Spring 1974) provides an excellent history of communitarian women.

Major collections of Shaker drawings and manuscripts are held by Shaker Community, Inc., at Hancock Shaker Village; the Shaker Museums at Sabbathday Lake, Maine, and Old Chatham, New York; the Western Reserve Historical Society, Cleveland; and the Fruitlands Museum, Harvard, Massachusetts. The Historic American Buildings Survey (HABS) and the Index of American Design offer good photographic documentation of Shaker architecture and design.

The best general history of the sect is Edward Deming Andrews, *The People Called Shakers: A Search for the Perfect Society*, rev. ed., New York, 1963, which is illustrated and includes the "Millennial Laws" of 1845. Henri Desroche, *The American Shakers: From Neo-Christianity to Presocialism*, tr. John K. Savacool, Amherst, Mass., 1971, probes motivation and organization.

Visual Materials (Not Illustrated)

Beers, Frederick W., *County Atlas of Berkshire, Massachusetts*, New York, 1876.

Douglas, William, "Map of the Town of Hancock, 1794," Library of Congress, Map Division.

"Map of the Spirit City of the Valley of Wisdom," n.d., Western Reserve Historical Society.

"A Trip to Hancock," MS photograph album, Shaker Museum, Sabbathday Lake, Maine, ca. 1935.

U.S. Department of the Interior, National Park Service, Historic American Buildings Survey, file of historical data sheets, measured drawings, and photographs of Hancock Shaker Village.

Walling, Henry F., "Map of the County of Berkshire, Mass.," 1858, Library of Congress, Map Division.

Community Publications

Authorized Rules of the Shaker Community and *Supplementary Rules of the Shaker Community*, Mount Lebanon, N. Y., 1894.

Avery, Giles B., *Sketches of 'Shakers and Shakerism,'* Albany, 1883. Includes views of most communities.

Green, Calvin, and Seth Y. Wells, eds., *A Summary View of the Millennial Church or United Society of Believers, Commonly Called Shakers*, 2d ed., Albany, 1848.

Johnson, Theodore, ed., "The 'Millennial Laws' of 1821," *Shaker Quarterly*, 7 (Summer 1967), 34-58.

Millennial Praises, Containing A Collection of Gospel Hymns, in Four Parts, Hancock, Mass., 1813.

Sawyer, Otis, *Who Built Our Shaker Home?* undated imprint, Shaker Museum, Sabbathday Lake, Maine.

The Shaker, Mount Lebanon, N. Y., 1871-1873 (later titled *Shaker and Shakeress*).

The Shaker Religious Concept, together with *The Covenant* (Hancock, Mass., 1830), Old Chatham, N.Y., 1959.

Members' Accounts

Blinn, Henry C., "A Journey to Kentucky, 1873," ed. Theodore Johnson, *Shaker Quarterly*, 5 (Summer 1965), 37-55. Description of Hancock, pp. 37-39.

Doolittle, Mary Antoinette, *Autobiography of Mary Antoinette Doolittle*, Mount Lebanon, N.Y., 1880. Feminist Eldress.

Evans, Frederick W., *Autobiography of a Shaker*, New York, 1869.

Lamson, David R., *Two Years' Experience Among the Shakers*, West Boylston, Mass., 1848. Apostate's account of life at Hancock.

White, Anna, and Leila S. Taylor, *Shakerism: Its Meaning and Message*, Columbus, Ohio, 1904.

Visitors' Accounts

Barber, John Warner, *Historical Collections . . . of Every Town in Massachusetts*, Worcester, Mass., 1839. Includes view of Hancock.

Buckingham, James S., *America, Historical, Statistic, and Descriptive*, 2 vols., New York, 1841. Account of visit to Niskayuna, vol. 2, pp. 56-87.

Dickens, Charles, *American Notes*, New York, 1842. Description of visit to Mount Lebanon and Hancock, pp. 79-80.

Frank Leslie's Illustrated Newspaper, "The Shakers," including sketches of Mount Lebanon Shakers (Sept. 6, 1873, 416-417; Sept. 13, 1873, 12-13).

Greeley, Horace, "A Sabbath with the Shakers," *The Knickerbocker*, 9 (June 1838), 532-537. Account of visit to Niskayuna.

Hazard, Rodman, "Hancock," in *A History of the County of Berkshire, Massachusetts*, by Gentlemen in the County, Clergymen and Laymen, Pittsfield, Mass., 1829.

Howells, William Dean, *Three Villages*, Boston, 1884. Description of Shaker Settlement at Shirley, Mass., pp. 67-113.

Lossing, Benson J., "The Shakers," *Harper's New Monthly Magazine*, 15 (July 1857), 164-177. Account of visit to Mount Lebanon.

Martineau, Harriet, *Society in America*, vol. 1, New

York, 1837. Visit to Hancock, pp. 309-315.

Nordhoff, Charles, *The Communistic Societies of the United States* (1875), New York, 1966. Account of visit to Mount Lebanon, pp. 117-258.

Sedgewick, Catherine Maria, *Redwood, A Tale*, New York, 1850. Description of Shaker meal, p. 317.

Taylor, Bayard, *At Home and Abroad: A Sketchbook of Life, Scenery, and Men*, London, 1802. Description of Hancock, pp. 335-336.

Other Works

Andrews, Edward Deming, *The Gift to Be Simple: Songs, Dances and Rituals of the American Shakers*, New York, 1940.

_____, *The Hancock Shakers*, Hancock, Mass., 1961.

_____, *The Communal Industries of the Shakers*, Albany, 1932.

Andrews, Edward Deming, and Faith Andrews, *Shaker Furniture: The Craftsmanship of an American Communal Sect*, New York, 1964.

_____, *A Shaker Meeting House and Its Builder*, Hancock, Mass., 1962.

_____, *Visions of the Heavenly Sphere*, Charlottesville, Va., 1969. Illustrated work on Shaker "spirit drawings."

Dodd, Eugene Merrick, *Melville and Hawthorne at Hancock*, Hancock, Mass., 1966.

Keig, Susan Jackson, and Elmer Ray Pearson, "Shaker Graphics of the Nineteenth Century," *Print*, 26 (Mar. 1972), pp. 40-47.

Lassiter, William, *Shaker Architecture*, New York, 1966. Includes HABS drawings of buildings at Mount Lebanon and Hancock barn.

Peladeau, Marius B., "The Shaker Meetinghouses of Moses Johnson," *Antiques*, 98 (Oct. 1970), 594-599.

Smith, Marian, "Shamanism in the Shaker Religion of Northwest America," *Man*, 181 (Aug. 1954).

Upton, Charles W., "The Shaker Utopia," *Antiques*, 98 (Oct. 1970), 582-587.

Williams, John S., "Consecrated Ingenuity: The Shakers and Their Inventions," Old Chatham, N. Y., 1957.

Whitehill, Walter, et al., *The Shaker Image*, Boston, 1974.

Bibliographies

Maclean, J. P., *A Bibliography of Shaker Literature*, Columbus, Ohio, 1905.

Richmond, Mary L., *Shaker Literature: An Annotated Bibliography in Two Volumes* (working title), Hanover, N.H., University Press of New England, forthcoming (late 1976).

Winter, Esther C., *Shaker Literature in the Grosvenor Library, A Bibliography*, Buffalo, N. Y., 1940.

The broad range of materials available on Mormons and Mormonism is frustratingly diverse and contradictory, especially for a non-Mormon scholar. Stanley Kimball's bibliography covers the sources of the Nauvoo period of Mormon history very well, and most materials he lists are available on microfilm for study at Southern Illinois University, Edwardsville campus. Official church historians in Independence, Missouri, and in Salt Lake City, Utah, supervise extensive manuscript collections and archives. Houghton Library, Harvard University, has an extensive collection of Mormon imprints and non-Mormon journalistic accounts of the Saints' activities. Buildings in Nauvoo, Illinois, are open to visitors, but all materials owned by Nauvoo Restoration, Inc., are located in the Salt Lake City office. (The collection was in transit, unfortunately, during the preparation of this manuscript and not available to the author.)

The most useful studies of Mormon ideologies and Mormon environments in Utah are Leonard Arrington's *Great Basin Kingdom: An Economic History of the Latter-Day Saints, 1830-1900*, Cambridge, Mass., 1958, and Richard V. Francaviglia's Ph.D. thesis, "The Mormon Landscape: Existence, Creation and Perception of a Unique Image in the American West," University of Oregon, 1970. Robert Flanders's monograph on Nauvoo (*Nauvoo: Kingdom on the Mississippi*, Urbana, Ill., 1965) is the most comprehensive treatment of Mormon history in Illinois, and his article "To Transform History: Early Mormon Culture and the Concept of Time and Space," *Church History*, 40.1 (Mar. 1971), 108-117, is an excellent discussion of these difficult issues.

Visual Material (Not Illustrated)

Hills, Gustavus, "Map of the City of Nauvoo," New York, 1842, New York Public Library. Includes sketch of Temple by William Weeks.

Holmes, J. W., and C. R. Arnold, "Map of Hancock County, Illinois," Chicago, Ill., 1859. Approximately 55" by 60", mounted on cloth. Includes sketch of Nauvoo by John Schroede. Illinois State Historical Library, Springfield, Ill.

Miller, Rowena J., "Map for Nauvoo Restoration, Inc.," Oct. 29, 1964, showing houses and commercial buildings in Nauvoo, compiled from tax records. Office of Nauvoo Restoration, Inc., Nauvoo, Ill.

Young, J[ames] H., "The Tourist's Pocket Map of the State of Illinois Exhibiting Its Internal Improvements, Roads, Distances, Etc.," Philadelphia, 1837. Newberry Library, Chicago.

Community Publications

Nauvoo *Neighbor*, Nauvoo, Ill., 1-2, May 3, 1843 to Oct. 29, 1845.

Smith, Joseph, Jr., *The Book of Doctrine and Covenants*, various editions.

————, tr., *The Book of Mormon*, various editions.

————, *History of the Church of Jesus Christ of Latter-Day Saints, Period I, History of Joseph Smith, the Prophet, by Himself*, 6 vols., Salt Lake City, 1912.

Times and Seasons, Commerce, Ill., and Liverpool, England, 1839-1846.

The Wasp, Nauvoo, Illinois, 1.1-51 (Apr. 16, 1842-Apr. 19, 1843).

Young, Brigham, *Discourses of Brigham Young*, ed. John A. Widtsoe, Salt Lake City, 1912.

Members' Accounts

Angell, Truman Osborne, St., papers, 1810-1887. Church Historian's Office, Salt Lake City. Angell was the official Church Architect for the Salt Lake Temple, also worked in Kirtland and Nauvoo.

Greenlaugh, James, *Narrative of James Greenlaugh, cotton-spinner, Egerton, Bolton-Le-Moors*, Liverpool, 1842. A disaffected English convert's story of his life in Nauvoo.

Hascall Family Letters, 1840-1854, Missouri Historical Society, Saint Louis.

Visitors' Accounts

Adams, Henry, "Charles Francis Adams Visits the Mormons in 1844," *Proceedings of the Massachusetts Historical Society*, 68 (Oct. 1944-May 1947).

Aitken, W., *A Journey Up the Mississippi River, From Its Mouth to Nauvoo, the City of the Latter Day Saints*, Ashton-under-Lyne, England, 1845.

Buckingham, J. H., *Illinois As Lincoln Knew It: A Boston Reporter's Record of a Trip in 1847*, ed. Harry E. Pratt, Springfield, Ill., 1938. Account of visit to Nauvoo, pp. 63-69.

Caswall, Henry, *The City of the Mormons: or Three Days at Nauvoo in 1842*, London, 1843. A religious polemic, few physical descriptions.

Kirk, John, "Letterbook," Chicago Historical Society. By a visitor to Nauvoo in 1853.

[Wistar, Isaac], *A Journey on the Mississippi River Being a Lecture Delivered Before the Lyceum of the Zane Street Public School of Philadelphia*, Philadelphia, 1847.

Other Works

Andrew, David S., and Laurel B. Blank, "The Four Mormon Temples in Utah," *Journal of the Society of*

Architectural Historians, 30.1 (Mar. 1971), 51-65.

Arrington, Leonard, "Early Mormon Communitarianism: The Law of Consecration and Stewardship," *Western Humanities Review*, 7 (Autumn 1953), 341-369.

_____, *Orderville, Utah: A Pioneer Mormon Experiment in Economic Organization*, Utah State Agricultural College Monograph Series, 2 (Mar. 1954).

Arrington, Joseph Earl, "Construction of the Nauvoo Temple or the Architecture and Construction of an Early Mormon Temple on the Mississippi River," MS, 4 vols., LDS Church Historian's Office, Salt Lake City.

Barber, John Warner, and Henry Howe, *Our Whole Country*, vol. 2, Cincinnati, 1861.

Brodie, Fawn, *No Man Knows My History, The Life of Joseph Smith, The Mormon Prophet*, New York, 1945.

Carmer, Carl, "A Panorama of Mormon Life," *Art in America*, 58.3 (May-June 1970), 52-65. Color reproductions of twenty-two paintings by Carl C. A. Christensen illustrating the early decades of Mormon life.

Colvin, Don, "A Historical Study of the Mormon Temple at Nauvoo, Illinois," unpublished M.A. thesis, Brigham Young University, 1962.

Faris, John T., *The Romance of Forgotten Towns*, New York, 1924. Reproduction of wood engraving of Nauvoo, opposite p. 225.

Flagg, Edmund, "Nauvoo," in Charles A. Dana, ed., *The United States Illustrated in Views of City and Country with Descriptive and Historical Articles*, vol. 1, New York, 1855, pp. 37-46.

Fox, Feramorz Y., "The Mormon Land System: A Study of the Settlement and Utilization of Land under the Direction of the Mormon Church," unpublished Ph.D. dissertation, Northwestern University, 1932.

_____, "Notes Concerning Joseph Smith's Plat of Zion City," mimeograph, Church Historian's Office, Salt Lake City.

Goeldner, Paul, "The Architecture of Equal Comforts: Polygamists in Utah," *Historic Preservation*, 24 (Jan.-Mar. 1972), 14-17.

Gregg, Thomas, *History of Hancock County, Illinois*, Chicago, 1880. Contains etching of the Nauvoo Temple, opposite p. 260.

_____, *The Prophet of Palmyra*, New York, 1890. Includes (inaccurate) sketch of baptismal font in Nauvoo Temple, p. 382.

Harrington, Virginia, and J. C. Harrington, *Rediscovery of the Nauvoo Temple; Report on the Archaeological Excavations*, Salt Lake City, 1971.

Hitchcock, Mrs. Peter, "Joseph Smith and His Kirtland Temple," *The Historical Society Quarterly*, Lake County, Ohio, 7.4 (Nov. 1965).

Jennings, Warren Abner, "Zion Is Fled: The Expulsion of the Mormons from Jackson County, Missouri," unpublished Ph.D. dissertation, University of Florida, 1962.

Kimball, Stanley B., "The Mormons in Early Illinois," *Dialogue*, 5 (Spring 1970).

Lasch, Christopher, "Burned-over Utopia," *New York Review of Books*, 7.1 (Jan. 26, 1967), 15-18. Review of Flanders; incorporates discussion of Mormon economic development to date.

Lewis, Henry, *Das illustrierte Mississippithal*, Düsseldorf, 1857. Includes sketches of Nauvoo and Nauvoo Temple.

Lifchez, Raymond, "Inspired Planning: Mormon and American Fourierist Communities in the Nineteenth Century," unpublished M.C.P. thesis, University of California, Berkeley, 1972.

Lillibridge, Robert M., "Architectural Currents on the Mississippi River Frontier: Nauvoo, Illinois," *Journal of the Society of Architectural Historians*, 19 (Oct. 1960), 109-114.

"List of Books in Seventies Hall, 1845-1846," mimeo, LDS Visitors Center, Nauvoo, Ill.

Nelson, Lowry, *The Mormon Village*, Salt Lake City, 1952.

O'Dea, Thomas F., *The Mormons*, Chicago, 1957.

_____, and Evan Z. Vogt, "A Comparative Study of the Role of Values in Social Action in Two Southwestern Communities," *American Sociological Review*, 18 (Dec. 1953), 645-654.

Reps, John, *The Making of Urban America*, Princeton, 1964. Chapter on "Cities of Zion."

Sellers, Charles, "Early Mormon Community Planning," *Journal of the American Institute of Planners*, 28 (Feb. 1962), 25.

Smith, Page, *As A City Upon A Hill: The Town in American History*, New York, 1966.

Snider, Cecil A., and Helen F. Snider, "The Attitudes Toward Mormonism in Illinois, 1839-46," compilation of non-Mormon newspaper accounts, Houghton Library, Harvard University.

Bibliographies

Kimball, Stanley B., *Sources of Mormon History in Illinois, 1839-1848*, Southern Illinois University Library, Carbondale, 1964.

The community's minutes and various other records are held by the Monmouth County Historical Association Library (MCHAL), Freehold, New Jersey. Letters concerning the colony and its members are included in the papers of James T. Fisher, held by the Massachusetts Historical Society and by the Houghton Library, Harvard University; in the Amédée Simonin Collection of the Library of Congress; in the correspondence of Horace Greeley, at the New York Public Library; and in the papers of Elijah Grant, at the University of Chicago Library. The Colt's Neck (New Jersey) Historical Society has some historic photographs.

The fullest historical study of the community is an unpublished book-length manuscript by Eric Schirber of Princeton, New Jersey, entitled "The North American Phalanx, 1843-1855," Department of History, Princeton University, 1972.

Community Publications and Records

North American Phalanx, "Conditions of Membership and Rules of Admission," n.d., MCHAL.

_____ , "Constitution," adopted August 12, 1843, MCHAL.

_____ , "Key to Scale of Primary Awards for Labor and the Use of Capital in the North American Phalanx, 1853," Houghton Library, Harvard University.

_____ , "Positive Sale of the Domain of the Phalanx," inventory of the domain, 1855, Houghton Library, Harvard University.

_____ , "Record of the Proceedings of the North American Phalanx" and "Minutes of the Sessions of the Executive Council and Resident Members," 1843-1855, MCHAL.

_____ , "Revised Constitution of the North American Phalanx," Sept. 30, 1849, MCHAL.

Sears, Charles, *Exposé of the Conditions and Progress of the North American Phalanx*, New York, 1853. Includes financial data, 1844-1853.

_____ , *Socialism and Christianity*, Phalanx, Monmouth County, N. J., 1854.

Members' Accounts

Fisher, James T., "Collected Papers, 1790-1865," Massachusetts Historical Society, Boston.

Longley, Alcander, "Life in the North American Phalanx," series of five articles published in the *Phalansterian Record*, Cincinnati, Ohio, 1.2-5 (Jan.-Apr. 1858), continued as *Social Record*, Dearborn Co., Ind., 1.8 (Sept. 1858).

Sears, Charles, "The North American Phalanx," letter from Silkville, Kansas, May 10, 1879, *American So-*

cialist, 4.21 (May 22, 1879), 163.

_____, "The North American Phalanx, An Historical and Descriptive Sketch," Prescott, Wis., 1886.

Visitors' Accounts
Bremer, Frederika, *The Homes of the New World*, tr. Mary Howitt, New York, 1853. Accounts of two visits, pp. 76-84, 611-624.

Macdonald, A. J., "Materials for a History of Communities," MSS, Beineke Library, Yale University, New Haven, Conn. Accounts of three visits made by Macdonald to the Phalanx, illustrated with sketches.

Noyes, John Humphrey, *History of American Socialisms* (1870), New York, 1966. Includes Macdonald's work in edited form and other accounts.

Olmsted, Frederick Law ("An American Farmer"), "The Phalanstery and the Phalansterians," letter to the New York *Tribune*, July 24, 1852.

"A Week in the Phalanstery," part 1, *Life Illustrated*, Aug. 11, 1855; part 2, Aug. 18, 1855.

Wolski, Kalikst, "A Visit to the North American Phalanx," tr. Marion M. Coleman, *Proceedings of the New Jersey Historical Society*, 83.3 (July 1965), 149-160. Wolski, a Polish engineer, visited in 1852.

Other Works
Beecher, Jonathan, and Richard Bienvenu, eds., *The Utopian Vision of Charles Fourier*, Boston, 1971.

Belz, Herman J., "The North American Phalanx: Experiment in Socialism," *Proceedings of the New Jersey Historical Society*, 81.4 (Oct. 1963), 215-247.

Bestor, Arthur E., Jr., "Albert Brisbane—Propagandist for Socialism in the 1840s," *New York History*, 28.2 (Apr. 1947), 128-158.

Brisbane, Albert, "Association," series of articles, New York *Tribune*, irregular intervals, 1842-1855.

_____, *A Concise Exposition of the Doctrine of Association or Plan for a Re-organization of Society*, New York, 1843.

_____, *Theory of the Functions of the Human Passions*, followed by an outline view of *The Fundamental Principles of Fourier's Theory of Social Science*, New York, 1856.

Brisbane, Redelia, *Albert Brisbane: A Mental Biography*, Boston, 1893.

Col[. . .], M.A., *The Fulfillment!! or Twelve Years Afterwards: Paris, June, 1858: To Texas!!* tr. James W. Phillips, DeGolyer Foundation Library, Dallas, Texas, occasional publication no. 2, 1963. A first-person account of life in Victor Considérant's colony at Réunion, Texas.

Considérant, Victor P., *Destinée sociale*, Paris, 1834.

_____, *Description du phalanstère et considérations sociales sur l'architectonique*, Paris, 1848.

_____, *Exposition abrégée du système phalanstérien de Fourier*, Paris, 1846.

de Gamond, Gatti, *The Phalanstery; or, Attractive Industry and Moral Harmony*, London, 1841.

Fourier, Charles, *Oeuvres complètes*, Paris, 1967.

Giles, Julia Bucklin, "Address to the Monmouth County Historical Association," undated (1922?), MS, MCHAL.

Greeley, Horace, *Industrial Association* (address to American Union of Associationists), Boston, 1850.

Greene, Maud Honeyman, "Raritan Bay Union, Eagleswood, New Jersey," *Proceedings of the New Jersey Historical Society*, 67.260 (Jan. 1950), 2-19.

Greenough, Horatio, "Fourier et Hoc Genus Omne," *The Crayon*, 1.34 (June 13, 1855), 371-372.

Godwin, Parke, *A Popular View of the Doctrines of Charles Fourier*, New York, 1844.

Hammond, William, and Margaret Hammond, *La Réunion: A French Settlement in Texas*, Dallas, 1958.

Hinds, William Alfred, *American Communities*, rev. ed., Chicago, 1902.

McLaren, Donald C., *Boa Constrictor, or Fourier Association Self-Exposed*, Rochester, N.Y., 1844.

Swann, Norma Lippincott, "The North American Phalanx," *Monmouth County Historical Association Bulletin*, 1.1 (May 1935), 35-65.

Publications of Other Fourierist Groups
The Harbinger, Boston and New York, 1-8, 1845-1849, weekly.

The Phalanx, New York, 1-5, Oct. 5, 1843-May 28, 1845, weekly, continued as *The Harbinger*.

Société de Colonisation Européo-Américaine au Texas, "Bulletin," 1857, 1858, 1860, Houghton Library, Harvard University.

The most complete collections of Oneida publications are those of the Oneida Community Historical Committee; the Houghton and Widener Libraries, Harvard University; the Syracuse University Library; and the Beineke Library, Yale University. The Oneida Community Historical Committee has a large collection of photographs and artifacts, including the community model made by Ethelbert Pitt and examples of the community's products. Oneida Ltd. in Kenwood, New York, has an extensive file of architectural drawings, including original full-scale details and watercolor renderings of the Second Mansion House. Maps in their collection document the community's land acquisition process between 1848 and 1870.

The best general historical study is Maren Lockwood Carden, *Oneida: Utopian Community to Modern Corporation*, Baltimore, 1969. Constance Robertson's two volumes, *Oneida Community: An Autobiography, 1851-1876*, and *Oneida Community: The Breakup, 1876-1881*, Syracuse, 1970, 1972 provide a descendent's view, more complete and more colorful, but perhaps less critical. Carden reports that descendents' embarrassment about the Perfectionists' sexual activities resulted in a major diary-burning spree after G. W. Noyes's death in 1941, but Robertson seems to have had access to privately held diaries. Some members' letters are available in the Evan Rupert Nash Family Papers at Stanford University Library. In 1974 Porcupine Press, Philadelphia, republished the *Daily Journal of the Oneida Community* (1866-1868) with an introduction by Robert Fogarty of Antioch College, who also has a personal collection of the *Quadrangle*.

Visual Materials (Not Illustrated)
Bailey, O. H. and Company, "View of Wallingford, Conn.," Boston, 1881. Shows community buildings.

Hinds, William Alfred, "Album," 1906, Oneida Community Historical Committee, Kenwood, N. Y. Community member's manuscript album with photographs and notes about community buildings and members at Oneida, Wallingford, and Niagara Falls.

"Map No. 1, Shows Total Land Purchased North of Seneca Turnpike by the 'Big 4,' " 1869, owned by Oneida, Ltd.

Noyes, Theodore R., "Map of the Home Domain of the Oneida Community," 1864, Oneida, Ltd.

Pitt, Ethelbert, model of community buildings, 1901, Oneida Community Historical Committee.

Skinner, J. J., "Map of Buildings and Southern Grounds of Oneida Community," 1869, Oneida, Ltd.

_____ , "Map of a Section of the Oneida Community Domain," 1872, Oneida, Ltd.

Skinner, T. H., "Map Showing Lands of Oneida Community," 1913, Oneida, Ltd.

Community Publications
The American Socialist, 1-4 (1876-1879), weekly, Oneida, N. Y. Articles and letters discuss many other experimental communities besides Oneida, including Amana, Bishop Hill, Guise, North American Phalanx.

Daily Journal of the Oneida Community, 1-31 (Jan. 1866-Mar. 1868).

Noyes, John Humphrey, *Confessions of John H. Noyes*, part 1, Oneida, N. Y., 1849.

_____ , *History of American Socialisms*, Oneida, N. Y., 1870. Much of this book is the work of A. J. Macdonald, a traveling journalist who interviewed members of many communities.

_____ , *Male Continence*, Oneida, N. Y., 1872. This pamphlet describes the process and religious justification of *coitus reservatus*, necessary for complex marriage.

Oneida Association, *First Annual Report . . . to Jan. 1, 1849*, Oneida Reserve, 1849.

_____ , *Second Annual Report . . . to February 20, 1850*, Oneida Reserve, 1850.

_____ , *Third Annual Report . . . to February 20, 1851*, Oneida Reserve, 1851.

Oneida Circular, 1-13 (1851-1876), weekly, Brooklyn, N. Y., Wallingford, Conn., and Oneida, N. Y., continued as *The American Socialist*.

Oneida Community, *Bible Communism; A Compilation from the Annual Reports and Other Publications of the Oneida Association and Its Branches*, Brooklyn, N. Y., 1853.

_____ , "Financial History of the Oneida Community" (1857-1865), appendix to *The Oneida Community: A Familiar Exposition*, 1865, pp. 28-32.

_____ , *Handbook of the Oneida Community; Containing a Brief Sketch of Its Present Condition, Internal Economy and Leading Principles*, Oneida, N. Y., 1871.

_____ , *Hand-Book of the Oneida Community*, Oneida, N. Y., 1875.

_____ , *The Oneida Community: A Familiar Exposition of Its Ideas and Practical Life, in a Conversation with a Visitor*, Wallingford, 1865.

Oneida Community Ltd., *The By-Laws and Charter of the Oneida Community Limited*, passed June 21,

1875, Kenwood, N.Y., 1881.

Oneida Community Ltd., *Oneida Community, Limited: 1848-1901*, n.p. (Kenwood, N. Y.?), n.d. (1901-1914?). Corporation brochure discussing its history. Illustrated.

The Quadrangle, 6-7 (Jan. 1913-Dec. 1914), Kenwood, N. Y. Issued by corporation and former members; includes many articles about community buildings by George E. Cragin.

Members' Accounts
Easton, Abel, *The Dissolution of the Oneida Community*, n.p., n.d. (after 1881).

Hinds, William Alfred, *American Communities*, Oneida, N. Y., 1878. Illustrated with wood engravings.

_____, *American Communities*, Chicago, 1902. Frontispiece is photograph of Ethelbert Pitt model of community.

Nash, Evan Rupert, Family Papers, 1827-1945, Stanford University Library, Palo Alto. Includes many letters from community members at Wallingford and Oneida.

Noyes, Corinna Ackley, *The Days of My Youth*, Kenwood, N. Y., 1960.

Noyes, George Wallingford, ed., *John Humphrey Noyes: The Putney Community*, Oneida, N. Y., 1931.

_____, ed., *Religious Experience of John Humphrey Noyes, Founder of the Oneida Community*, New York, 1923.

Noyes, Hilda Herrick, M.D., and George Wallingford Noyes, "The Oneida Community Experiment in Stirpiculture," *Eugenics, Genetics, and the Family*, 1 (1923), 374-386.

Noyes, Pierrepont B., *My Father's House: An Oneida Boyhood*, New York, 1937.

Seymour, Henry J., *The Oneida Community: A Dialogue*, n.p., n.d. (before 1881?). Member's pamphlet discussing theology.

Visitors' Accounts
Dixon, William Hepworth, *Spiritual Wives*, London, 1875.

Reed, Isaac G., Jr., "The Oneida Community of Free Lovers," *Frank Leslie's Illustrated Weekly Newspaper*, 30 (April 2, 1870), 54-55; 30 (April 9, 1870), 38-39. Illustrated with wood engravings.

Nordhoff, Charles, *The Communistic Societies of the United States* (1875), New York, 1966.

Other Works
[Carden], Maren Lockwood, "The Experimental Utopia in America," in Frank E. Manuel, ed., *Utopias and Utopian Thought*, Boston, 1966.

"Early Site of Masonic Home Occupied by Strange People," *The Connecticut Square and Compasses* (Jan. 1958), 7ff. Describes Wallingford dwelling. Illustrated.

Eastman, Hubbard, *Noyesism Unveiled: A History of the Sect Self-Styled Perfectionists*, Brattleboro, Vt., 1849. A polemical work by a minister determined to expose Noyes's "heresies."

Schuster, Eunice Minette, "Native American Anarchism: A Study of Left Wing American Individualism," *Smith College Studies in American History*, 17 (1931-1932). Deals with John Humphrey Noyes, as well as Adin Ballou, Josiah Warren, Frances Wright, and Wilhelm Weitling.

Smith, Goldwin, "The Oneida Community and American Socialism," appendix to *Essays on Questions of the Day, Political and Social*, New York, 1893.

Worden, Harriet M., *Old Mansion House Memories*, Kenwood, N. Y., 1950.

Bibliography
Wells, Lester G., *The Oneida Community Collection in the Syracuse Library*, Syracuse, N. Y., 1961.

The Inspirationists were not eager to advertise the virtues of their community, so the community newspapers and members' correspondence which exist for other groups are lacking here. The group published chiefly religious works in German. Extensive manuscript records of a religious nature exist in the Middle Amana *Archiv* of the Amana Church Society but I have not used this material. The Amana Society has an extensive inventory of buildings made in 1932 just before the "Great Change."

The best general historical work is Bertha M. H. Shambaugh, *Amana: The Community of the True Inspiration*, Iowa City, 1908 (reprinted in 1932 as part of *Amana That Was and Amana That Is*). In terms of physical design, the fullest maps are published in Darrell H. Davis, "Amana, A Study of Occupance," *Economic Geography*, 12.3 (July 1936), 217-230, but the plans do not show kitchen house locations since they were published just after the "Great Change."

Visual Material (Not Illustrated)

Green, Howard R. and Co., Engineers, plats of all Amana Villages, Cedar Rapids, Iowa, June 14, 1932. Held by Main Office, Amana Society, Amana, Iowa.

"Kenneberg in Canada," watercolor, collection of Museum of Amana History, Amana, Iowa. (Kenneberg is Caneborough or Canboro.)

Warner, George E., and C. M. Foote, "Plat of Lenox and Amana," *Plat Book of Iowa County, Iowa*, Minneapolis, 1886.

Community Publications and Records

Amana Society, *Annual Reports*, vols. 2-18, 1934-1949. These are corporation reports.

Amana Society, *Bulletin* (mimeographed newsletter), 1.1 (May 12, 1932) to 11.52 (Apr. 22, 1943). These are chatty versions of the corporation reports.

Amana Society, "Village Appraisals," printed forms with manuscript infill. I, "Amana, Middle, East"; II, "High, West, South, Upper South, Homestead," 1932. Locates, dates, and describes every building. Main Office, Amana Society, Amana, Iowa. Keyed to plats drawn by Howard R. Green Co., Engineers, Cedar Rapids, June 14, 1932.

Noe, Charles F., "A Brief History of the Amana Society, 1714-1900," *Iowa Journal of History and Politics*, 2 (Apr. 1904), distributed as a pamphlet and as an unpaged reprint. A member's version of Amana history officially sanctioned by the community.

Scheuner, Gottlieb, *Inspirations-Historie*, 2 vols., 1884.

Members' Accounts

Barlow, Arthur, *Recollections . . . The Amana Society's "Great Change,"* n.p., 1971. A businessman recalls the economic and administrative shifts in 1932.

Yambura, Barbara S., with Eunice W. Bodine, *A Change and a Parting: My Story of Amana*, Ames, Iowa, 1960. Yambura grew up in Homestead just before the "Great Change" and gives her account of community rituals and daily life.

Visitors' Accounts

Blakeman, Elisha, *A brief account of the society of Germans, called the True Inspirationists, residing seven miles southeast of Buffalo . . . from recollections of Peter H. Long and himself after visiting them in the month of August 1846*, New Lebanon, N. Y., 1846.

Chafee, Grace Earhart, "A Sociological Investigation of the Amana and Amish-Mennonite Communities," unpublished M.A. thesis, Department of Sociology and Anthropology, University of Chicago, 1927.

Ely, Richard T., "Study of Religious Communism," *Harper's Magazine*, 105 (Oct. 1902), 659-668, reprinted in *The Palimpsest*, 52.4 (Apr. 1971), 177-197. Account of a visit to Amana by a political economist.

Hinds, William Alfred, *American Communities*, Chicago, 1902, chapter on "The Amana Community," 263-286.

Infield, Henrik F., *Utopia and Experiment: Essays in the Sociology of Cooperation*, New York, 1955. Pp. 74-80 deal with Amana.

MacClure, Lulu, "Life in Amana" (ca. 1885), *The Palimpsest*, 52.4 (Apr. 1971), 219-222.

Nordhoff, Charles, *The Communistic Societies of the United States* (1875), New York, 1966, chapter on "The Amana Society," pp. 25-64. Account of visit illustrated with wood engravings.

Perkins, William Rufus, and Barthinius L. Wick, *History of the Amana Society or Community of the True Inspiration*, State University of Iowa Publications, Historical Monograph no. 1, Iowa City, 1891.

Rice, Richard Millburn, "Eighty-Nine Years of Collective Living," *Harper's Magazine*, 177 (Oct. 1938), 522-524, reprinted in *The Palimpsest*, 52.4 (Apr. 1971), 198-213.

Shaw, Albert, "Life in the Amana Colony," *Chautauquan* (Feb. 1888), reprinted in *The Palimpsest*, 52.4 (Apr. 1971), 163-176.

Other Works

Duval, Francis Alan, "Christian Metz, German American Religious Leader and Pioneer," unpublished Ph.D. dissertation, Department of German, State University of Iowa, 1948. Includes extremely detailed accounts of Metz's activities in New York, Kansas, and Iowa.

"How it was in the Community Kitchen," published by Marie's Gift Shop, Middle Amana, Iowa, n.d. (1973?).

Godwin, Parke, "Letters from America: A New Community in America," *People's Journal* (London), 4 (Oct. 9, 1847), 218-219.

Murtagh, William J., *Moravian Architecture and Town Planning*, Chapel Hill, N. C., 1967.

Lankes, Frank J., *The Ebenezer Community of True Inspiration*, Gardenville, N. Y., 1949. Includes clear maps of four villages at Ebenezer based upon original drawings by William Noe and author's observations. Maps are not to scale.

Reps, John W., *The Making of Urban America*, Princeton, 1964. Pp. 443-463 deal with the town plans of the Moravian, Harmonist, Aurora, Bethel, and Amana communities.

Schultz-Beherend, G., "The Amana Colony," *American German Review*, 7 (Dec. 1940). Illustrated.

Snyder, Ruth Geraldine, "The Arts and Crafts of the Amana Society," unpublished M.A. thesis, Department of Fine Arts, State University of Iowa, 1949. Includes photographs, town plans, and drawings of architectural details, as well as information on painting and crafts.

Ungers, O[swald] M[atthias], and Liselotte Ungers, "Utopische Kommunen in Amerika, 1800-1900, Die Amana-Community," *Werk* (Aug. 1970), 543-546. Site plan shows inaccurate block configurations.

United States Department of Commerce, Bureau of the Census, "Communistic Societies: Statistics, Denominational History, Doctrine, Organization" (from 1926 Census of Religious Bodies), Washington, D.C., 1928. Deals with Amana community and Shakers.

West Seneca (N. Y.) Centennial Society, *1851-1951 West Seneca Centennial Celebration*, West Seneca, 1951. Includes discussion of Ebenezer town plans and industries, illustrated.

Zug, Joan Liffring, and John Zug, *The Amanas Today: Seven Historic Iowa Villages*, n.p., 1972. Tourist pamphlet including many historic photographs.

Some Colony records are held by the Greeley Municipal Museum, but James F. Willard has reprinted much material in *The Union Colony at Greeley, Colorado, 1869-1871*, Boulder, 1918, including members' correspondence and visitors' accounts.

The most complete historical work is David Boyd, *A History: Greeley and The Union Colony of Colorado*, Greeley, 1890, but it suffers from rehashing old community issues from the author's point of view.

Visual Material (Not Illustrated)

Kelly, William, "The Union Colony Lands, 1870," sketch showing canals, railroads, and fence, undated, Greeley Municipal Museum.

"Map of Colony Lands as Laid Out by the Union Colony of Colorado," 1871, Greeley Municipal Museum, drawn by Rebecca G_____ (illegible).

"Map of Colony Lands as Laid Out by the Union Colony of Colorado," 1873, Greeley Municipal Museum.

"Map of the Town of Greeley, Weld County, Colorado," June 29, 1871, Greeley Municipal Museum.

"Map of the Town of Greeley, Weld County, Colorado," Jan. 8, 1873, Greeley Municipal Museum.

"Union Colony Fence 1871-1874," unsigned, undated sketch, Greeley Municipal Museum.

Members' Accounts

Boyd, David, *A History: Greeley and the Union Colony of Colorado*, Greeley, Colo., 1890. Fullest historical treatment of colony, by a former colonist.

Clark, J. Max, *Colonial Days*, Denver, 1902. A more anecdotal history, by a former colonist.

Green, A[nnie] M[aria], *Sixteen Years on the Great American Desert*, Titusville, Pa., 1887. Contemporary account by pioneer woman.

"Village Improvement from the Foundations," unsigned, undated MS, Greeley Municipal Museum. Deals with town planning and women's activities.

Community Publications and Records

"Applications for Membership in the Union Colony of Colorado," folder of MS forms, Greeley Municipal Museum, Greeley, Colorado.

The Greeley Tribune, ed. Nathan C. Meeker, 1870-1875.

[Pabor, William E.], *First Annual Report of the Union Colony of Colorado, Including a History of the Town of Greeley*, New York, 1871.

Union Colony of Colorado, "Record Book No. 3, Min-

Llano del Rio

utes from July 5, 1871 to October 29, 1872," MS, Greeley Municipal Museum.

_____ , "Record Book No. 4, Minutes from Nov. 5, 1872 to March 4, 1882," MS, Greeley Municipal Museum.

Other Works

Colorado Territory, Board of Immigration, *Resources and Advantages of Colorado*, Denver, 1873. Discusses several Colorado colonies as part of a settler's guide.

Fox, Feramorz Young, "The 'Mormon' Farm-Village in Colorado," *Improvement Era*, 46 (Aug. 1943), 451 ff. Mormon historian compares Greeley with Mormon settlements.

Greeley, Colorado, Board of Trade, *Farming in Colorado*, Greeley, 1887.

"The Union Colony," *The Greeley Tribune*, Illustrated Extra, July 1880, 1-4.

Jackson, J. B., "The Almost Perfect Town," *Landscapes*, Amherst, Mass., 1970. The descriptions in the chapter on "The Almost Perfect Town" could apply to Greeley.

Meeker, Nathan Cook, "Lecture on Association (no. 1)" October 9, 1843, MS, Greeley Municipal Museum.

_____ , letters concerning the Trumbull Phalanx, reprinted in John Humphrey Noyes, *History of American Socialisms* (1870), New York, 1966.

_____ , *Life in the West, or Stories of the Mississippi Valley*, New York, 1868.

Smith, Page, *As A City Upon A Hill: The Town in American History*, New York, 1966. Discusses Greeley as extension of Puritan covenant communities.

Willard, James F., ed., *The Union Colony at Greeley, Colorado, 1869-1871*, University of Colorado Historical Collections vol. 1, Colony Series, vol. 1, Boulder, 1918. Reprints Colony records, minutes, correspondence, and journalistic accounts.

Willard, James F. and Colin B. Goodykoontz, eds. *Experiments in Colorado Colonization, 1869-1872*, University of Colorado Historical Collections, vol. 3, Colony Series, vol. 2, Boulder, 1926.

Community source material was rather limited until 1969, when the Huntington Library acquired correspondence and records of Mellie Miller Calvert, describing the activities of dissident members in the Llano del Rio Welfare League in 1915. In 1973, the California Historical Society was given correspondence describing the ruling clique's version of events, the papers of Walter Millsap (1911-1962). The papers of George T. Pickett (1883-1960), covering Llano colonies in California and Louisiana, are held by Louisiana State University, Baton Rouge, Louisiana. Deed records for Los Angeles County chronicle a maze of land deals ignored in existing histories, which merit careful study.

Two general treatments of the community's history were prepared before much material on Llano factions was available. Paul Conkin, *Two Paths to Utopia: The Hutterites and the Llano Colony*, Lincoln, Nebraska, 1964, deals with Llano in California and in Louisiana and includes a bibliographical essay; Robert V. Hine, *California's Utopian Colonies*, San Marino, 1953, includes a chapter on Llano in California. Paul Kagan, "Llano del Rio: Portrait of a California Utopia," *California Historical Quarterly*, 51.2 (Summer 1972), 130-154, includes historical and contemporary photographs. His excellent collection of photographs on California utopias is well represented in his book, *New World Utopias: A Photographic History of the Search for Community*, Baltimore, 1975.

Community Publications and Records

"Constitution of the Llano del Rio Community," draft copy with MS corrections, Huntington Library, San Marino, California.

Llano Colonist, issued at Llano, California (1917), Newllano, Louisiana (1921-1937), and Los Angeles (1947 and 1960). The Los Angeles Public Library has preserved vol. 1, nos. 32, 33, and 37 from 1917. The Leesville, La. Public Library has microfilms of the 1921-1937 run. The Huntington Library, San Marino, Calif., has nos. 1-14 from 1947. The California Historical Society, San Francisco, has a single issue, *The Colonist*, Aug. 1960.

Llano Colony Press Department, *The gateway to freedom. Cooperation in action. A story of the endeavor and achievements of the Llano del Rio Cooperative Colony at Llano, California*, Llano, Calif., 1915.

Llano del Rio Company of Nevada, "Agreement to Purchase Stock and Agreement of Employment," Dec. 1, 1916. Huntington Library, San Marino, Calif.

Llano del Rio Colony, Board of Commissioners, "Minutes of Meetings and Correspondence," February 1915 to August 1915, Huntington Library, San Marino, Calif.

Llano del Rio Co-operative Colony, *The Gateway to Freedom*, Llano, Calif., 1916.

———, "Application for Membership," California Historical Society, San Francisco.

Llano Publications, *Llano Viewbook*, Llano, Calif., 1917.

101 Questions that have been most frequently asked about the Llano del Rio Cooperative Colony of Llano, Los Angeles County, Cal., Llano, Calif., n.d. (after May 1, 1917).

Welfare League of the Llano del Rio Colony, "Preamble," "Declaration of Purpose," and memos to the directorate, mimeo, Dec. 1915, Huntington Library, San Marino, Calif.

Western Comrade, 1-4 (1913-1917), Los Angeles and Llano, Calif., becomes *The Internationalist*, Leesville, La., 5-6 (1917-1918).

Wood, H. M., and J. E. Wallace, "Survey and Inventory," Llano del Rio Community, September 15, 1915, mimeo, Huntington Library, San Marino, Calif.

Members' Accounts

Calvert, Mellie M., "The Llano del Rio Cooperative Colony," unpublished memoir, n.d. (1962-1969?), Huntington Library, San Marino, Calif.

McCorkle, Gentry Purviance, notes from "Wayside Memories of a Tennessee Rebel," unpublished memoir [1962], Huntington Library, San Marino, Calif.

McDonald, A. James, *The Llano Co-operative Colony and What It Taught*, Leesville, La., 1950.

Miller, F[rank] W., "Experiences of F. W. Miller during his First Three Months at the Llano del Rio Colony (in 1915)," MS, Huntington Library, San Marino, Calif.

Miller, Frank W., and Mrs. Frank W. (Josephine) Miller, MS letters to Mellie (Miller) Calvert and Herbert S. Calvert, Llano, Calif., 1915-1916, Huntington Library, San Marino, Calif.

Millsap, Walter, "The History of United Cooperative Industries," mimeo, August 1966, California Historical Society, San Francisco.

———, transcript of interviews with Abe Hoffman, U.C.L.A. Oral History Project, July 15, 1962, U.C.L.A. Library, Los Angeles.

Wooster, Ernest S., *Communities of the Past and Present*, Newllano, La., 1924.

———, "They Shared Equally," "Bread and Hyacinths," "The Colonists Win Through," series of articles for *Sunset Magazine*, 53 (July 1924), 21-23ff.; 53 (Aug. 1924), 21-23ff.; 53 (Sept. 1924), 30-33ff.

Young, Sid, *The Crisis in Llano Colony, 1935-1936: An Epic Story*, Los Angeles, 1936. Describes controversy over George Pickett's leadership at Newllano.

Visitors' Accounts

Austin, Alice Constance, "Building a Socialist City," and "The Socialist City," series of seven articles, *Western Comrade* (Oct. and Nov. 1916; Jan., Feb., Mar., Apr., and June 1917).

Clifton, A[rchie] R[oy], "History of the Communistic Colony Llano del Rio," *Annual Publications, Historical Society of Southern California*, 9.1 (1918), 80-90. This article is based on personal interviews and summarizes an unpublished M.A. thesis for the University of Southern California, 1918.

Other Works

Austin, Alice Constance, *The Next Step: How to Plan for Beauty, Comfort and Peace with Great Savings Effected by the Reduction of Waste*, Los Angeles, 1935.

Cantrell, Edward Adams, "Harrimanism: Have We Had Enough of It?," open letter to Socialist Party of California, Los Angeles, n.d. (1912?).

Farm, Field and Fireside and Western Rural Colony Department, *Sunset Colonies: Fair Oaks and Olive Park in the Heart of California*, Chicago, 1894. Mentions the "successful" Rio del Llano or Almondale enterprise.

Howard, Ebenezer, *Garden Cities of To-Morrow* (1902), London, 1970.

Huxley, Aldous, "Ozymandias, the Utopia That Failed," *California Historical Quarterly*, 51.2 (Summer 1972), 119-129.

Bibliographies

Bauer, Patricia M., "Cooperative Colonies in California," bibliography of printed and MS materials in Bancroft and Doe Libraries, Berkeley, Calif., n.d.

Sources and Credits for Illustrations

Chapter 2. The Ideal Community: Garden, Machine, or Model Home?

2.1 Maps by D. Hayden based on list by Arthur E. Bestor in *Backwoods Utopias: The Sectarian Origins and the Owenite Phase of Communitarian Socialism in America, 1663 to 1829*, 2d ed., rev. and enl., Philadelphia, 1970. (See Appendix B for list.)

2.2 Martha B. Smith, "The Story of Icaria," *Annals of Iowa*, 3rd series, 38 (Summer 1965), 44-45.

2.3 L.H. Everts and Co., *Combination Atlas Map of Tuscarawas County* (Ohio), Philadelphia, 1875.

2.4 Photograph by Bill Logan, 1971.

2.5 Photograph by Bill Logan, 1971.

2.6 *The Co-operative Magazine and Monthly Herald*, 1 (Jan. 1826), frontispiece. Photograph courtesy Arthur E. Bestor.

2.7 "Vue générale d'un Phalanstère ou Village organisé d'après la théorie de Fourier, réduction du grand dessin lithographié par Jules Arnoult," Paris, ca. 1848, collection Oneida Community Historical Committee, found by author in Oneida Mansion House attic, 1971.

2.8 Reprinted from Leonardo Benevolo, *The Origins of Modern Town Planning*, Cambridge, Mass., MIT Press, 1971, pp. 36-37.

2.9 Pennsylvania Prison Society, Philadelphia.

2.10, 2.11 *The Shaker Manifesto*, 8.1 (Jan. 1878), opp. p. 24 and p. 26.

2.12 Jean-Baptiste Godin, *Social Solutions*, New York, 1880.

2.13 *Frank Leslie's Illustrated Newspaper*, 34. 937 (Sept. 13, 1873), 12.

2.14 *Frank Leslie's Illustrated Newspaper*, 30. 757 (Apr. 2, 1870), 40.

2.15 Undated sketch courtesy Old Salem Restoration, Winston-Salem, N.C.

2.16 Catharine E. Beecher and Harriet Beecher Stowe, *The American Woman's Home*, New York, 1869, title page.

2.17, 2.18 Ray Reynolds, *Cat's Paw Utopia*, El Cajon, Calif., 1972.

Chapter 3. The Communal Building Process

3.1 Helen Rosenau, *The Ideal City in Its Architectural Evolution*, London, Routledge and Kegan Paul, 1959, p. 38, after original in Biblioteca Nazionale, Florence.

3.2 Ibid., p. 59.

3.3 *The Winter's Island Co-operator*, 1 (Nov. 1895), 1, courtesy the Bancroft Library.

3.4 J. Madison Allen plan, in Josiah Warren, *Practical Applications of the Elementary Principles of 'True Civilization' to the Minute Details of Every Day Life*, Princeton, Mass., 1873, pp. 46-47, redrawn by W. Tibbs.

3.5 Ray Reynolds, *Cat's Paw Utopia*, El Cajon, Calif., 1972.

3.6 Joseph Paxton, Crystal Palace, London, 1851, reprinted from George F. Chadwick, *The Works of Sir Joseph Paxton, 1803-1865*, London, The Architectural Press, 1961, p. 130, after original in Victoria and Albert Museum.

3.7 O[rson] S[quire] Fowler, *A Home For All, or, The Gravel Wall and Octagon Mode of Building*, New York, 1854, frontispiece.

3.8 Undated photograph, California Historical Society, Paul Kagan Collection.

3.9 Undated photograph, State Historical Society of Iowa.

3.10 Undated photograph, Oneida Community Historical Committee.

3.11 "Design for a Social Palace or Symposium," Fountaingrove, Calif., 1894 (tracing dated 1922 initialed "L.C."), courtesy Horrman Library, Wagner College, Staten Island, N.Y.

3.12 Longitudinal section of 3.11.

3.13 Photograph by D. Hayden, 1972.

3.14 Undated photograph, California Historical Society, Paul Kagan Collection.

3.15 Undated photograph, California Historical Society, Paul Kagan Collection.

3.16 Reprinted from Charles M. Stotz, *The Early Architecture of Western Pennsylvania*, by permission of the University of Pittsburgh Press, © 1936, p. 196.

3.17 Photograph by Bill Logan, 1971.

3.18 Cyrus Teed, *The Cellular Cosmogony*, or, *The Earth a Concave Sphere*, Chicago, 1901, etching 8, opp. p. 156.

Chapter 4. Heavenly and Earthly Space

4.1 Charles Nordhoff, *The Communistic Societies of the United States*, 1875.

4.2 Department of Public Information, State of Kentucky, Frankfort, Ky.

4.3 Edward Deming Andrews and Faith Andrews, *Shaker Furniture: The Craftsmanship of an American Communal Sect*, New York, Dover Publications, 1964, plate 4.

4.4, 4.5 Courtesy Shaker Community, Inc., Hancock, Mass.

4.6 D.W. Kellogg, "Square Order Shuffle," The Shaker Museum, Old Chatham, N.Y.

4.7 "The Whirling Gift," woodcut from David R. Lamson, *Two Years' Experience among the Shakers*, West Boylston, Mass., 1848.

4.8 Site plan, D. Hayden and M. Jones, based on various historic maps and using field notes by Robert Meader.

4.9 Diagram of organization, Hancock, 1840, D. Hayden.

4.10 John Warner Barber, *Historical Collections . . . of Every Town in Massachusetts*, Worcester, Mass., 1839.

4.11 Giles B. Avery, *Sketches of "Shakers and Shakerism,"* Albany, 1883.

4.12 Courtesy the Shaker Museum, Old Chatham, N.Y.

4.13 Photograph by Bill Logan, 1971.

4.14 Schematic plans, W. Tibbs.

4.15 Undated, number 9 from a portfolio of drawings, collection of Shaker Community, Inc., Hancock, Mass.

4.16 Photograph by Bill Logan, 1971.

4.17 *Frank Leslie's Illustrated Newspaper*, 36 (Sept. 6, 1873), 417.

4.18 Photograph by Jack Boucher for Historic American Buildings Survey (HABS), Washington, D.C., 1962.

4.19 Photograph by Jack Boucher for HABS, 1962.

4.20 Undated, number 1 from a portfolio of drawings, collection of Shaker Community, Inc., Hancock, Mass.

4.21 Schematic sections, D. Hayden and M. Jones.

4.22 Photograph by Jack Boucher for HABS, 1962.

4.23 Photograph by Jack Boucher for HABS, 1962.

4.24 Photograph by Jack Boucher for HABS, 1962.

4.25 Photograph by N.E. Baldwin for HABS, 1939.

4.26 Photograph by Bill Logan, 1971.

4.27 Plans and section, HABS.

4.28 Photograph by Bill Logan, 1971.

4.29 Photograph by Bill Logan, 1971.

4.30 Photograph by Bill Logan, 1971.

4.31 Photograph by Bill Logan, 1971.

4.32 Lamson, *Two Years' Experience.*

4.33 Photograph, ca. 1960, Shaker Community, Inc., Hancock, Mass.

4.34 Shaker Community, Inc., Hancock, Mass.

Chapter 5. Eden versus Jerusalem
5.1 Map, D. Hayden and M. Jones.

5.2 Diagram, Paul Anderson.

5.3 LDS Church Historian's Office, Salt Lake City.

5.4 John William Larner, "Nails and Sundrie Medicines," *Western Pennsylvania Historical Magazine*, 45.2 (June 1962), 126.

5.5 Photograph by Bill Logan, 1971.

5.6 Diagrammatic site plan, D. Hayden and W. Tibbs.

5.7 Henry Lewis, *Das illustrierte Mississippithal*, Düsseldorf, 1857, courtesy the Edward E. Ayer collection, The Newberry Library, Chicago.

5.8 Regional plan, D. Hayden and W. Tibbs.

5.9 Diagram, D. Hayden and W. Tibbs.

5.10 Photograph by Bill Logan, 1971.

5.11 Photograph by Bill Logan, 1971.

5.12 Photograph, ca. 1900, courtesy Illinois State Historical Library, Springfield.

5.13 Photograph by D. Hayden, 1972.

5.14 Photograph by Bill Logan, 1971.

5.15 Photograph by Bill Logan, 1971.

5.16 Unsigned drawing from portfolio of drawings, LDS Church Historian's Office, Salt Lake City. Portfolio contains work by William Weeks, but Robert Flanders cites Lucian Woodworth as architect of this building.

5.17 Lynn E. Smith, Independence, Mo.

5.18 Drawing by Henry Howe, 1846, photograph LDS Church Historian's Office.

5.19 HABS.

5.20 HABS.

5.21 Portfolio of drawings by William Weeks, LDS Church Historian's Office, Salt Lake City. Signed "Isle of Man, Sept. 1842, J. McC."

5.22, 5.23, 5.24, 5.25 William Weeks, portfolio of drawings, LDS Church Historian's Office, Salt Lake City.

5.26 Courtesy Illinois State Historical Library, Springfield.

5.27 *Thuilleur des trente-trois degrés de l'écossisme du rit ancien dit accepté*, Paris, rev. ed., 1821, frontispiece.

5.28 Unsigned sketch, included in portfolio of drawings by William Weeks, LDS Church Historian's Office, Salt Lake City.

5.29 *American Architect and Building News*, 1 (Feb. 12, 1876), 52.

5.30 Robert Hytten, research by Stanley B. Kimball, in R. Don Oscarson, ed., *A Traveller's Guide to Historic Mormon America*, Salt Lake City, Book Craft, 1965.

5.31 Conjectural plans and sections, D. Hayden and W. Tibbs.

5.32 Missouri Historical Society, St. Louis.

5.33 Church Archives, The Church of Jesus Christ of Latter-day Saints, Salt Lake City.

5.34 Carl C.A. Christensen, LDS Church Historian's Office, Salt Lake City.

5.35 Richard V. Francaviglia, "The Mormon Landscape: Existence, Creation, and Perception of a Unique Image in the American West," Ph.D. dissertation, University of Oregon, 1970.

5.36, 5.37 LDS Church Historian's Office, Salt Lake City.

Chapter 6. The Architecture of Passional Attraction
6.1, 6.2 Victor Considérant, *Description du phalanstère*, Paris, 1848.

6.3 H. Fugère, editor, Charles Daubigny, designer, published by Librairie Phalanstérien, Paris (ca. 1848), by permission of the Harvard College Library.

6.4 Diagram, D. Hayden.

6.5 Site plan, D. Hayden and W. Tibbs.

6.6 "Map of the Domain of the North American Phalanx," based on a survey made by Alfred Walling, Sept. 1855, by permission of the Harvard College Library. (Accompanied by inventory, "Positive Sale of the Domain of the Phalanx.")

6.7 Detail of 6.6.

6.8 Detail of 6.6.

6.9 Detail of 6.6.

6.10 Schematic plans, D. Hayden and W. Tibbs.

6.11 T[homas] W. Whitley, "North American Phalanx, Monmouth County, New Jersey," watercolor and "Historical Sketch," 1852 (Phalanstery dining wing shown in incorrect position), by permission of the Harvard College Library.

6.12 "Grand Unitary Edifice," front elevation and plan of the upper floors, designed by J[ames] Sartain, drawn by Henry Sartain, published with "Constitution of the Philadelphia Unitary Building Association," Philadelphia, 1849.

6.13 Site plan, D. Hayden and W. Tibbs.

6.14 Schematic plans, drawn from existing building, D. Hayden and W. Tibbs. Dining wing is reconstructed from verbal descriptions given by Ann Vernell, Lincroft, N.J., June 1972.

6.15 Photograph, ca. 1900, courtesy Ann Miles, Colt's Neck, N.J.

6.16 Undated photograph (before 1938), collection Arthur E. Bestor.

6.17 Photograph by Bill Logan, 1971.

6.18 Photograph by D. Hayden, 1971.

6.19 Photograph by Arthur E. Bestor, 1938.

6.20 Detail of 6.19.

6.21 "Eagleswood House," from map of Perth Amboy, Staten Island, and South Amboy, by Thomas A. Hurley, 1858, courtesy New Jersey Historical Society.

6.22 "Plan des Terres Appartenant à la Société de Colonisation Européo-Américaine dans le Comté de Dallas, Texas," with "Plan des Lots à Bâtir et de Jardins de Réunion," engraved by Delamare, Paris (ca. 1854), by permission of the Harvard College Library.

Chapter 7. The Architecture of Complex Marriage
7.1 Photograph, ca. 1863, Oneida Community Historical Committee.

7.2 Diagram, D. Hayden.

7.3 *Oneida Circular*, 7.1 (Mar. 21, 1870), 7.

7.4 *Bible Communism: A Compilation from the Annual Reports and Other Publications of the Oneida Community and Its Branches*, Brooklyn, N.Y., 1853.

7.5 *Handbook of the Oneida Community*, Oneida, N.Y., 1871.

7.6 *Frank Leslie's Illustrated Newspaper*, 30 (Apr. 2, 1870), p. 37.

7.7 Site plan, D. Hayden and M. Jones.

7.8 Drawn by M. Jones after an original plan owned by Oneida, Ltd.

7.9 William Alfred Hinds, *American Communities*, 2d ed., Chicago, 1902, frontispiece. Model is in the collection of Oneida Community Historical Committee.

7.10 Lunch bag, *Oneida Circular*, 2.11 (May 29, 1865), 85; "Final Shoe," Ibid., 5.43 (Jan. 11, 1869), 344.

7.11 Drawn by J.J. Skinner, 1869, Oneida, Ltd.

7.12 Diagram, D. Hayden.

7.13 Oneida, Ltd.

7.14 Oneida, Ltd.

7.15 Photograph by Bill Logan, 1971.

7.16 Photograph, ca. 1960, courtesy Oneida Community Historical Committee.

7.17 Photograph, ca. 1875, courtesy Oneida Community Historical Committee.

7.18 Diagram, D. Hayden and M. Jones. Based on verbal descriptions in Harriet Worden, *Old Mansion House Memories*, Kenwood, N.Y., 1950.

7.19 Schematic plans, D. Hayden and W. Tibbs. Drawn from verbal descriptions and examinations of structure, 1971, and measured drawings, ca. 1925 (after renovation as apartment house), in the collection of Oneida, Ltd.

7.20 Andrew Jackson Downing, *The Architecture of Country Houses*, New York, 1850, Figures 168 and 169.

7.21 Diagram, D. Hayden.

7.22 Detail of 7.8.

7.23 *Frank Leslie's Illustrated Newspaper*, 30 (Apr. 9, 1870), 57.

7.24 Ibid., p. 41.

7.25, 7.26 Ibid., p. 56.

7.27 Photograph by Bill Logan, 1971.

7.28 Photograph by Bill Logan, 1971.

Chapter 8. Communes within Communes
8.1 Richard Ely. "Study of Religious Communism," *Harper's Magazine*, 105 (Oct. 1902), 662.

8.2 Museum of Amana History, Amana, Iowa.

8.3 Diagram, D. Hayden.

8.4 Site plan, D. Hayden and W. Tibbs.

8.5 Darrell Davis, "Amana: A Study of Occupance," *Economic Geography*, 12. 3 (July 1936), 222.

8.6 Photograph by Bill Logan, 1971.

8.7 State Historical Society of Iowa, Iowa City.

8.8 Photograph by Bill Logan, 1971.

8.9 F.J. Lankes, after original drawings by William Noe, ca. 1843-1852, *The Ebenezer Community of True Inspiration*, Gardenville, New York, 1949.

8.10 Photograph by William F. Noe, State Historical Society of Iowa.

8.11 Photograph by Bill Logan, 1971.

8.12 Davis, "Amana, a Study of Occupance," 224, 226. Kitchen houses are not indicated.

8.13 Diagram, based on Amana Society records, 1932, D. Hayden and W. Tibbs.

8.14, 8.15 Charles Nordhoff, *The Communistic Societies of the United States*, New York, 1875.

8.16 Photograph by Bill Logan, 1971.

8.17 Drawn by W. Tibbs after Ruth Geraldine Snyder, "The Arts and Crafts of the Amana Society," unpublished M.A. thesis, Department of Fine Arts, State University of Iowa, 1949.

8.18 Schematic plan, D. Hayden and W. Tibbs.

8.19, 8.20 Undated photographs (ca. 1900), State Historical Society of Iowa, Iowa City.

8.21 Schematic plan, D. Hayden and W. Tibbs.

8.22 W. Tibbs, after Ruth Geraldine Snyder, "The Arts and Crafts of the Amana Society."

8.23 Photograph by Bill Logan, 1971.

8.24 Photograph by Lillian Snyder, 1964.

8.25 Photograph by Bill Logan, 1971.

8.26 Photograph, 1932, State Historical Society of Iowa.

8.27 Photograph by Peter Marris, 1974.

8.28 Undated photograph, State Historical Society of Iowa, Iowa City.

8.29 Photograph by Peter Marris, 1974.

8.30 Nordhoff, *Communistic Societies of the United States*.

Chapter 9. The Disintegration of Association
9.1 Photograph, 1870, Greeley Municipal Museum.

9.2 Diagram, D. Hayden.

9.3 Diagram, D. Hayden and W. Tibbs.

9.4 Conjectural site plan, D. Hayden and W. Tibbs.

9.5 Plan, 1871, Greeley Municipal Museum.

9.6 Photograph, 1870, Greeley Municipal Museum.

9.7 Photograph, 1871, Greeley Municipal Museum.

9.8 Photograph, 1870, Greeley Municipal Museum.

9.9 Photograph, 1870, Greeley Municipal Museum.

9.10 Woodcut from Greeley *Tribune*, Extra, July 1880, p. 2.

9.11, 9.12, 9.13, 9.14 Undated photographs, Greeley Municipal Museum.

9.15 Photograph, 1870, Greeley Municipal Museum.

9.16 Photograph, 1871, Greeley Municipal Museum.

9.17 Undated photograph, Greeley Municipal Museum.

9.18 Undated photograph, Greeley Municipal Museum.

9.19 Undated photograph, Greeley Municipal Museum.

9.20 Beck and Paul, lithograph, 1882, published by J.J. Stoner, Madison, Wisconsin, Greeley Municipal Museum.

9.21 Photograph by D. Hayden, 1972.

Chapter 10. Feminism and Eclecticism
10.1 Group of colonists, Christmas 1914, *Western Comrade*, 2.9-10 (Jan.-Feb. 1915), 27, courtesy The Bancroft Library.

10.2 Diagram, D. Hayden.

10.3 Detail from E.T. Wright, "Official Map of the County of Los Angeles," 1898, California Historical Society, San Francisco.

10.4 Drawn by D. Hayden after a map by R.E.P. (Ray E. Proebstel), May 20, 1917, California Historical Society, San Francisco.

10.5 Conjectural site plan, prepared from site evidence, deed surveys, photographs, and verbal evidence, D. Hayden and M. Jones.

10.6 Photograph, ca. 1815-1917, courtesy Paul Kagan.

10.7 "Type of the Temporary Clay Brick Houses at Llano," *Western Comrade*, 3.6 (Oct. 1915), 18, courtesy The Bancroft Library.

10.8 "A Llano Home," *Western Comrade*, 4.5 (Oct. 1916), 14, courtesy The Bancroft Library.

10.9 *Western Comrade*, 2.11 (Mar. 1915).

10.10 *Llano Viewbook*, 1917, courtesy Department of Special Collections, UCLA.

10.11 *Garden Cities of To-Morrow* (1902), London, 1970, p. 53.

10.12 Alice Constance Austin, *The Next Step*, Los Angeles, 1935, opposite p. 46.

10.13 Josephine Miller, MS. letter to Mellie Miller Calvert, Llano, Calif., Sept. 1915, tracings by permission of The Huntington Library, San Marino, Calif.

10.14 Photograph, 1916, courtesy Paul Kagan.

10.15 Esther McCoy, *Five California Architects*, Reinhold Publishing Co., New York, 1960, p. 84.

10.16, 10.17, 10.18 Austin, *The Next Step*, Los Angeles, 1935, opposite p. 18.

10.19 Ibid., opposite title page.

10.20, 10.21 Undated photographs, courtesy Paul Kagan.

10.22 Schematic plan, D. Hayden and W. Tibbs. Information on interior furnished by Adolph Davis, Newllano.

10.23 Undated photograph, courtesy Paul Kagan.

10.24, 10.25 Photographs by D. Hayden, 1973.

10.26 Schematic plan, D. Hayden and W. Tibbs.

10.27 "Llano Cooperative Colony, Vernon Parish, Louisiana," from *Llano Colonist*, 14 (Nov. 13, 1947), cover, collection Huntington Library, San Marino, Calif.

Chapter 11. Communal Building Today
11.1 From (John Minter Morgan), *Hampden in the Nineteenth Century; or Colloquies on the Errors and Improvement of Society*, vol. 2, London, 1834, plate facing p. 100, illustrating section entitled "Mr. Owen visits America." Photograph courtesy Arthur E. Bestor.

11.2 Village of Arts and Ideas, *Village One*, Berkeley, 1972.

11.3 Martha B. Smith, "The Story of Icaria," *Annals of Iowa*, 3rd series, 38 (Summer 1965), 44.

11.4 *New York Times*, Aug. 3, 1970, p. 28.

11.5 Synanon, "The Words to Our Song," 1972.

11.6 "Blueprint for a Communal Environment," *The Berkeley Tribe* (1969?), reprinted in Theodore Roszak, ed., *Sources*, New York, Harper Colophon Books, 1972, pp. 396, 401, 403.

11.7 Ernest Miller, "Utopian Communities in Warren County, Pennsylvania," *Western Pennsylvania Historical Magazine*, 49, opposite p. 303, and Paul Kegan Collection, California Historical Society.

11.8 Steve Baer, *Dome Cookbook*, Corrales, N.M., 1969, p. 33.

11.9 Paul Kagan Collection, California Historical Society.

11.10 Photograph by D. Hayden, 1972.

11.11 California Historical Society.

11.12 Ken Kern, "The Owner-built Homestead," *The Mother Earth News*, 5 (Sept. 1970), 73.

11.13 *Casabella*, 35. 358 (1971), 18 ff.

Index

Economy, Pennsylvania (*continued*)
  brick houses (ca. 1825) at, 112f
  communal dwellings (after 1824) in, 249f
  gardens, 19f, 25
"Ecotecture," 323
"Eden," imagery of. *See* Symbolism and imagery
Eden, Virginia, 3
"Edge City," 323, 325
Electric Kool Aid Acid Test (Wolfe), 326
Elkins, Elder Hervey, 98
Elkins, Meyer, family, 299
Ellis, Charles, 197
Elysian Valley, California, 3
"Emblem of the Heavenly Sphere, An" (Shaker drawing), 73f
Emerson, Ralph Waldo, 9, 103n.49, 321
Enfield, Connecticut, 81, 86f, 362
Enfield, New Hampshire, 355, 362
Engels, Friedrich, 3, 65, 149
Environment. *See also* Architecture; Housing; Housing, communal; Land and natural resources; Territory
  capitalism and, 33
  and environmental psychology, 42, 92, 100-101, 154, 161, 218, 339
  "invisible," 4
  physical, 76, 142, 143, 251. *See also* Landscape design
    Fourierists (North American Phalanx) and, 42, 150, 154, 159, 161
    Oneidans and, 42, 101, 188, 190, 191, 196, 218, 251
  pollution of, 142
  and recycling, 43, 76, 323, 338-339
  replicable. *See* Duplication of model
  and "sociofugal," "sociopetal" space. *See* Space
  technology and, 14
  unique, and collective identity, 47-49, 56. *See also* Design and construction
Ephrata Pietists, 34, 362
Esalen ("growth center," California), 329
Estero, Florida, 47, 59f
Europeans, 14, 35
Evans, Elder Frederick, 76, 188
Evanston, Illinois, 262
Evening and Morning Star (Mormon newspaper), 113

Familistère, Guise, France, 26f, 181
Family. *See also* Children and child care facilities; Marriage
  "ambition" of, 260, 273. *See also* 276f
  Church. *See* Shaker sect
  under Fourierism, 24-25, 159, 164, 173, 174, 334
  isolation of, 24-25, 107, 206, 212, 273, 353. *See also* 208f; and single-family home, *below*
  Mormon view of, 107, 110
  nuclear (dissolution vs. retention of), 43, 45, 262, 274, 284, 328

  and Shaker "family system," 43, 45, 67, 68, 77, 78f, 230
  and single-family home, 28f, 34
    Catharine Beecher and, 25
    vs. communal, 334, 353. *See also* Territory
    Inspirationist, 243-244
    Llano del Rio, 45, 289, 301-302, 309-310
    Mormon, 45, 118, 119-120, 142, 225, 244, 261, 273
    North American Phalanx, 24-25, 173, 174, 334
    suburban American (contemporary), 326
    Union Colony, 244, 262, 273-274, 334
  size, 145n.13, 230
  suites, 29f, 173, 176f, 177f, 243, 334, 353
Family, The (contemporary commune), 328, 332
Family, The (of Rigdon, Kirtland, Ohio), 106, 107, 363
Farm, Field and Fireside magazine, 293
Farm, The (contemporary commune), 329
Farming. *See* Agriculture
Farr, Winslow, and Winslow Farr House, 120, 123f
Far West, Missouri, 111, 113, 141
"Fat City," 323, 325
Feminism. *See* Women
Feminist Studio Workshop, 328
Fences. *See* Boundaries, approaches, and vantage points
Filarete, 339
  Sforzinda of, 36f
Fisher, James T., 157, 164, 174
Fishkill, New York, octagonal house, 35, 38f
Flansburgh, David and Ogden, 164
Fogarty, Robert, 365
Fort Collins, Colorado, 284
Fort Hill (Roxbury, Massachusetts), 329
Foster, Robert, 124
Fountain Colony (later Colorado Springs). *See* Colorado
Fountaingrove, California, "Social Palace," 35, 48, 50-51f, 52-53f, 182, 351
Fourier, Charles, 3, 4, 9, 20, 111, 181, 325, 340, 352. *See also* Fourierists
  background and beliefs of, 149-150, 154-155, 221n.21, 273, 301
  Brisbane and, 155. *See also* Brisbane, Albert
  and circulation paths ("galleries of association"), 46, 150-151, 172, 190, 196, 197, 238, 334, 353
  and landscape design, 154-155, 159, 161, 191, 238, 353
  phalanstery designed by, 21f, 34, 35, 150-151, 191
  and "Phalanx," 148, 154, 159
  shown in Daubigny's "View of a Phalanx," 153f
  and unitary dwellings, 244, 353
  writings of, 149, 339
Fourierists, 5, 14, 15, 145n.1, 219, 258n.3, 261, 284, 321, 326. *See also* Fourier, Charles; North American Phalanx
  architecture and design, 28, 34-35, 40, 41, 50-51f,

"Real City," 323, 325
Red Bank, New Jersey, 159, 180
Re-Education Foundation, 329
Religion and religious authority. *See also* Mormons; Sects, religious; Shaker sect
  communism, and survival of, 227
  comparative chart of, 358-359
  contemporary, 332
  Fourierists/North American Phalanx and, 149, 159, 262
  Inspirationist/Amana, 225, 227, 242, 251
  millennial. *See* "Millennium, the"
  Oneidan, 41, 187, 188, 197, 218-219
  revival of, 106, 155, 188
  and ritual. *See* Rituals
  in Union Colony, 277
  and visions and revelations. *See* Symbolism and imagery
Resident Hotel or "Unitary Dwelling." 29f. *See also* Housing, communal
Réunion (Texas), 35, 180, 181, 182f. *See also* North American Phalanx
Revelations and visions. *See* Symbolism and imagery
Richmond, Massachusetts, 77
Ridgeway, Richard, 310
Rigdon, Sidney, 106, 107, 110, 145nn.2, 9
Ripley, George, 155. *See also* 166f
Ripon, Wisconsin, 364. *See also* North American Phalanx
  and Wisconsin Phalanx, 173, 176f
Rituals, 43, 45. *See also* 50-51f. *See also* Symbolism and imagery
  Amana, 242
  Mormon, 107, 110, 125, 130-131, 141, 143
  Oneidan, 188, 219
  Shaker, 46, 65, 71, 74f, 76, 92, 98, 99f, 100, 101f, 311
Riverside, Illinois, 18
Rock, Johann Friedrich, 225
Romney, Hugh, 320
Round Barn (Hancock), 92, 94f, 95f
Roxbury, Massachusetts, 329
Rural-urban conflict. *See* Urbanism

Sabbathday Lake, Maine, 66, 362
St. Louis *Gazette*, 131
St. Nicholas Hotel, New York, 222n.55
Salem, North Carolina, 18, 244
Salt Lake City, Utah, 45, 130, 143, 262, 365
  Temple, 141, 142-143, 144f, 146-147n.47
San Diego New Alchemy Institute *Bulletin*, 325
Sanitary Engineer, The (publication), 75-76
Sartain, James: design of, 166f
Scandinavia, 14, 35
Schwitters, Kurt, 338, 341
Sears, Charles, 157, 181, 183n.3
"Second Coming." *See* "Millennium, the"
Sects, religious, 5, 14, 65. *See also* Mormons; Religion

and religious authority; Shaker sect
  and "divine will" in community planning, 39-40, 92. *See also* Symbolism and imagery
  German, 15, 106, 225, 226f, 227
  Hutterian Brethren, 57, 253, 321
  Jansenists, 35, 244, 365
  Moravian Brethren, 18, 20, 27f, 35, 225, 227, 244, 355, 362, 365
  nonsectarian communities, 5, 14, 34, 40, 159, 188, 262, 332, 358, 359
  Puritan covenant communities, 9, 16, 24, 30n.7, 35, 110, 113, 270
  Separatists, 35, 43, 227, 362
  in Union Colony, 277
Separatists. *See* Sects, religious
Seristery (Phalanx workshop), 161, 163f
Sermon on the Mount, 15
Sex(es)
  and celibacy, 46, 66, 229, 243, 358
  and "complex marriage" (sexual revolution). *See* Marriage
  as issue in communal dwellings, 43, 243, 334
  and Mormon polygamy, 110, 142, 145n.13, 147n.58, 358
  roles, 328, 330, 331. *See also* Women
  segregation
    Amana, 242, 243
    Shaker, 69, 70f, 71, 81, 87f, 225
  sexual organization of communities charted, 358-359
  and sexual politics, 24. *See also* 26f
Sforzinda, by Filarete, 36f
Shaker Mountain ("Mount Sinai"), 77, 99f, 100
Shaker sect (United Society of Believers), 5, 145n.1, 225, 229, 258n.3, 261, 321, 331, 340, 358. *See also* Hancock, Massachusetts, Shaker settlement; New Lebanon, New York, Shaker settlement
  agriculture, 16, 18, 75, 76, 77, 92, 161, 323
  architecture and building materials, 28, 35, 39, 49, 76, 81-92, 225, 252, 253, 349, 353. *See also* and "living building," *below*
  buildings remodeled, 355
  Church Family, 68, 77, 80f, 81, 82-83f, 84f, 90f, 91f, 92, 93f-97f, 99f, 101f
  and rural-urban conflict, 15, 325
  and "Cleansing Gift," 46, 98
  color use, 43, 49, 77, 81, 92, 252, 352
  communal dwellings, 77, 78f, 80f, 81, 84-85f, 87f, 243
  community design, 75-76, 77, 78f, 80f, 81, 92, 100-101, 155, 270
  decline of, 66, 92
  and duplication of model, 20, 35, 47, 65-66, 92, 100, 101
  economic system, 66, 75, 77, 81, 92, 273, 358
  entrances to men's and women's rooms, communal dwelling, New Lebanon (1873), 87f
  and environmental psychology, 42, 92, 100-101, 218

Space (*continued*)
    Oneidan "changeability" in, 199, 206-207, 399
    Shakers and, 45, 92
    "earthly and heavenly," Shakers and, 58, 69-71, 74, 100, 354. *See also* 97f
    personal, Shakers' unorthodox use of, 57-58, 69-71, 75-76, 197, 332
    "sociofugal," "sociopetal," 42, 150, 151, 154, 181, 197, 206
    and spatial commitment, 56-59
    and time, Mormon concept of, 61n.41
Sparta Township, Indiana, 181
Spiritual Springs, New York, 336f, 365
Spring, Marcus, 157, 164, 174
    phalanstery commissioned by, 178f
    private residences of, 165f, 173, 177f, 179f
Square Pigeon community, 334, 339
Stables, Louisiana, 309. *See also* Newllano, Louisiana
Standardization, 49, 71. *See also* Duplication of model and prefabrication, 34, 38f, 49
Standerin, Abraham, 65
Stowe, Harriet Beecher, 223n.55
    The American Woman's Home, 25. *See also* 28f
Style, vernacular, 35, 48-49, 353. *See also* Design and construction
    Amana, 227, 251-254, 353
    contemporary, 326, 328, 330, 338-341
    indecision in, 289, 310
    Mormon (Nauvoo), 110, 120, 125, 142, 143, 353
    Shaker, 76, 252, 353
Sun, Andrew, 339
Sunrise Hill Community (Conway, Massachusetts), described, 330
Superstudio of Milan, 339-340
Synanon (San Francisco and Oakland), 323, 329, 334, 352
    plan for warehouse rehabilitation, 333f
Symbolism and imagery, 14, 33, 40, 49. *See also* Temple(s)
    and choice of site, 15, 47, 191
    of contemporary communes, 322-323, 326, 329, 340
    and "divine will" in community planning, 39-40, 92
    and "Garden of Eden" imagery, 15, 17f, 18, 34, 38f, 104, 105, 111, 113, 117-118, 119, 120, 143, 218, 231, 266, 285, 322
    geometric, 38f, 335
    and "Jerusalem"
        of Mormons, 34, 105, 106, 110-111, 117, 125, 131, 143
        of Shakers, 15, 34, 67-68, 100
    Masonic, 40, 102n.14, 131, 134f, 146n.47
    and spatial reference, 57-58
    of visions and revelations, 39, 106, 107, 130-131, 142, 227, 231, 251
    and "Zion"
        of Mormons, 106, 119, 125. *See also* Mormons
        of Shakers, 68, 69, 98

Taconic Mountains, 77
Talcott, Josiah, 77
Tanzania, *ujamaa* (communal) villages in, 4, 350
Taos, New Mexico, 328, 332
    Kingdom of Heaven commune, 327f
Taylor, John, 142
Technology, 14, 15
    "alternative," 325, 326, 328
    and technological ideal, 9, 41, 323, 325-326
Teed, Cyrus, design for "Cellular Cosmogony," 59f
Temperance, Union Colony and, 262, 284
Temple(s). *See also* Symbolism and imagery
    of Jerusalem (Solomon's), 34, 68, 81, 102n.14, 125, 131, 145n.2
    Mormon, 4, 110
        Kirtland, Ohio, 35, 39, 128f, 130, 131, 143
        Nauvoo, Illinois, 39, 43, 48, 104f, 107, 115f, 117-118, 124, 125, 129f, 130-131, 133f, 135f, 136-138f, 139f, 140f, 141, 143, 349
        Salt Lake City, Utah, 141, 142-143, 144f, 146-147n.47
Tent colony (Advance, California), 344f
"Tent Room" (Oneida), 45, 206, 207, 208f, 212, 351
Territory. *See also* Environment; Land and natural resources; Property ownership
    boundaries of. *See* Boundaries, approaches, and vantage points
    circulation paths in. *See* Space
    communal vs. private, 5, 39, 42-46, 143, 149, 173, 174, 206-207, 212, 218, 244, 251, 253, 254, 261, 262, 270, 273-274, 302, 308, 329, 331-335, 350, 352-353. *See also* Family; Identity, collective
    and isolation
        of community, 42-43, 105, 222n.31, 237. *See also* 21f
        of family, 24-25, 107, 206, 212, 273, 352. *See also* 208f; Family
    and sex segregation. *See* Sex(es)
Texas, State of, 174, 180
    plans for "Réunion," 35, 180, 182f
    Texas Emigration Union bulletin, 174
Thacker, Henry, 191, 198
Theosophists. *See* Point Loma, California, Theosophists
Thoreau, Henry David, 322
Thunder Mountain, Nevada, 338, 340-341
    1972 photograph of, 343f
Times and Seasons (Mormon publication), 104, 119
Topolobampo, Mexico, 24, 48, 181
    geometric plan for, 37f
    "unitary dwelling" proposed for, 29f
Total Loss Farm (Mungo), 322
Trinidad, Colorado, 331
Troy, New York, 262
True Inspiration Congregations. *See* Amana, Iowa, Inspirationists